FOR DUMMIES

BUSINESS
BOOK SERIES
FROM IDG

Taxe$ For Dummie$

20 Tips and Teasers to Take th̶...̶...̶...̶ ̶ ̶ ̶ ̶ ̶ ̶ ̶ ̶ ̶ ̶̶
(and Save You̶...̶

1. **Don't gripe so much about taxes.** Although it's tempting and ̶...̶...̶...̶ ̶ ̶ government and taxes, remember that without taxes we wouldn't have p̶...̶...̶...̶...̶ ̶ ̶oads, bridges, national parks, museums, defense, and a whole lot of other things that make our lives better.

2. **You can control your taxes.** Although death and taxes may be certainties, both can be legally postponed if you practice healthy habits.

3. **You can learn how to reduce your taxes.** If you educate yourself about the tax laws and incentives, you can dramatically and permanently reduce the taxes you'll pay over the course of your lifetime. The less you pay in taxes, the more money you'll have to spend on the fun stuff: vacations, gifts for loved ones, and more *For Dummies* books to maintain your sanity!

4. **Do it yourself.** Learn enough about the tax laws so that you can prepare your own return, or at least so that you can intelligently review your return prepared by someone you hire.

5. **Get good help, if you need it.** Hire tax and financial advisors who charge a fee for their time to help with making major decisions. Never delegate full control to these advisors and avoid those who sell products for commissions — they're salespeople, not advisors.

6. **Use preparers only when you need them.** If your situation hasn't changed since last year, you're probably wasting your hard-earned dollars paying a tax preparer to plug your new numbers into this year's return. Unless your finances are complicated or the tax laws have dramatically changed in an area that affects you, try preparing your own return. If you get stuck or want another opinion, you can always take it to a preparer at that point.

7. **Get and stay organized.** Try to keep your tax and financial documents organized year-round. This practice will save many hours when it comes time to prepare your tax return and make important financial decisions.

8. **Learn from life and taxes.** Okay, forgive us for being a bit philosophical. But because you've gone to all the time and trouble of preparing your tax return and paying all those taxes, you can now use your completed return as a tool to identify areas for improvement for next year.

9. **Be happy with success.** Taxes are the inevitable result of making money. The more you make, the more you'll pay. If you pay a lot, be happy that you're earning a lot in the first place.

...For Dummies: The Best-Selling Book Series

Taxe$ For Dummie$

Quick Reference Card

10. **Don't panic when the IRS calls.** If you haven't knowingly cheated and defrauded the IRS, you have little to fear from audit notices or other IRS letters. Calmly organize your supporting documents to prove your case. If you can't bear to face the IRS alone, you can always hire a tax advisor to represent you.

11. **The IRS isn't always right.** Whether by providing advice over the phone or challenging taxpayers' returns, the IRS has made more than its fair share of mistakes. Don't be surprised if they make a mistake with you.

12. **Taxing political arguments — to help you follow the tax debates.** Here's a *For Dummies* approved tax definition of political parties: Democrats are idealistic about how efficiently government can provide services and other things with your tax dollars. Republicans are idealistic about the private sector's ability to be fair and provide needed services for everyone.

13. **Spend less! Save more!** Please say it again — it's a good learning formula. Many of the best tax breaks available for people at *all* income levels are accessible only if you are able to save money to invest. But if you spend all your hard-earned income on other stuff, you won't be able to take advantage of those terrific tax breaks. Therefore, you may have to reduce your spending before you're able to reduce your taxes.

14. **The more you consume, the more you'll pay in taxes.** As you earn income and spend it, you not only must pay income tax on your earnings, but you also incur sales tax and other taxes on your purchases.

15. **Bad financial stuff costs you.** The things that are worst for your finances are also the most tax-costly. Remember credit-card and auto-loan interest rates are high and not tax deductible.

16. **Invest for your future.** The best way for people at all income levels to reduce their income taxes is to use retirement accounts. You not only reduce your taxes by contributing to these accounts now, but after the money is inside the account, the earnings on the investment compound without taxation.

17. **Invest tax-wisely.** Don't overlook tax implications when investing your money. Just because one investment is expected to increase in value more than another doesn't necessarily make it better for you if you end up paying a lot of taxes on your profits.

18. **Don't buy real estate only for tax purposes.** Owning your own home and other real estate can be an investment that helps to reduce your taxes. But don't purchase real estate because of the tax benefits — these benefits are already reflected in the price you pay for a property.

19. **Know when estate planning matters.** Read up on this issue so that you know when and what you should do to arrange your financial affairs.

20. **Keep taxes in perspective.** Taxes are another of the many reminders that there's more to life than working and making money. If you do such a good job reducing your taxes that you gain great wealth, don't forget to enjoy and share it with others.

Praise for Eric Tyson

"Eric Tyson is doing something important — namely, helping people at all income levels to take control of their financial futures. This book is a natural outgrowth of Tyson's vision that he has nurtured for years. Like Henry Ford, he wants to make something that was previously accessible only to the wealthy accessible to middle-income Americans."

> — James C. Collins, coauthor of the national bestseller *Built to Last* and *Beyond Entrepreneurship,* Lecturer in Business, Stanford Graduate School of Business

"Smart advice for dummies … skip the tomes … and buy *Personal Finance For Dummies,* which rewards your candor with advice and comfort."

> — Temma Ehrenfeld, *Newsweek*

"*Personal Finance For Dummies* offers a valuable guide for common misconceptions and major pitfalls. It's a no-nonsense, straightforward, easy-to-read personal finance book… With this book, you can easily learn enough about finances to start thinking for yourself."

> — Charles R. Schwab, Chairman and CEO, The Charles Schwab Corporation

"Worth getting. Scores of all-purpose money-management books reach bookstores every year, but only once every couple of years does a standout personal finance primer come along. *Personal Finance For Dummies,* by financial counselor and columnist Eric Tyson, provides detailed, action-oriented advice on everyday financial questions … Tyson's style is readable and unintimidating."

> — Kristin Davis, *Kiplinger's Personal Finance Magazine*

"Best new personal finance book."

> — Michael Pellecchia, syndicated columnist

"Eric Tyson … seems the perfect writer for a …*For Dummies* book. He doesn't tell you what to do or consider doing without explaining the why's and how's — and the booby traps to avoid — in plain English … it will lead you through the thickets of your own finances as painlessly as I can imagine."

> — Clarence Peterson, *Chicago Tribune*

"*Personal Finance For Dummies* is, by far, the best book I have read on financial planning. It is a simplified volume of information that provides tremendous insight and guidance into the world of investing and other money issues."

> — Althea Thompson, producer, "PBS Nightly Business Report"

Praise for David J. Silverman

Here is what critics have said about David J. Silverman's book, *Battling the IRS*:

"A comprehensive self-help manual for IRS problems. It addresses every situation methodically in a 'how-to' fashion... the average taxpayer will find it extremely helpful... a great survival manual."
— National Taxpayers Union

"The IRS loves to send out notices. Each year it mails out good news in the form of 26.6 million penalty notices, 3.5 million notices informing tax payers they didn't report all their income, 3 million notices to taxpayers stating they failed to file a tax return and tens of millions of notices — the exact number is not knowable — stating that taxpayers failed to pay what they owed or made a mistake in preparing their tax return. Fortunately, Mr. Silverman's book provides replies to nearly every type of communication the IRS dispatches. It also tells you when you should seek professional assistance and when you can take the agency on alone."
— *The Wall Street Journal*

"Written in easy-to-understand language... A valuable source for the general consumer."
— *The National Public Accountant*

"David J. Silverman's book should help take the terror out of audits. It is a guide to notices and assessment from the Internal Revenue Service, and includes letters taxpayers can copy to deal with a variety of grievances, as well as a thorough explanation of taxpayer's rights."
— *The New York Times*

"Should the IRS come after you, defend yourself with David Silverman's excellent book."
— *Money* magazine

"This volume is the most definitive and informative compendium for dealing with the IRS that we have ever seen."
— *The New England Review of Books*

What readers say about ...For Dummies™ Business Books

"The minute I read the table of contents, I knew this was a book I should have had 30 years ago. I strongly believe that all young people just starting out in their first job should have this book."
— Ellinor Juarez, Alameda, Calif.

"This book cuts through all the jargon so that a novice like myself can understand how to manage money."
— Ronnell Mitchell, New York, N.Y.

"This book answered so many questions. Truly, I was completely illiterate financially — now I am becoming the family guru."
— Jean M., Holt, Mo.

"I purchased copies for each of my children."
— M.G. Sher, Marblehead, Mass.

"Covers important information clearly and concisely — it will be my reference guide as I start my 'adult life' with my first post-college salaried job."
— Andrew Potter, Washington, D.C.

"*Personal Finance For Dummies* is a great book. It addresses everything and helps me feel secure about my finances."
— Phyllis Haber, Kansas City, Mo.

"Well-written, good format. I gave a copy to my 25-year-old, newly married daughter. Her reaction: 'The book is a real eye opener.'"
— Reece Little, Louisville, Ky.

"Fun to read, informative. I wish all financial magazines and prospectuses were as fun to read.
— Mike Mendiola, Whittier, Calif.

"Simplified and demystified personal finance. This book actually made me excited about future investments and taking control of my finances."
— Kathy West, Chicago, Ill.

"Easy to understand ... made sense of a complex subject."
— Melody Edwards, Martinez, Ga.

References for the Rest of Us™

BUSINESS BOOK SERIES FROM IDG

Are you intimidated and confused by personal finance and business issues? Do you find that traditional books are overloaded with technical details and advice that you'll never use? Do you postpone important financial decisions because you just don't want to deal with them? Then our *...For Dummies™* business book series is for you.

... For Dummies™ business books are written for those frustrated and hard-working souls who know they aren't really dumb but find that that the myriad of personal finance and business issues and the accompanying horror stories make them feel helpless. *...For Dummies™* books use a lighthearted approach, a down-to-earth style, and even cartoons and humorous icons to diffuse fears and build confidence. Lighthearted but not lightweight, these books are perfect survival guides to solving your personal finance and business problems.

> *"More than a publishing phenomenon, 'Dummies' is a sign of the times."*
> — The New York Times

> *"This is the best book ever written for a beginner."*
> — Clarence Peterson, Chicago Tribune, on DOS For Dummies ®

> *"... you won't go wrong buying them."*
> — Walter Mossberg, Wall Street Journal, on IDG's ...For Dummies™ books

Already, hundreds of thousands of satisfied readers agree. They have made *...For Dummies™* the #1 introductory level computer book series and a best selling business book series. They have written asking for more. So if you're looking for the best and easiest way to learn about personal finance and business, look to *...For Dummies™* to give you a helping hand.

IDG BOOKS

TAXE$ FOR DUMMIE$™

by Eric Tyson, MBA

Financial Counselor and Author of the National Bestseller
Personal Finance For Dummies

and David J. Silverman, EA

Tax Advisor and
Author of the Critically Acclaimed *Battling the IRS*

	Technical Review by
folio. IDG thing, a page number then placed at the outside of the running head at the top of the page. If placed at the	**KPMG Peat Marwick LLP,** the world's largest accounting firm

IDG
BOOKS

IDG Books Worldwide, Inc.
An International Data Group Company

Foster City, CA ♦ Chicago, IL ♦ Indianapolis, IN ♦ Braintree, MA ♦ Dallas, TX

Taxe$ For Dummie$, 1995 Edition

Published by
IDG Books Worldwide, Inc.
An International Data Group Company
919 E. Hillside Blvd., Suite 400
Foster City, CA 94404

Library of Congress Catalog Card No.: 94-72819

ISBN: 1-56884-220-1

Printed in the United States of America

10 9 8 7 6 5 4 3 2 1

1A/RV/RS/ZU

Distributed in the United States by IDG Books Worldwide, Inc.

Distributed by Macmillan Canada for Canada; by Computer and Technical Books for the Caribbean Basin; by Contemporanea de Ediciones for Venezuela; by Distribuidora Cuspide for Argentina; by CITEC for Brazil; by Ediciones ZETA S.C.R. Ltda. for Peru; by Editorial Limusa SA for Mexico; by Transworld Publishers Limited in the United Kingdom and Europe; by Al-Maiman Publishers & Distributors for Saudi Arabia; by Simron Pty. Ltd. for South Africa; by IDG Communications (HK) Ltd. for Hong Kong; by Toppan Company Ltd. for Japan; by Addison Wesley Publishing Company for Korea; by Longman Singapore Publishers Ltd. for Singapore, Malaysia, Thailand and Indonesia; by Unalis Corporation for Taiwan; by WS Computer Publishing Company, Inc. for the Philippines; by WoodsLane Pty. Ltd. for Australia; by WoodsLane Enterprises Ltd. for New Zealand.

For general information on IDG Books in the U.S., including information on discounts and

premiums, contact IDG Books at 800-434-3422 or 415-655-3000.

For information on where to purchase IDG Books outside the U.S., contact IDG Books International at 415-655-3021 or fax 415-655-3295.

For information on translations, contact Marc Jeffrey Mikulich, Director, Foreign & Subsidiary Rights, at IDG Books Worldwide, 415-655-3018 or fax 415-655-3295.

For sales inquiries and special prices for bulk quantities, write to the address above or call IDG Books Worldwide at 415-655-3000.

For information on using IDG Books in the classroom, or ordering examination copies, contact Jim Kelly at 800-434-2086.

 is a registered trademark of
IDG Books Worldwide, Inc.

About the Authors

Eric Tyson

Eric Tyson is a nationally recognized personal financial counselor, writer, and lecturer based in San Francisco. He has taught thousands of people from all income levels. So he knows the financial and tax concerns and questions of real folks just like you. Eric also teaches the Bay Area's most highly attended personal financial management course, at the University of California, Berkeley.

Despite being handicapped by a joint B.S. in Economics and Biology from Yale and an M.B.A. from Stanford, Eric remains a master at "keeping it simple." After toiling away for a number of years as a management consultant to Fortune 500 financial-service firms, Eric finally figured out how to pursue his dream. He took his inside knowledge of the banking, investment, and insurance industries and committed himself to making personal financial management accessible to us all.

An accomplished freelance personal finance writer, Eric is the author of the national bestseller *Personal Finance For Dummies* and writes a column for the Sunday *San Francisco Examiner*. His work has been featured and quoted in numerous local and national publications, including *Newsweek*, *The New York Times, Forbes, Kiplinger's Personal Finance Magazine, Parenting, Bottom Line/ Personal*, and on the NBC "Today Show," ABC, CNBC, PBS's "Nightly Business Report," CNN, FOX-TV, CBS national radio, Bloomberg Business Radio, and Business Radio Network. He's been a featured speaker at a White House conference on aging and retirement.

David J. Silverman, EA

David J. Silverman is an enrolled agent and is enrolled to practice before the Internal Revenue Service. He has served on the Advisory Group to the Commissioner of Internal Revenue. David has a Certificate in Taxation from New York University and has been in private practice in Manhattan for over twenty-five years.

David regularly testifies on tax issues before both the Senate Finance Committee and the House of Representatives Committee on Ways and Means. As the result of his suggestions regarding penalty reform that he made while testifying before these committees, legislation was enacted that reduced the amount of penalties that may be assessed in a number of key areas.

He is the author of *Battling the IRS*, which has received critical acclaim in *The New York Times, Money*, and *The Wall Street Journal*. As a contributing editor, David's monthly tax column appears in *SmartMoney* magazine. David is frequently interviewed on national TV and radio as an expert on tax issues.

Welcome to the world of IDG Books Worldwide.

IDG Books Worldwide, Inc. is a subsidiary of International Data Group, the world's largest publisher of business and computer-related information and the leading global provider of information services on information technology. IDG was founded more than 25 years ago and now employs more than 7,000 people worldwide. IDG publishes more than 220 computer publications in 65 countries (see listing below). More than fifty million people read one or more IDG publications each month.

Launched in 1990, IDG Books Worldwide is today the fastest-growing publisher of computer and business books in the United States. We are proud to have received 3 awards from the Computer Press Association in recognition of editorial excellence, and our best-selling ...*For Dummies*™ series has more than 12 million copies in print with translations in more than 24 languages. IDG Books, through a recent joint venture with IDG's Hi-Tech Beijing, became the first U.S. publisher to publish a computer book in the People's Republic of China. In record time, IDG Books has become the first choice for millions of readers around the world who want to learn how to better manage their businesses.

Our mission is simple: Every IDG book is designed to bring extra value and skill-building instructions to the reader. Our books are written by experts who understand and care about our readers. The knowledge base of our editorial staff comes from years of experience in publishing, education, and journalism — experience which we use to produce books for the '90s. In short, we care about books, so we attract the best people. We devote special attention to details such as audience, interior design, use of icons, and illustrations. And because we use an efficient process of authoring, editing, and desktop publishing our books electronically, we can spend more time ensuring superior content and spend less time on the technicalities of making books.

You can count on our commitment to deliver high-quality books at competitive prices on topics consumers want to read about. At IDG, we value quality, and we have been delivering quality for more than 25 years. You'll find no better book on a subject than an IDG book.

John J. Kilcullen

John Kilcullen
President and CEO
IDG Books Worldwide, Inc.

IDG Books Worldwide, Inc. is a subsidiary of International Data Group, the world's largest publisher of computer-related information and the leading global provider of information services on information technology. International Data Group publishes over 220 computer publications in 65 countries. More than fifty million people read one or more International Data Group publications each month. The officers are Patrick J. McGovern, Founder and Board Chairman; Kelly Conlin, President; Jim Casella, Chief Operating Officer. International Data Group's publications include: **ARGENTINA'S** Computerworld Argentina, Infoworld Argentina; **AUSTRALIA'S** Computerworld Australia, Computer Living, Australian PC World, Australian Macworld, Network World, Mobile Business Australia, Publish!, Reseller, IDG Sources; **AUSTRIA'S** Computerwelt Oesterreich, PC Test; **BELGIUM'S** Data News (CW); **BOLIVIA'S** Computerworld; **BRAZIL'S** Computerworld, Connections, Game Power, Mundo Unix, PC World, Publish, Super Game; **BULGARIA'S** Computerworld Bulgaria, PC & Mac World Bulgaria, Network World Bulgaria; **CANADA'S** CIO Canada, Computerworld Canada, InfoCanada, Network World Canada, Reseller; **CHILE'S** Computerworld Chile, Informatica; **COLOMBIA'S** Computerworld Colombia, PC World; **COSTA RICA'S** PC World; **CZECH REPUBLIC'S** Computerworld, Elektronika, PC World; **DENMARK'S** Communications World, Computerworld Danmark, Computerworld Focus, Macintosh Produktkatalog, Macworld Danmark, PC World Danmark, PC Produktguide, Tech World, Windows World; **ECUADOR'S** PC World Ecuador; **EGYPT'S** Computerworld (CW) Middle East, PC World Middle East; **FINLAND'S** MikroPC, Tietoviikko, Tietoverkko; **FRANCE'S** Distributique, GOLDEN MAC, InfoPC, Le Guide du Monde Informatique, Le Monde Informatique, Telecoms & Reseaux; **GERMANY'S** Computerwoche, Computerwoche Focus, Computerwoche Extra, Electronic Entertainment, Gamepro, Information Management, Macwelt, Netzwelt, PC Welt, Publish, Publish; **GREECE'S** Publish & Macworld; **HONG KONG'S** Computerworld Hong Kong, PC World Hong Kong; **HUNGARY'S** Computerworld SZT, PC World; **INDIA'S** Computers & Communications; **INDONESIA'S** Info Komputer; **IRELAND'S** ComputerScope; **ISRAEL'S** Beyond Windows, Computerworld Israel, Multimedia, PC World Israel; **ITALY'S** Computerworld Italia, Lotus Magazine, Macworld Italia, Networking Italia, PC Shopping Italy, PC World Italia; **JAPAN'S** Computerworld Today, Information Systems World, Macworld Japan, Nikkei Personal Computing, SunWorld Japan, Windows World; **KENYA'S** East African Computer News; **KOREA'S** Computerworld Korea, Macworld Korea, PC World Korea; **LATIN AMERICA'S** GamePro; **MALAYSIA'S** Computerworld Malaysia, PC World Malaysia; **MEXICO'S** Compu Edicion, Compu Manufactura, Computacion/Punto de Venta, Computerworld Mexico, MacWorld, Mundo Unix, PC World, Windows; **THE NETHERLANDS'** Computer! Totaal, Computable (CW), LAN Magazine, Lotus Magazine, MacWorld; **NEW ZEALAND'S** Computer Buyer, Computerworld New Zealand, Network World, New Zealand PC World; **NIGERIA'S** PC World Africa; **NORWAY'S** Computerworld Norge, Lotusworld Norge, Macworld Norge, Maxi Data, Networld, PC World Ekspress, PC World Nettverk, PC World Norge, PC World's Produktguide, Publish& Multimedia World, Student Data, Unix World, Windowsworld; **PAKISTAN'S** PC World Pakistan; **PANAMA'S** PC World Panama; **PERU'S** Computerworld Peru, PC World; **PEOPLE'S REPUBLIC OF CHINA'S** China Computerworld, China Infoworld, China PC Info Magazine, Computer Fan, PC World China, Electronics International, Electronics Today/Multimedia World, Electronic Product World, China Network World, Software World Magazine, Telecom Product World; **PHILIPPINES'** Computerworld Philippines, PC Digest (PCW); **POLAND'S** Computerworld Poland, Computerworld Special Report, Networld, PC World/Komputer, Sunworld; **PORTUGAL'S** Cerebro/PC World, Correio Informatico/Computerworld, MacIn; **ROMANIA'S** Computerworld, PC World, Telecom Romania; **RUSSIA'S** Computerworld-Moscow, Mir - PK (PCW), Sety (Networks); **SINGAPORE'S** Computerworld Southeast Asia, PC World Singapore; **SLOVENIA'S** Monitor Magazine; **SOUTH AFRICA'S** Computer Mail (CIO),Computing S.A.,Network World S.A., Software World; **SPAIN'S** Advanced Systems, Amiga World, Computerworld Espana, Communicaciones World, Macworld Espana, NeXTWORLD, Super Juegos Magazine (GamePro), PC World Espana, Publish; **SWEDEN'S** Attack, ComputerSweden, Corporate Computing, Macworld, Mikrodatorn, Natverk & Kommunikation, PC World, CAP & Design, DataIngenjoren, Maxi Data,Windows World; **SWITZERLAND'S** Computerworld Schweiz, Macworld Schweiz, PC Tip; **TAIWAN'S** Computerworld Taiwan, PC World Taiwan; **THAILAND'S** Thai Computerworld; **TURKEY'S** Computerworld Monitor, Macworld Turkiye, PC World Turkiye; **UKRAINE'S** Computerworld, Computers+Software Magazine; **UNITED KINGDOM'S** Computing/Computerworld, Connexion/Network World, Lotus Magazine, Macworld, Open Computing/Sunworld; **URAGUAY'S** PC World Uruguay; **UNITED STATES'** Advanced Systems, AmigaWorld, Cable in the Classroom, CD Review, CIO, Computerworld, Computerworld Client/Server Journal, Digital Video, DOS World, Electronic Entertainment Magazine (E2), Federal Computer Week, Game Hits, GamePro, IDG Books, Infoworld, Laser Event, Macworld, Maximize, Multimedia World, Network World, PC Letter, PC World, Publish, SWATPro, Video Event; **VENEZUELA'S** Computerworld Venezuela, PC World; **VIETNAM'S** PC World Vietnam.

Dedications

Our families and friends have been a tremendous source of inspiration, good ideas and support. My wife Judy deserves special mention for putting up with me while I babbled about taxes over dinner and in my sleep since I worked too many hours finishing this book. — Eric Tyson

To my wife Betsy who provided the inspiration, my late father Louis whose writing skills I hope I inherited, and my daughters Joanna and Lisa who assisted with the essential research and editing. — David J. Silverman

Acknowledgments

Many terrific people contributed to this book. We'd like to highlight and thank those who stand out in our minds for their thoughtfulness, insight, and hard work. First, we'd like to thank our counseling clients, students, and readers who have helped us to learn what issues and questions people at all income levels have.

We would also like to thank the journalists and other leaders in their fields for citing, complimenting and critiquing our previous writing. There's not much point in writing if others don't know we're doing it! And to those who still don't get the fact that Dummies is supposed to be funny and not insulting, get a life. Heck — even William F. Buckley uses ...*For Dummies*™ books!

Special thanks to the many people from the accounting firm of KPMG Peat Marwick LLP. While we were a bit hesitant to ask a firm with funny initials in front of their name to work with us as technical reviewers, we're glad we did. Now we know why these guys and gals have grown into the world's largest accounting firm — can you believe they have 76,200 employees?!

Led by a team headed by Dennis Ito — a really bright partner with 21 years at Peat Marwick — every chapter in this book was improved by their knowledge, insights and experience. It was also heartening to see that even though they work full-time preparing taxes for companies large and small as well as individuals, they have a sense of humor. Hey, they successfully completed our editing process! (It's interesting to note that they do strategic planning to help companies grow — which creates more demand for their tax work — we told you these people were sharp). In addition to Dennis Ito, we would also like to make special mention at Peat Marwick of Robert K. Taylor, Jeanine T. Patrick, and Mark T. Watson and their colleagues and assistants. KPMG Peat Marwick LLP folks are nice people; they treat their employees well and give tons to charities and other good causes. They even made it to the finals of the Malcolm Baldridge National Quality Award.

And finally, we'd like to thank all the good people at IDG Books. Special recognition goes to Andy Cummings for a super job as project editor, Bill Helling for his overachieving work as copy editor, and Kathy Welton and John Kilcullen as ever capable chiefs at IDG. Beth Jenkins, Cindy Phipps, Steve Peake, Tony Augsburger, Paul Belcastro, Cameron Booker, Linda Boyer, Mary Breidenbach, Chris Collins, Tyler Connor, Sherry Gomoll, Drew Moore, Carla Radzikinas, Dwight Ramsey, Tricia Reynolds, Kathie Schnorr, Gina Scott, Kristin Cocks, Jeff Waggoner, Jennifer Wallis, Kathy Cox, Michael Simsic, Mike Kelly, Diane Giangrossi, Stacey Holden Prince, Tammy Castleman, Diane Steele, and Mary Bednarek also deserve a round of applause.

P.S. We guess we should thank the IRS and the politicians for tinkering with the tax code for so many years that this book was needed to explain the resulting mess to those who have to work for a living and deal with taxes and their personal finances.

(The publisher would like to give special thanks to Patrick J. McGovern, without whom this book would not have been possible.)

Credits

VP & Publisher
Kathleen A. Welton

Brand Manager
Stacy S. Collins

Production Director
Beth Jenkins

Project Coordinator
Cindy L. Phipps

Editorial Assistants
Tammy Castleman
Stacey Holden Prince

Pre-Press Coordinator
Steve Peake

Production Staff
Tony Augsburger
Paul Belcastro
Cameron Booker
Linda Margaret Boyer
Mary Breidenbach
Chris Collins
J. Tyler Connor
Sherry Dickinson Gomoll
Drew R. Moore
Carla Radzikinas
Dwight Ramsey
Patricia R. Reynolds
Kathie Schnorr
Gina Scott

Project Editor
Andy Cummings

Editors
Bill Helling
Kristin A. Cocks
Jeffrey Waggoner
Michael Simsic
Jennifer Wallis
Kathleen M. Cox
Diane L. Giangrossi
Michael Kelly

Technical Reviewers
Dennis Ito
Robert K. Taylor
Jeanine T. Patrick
Mark T. Watson

Proofreaders
Michelle Worthington
Linda Langan

Indexer
Sharon Hilgenberg

Cover Design
Kavish + Kavish

Contents at a Glance

Cartoons at a Glance

By Wiley

Reprinted with permission

page 7

page 73

page 77

page 263

page 306

page 325

page 435

page 424

Table of Contents

Chapter 13: The Rest of the 1040 and Other Yucky Forms 243

Introduction

*W*elcome to *Taxes For Dummies* — the no-nonsense book that answers both your tax preparation and tax planning questions in plain English without putting you to sleep. Should the IRS ever come after you, this book will help you get and stay out of trouble. For more than 80 years, the Internal Revenue Service (the government division responsible for collecting taxes) and Congress (whose benevolent lawmakers keep tinkering with our tax code) have been making our taxes more complex and making us more miserable.

Taxes For Dummies can relieve your pain and misery. Like the trainer who tapes your ankle so you can play in the big games, or like the long-overdue highway sign announcing the next rest stop, *Taxes For Dummies* helps you to get through your tax return with a minimum of discomfort. And this book can also help you keep your mind on your taxes while you plan your finances for the upcoming year. In addition to learning how to deal with federal taxes, you also learn how to handle some of those pesky and not-so-insignificant taxes slapped on by states and other tax-collecting bodies. Finally, *Taxes For Dummies* teaches you how to keep from breaking laws, which is an easy thing for even an honest person to do.

Most people's tax concerns fall into three categories: filling out their forms properly, keeping as much of their money as possible out of the government coffers, and avoiding any penalties. *Taxes For Dummies* addresses these concerns.

This Tax Book Is (Thankfully) Different

In case you haven't sampled the other fare yet, we can honestly tell you that there are basically two major types of tax books in bookstores today: gigantic preparation books that weigh more than the Manhattan telephone book (and are often less interesting to read) and advice books that tell you most of the things you should have been doing for years. Neither type of book does a good job at meeting the needs that typical taxpayers have when completing their annual tax returns or managing and planning their personal finances.

Many of the annual preparation books try to cover every possible question on filling out tax forms. At their worst, these books are as dreadful as the IRS instruction booklets themselves — bulky, bureaucratic, and jargon-filled. In some cases, preparation books have simply reproduced dozens of pages of IRS instructions! At their best, these books tell you things you won't find in the IRS instructions — but the golden nuggets are buried in massive piles of granite. *Taxes For Dummies* lays out those golden nuggets in nice, clean display cases so you won't miss a single one. There's still plenty of granite, but we promise not to bury you *or* the key insights.

Too many tax advice books start off with ominous grumblings about how the government has jacked up your taxes again; and, of course, the only way to save yourself from abject poverty is to read the book. By the way, most of these tax advice books are written by large accounting firms that charge upwards of $300 per hour. Such firms are used to hearing their clients — senior executives and other muckety-mucks — complain about their tax burdens.

If you're not already a senior-level executive with a six-figure salary, *Taxes For Dummies* shows you, for example, how to file your taxes and plan your finances year-round. If you *are* a big income earner, you discover — just like the rest of the class — sound and legal strategies for reducing your tax bill. Everyone will learn how to jump obediently and happily through all the proper hoops to keep the taxing authorities from sending threatening notices and bills. If you do get a nasty letter from the tax patrol, we even tell you how to deal with that dreaded situation in a calm, level-headed manner to get the IRS off your case.

How to Use This Book

Life in America is always delightful because you have choices and you can pick the option that best meets your needs! You can use this book in several ways:

- ✔ **As a reference.** Maybe you know a fair amount about your taxes but you don't know how to report the puny dividends you got last year from the five shares of stock your Great-Aunt Maye gave you for Christmas. Just use the table of contents or index to find the right spot in the book to answer your questions.

- ✔ **As an advisor.** Maybe you're self-employed and you've known that you should be salting some money away so that you can someday cut back on those 12-hour days. No problem. You can turn to Chapter 19 and learn all about the different types of retirement accounts and which one may be right for you, how it can slash your taxes, and even where to set one up.

- ✔ **As a textbook.** Maybe you just want to know everything. If you have the time, desire, and discipline, by all means, go for it and read the whole shebang. And please be sure to drop us a line and let us know of your triumph!

The Roadmap

If you've already peeked at the table of contents, you know that this book contains chapters that are organized into five major sections. (We entertained the possibility of using a roulette wheel to determine the order of topics — because there is no number-one tax fact that everyone needs to know — but our sensible editors at IDG Books advised us otherwise. The burden of keeping customers happy so that they'll come back for more was just too powerful. So we gave it some thought and organized in a way that should make sense for you, the reader.)

Here is a brief description of what you'll find in each of the five major parts:

Part I: On Your Mark, Get Set...

Don't worry, you won't have to put on running shoes or squeeze into a tank top. This part helps you understand how and why taxes work in the way that they do. You'll learn how to fit taxes into your financial life. Here, you'll also master time-tested and accountant-approved ways to get organized and be ready to file your annual return, along with all those other tedious tax forms that may be required at random times of the year.

Part II: GO!

In this part, we walk you through the process of completing a tax return containing the typical challenges that taxpayers face. We answer the questions that are confronted by about 98 percent of taxpayers, and we do it quickly and clearly so you can get the darn forms into the mailbox and return to your real life. And we do it without reprinting pages and pages from the incomprehensible IRS manuals. (If we do sometimes sound like an official IRS publication, please forgive us! Some tax stuff is just so complicated. But we promise to keep IRS-speak to a minimum.)

If you're among the 2 percent of taxpayers with complicated situations, fear not! You won't be left high and dry. In fact, you'll be pleased to know that we high-light the places where answering a complicated tax issue with a book would probably be like trying to perform a root canal while reading a step-by-step instruction manual. We point out the problem and tell you where you can get the advice — and the anesthetic — that you need!

Part III: About Face! Dealing with the IRS

No matter how hard you try to ward off nasty letters from the IRS, sooner or later you may receive that dreaded thin envelope from the friendly tax folks with a message challenging your return. The operative word here is *challenge*. As long as you think of this situation as a wonderful opportunity to show off your financial stuff, you'll do fine.

So you'll be tickled to know that *Taxes For Dummies* goes beyond just dealing with the annual ritual of filing your tax return by offering tips, counsel, and a shoulder to cry on. You learn how to sweep the IRS off your doorstep swiftly, deftly, and without breaking a sweat. And you'll keep those pesky IRS agents out of your bank account while you keep yourself (and your loved ones) out of jail.

Part IV: Training for a Better Race Next Time

Because taxes are a year-round obligation and an important piece of your personal finance puzzle, this part provides tons of practical planning advice that you can use in July, in September, and during the rest of year — as well as in April. You'll learn how to accomplish important financial goals such as purchasing a home, or squirreling away enough loot that you don't have to work into your 80s — all in a tax-wise manner. You may be tempted to skip this section once you've made it past April 15. Don't make such a mistake. Part IV can pay off in tens of thousands of dollars someday, saving you headache and heartache when you file returns each and every year.

Part V: The Part of Tens

A ...*For Dummies* book just wouldn't be the same without irreverent authors, humor, and Top Ten lists. These lists often cover big-picture issues that cried out for top billing in their very own section. You'll also enjoy plowing through these short but highly useful chapters in record time.

Other stuff we stuck at the end

Appendixes usually include horrible, little technical details that are best avoided by normal readers. In this book, however, you can find a treasure trove of goodies back here, such as a list of IRS publications, addresses, phone numbers, and an extension form in case you miss important dates.

Best of all, you'll find a reader response card that allows you, postage-free, to write the good folks at IDG Books and tell them what you thought of this book and how we can make it better for you in the next edition. If you're the first to make a really good suggestion that we incorporate into the next round, we'll make sure you get a free copy of the next edition! (Just be sure to include your address.) What an incentive!

Icons Used in This Book

This target flags strategy recommendations for making the most of your taxes and money (for example, pay off your non-tax-deductible credit-card debt with your lottery winnings).

This highlights the best resources and products to implement strategy recommendations (for example, call Tax-Friendly Mutual Funds to learn more).

This will be of great notice to folks who want to learn a way to reduce their taxes — hey, this stuff is all legal, really.

This is a friendly reminder of information discussed elsewhere in the book or stuff you'll definitely want to remember.

This marks things to avoid and common mistakes people make with their taxes.

This alerts you to scoundrels, bad advice, and scams that prey on the unsuspecting.

This nerdy guy appears beside discussions that aren't critical if you just want to learn basic concepts and get answers to your tax questions. Reading them will deepen and enhance your knowledge. This stuff may also come in handy if you're ever on *Jeopardy*.

Part I
On Your Mark, Get Set...

In this part...

*I*f you feel disorganized, don't know where to turn for tax help, or are otherwise grumpy about all the forms you must complete and the taxes you have to pay, this part will be like a spoonful of sugar. You'll learn how to think about your taxes in the context of your overall financial situation and what our great politicians do with all the money you send them. But maybe you already know that! Although it's not as much fun as complaining about government waste, you'll also learn how to get organized — and stay organized — throughout the year. And we explain how to find competent tax help should you be at your wit's end.

Chapter 1

The Big Picture: Understanding, Preparing, and Planning Your Taxes

In This Chapter

▶ Taxes! Taxes! Taxes!

▶ Lost in the system

▶ Ignorance is not bliss (when it comes to taxes)

▶ Total and marginal taxes

▶ Federal, state, and the Alternative Minimum Tax systems

*U*nless you're a professional tax preparer or an IRS employee, taxes are a big, fat, unmitigated pain in the gluteus maximus — and sometimes in the neck and lower back. The mere thought of filing a tax return makes most people's blood pressure skyrocket and turns their stomachs into churning froths of painful acids.

First, there's the chore of gathering all sorts of official — and ugly — documents to complete the annual ritual. Then, if your past financial year was not exactly like the preceding one, you may have to get some new forms you've never heard of. Then you have to answer a bunch of questions that give you an all-too-real historical perspective on the Spanish Inquisition.

Maybe you have to figure out how to submit a quarterly tax payment if you no longer work for a company and have self-employment income from contracting work you do. Perhaps you sold some investments such as stocks or mutual funds or real estate — unbelievably — at a profit, and don't know how much (if any) tax you owe.

Unfortunately, too many people think of taxes only in the spring when it comes time to file the annual return. Throughout this book, you'll find all sorts of warnings, tips, and other suggestions that help you see the important role that taxes play in your entire personal financial situation. In fact, a big part of the book (Part IV) is devoted to teaching you how to accomplish your financial goals while legally reducing your taxes.

A (Brief) History of Taxes

It has been said that the only certainties in life are death and taxes. It is one of our goals to dispel at least 250 incorrect adages in our lifetime, so here it goes.... This saying is wrong because the good news is that some taxes, unlike death, can be avoided — or at least minimized.

Federal taxes, at least, were not always a certainty. Earlier in this century, you still could live without being bothered by the federal income tax — or by televisions, microwaves, computers, voicemail, and all those other complications. Beginning in 1913, Congress set up a system of graduated tax rates, starting with a rate of just 1 percent and going up to 7 percent. Most Americans didn't even have to file because the system mainly taxed mainly people who earned big incomes — incomes that don't sound big by today's standards because a dollar actually *bought* a lot in 1913.

Carolyn Webber and Aaron Wildavsky, in *History of Taxation and Expenditure in the Western World,* state that the flat 1 percent rate was for all individual incomes exceeding $3,000 and incomes exceeding $4,000 for married couples "whether derived from wages, rents, dividends, salaries, interest, entrepreneurial incomes, or capital gains." And just 2 percent of the U.S. population between 1913 and 1915 had to pay federal income taxes — the average personal income was not much more than $600!

Those were indeed the "good old days." Since then, thanks to endless revisions, enhancements, and "simplifications," the federal tax laws — along with all the IRS and court "clarifications" of them — can (and should) fill several dump trucks. In 1913, the forms, instructions, and clarifications would have filled just one small three-ring binder! (And we're not even sure if three-ring binders existed back then.) In the four decades after World War II, the girth of the federal tax code swelled by nearly 400 percent!

The system

It seems that any time money passes through your hands, you pay some kind of tax. Consider the following scenarios:

When you earn income from work, you pay tax on your earnings.

After paying taxes on your earnings and spending money on things you need (and paying more taxes), you may have some money left over for saving. Guess what? Your reward for being a saver is that you pay tax on the interest you earn on your savings.

That's the bad news. The good news is, if you can learn strategies for reducing your taxes at every step along the way, you can keep a lot more of your money in your own wallet:

You may be able to tax-shelter your earnings from work in some sort of retirement account. This strategy slashes your current taxes, allows your money to compound tax-free, and helps you work toward the goal of retirement.

The less you buy, the less sales tax you pay. You can buy a more fuel-efficient car, for example, and learn other ways to spend wisely.

When you invest, you can invest in a way that fits your tax situation. This makes you happier and wealthier come tax time. For example, you can choose tax-friendly investments that reduce your tax bill and increase your investment returns.

If *Taxes For Dummies* at least helps you learn how the tax system works (while showing you here and there how to make it work for you), our effort has not gone for naught. And it's very possible that this book will show you some things about the tax system that don't seem very fair. Maybe these things will bother you. But even if you don't agree with the whole tax system, you still have to play by the rules. It definitely doesn't help your situation to get angry and have the veins in your neck bulge. Your newfound insights can help improve your political vision at election time, or perhaps can cause you to call your travel agent for a one-way ticket to a low-tax tropical island.

The value of understanding the system

If you don't understand the tax system, you almost certainly pay more in taxes than necessary. Your tax ignorance can cause mistakes, which are costly if the IRS and your state government catch your errors. With the proliferation of computerized information and data tracking, discovering gaffes has never been easier for the tax cops. And when they discover boo-boos, you have to pay the tax you originally owed *and* interest (*and* possibly penalties).

The tax system, like other public policy, is built around incentives to encourage *desirable* behavior and activity. Home ownership, for example, is considered desirable because it encourages people to take more responsibility for maintaining buildings and neighborhoods. Clean, orderly neighborhoods are supposed to be the result of home ownership. Therefore, the government offers all sorts of tax benefits *(allowable deductions)* to encourage people to own homes.

To understand the tax system is to understand what your government thinks you should be doing. Naturally, not everyone follows the path that the government encourages. After all, it's a free country. You've spent years rebelling against your parents. Why should the government get better treatment?

Of course, the difference between being a rebellious child and being a rebellious taxpayer is that, as a taxpayer, the cost comes out of your pocketbook. (We haven't heard of many parents who penalize a child's defiance in *cash.*) If you understand the options, you can choose the behaviors that fit into your lifestyle and your stages of financial life.

Many people resent the taxes they pay — they feel that they pay too much and get too little in return. Therefore, another benefit to understanding the tax system is that you can become a more informed voter and citizen in the democratic process.

Getting lost in the bureaucratic abyss

You say that you want to understand more. If you're like most people, though, making sense of the tax jungle is more daunting than hacking your way out of a real jungle with a rusty machete. Even if you're an honest, earnest, well-intentioned, and law-abiding citizen, odds are that you don't understand the tax system. This ignorance wreaks havoc with your personal finances, because you end up paying more in taxes than you need to. Unless you're a really high-income earner and spend far less than you earn — a very un-American thing to do — your finances may already be in shambles *before* you even look at taxes.

To add insult to injury, you can step on a tax land mine. Like millions of citizens who have come before you, you may unwittingly be in noncompliance with the myriad and ever-changing tax laws at the federal, state, and local levels. And if you've ever tried to read (and make sense of) the tax laws, you know that you're probably more likely to win your state's lottery than you are to figure out the tax code. That's one of the reasons that tax lawyers and accountants get paid so much — to compensate them for the intense and prolonged agony of deciphering the tax code day after day after day.

The tax code has been changed incrementally over the years but has never been examined globally or given a complete overhaul. Of course, some major revisions have been made. However, despite many sensible people saying we need to *start over and truly simplify* the system, it hasn't happened yet.

Our tax system is so complicated because of an interesting phenomenon: We don't like it but we just can't seem to leave it alone. Nearly every year, elected officials make revisions to the tax code — changing, amending, deleting, and adding to the written rules and regulations that determine what is taxable, which deductions are legal, which aren't, and so on. The revisions result from political bargaining that often seems to toss aside your best interests. In fact, it seems that common sense is often forgotten.

So don't feel like a dummy when it comes to understanding our tax system, because it's not you — it's the system. Nevertheless, even if you hire a tax advisor to help you navigate the tax morass, it's worth some of the time to understand how the system treats certain financial moves you make. We help you do this throughout the book, and we promise not to make you read any of the tax laws.

Beyond April 15: What you don't know can hurt you

Every spring, more than 100 million tax returns (and several million extension requests) are filed with the IRS. The by-product of this effort is guaranteed employment for more than 1 million accountants and auditors and 2 million bookkeeping and accounting clerks. Accounting firms rake in about $30 billion helping the bewildered and the desperately confused figure out all those tax laws. So that you can feel okay about this situation, keep in mind that at least some of the money paid to the tax scorekeepers winds up in the government coffers as taxes!

Given all the hours that you put into filing necessary documents during the year — and into actually completing the dreaded return — we're sure that you feel more than justified in forgetting about your taxes once your return is in — until next year. This avoidance is a costly mistake.

During the tax year, you can do many simple things to ensure not only that you're in compliance with the ever-changing tax laws, but also that you're minimizing your taxes. Given your limited income, you need to understand the tax code in order to make it work for you and help you accomplish your financial goals.

A pound today or two pounds tomorrow

Take the case of Sheila and Peter, the proud owners of a successful and rapidly growing manufacturing business. They became so busy running the business and taking care of their children that they hardly had time to call a tax advisor. In fact, not only did they fail to file for an extension by April 15, but they also didn't pay any federal or state income tax.

By the following August, they finally had time to focus on the prior year's taxes, but by then they had gotten themselves into some problems and incurred more taxes. The first cost is failure to file which is 5 percent a month for a maximum of 25 percent. Then comes interest at about 9 percent per year. Another cost, caused by lack of planning, was far more expensive. Because they had incorporated their business, Peter and Sheila were on the payroll for salary during the year. Despite the high level of profitability of their business, they had set their pay at a low level.

A low salary wouldn't seem to be a problem if you're the owner and the only employee of a company. The worst that you'd think would have happened to Peter and Sheila is that they might have eaten more peanut butter and jelly sandwiches during the year. But because they received small salaries, they could only make contributions into tax-deductible retirement accounts based on a percentage of small salaries. The rest of the business profits, however, had to be taken by Sheila and Peter as taxable income because they had their company set up as an *S Corporation*. (You learn all about the different tax types of corporations in "To Incorporate or Not to Incorporate" in Chapter 20.)

Sheila and Peter actually lost *more* than the $10,000 in additional taxes by not being able to make larger retirement account contributions. Once money is inside tax-sheltered retirement accounts, it compounds (tax-deferred) over time. So over the 25-plus years that Sheila and Peter's money would have been in their retirement accounts, it would have grown by some tens of thousands of dollars by the time they took it out, even after payment of taxes.

Shoot first, aim later

Another common mistake made by otherwise intelligent folks is jumping into a financial decision *before* understanding the consequences and the other options. To our credit, human beings are rational in that we tend to do this kind of stuff in other parts of our lives as well!

Had enough of Sheila and Peter? Well, meet Bob and Mary, who are kind enough to illustrate this common mistake. They were in their early 60s when they met, fell for each other, got married quickly, and jetted off on a terrific honeymoon. When they returned home, they sat down with a tax preparer. They planned to sell their homes and buy one together.

You can imagine their disappointment when they learned that their rush to get married cost them about $43,000 in capital gains taxes. Why? As you learn in Chapter 22, when you've met certain requirements, you can sell your home once after age 55 and not pay capital gains tax on your first $125,000 of profit.

The tax mistake that Bob and Mary made was in selling their homes *after* they got married rather than *before*. After they were married, the IRS treated them as one. If they had sold their homes while they were still single, they each could have taken the "once-in-a-lifetime" capital gains exclusion.

My Taxes Are How High?

You pay a great deal of money in taxes — probably more than you realize. Most people remember only whether they got tax refunds or owed money on their tax returns. But you should also care about the *total* and the *marginal* taxes you pay.

When you file your tax return, all you're doing is balancing your checkbook, so to speak, against the federal and state governments' versions of your checkbook. You're settling up with tax authorities over the amount of taxes you paid during the year versus the total tax that you still owe based on your income and deductions.

Some people feel lucky when they get a refund, but really all a refund indicates is that you overpaid in taxes during the year. You could have had this money in your own account all along.

Total taxes

The only way to know the total taxes you pay is to get out your federal and state tax returns. On each of those returns is a line that shows the *total tax* (line 53 on federal 1040 returns). Add the totals from your federal and state tax returns and you'll probably see one of the single largest expenses of your financial life (unless you have an expensive home or a huge gambling habit).

Taxes are such a huge portion of most people's expenditures that any budget or spending plan that doesn't address, contain, and reduce your taxes is probably doomed to failure. Throughout this book, we highlight strategies for reducing your taxes right now as well as in the future.

Your marginal income tax rate

"What's marginal about my taxes?" we hear you asking. "They're huge! They're not marginal at all!" *Marginal* is a word that people often use when they mean small or barely acceptable. Sort of like getting a C– on a school report card (or an A– if you're from an overachieving family).

But when you're talking about taxes, marginal has a different, and very specific meaning. Your marginal tax rate is the rate you pay on the last dollar you earn. For example, if you earned $35,000 last year, the marginal rate is the rate you paid on the dollar that brought you from $34,999 to $35,000. The reason this subject comes up in the first place is that the government charges you different rates for different parts of your annual income.

After you understand the powerful concept of marginal tax rates, you can understand the value of many financial strategies that affect the amount of taxes you pay. Because you pay taxes on your employment income as well as on the earnings from your investments held outside of retirement accounts, a great number of your money decisions are at stake.

When it comes to taxes, *not all income is treated equally.* This fact is not self-evident. If you work for an employer and have a constant salary during the course of a year, a steady and equal amount in federal and state taxes is deducted from your paycheck. It sure looks as though all that earned income is being taxed equally.

In reality, however, you pay less tax on your *first* dollars of earnings and more tax on your *last* dollars of earnings. For example, if you're single and your taxable income totaled $30,000 during 1994, you paid federal tax at the rate of 15 percent on the first $22,749 of taxable income and 28 percent on income from $22,750 up to $30,000.

Taxable income is defined as the amount of income on which you actually pay taxes. You don't pay taxes on your total income for the following two reasons:

✔ **Not all income is taxable.** For example, you pay federal tax on the interest you earn on a bank savings account but not on the interest from municipal bonds.

✔ **You get to subtract deductions from your income.** Some deductions are available just for being a living, breathing human being. In 1994, single people receive an automatic $3,800 standard deduction and married couples filing jointly get $6,350. (People older than age 65 and those who are blind get slightly higher deductions.) Other expenses, such as mortgage interest and property taxes, are deductible to the extent that your total deductions exceed the standard deductions.

Table 1-1 gives federal tax rates for singles and for married households filing jointly.

Table 1-1	**1994 Federal Income Tax Brackets and Rates**	
Singles Taxable Income	*Married-Filing-Jointly Taxable Income*	*Federal Tax Rate*
Less than $22,750	Less than $38,000	15%
$22,750 to $55,100	$38,000 to $91,850	28%
$55,100 to $115,000	$91,850 to $140,000	31%
$115,000 to $250,000	$140,000 to $250,000	36%
More than $250,000	More than $250,000	39.6%

Your marginal tax rate is the rate of tax that you pay on your *last* or so-called *highest* dollars of income. In the example of a single person with taxable income of $30,000, that person's federal marginal tax rate is 28 percent. In other words, he or she effectively pays a 28 percent federal tax on his or her last dollars of income — those dollars earned between $22,750 and $55,100.

Your marginal tax rate allows you to quickly calculate additional taxes that you would pay on additional income. Conversely, you can delight in quantifying the amount of taxes that you save by reducing your taxable income, either by decreasing your income or by increasing your deductions.

Your marginal tax rate — the rate of tax you pay on your last dollars of income — should be higher than your average tax rate — the rate you pay, on average, on all your earnings. The reason your marginal tax rate is more important is that it tells you the value of reducing your taxable income.

TECHNICAL STUFF

Is it fair? You be the judge

Few issues, except maybe abortion, gun control, or whether to watch *Melrose Place* or *Murphy Brown* on Monday nights, inspire as much emotionally charged dialogue (and preachy monologues from radio talk show commentators) than the issue of whether our tax system is fair. By fair we mean how much total tax we are asked to pay and how that total compares with our neighbors, with our coworkers, and with the guy in Crawfordsville, Indiana.

If you're like most Americans, you probably feel that you pay too much in taxes. It may not be much comfort to you, but the average total taxes we pay are low in comparison to other industrialized countries in Europe and Asia. However, low- and moderate-income earners in the U.S. pay higher income taxes than do our overseas friends.

There is tremendous debate and gnashing of teeth over how much high-income earners and the wealthy, relative to others, should pay in taxes. Folks such as Malcolm Forbes Jr. and Rush Limbaugh argue that it's unfair and economically harmful to burden — with onerous taxes — those who "work hard and generate jobs" (that is, the high-income earners). At the other end of the spectrum, you hear the likes of Jesse Jackson and Ted Kennedy pleading that the well-heeled don't pay their fair share and should face higher taxes to help pay for "deserving programs for the poor and disadvantaged."

As with many disagreements, those at the polar extremes feel that they are right — intellectually, not politically speaking — and that the other side is wrong. Our advice is to keep an open mind, listen to both sides, and remember the big picture. Back in the 1950s (an economic boom time), for example, the highest federal income tax rate was a whopping 90 percent. Today, it's less than half that, thanks to tax law changes made in the 1960s and 1980s. And whereas, during most of this century, the highest-income earners paid a marginal rate that was double to triple the rate paid by moderate-income earners, that gap was greatly reduced during the 1980s.

And although we can agree that easy access to tax revenue encourages some wasteful government spending and pork-laden programs, we also know that taxes must come from somewhere. The questions are *how much* and *from whom?* The politically liberal have a tendency to idealize how well government solves problems and therefore advocate more taxes for more programs. On the other hand, the politically conservative have a tendency to idealize how well the private sector meets the needs of society at large in the absence of government oversight and programs.

State taxes

As you are painfully aware, you don't pay just federal income taxes. You also get hit with state income taxes — that is, unless you live in Alaska, Florida, Nevada, South Dakota, Texas, Washington, or Wyoming. Those states have no state income taxes. It is important to note that your *total marginal rate* includes your federal *and* state tax rates.

TIP

You can look up your state tax rate by getting out your most recent year's state income tax preparation booklet. Alternatively, we've been crazy — but kind — enough to prepare a helpful little (okay, not so little) table that should give you a rough idea of what your state taxes are (see Table 1-2).

Table 1-2		State Income Tax Brackets			
			Taxable Income		
State	**Filing Status**	**$25,000**	**$50,000**	**$100,000**	**$250,000**
Alabama	all	5%	5%	5%	5%
Alaska	all	none	none	none	none
Arizona	singles	5.3%	6.5%	6.5%	7%
	marrieds	4.4%	5.3%	6.5%	6.5%
Arkansas	all	7%	7%	7%	7%
California	singles	8%	9.3%	9.3%	11%
	marrieds	4%	8%	9.3%	10%
Colorado	all	5%	5%	5%	5%
Connecticut	all	4.5%	4.5%	4.5%	4.5%
Delaware	all	6.6%	7.7%	7.7%	7.7%
District of Columbia	all	9.5%	9.5%	9.5%	9.5%
Florida	all	none	none	none	none
Georgia	all	6%	6%	6%	6%
Hawaii	singles	10%	10%	10%	10%
	marrieds	8.8%	10%	10%	10%
Idaho	all	8.2%	8.2%	8.2%	8.2%
Illinois	all	3%	3%	3%	3%
Indiana	all	3.4%	3.4%	3.4%	3.4%
Iowa	all	7.6%	10%	10%	10%
Kansas	singles	7.5%	7.8%	7.8%	7.8%
	marrieds	3.5%	6.3%	6.5%	6.5%
Kentucky	all	6%	6%	6%	6%
Louisiana	all	4%	4%	6%	6%
Maine	singles	8.5%	8.5%	8.5%	8.5%
	marrieds	7%	8.5%	8.5%	8.5%
Maryland	all	5%	5%	5%	6%
Massachusetts[1]	all	6%	6%	6%	6%

(continued)

Table 1-2 *(continued)*

State	Filing Status	\$25,000	\$50,000	\$100,000	\$250,000
Michigan	all	4.6%	4.6%	4.6%	4.6%
Minnesota	singles	8%	8%	8.5%	8.5%
	marrieds	8%	8%	8.5%	8.5%
Mississippi	all	5%	5%	5%	5%
Missouri	all	6%	6%	6%	6%
Montana	all	9%	10%	11%	11%
Nebraska	singles	6%	7%	7%	7%
	marrieds	4%	7%	7%	7%
Nevada	all	none	none	none	none
New Hampshire[2]	all	none	none	none	none
New Jersey	singles	2.5%	6.5%	7%	7%
	marrieds	2.5%	3.5%	6.5%	7%
New Mexico	singles	7%	8.5%	8.5%	8.5%
	marrieds	6%	8.5%	8.5%	8.5%
New York	singles	7.9%	7.9%	7.9%	7.9%
	marrieds	7%	7.9%	7.9%	7.9%
North Carolina	all	7%	7%	7.8%	7.8%
North Dakota	all	9.3%	12%	12%	12%
Ohio	all	4.5%	5.2%	6.9%	7.5%
Oklahoma	all	7%	7%	7%	7%
Oregon	all	9%	9%	9%	9%
Pennsylvania	all	2.8%	2.8%	2.8%	2.8%
Rhode Island[3]	all	n/a	n/a	n/a	n/a
South Carolina	all	7%	7%	7%	7%
South Dakota	all	none	none	none	none
Tennessee[4]	all	none	none	none	none
Texas	all	none	none	none	none
Utah	all	7.2%	7.2%	7.2%	7.2%
Vermont[3]	all	n/a	n/a	n/a	n/a
Virginia	all	5.8%	5.8%	5.8%	5.8%

State	Filing Status	Taxable Income $25,000	$50,000	$100,000	$250,000
Washington	all	none	none	none	none
West Virginia	all	4%	6%	6.5%	6.5%
Wisconsin	all	6.9%	6.9%	6.9%	6.9%
Wyoming	all	none	none	none	none

[1]Massachusetts taxes non-bank interest, dividends, and capital gains at the rate of 12%.

[2]New Hampshire taxes interests and dividends from bonds and other debts at 5%.

[3]Rhode Island and Vermont. Rate is applied to federal income tax, not taxable income.

[4]Tennessee taxes interests and dividends from stocks and bonds at 6%.

The second tax system: Alternative Minimum Tax

You may find this hard to believe, but (as if the tax system weren't already complicated enough) there is actually a *second* federal tax system. This second system may raise your taxes higher than they would have been otherwise. Let us explain.

Over the years, as the government has grown hungrier for revenue, taxpayers who slash their taxes by claiming lots of deductions have come under greater scrutiny. So the government created a second tax system — the *Alternative Minimum Tax* (AMT) — to ensure that those with high deductions pay at least a certain amount of taxes on their income.

If you have a lot of deductions from state income taxes, real estate taxes, certain types of mortgage interest, and passive investments (for example, limited partnerships and rental real estate), you may fall prey to the AMT. The AMT is a classic case of the increasing complexity of our tax code. As incentives were placed in the tax code, people took advantage of them. Then the government said, "Whoa Nelly! We can't have people taking that many write-offs." Thus was born the AMT.

At the federal level lurk two AMT tax brackets: 26 percent for AMT income up to $175,000 and 28 percent for everything over that amount. The AMT restricts you from claiming certain deductions and requires you to increase your taxable income. So you have to figure your tax under the AMT system *and* under the other system and pay whichever amount is *higher* (ouch!). Unfortunately, the only way to know for certain if you're ensnared by this second tax system is to complete— you guessed it— another tax form. We tell how to do this in Chapter 13.

Taxing perspectives

"In this world nothing can be said to be certain, except death and taxes."
                    - Benjamin Franklin

"The power to tax involves the power to destroy."
                    - John Marshall

"The wisdom of man never yet contrived a system of taxation that would operate with perfect equality."
                    - Andrew Jackson

"The avoidance of taxes is the only intellectual pursuit that still carries any reward."
                    - John Maynard Keynes

"An economy hampered by restrictive tax rates will never produce enough revenues to balance our budget, just as it will never produce enough jobs or enough profits."
                    - John F. Kennedy

"There is one difference between a tax collector and a taxidermist — the taxidermist leaves the hide."
                    - Mortimer Caplan

"People hate taxes the way children hate brushing their teeth — and in the same shortsighted way."
                    - Paul A. Samuelson

"The nation should have a tax system which looks like someone designed it on purpose."
                    - William E. Simon

"The entire graduated income tax system was created by Karl Marx."
                    - Ronald Reagan

"The last important human activity not subject to taxation is sex."
                    - Russell Baker

Chapter 2

Who's Gonna Do It? You, Software, or a Preparer?

*P*lanning ahead may sound like the impossible dream, but when it comes to taxes, a little planning can pay big dividends. By the time you actually file your return, it's usually too late to take advantage of many (but not all) tax-reduction strategies. And what is more aggravating than, on April 14, finding a golden nugget of tax advice that works great — for those who knew about it last June? Shoulda, woulda, coulda been a millionaire. So be sure to review Part IV, which covers the important planning issues you should take advantage of *after* you complete the annual chore of filing your tax return.

If you're now faced with the daunting task of preparing your return, you're probably trying to decide how to get it done with a minimum of pain and a maximum of dollars saved. You have some basic options. The choice that makes sense for you depends on how complex your situation is, how much you know about taxes, and how much you enjoy a challenge.

Doing It Yourself

Perhaps you already do many things for yourself. You dress yourself every morning. You choose your own shampoo. Maybe you cook for yourself, do home repairs, or even change the oil in your car. You may do these chores because you enjoy them, because you save money by doing them yourself, or because you want to develop a particular skill.

Preparing your own tax return is the cheapest way to get it done — as long as you don't figure in the value of lost leisure time, of course. This solution is especially good if your financial situation doesn't change much from year to year because you can just pull out last year's return, fill in the new numbers for this year, add them up, put it in the mail, and forget about taxes until next year. You may need to do a little reading to keep up with the small number of changes in the tax system and laws that affect your situation.

The down side to preparing your own taxes is that you probably just keep on doing what you're doing with taxes — year after year — which means that you may be missing some easy ways to keep more money in your bank account.

You bought this book, so you must feel somewhat confused. If that feeling continues, you probably shouldn't try to do your return yourself. Give our advice in Part II a try before you throw in the towel and pay hundreds of dollars in tax-preparation fees. And if you stay alert while preparing your return, reading the list of deductions that don't apply to you may motivate you to make changes in your financial habits so you can qualify to take some of those deductions next year.

IRS assistance

If you have a simple, straightforward tax return, filing it on your own using only the IRS instructions is fine. This approach is as cheap as you can get. The only costs are time, patience, photocopying expenses (you should always keep a copy for your files), and postage to mail the completed tax return.

This approach has a lot in common with an Easter egg hunt. If you've ever hunted Easter eggs, you know the prizes are well hidden (from a child's perspective, anyway) and require some real searching to find. In our own egg-hunting experience, we don't recall any large, flashing neon signs reading DON'T MISS THIS ONE! pointing to hidden eggs.

Likewise, IRS publications don't, in general, have helpful icons like this book. For example, here's something you don't see in an IRS publication:

```
STOP! One of the most commonly overlooked deductions is a
tax-deductible retirement contribution. You still have time
to start one and whack off hundreds — maybe thousands — of
dollars from your tax bill! HURRY!
```

Another danger of relying on the IRS is that it has been known to give wrong information on a more-than-infrequent basis. If you call the IRS with a question, be sure to take notes about your conversation to protect yourself in the event of an audit. Date your notes and include the name of the IRS employee you talked to, what you asked, and the employee's responses. File your notes in a folder with a copy of your completed return.

In addition to the standard instructions that come with your tax return, the IRS offers some free and helpful books that you can request by phone. Publication 17 *(Your Federal Income Tax)* is designed for individual tax-return preparation. Publication 334 *(Tax Guide for Small Businesses)* is for (you guessed it) small-business tax-return preparation. These guides serve as useful references and provide more detail and insight than the basic IRS publications. Call 800-TAX-FORM to have the guides sent to you free of charge. (Actually, nothing is free. You've already paid for IRS guides through your taxes!)

The IRS also offers more in-depth booklets focusing on specific tax issues. We've listed them in the appendix for those gluttons for punishment who can't wait to read this kind of stuff. However, if your tax problem is so complex that this book (and Publication 17) can't address it, you should think long and hard about getting help from a tax advisor (see the "Hired Help" section later in this chapter) or from one of the other sources recommended in this chapter.

The IRS books are like law books. They have to give you the facts, but they don't have to make it easy for you to find the facts and advice you really need. The best way to use these publications is for you to confirm facts that you already think you know or to check the little details.

Preparation and advice guides

Books about tax preparation are invaluable if they highlight common problems in clear, simple English. *Taxes For Dummies,* we hope you'll agree, is top of the line in this category.

These books make it easier to find the facts you need in the official instruction and they help you complete your return correctly while saving you as much money as possible. The amount of money invested in a book or two is vastly smaller than the annual cost of a tax expert! (And, by the way, it helps keep authors and publishers in business, too!)

Taxes For Dummies covers the important preparation and planning issues that hit the vast majority of taxpayers. There are some nit-picky issues that a minority of taxpayers run into because of an unusual event in their lives or because of extraordinary changes in their income or assets. For these folks, this book may not be enough. More comprehensive books exist, and our favorites are:

- ✔ J.K. Lasser's *Your Income Tax*
- ✔ Consumer Reports' *Guide to Income Tax*

Software

If you have access to a computer, tax-preparation software can be a great tool. Think of it as having a squadron of excellent accountants living on your desktop. Plus, you don't have to race to the library to get all the forms for your particular return — only to discover that the library is out of them. And you don't have to call the IRS and wait for weeks for your forms to arrive in the mail. Your software has all the forms you're likely to need!

Software also has the virtue of automatically recalculating all the appropriate numbers on your return when one number changes — no more whiting out math errors or recalculating a whole page of figures because your dog was sleeping on some of the receipts.

Software is not without its drawbacks, however. Here are the main ones:

- ✔ **Garbage in, garbage out.** A tax return prepared by a software program is only as good as the quality of the data you enter into it. Of course, this drawback exists no matter who is actually filling out the forms — some tax preparers don't probe and clarify to make sure you've given all the right stuff.

- ✔ **Where's the beef?** A number of the tax software packages on the market give little in the way of background help, advice, and warnings. This lack of assistance can lull you into a false sense of security about the completeness and accuracy of the return you are preparing.

- ✔ **Think, computer, think!** Computers are good at helping you access and process information. They don't exercise judgment or think for you (although someday they may do more if the artificial intelligence gurus realize their dreams). In the meantime, remember that your computer is great at crunching numbers but has a lower IQ than you.

On-line and Internet tax information

In addition to using your computer to prepare your tax return, you can do an increasing number of other tax activities on the information superhighway. But if you don't own a computer or know how to access on-line services and the Internet, we wouldn't recommend learning the services or spending the monthly usage fees just for the tax information. You're not missing much that you can't find or do through other, often more convenient, means.

The major on-line services such as CompuServe and America Online have financial forums where you can post messages and discuss issues. We would not recommend that you depend on the accuracy of the answers you get there for tax questions. The problem: You have no idea of the background, expertise, and identity of the person who you are trading messages with. If you enjoy chatting and getting multiple opinions on a vexing issue, it's fine to use an on-line service as one of the sources.

Once you've learned how to hop on and navigate the information highway, use it for what it's best at — possibly saving you time tracking down factual information or other stuff.

CompuServe currently offers the largest array of tax materials and services. For example, you can download, for a fee of course, hundreds of IRS income tax forms and instructions. So if you don't want to spend money on tax software that includes most of the forms you need, CompuServe might save you a trip to a government office to retrieve forms. IRS tax forms are also available on **FedWorld**, a government-run Internet bulletin board.

CompuServe also allows you to get on-line technical support from the larger publishers of tax preparation software. Alternatively, you can obtain help by calling or faxing, sometimes through a toll-free 800 number.

On the Internet, a number of newsgroups, such as **misc.taxes**, offer information and discussion of tax issues. Again, take advice and counsel from other net users at your peril.

If you want to liven up your life — and taxes make you mad — a number of political forums allow you to converse and butt heads with others. You can complain about recent tax hikes or explain why you think the wealthy still don't pay enough taxes!

The best tax preparation software is easy to install and use on your computer, provides high-quality help if you get stuck, and highlights deductions you may be overlooking. Some of the packages even let you import data you've been collecting throughout the year from other software, including checkbook packages such as Quicken, Microsoft Money, and others. If you get a headache trying to figure out how to do something in the software, the best packages have accessible and helpful technical support people you can call in your time of need. (Remember, though, that these people are software techies, not tax techies. Don't expect to get an explanation of whether or not you can deduct your last trip to Hawaii as a business expense.)

Among the better tax-preparation software packages on the market are:

- ✔ Kiplinger Taxcut (for DOS, Windows, and the Macintosh)
- ✔ TurboTax (for Windows and DOS) and MacinTax (for the Macintosh)

If you're undecided about which package to purchase, check to see if the one you're considering offers a separate package for your state. Another way to break a tie between software is price — you may be able to get a better deal on one or the other. This is a case where procrastinating has its benefits, because the longer you wait to buy the software, the cheaper it gets, especially if you buy it after filing for an extension. Also, be sure to check if the one you buy imports data from the checkbook software you may have been using to track your tax-deductible expenses throughout the year.

Hired Help

Some people hire a contractor to help with a home-remodeling project because they lack the time, interest, energy, or skill to do it themselves. And they think they can afford to pay a contractor to do the work for them (although sometimes this last part isn't true and they wind up with more debt than they can afford!). For the same reasons, some people choose to hire a tax advisor.

Competent tax specialists can save you money — sometimes more than enough to pay their fees — by identifying tax-reduction strategies you may overlook. They may also reduce the likelihood of an audit, which can be triggered by blunders you might make.

The best tax advisors won't usually cold-call you at home trying to get your business. The hard part for you is to uncover those busy advisors who do terrific work and charge reasonable fees. Here are some resources to find those publicity-shy tax preparers:

- ✔ **Friends.** Some of your friends probably use a tax advisor and can steer you to a decent one or two for an interview. Later in this chapter we list questions that we suggest you ask potential tax preparers in advance.
- ✔ **Coworkers.** Ask people in your field who they use. This strategy can be especially useful if you're self-employed.

✔ **Other advisors.** Financial and legal advisors can be helpful as well, but don't assume that they know more about the competence of a tax person than you do. There is a common problem to beware of: these folks may simply be referring you to tax preparers who send them work.

✔ **Associations.** Both enrolled agents (EAs) and certified public accountants (CPAs) maintain professional associations that can refer you to members in your local area. Their toll-free 800 numbers are listed in the sections that follow.

Tax practitioners come with various backgrounds, training, and credentials. One type of professional is not necessarily better than another. Think of them as different types of specialists who are appropriate for different circumstances. The four main types are preparers, enrolled agents, certified public accountants, and tax attorneys.

Preparers

Among all the tax practitioners, preparers *generally* have the least amount of training, and a greater proportion of them work part time. As with financial

Can I do my return without a preparer?

This is not a simple question to answer. Odds are you can. Most people's returns don't vary that much from year to year. So you have a head start if you get out last year's return (which, of course, you copied and saved in a well-marked place!) and hit the ground running.

This strategy won't work as well if your situation has changed in some way — if you bought or sold a house, started your own business, or retired. In that case, start by focusing on the sections of this book in Part II that deal with those preparation issues. If you want more planning background, check out the relevant portions in Part IV.

Don't give up and hire a preparer because you can't bear to open your tax preparation booklet and get your background data organized. Even if

you hire a tax preparer, you need to get your stuff organized before a consultation.

As hard and as painful as it is, confront preparing your return as far in advance of April 15 as you can. That way, if you don't feel comfortable with your level of knowledge, you have enough time to seek help. The more organizing you can do before hiring a preparer, the less it should cost you. Avoid waiting until the 11th hour to hire an advisor — you won't do as thorough a job selecting a competent person, and you'll probably pay more for a rush job. If you get stuck preparing the return, you can get a second opinion from another preparation resource, such as a more technical tax book or a good software package (recommended earlier in this chapter).

planners, no national regulations apply to preparers, and no licensing is required. In most states, almost anybody can hang out their tax-preparation shingle and start preparing. Most preparers, however, complete some sort of training program before working with clients.

H&R Block, with about 9,000 offices nationwide, is the largest and most well-known tax-preparation firm in the country. In addition to H&R Block and other national firms such as Jackson Hewitt and Triple Check, there are also lots of mom-and-pop shops. The appeal of preparers is that they are relatively inexpensive; they can do most basic returns for $100 or less. The drawback, of course, is that you may be hiring a preparer who doesn't know much more than you do.

Preparers make the most sense for folks who don't have a lot of complications in their financial lives, who are budget minded, and who hate doing their own taxes. If you're not good about hanging onto receipts or don't want to keep your own files with background details about your taxes, you should definitely shop around for a tax preparer who's going to be around for a few years.

You may need all that paperwork stuff someday for an audit, and many tax preparers keep and organize their clients' documentation rather than return everything each year. (Can you blame them for keeping it after they went to the trouble of sorting it all out of the shopping bags?) Also, it may be safer to go with a firm that is open year-round in case tax questions or problems arise (some small shops are open only during tax season).

Please note that the IRS recognizes three types of people that can represent a taxpayer should they be audited: CPAs, EAs, and attorneys. When someone else — like a tax preparer — helps you with your taxes, that person cannot act as your advocate during an audit or other IRS encounter.

Enrolled agents (EAs)

A person must pass IRS scrutiny in order to be called an *enrolled agent*. This license allows the agent to represent you before the IRS in the event of an audit. Continuing education is also required. The training to become an EA is generally longer and more sophisticated than that of a typical preparer. EAs must complete at least 24 hours of continuing education each year to maintain their license.

Enrolled agents' prices tend to fall between those of a preparer and a CPA. Returns with a few of the more common schedules (such as Schedule A for deductions and Schedule B for interest and dividends) shouldn't cost more than a couple hundred dollars to prepare. If you live in a high-cost city such as New York or Los Angeles, you may pay more.

ıain difference between enrolled agents and CPAs and attorneys is that
ork exclusively in the field of taxation. Not all CPAs and attorneys do. In
ɔn to preparing your return (including simple to complex forms), some
·lp with tax planning, representing you at audits, and getting the IRS off
ack. You can get names and telephone numbers of EAs in your area by
ting the National Association of Enrolled Agents (800-424-4339).

tified public accountants (CPAs)

ed public accountants go through significant training and examination to
e the CPA credential. In order to maintain this designation, a CPA must
mplete a fair number of continuing education classes every year — at
least 40 hours worth.

CPA fees vary tremendously. Most charge around $100 per hour, but CPAs at
large companies and in high cost-of-living areas tend to charge somewhat more.

Competent CPAs are of greatest value to people completing some of the more
unusual and less user-friendly schedules, such as K-1 for partnerships, Schedule
C for self-employed folks, or Form 8829 for home office deductions. CPAs are
also helpful for people who had a major or first-time tax event during the year,
such as the sale of a home, retirement, or childcare tax-credit determination.
(Good EAs and other preparers can do these things as well.)

If your return is uncomplicated and your financial situation is stable, hiring a
high-priced CPA year after year to fill in the blanks is a waste of money. A CPA
once bragged that he was effectively making about $500 per hour from some of his
clients' returns that required only 20 minutes of an assistant's time to complete.

Paying for the additional cost of a CPA on an ongoing basis makes sense if you
can afford it and if your situation is reasonably complex or dynamic. If you are
self-employed and/or file lots of other schedules, it may be worth hiring a CPA.
But you needn't do so year after year. If your situation grows complex one year
and then stabilizes, consider getting help for the perplexing year and then using
preparation guides, software, or a lower-cost preparer or enrolled agent in the
future. You can obtain the names and phone numbers of CPAs in your local
area by checking your local pages under "Accountants — Certified Public."

Tax attorneys

Tax attorneys are hired guns who can tackle major tax problems and issues.
Attorneys, for example, handle court cases dealing with tax problems or
disagreements, or other complicated matters, such as the purchase or sale
of a business.

Who's best qualified? EA, CPA, or preparer.

It really depends on the individual. The CPA credential is just that, a credential. Some people who have the credential will try to persuade you not to hire someone without it, but don't always believe this advice.

Some of the tax-preparation books also perpetuate this myth. Consider the *Ernst & Young Tax Guide*. In a chapter about choosing a tax preparer, misleadingly entitled "How to Prepare for Your Accountant," the authors say that "choosing an accountant is not something that should be done casually. There are over 300,000 certified public accountants." These authors also recommend that you ask a potential preparer "Are you a certified public accountant?"

What about all the non-CPAs who do a terrific job helping their clients prepare their returns and plan for their taxes throughout the year?

As you may know or have guessed by now, Ernst & Young is a CPA firm that works primarily for big businesses and affluent people. If you can afford to and want to pay hundreds of dollars per hour, hiring this type of firm may make sense. But for the vast majority of taxpayers, it's unnecessary and wasteful to spend this kind of money. And there are many enrolled agents and other tax preparers who do super work for far less.

Unless you're a super high-income earner with a complex financial life, it's prohibitively expensive to hire a tax attorney to prepare your annual return. In fact, many tax attorneys don't prepare returns as a normal practice. Because of their level of specialization and training, tax attorneys tend to have the highest hourly billing rates — $200 to $300 per hour is not unusual.

The more training and specialization a tax practitioner has (and the more affluent the clients), the higher the hourly fee. Select the one that best meets your needs. Fees and competence at all levels of the profession vary significantly. If you're not sure of the quality of work performed and the soundness of the advice, try getting a second opinion.

Ten questions to ask a tax advisor you may hire

What tax services do you offer?

Most tax advisors prepare tax returns. We use the term tax *advisors* since most tax folks do more than simply prepare returns. Many advisors will help you plan and file other important tax documents throughout the year. Some firms will also assist your small business with bookkeeping and other financial reporting, such as income statements and balance sheets. These services can be very helpful if you suddenly need to get a loan or if you need to give clients or investors detailed information about your business.

Working with other advisors

There's more to your financial life than taxes, thank goodness. Your tax situation is an important piece to your personal finance puzzle. But so are your spending habits, your investment and retirement plans, your real estate decisions, your insurance coverage, and so on. Sometimes you're going to need to work with practitioners in these other areas and factor in the tax ramifications of an important financial decision. How this cooperation gets coordinated is important.

You can be the person who puts these pieces together. A good tax advisor who is adept at seeing the big picture can be a voice of reason and counsel, particularly if you're in the clutches of a salesperson with a vested interest in your decision. An objective financial advisor who consults on an hourly basis, like a tax advisor, can help as well. In Part IV, we discuss the important issues that confront you in factoring tax issues into important financial planning decisions.

Ask any potential tax advisors to explain how they work with clients. Look for those who probe their clients and ask questions to understand the big picture. Beware of tax preparers who view their job as simply plugging into tax forms the information that you bring them.

You're hiring the tax advisor because of your lack of knowledge of the tax system. If your tax advisor doesn't prod and explore your situation, it can mean you're walking into a situation where "the blind are leading the blind." A good tax advisor can help you make sure that you're not overlooking deductions and making other costly mistakes that might lead to an audit, penalties, and interest.

Do you have areas that you focus on?

This is an important question. If, for example, a tax preparer works mainly with people who receive regular paychecks from an employer, he or she may have less expertise in helping small business owners complete the blizzard of paperwork that the IRS requires.

It's critical to find out if the tax advisor has expertise in handling whatever unusual financial events you're dealing with this year — or what events you expect in future years. For example, if you need help completing an estate tax return for a deceased relative, ask how many of these the tax preparer has completed in the past year.

What other services (legal, financial planning, and so on) do you offer?

Ideally, you want to work with a professional who is 100 percent focused on taxes. We know it's hard to imagine that there are people who eat, sleep, and breathe this stuff, but there are — and lucky for you!

A multitude of problems crop up when a person tries to prepare tax returns, sell investments, and appraise real estate — all at the same time. They may not be fully competent or current in any of these areas. Another concern is that, maybe, they need to practice in other professions to earn a living because they're not good enough in one.

By virtue of their background and training, some tax preparers also offer consulting services for business owners or financial planning services. Because they already know a great deal about your personal and tax situation, a competent tax professional may be able to help in these areas. Just make sure that this help is on a fee-for-service or hourly consulting basis. Avoid tax advisors who sell financial products that pay them a commission — this situation inevitably creates conflicts of interest.

Who will be preparing my return?

If you're talking to a solo practitioner, the answer to this question should be simple — the person you're talking to. But if your tax advisor has assistants and other employees, make sure you know what level of involvement these different people will have. It's not necessarily bad if a junior-level person does the preliminary tax return preparation that your tax advisor will review and complete. In fact, this procedure can save you money in tax preparation fees if the firm bills you at a lower hourly rate for a junior-level person.

Be wary of firms that charge you a high hourly rate for the tax advisor who delegates most of the work to a junior-level person.

How aggressive or conservative are you regarding the tax law?

Some tax preparers, unfortunately, view their role as enforcement agents for the IRS. This attitude is often a consequence of one too many seminars put on by local IRS folks who admonish preparers with the threats of audits. On the other hand, some preparers are too aggressive and try tax maneuvers that put their clients on thin ice — subjecting them to more audits, additional taxes, penalties, and interest.

This is a difficult issue for you to assess, but start by asking what percentage of the tax preparer's clients get audited (see the next question). You can also ask the tax advisor for references from clients for whom the advisor helped unearth overlooked opportunities to reduce tax bills.

What's your experience with audits?

As a benchmark, you should know that about 1 percent of all taxpayer returns get audited. If the tax advisor works with a more affluent client base or small business owners, expect a higher audit rate — somewhere in the neighborhood of 2 percent to as much as 5 percent.

If the tax preparer proudly claims no audited clients, be careful. He's either not telling you the truth or he's ultraconservative. A tax preparer who has been in business at least a couple of years will have gone through audits. Ask the preparer to explain his last two audits, what happened, and why. This explanation will shed light not only on a preparer's work with clients, but also on a preparer's ability to communicate in plain English.

How does your fee structure work?

Accountant fees, like attorney and financial planner fees, vary all over the map — from $50 to $300 or more per hour. Many preparers will simply quote you a total fee for preparation of your tax return.

Ultimately, the tax advisor is charging you for time, so you should ask what the hourly billing rate is. If the advisor balks at answering this question, try asking about the fee for a one- or two-hour consultation. You may want a tax advisor to work on this basis if you've prepared your return yourself and want it reviewed as a quality control check. You also may seek an hourly fee if you are on top of your tax preparation in general but have some very specific questions about an unusual or one-time event, such as the sale of your business.

Clarify whether the accountant's set fee includes follow-up questions that you may have during the year, or if this fee covers IRS audits on the return. Some accountants include these functions in their set fee, but others charge for everything on an as-needed basis. The advantage of the all-inclusive fee is that it removes the psychological obstacle for your feeling that the meter's running every time you call with a question. The drawback can be that you're paying for additional services you may not need or use.

What work and educational experience qualify you to be a tax advisor?

Tax advisors come with a variety of backgrounds. The more tax and business experience they have, the better. But don't be overly impressed with credentials. As discussed earlier in the chapter, tax advisors can earn certifications such as CPAs and EAs. Although gaining credentials takes time and work, these certifications are no guarantee that you get high quality tax assistance or that you won't be overcharged.

Generally speaking, more years of experience are better than less, but don't rule out a newer advisor who lacks gray hair or time spent slogging through thousands of returns. Intelligence and training can easily make up for less experience. Newer advisors also may charge less in order to build up their practices.

Do you carry liability insurance?

If an accountant makes a major mistake or gives poor advice, you could lose thousands of dollars. The greater your income, assets, and importance of your financial decisions, the more financial harm can be done. We know you're not a litigious person, but your tax advisor should carry goof-up insurance, sometimes known as errors and omissions, or liability insurance. You could, of course, simply sue an uninsured advisor and hope the advisor has enough personal assets to cover a loss, but don't count on it. Besides, you'll have a much more difficult time getting your due compensation this way!

You may also ask the advisor if he or she has ever been sued and what the result was. It doesn't occur to most people to ask this type of question, so make sure you tell your tax advisor that you're not out to strike it rich on a lawsuit. If you want independent verification that a tax advisor hasn't gotten into any hot water, you can check with their professional organization.

Can you provide references of clients similar to me?

You need to know that the tax advisor has handled cases and problems like yours. For example, if you're a small business owner, ask to speak with other small business owners. Don't be overly impressed by accountants who claim that they work mainly with physicians, for example. While there is value in understanding the nuances of a profession, accountants are ultimately generalists — as are the tax laws.

When all is said and done, make sure that you feel comfortable with the tax advisor. We're not suggesting that you evaluate an advisor the way you would a potential spouse! But if you're feeling uneasy and can't understand what your tax advisor says to you in the early stages of your relationship, it'll probably get worse instead of better.

Chapter 3

Are You Organized?

- -

In This Chapter

▶ Benefits of good records

▶ Organize, organize, organize

▶ Statute of limitations

▶ What to do when records aren't available

▶ The Cohan Rule

- -

Do you want to make your tax preparation easier? Keep good records. Do you want to make sure you can claim every deduction you're entitled to? Keep good records. Do you want to survive an IRS audit and not pay additional tax, interest, and penalties? Keep good records. Do you want to save money by not paying tax preparers $50 to $200 an hour to organize your stuff? Keep good records.

We know we're repeating ourselves here, but this is a point worth saying over and over. If you're like most people, you probably aren't a very good book-keeper. But without good records, you could be in trouble. Furthermore, some tax preparers and accountants love to see people walk into their offices with shoeboxes full of receipts. They charge you a hefty hourly fee and then turn around and pay someone $20 an hour to organize your receipts.

You may be realizing now (as you sit down to complete your tax return) that you are going to have to rummage through a box of paper scraps containing not only your important tax records, but also cool things like your homework assignments from seventh grade and your 1986 Christmas list.

Or else you're sure that this is the year you know you can itemize deductions and save those big bucks — if only you could remember where you stashed your medical bills and the receipts from your favorite charity.

Finally, you can easily imagine yourself the night before an IRS audit wondering how you're going to support your claim for all those business entertainment costs. Do you know what happens if you're audited and can't document your claims? First, you'll owe additional tax and interest. Then come the penalties, and the IRS has a lengthy list of them.

But enough horror stories! You know that you must take some steps now to avoid the misery of not having good records. It may be too late for you this time around, but it's never too late to get into good habits for next time. In this chapter, you learn a few tried and proven ways to keep track of everything you need, to survive not only this tax preparation season, but future tax situations as well.

Here's an important point. To deal effectively with the IRS, you need documentation, because the tax laws place the burden of proof on the taxpayer. (Do you think this policy means that you're guilty until proven innocent? Unfortunately, the answer is *yes*.) But if the tax records you need to support your case are unavailable, don't throw in the towel yet. This chapter also shows you how to overcome such a problem — just in case you failed Recordkeeping 101.

Good Records

Tax records pose a problem for many people, because the IRS doesn't require a particular form of recordkeeping. In fact, the IRS recommends, in general terms, that you keep records in order to file a "complete and accurate" return. Need a bit more detail? Read on.

Your "complete and accurate" tax return

"Hey, my return is complete and accurate," you say, adding, "all the numbers are within the lines and neatly written without any math errors." In case you don't feel like flipping through countless pages of government instructions on what constitutes a "complete and accurate" return, we thought you'd like to see at a glance several common problem areas and the types of records normally required.

> ✔ **Charitable contributions.** No longer will a canceled check alone be allowed to support this deduction. If your donation is valued at $250 or more, you now need a written receipt from the charity indicating the amount of money you gave or a description of the property you donated (see "Lines 15-18: Gifts to Charity" in Chapter 8 for more information).

✔ **Dependent care expenses.** If you plan to claim someone as a dependent, you need to be able to prove that you provided over 50 percent of that person's total support. This case applies especially to children of divorced parents and college students. The length of time you provide the support doesn't mean anything — it's the total cost that matters. So be ready to show how much you paid for your dependent's lodging, food, clothes, health care, transportation, and any other essential support stuff.

✔ **Car expenses.** If, for the business use of your car, you choose to deduct the actual expenses instead of the standard mileage rate, you need to be able to show the cost of the car and when you started using the car. You also have to record your business miles, your total miles, and your expenses, such as insurance, gas, and maintenance — you'll need a combination of a log and written receipts, of course! (See "Line 10: Car and truck expenses" in Chapter 10.)

✔ **Home expenses.** Besides the records of your purchase price and purchase expenses, don't neglect to file all receipts and records of improvements and additions that affect the cost of your residence (see Chapter 22).

✔ **Business expenses.** The IRS is especially careful in this area, so be sure to provide detailed proof of any expenses claimed. This proof can consist of many items, such as receipts of income, expense account statements, and so on. Remember that canceled checks alone will not always be accepted as substantiation, so keep any written statements you can (see Chapter 10 if you're self-employed and Chapter 8 if you're an employee).

Organize, organize, organize

The tax year is a long time to keep track of what records you'll need (and where you put them) once the filing season arrives. So here are some easy things you can do to make your tax-preparation burden a little lighter:

✔ Invest in an accordion file. You can buy one that's already labeled with slots by month, by category, or by alphabet, or you can make your own filing system with the extra labels — all this can be yours for less than $10.

✔ If $10 is too much, you can purchase a dozen or so of those manila file folders for about $3. Decide on the organization that best fits your needs and get into the habit of saving all bills, receipts, and records that you think you can use someday for your tax purposes, as well as things that affect your overall financial planning. This basic advice is good for any taxpayer, whether you file a simple tax return on Form 1040EZ or a complicated Form 1040 with lots of supplemental schedules. Remember that this is only a minimal plan, but it's much better than the shoebox approach to recordkeeping.

✔ If your financial life is uncomplicated, then each new year set up one file folder that has the year on it (so in January, 1995, you establish your "1995" file). During the year, as you receive documentation that you think you'll use in preparing your return, stash it in the folder. In January, 1996, when you receive your dreaded Form 1040 booklet, toss that in the file, too. Come springtime 1996, when you finally force yourself to sit down, hopefully you'll have everything in this one bulging file.

✔ If you're a 1040 user and really a perfectionist, you can arrange your records in a file by schedules and forms that you know you'll need. For example, you can set up folders such as these:

Schedule A: deductible items (such as automobile expenses)
Schedule B: interest and dividend income stuff
Form 2119: papers on the sale of your home

And so on. You 1040 filers have so many options that you really should take the time to learn about your return — we'll help you there — so that you can anticipate your future tax needs.

Computerized recordkeeping

A number of financial software packages may be able to help you with tracking your spending for tax purposes. Just don't expect to get the benefits without a fair amount of up-front and continuing work. You need to learn how to use the software and you need to enter a great deal of data in order for it to be useful to you come tax time.

If you're interested in software, check out a package called Quicken, formerly by Intuit (they are in the process of getting swallowed by Microsoft). With Quicken, you can keep track of your stock portfolio, pay your bills, balance your checking account, and, best of all, get help with tabulating your tax information. Just remember that the package tabulates only what you enter. So if you use it to write your monthly checks but neglect to enter data for things you pay for with cash, for example, you won't have the whole picture.

For how long?

One of the most frequently asked questions is how long a taxpayer should keep tax records. The answer is easy — a minimum of three years. That's because there's a three-year statute of limitations on tax audits and assessments. If the IRS doesn't adjust or audit your 1991 tax return by April 17, 1995, it has missed its chance. On April 18, you can start disposing of your 1991 records if you want. Because in 1995 April 15 falls on a Saturday, you get two extra days to file your return — but the IRS gets two extra days, too.

Watch out for state differences

Although the IRS requires only that you keep your records for three years, the statute of limitations for your state may be longer. For example, say you pitch out your receipts after three years. Then the fellow who built your garage four years ago sues you, asserting that you never paid the bill. You may be out of luck in court if you don't have the canceled check showing that you paid.

The moral is to hang on to records that may be important (such as home improvement receipts) for longer than three years — especially if there is a possible dispute. Check with a legal advisor if you have a concern, because statutes of limitations vary from state to state. Also, your state may have a longer statute of limitations with regard to state income tax audits.

But in situations where the IRS suspects that income was not reported, IRS agents can go back as far as six years. And if there is an instance of possible tax fraud, forget all time restraints!

There is one point to add to the general three-year rule, however. Save all records for those assets you continue to own, such as purchase slips for stocks and bonds, automobiles, the purchase of your home (along with its improvements), and expensive personal property such as jewelry, video cameras, or computers. Keep these records in a safety deposit box in case you suffer a deductible casualty loss such as a fire. You don't want these records going up in smoke! Some taxpayers have taken the practical measure of videotaping their home and its contents (make sure to keep that record outside your home as well — save money on safety deposit box fees by leaving your video with relatives who might enjoy watching it because they don't see you often enough).

When Tax Records Are Not Available

The inscription above the entrance to the National Office of the Internal Revenue Service reads, "Taxes are what we pay for civilized society." But any taxpayer who has ever had a tax return examined would probably enjoy a little less civilization.

Our experience has shown us that the number-one reason taxpayers have to cough up additional tax when they get audited is due to lousy recordkeeping. This situation is not due to fabricated deductions. Rather, it's because most taxpayers are not very good bookkeepers — they fail to produce the records they need to properly substantiate the deductions that they claimed.

When taxpayers misplace tax records, or simply don't save the tax records they need in order to claim any of the deductions allowed under the law, all is not lost. There are other ways to get the evidence that will establish what was actually spent — but obtaining the necessary evidence may prove to be time consuming. However, when you consider the other option — paying additional tax, interest, and penalties on disallowed deductions from an audit where you couldn't prove what you spent — the time and energy expended will be more than rewarded. What follows are some ways to reconstruct records when they don't exist. You may also want to look at Chapter 15, which tells you how to fight back against the IRS when it comes to tax records.

Property received by inheritance or gift

The starting point for determining whether you made or lost money on a sale of a property is the property's *tax basis*. Tax basis is an IRS term for cost. Your cost is usually what you paid for something.

However, the rule for determining tax basis for property you inherited or received as a gift is different. Because you don't know the cost, the tax basis for determining the taxable gain or loss of property is the fair market value of the property on the date of the title holder's death. For property received by gift, the tax basis is the donor's cost. But in some instances it could also be the fair market value on the date of the gift (see Chapter 11).

A rather simple rule exists — at least in theory. IRS instructions state that when taxpayers sell property received by gift or inheritance, the taxpayers should use the values as stated in the decedent's Form 706 (Estate Tax Return) or in the donor's Form 709 (Gift Tax Return). The only problem is that these tax returns are probably no longer available or no longer exist when you need them, especially when someone sells an asset that they inherited many years earlier.

Establishing the value of real estate (farm or residence) received by inheritance, when original tax records aren't available, is not as formidable a task as it may first appear. Taxpayers can use four methods to compute their tax basis. These methods include the use of newspaper ads, local real estate board and broker records, the assessed value of the property, and the Consumer Price Index (CPI). You know what they mean by CPI: what cost $10 last month costs $50 this month. Seriously, it probably costs $10.02 and the CPI is an official government measure that tells how much prices increase over time.

Newspaper ads

If the property value you're trying to determine is for property acquired by gift, the deed tells you when the donor acquired the property. If the property was inherited, it's the date-of-death value that you have to determine. With this plan in hand, you're ready to proceed.

Start at your local library or your local newspaper to obtain a copy of the newspaper printed on the date you're trying to establish the value for. The classified ads in the real estate section should reveal the price that similar property was being offered for at the time. Back issues often are kept on microfilm, so it shouldn't be too difficult to go back or forward six months or so, in case you come up blank for a particular date.

If a piece of real estate exactly like yours wasn't offered for sale, you may have to find an ad for one as close as possible in description and just estimate the price. For example, say you are trying to figure out how much Uncle Jesse's farm was worth when he left it to you in 1970. You now want to sell the 100-acre farm and are searching for its 1970 value. You check out some 1970 ads from *The Daily Bugle* and find the following information:

- ✔ an ad showing a house and 50 acres for $75,000
- ✔ an ad showing a house and 60 acres for $85,000

Because the farm with ten more acres was selling for $10,000 more, assume that an acre was worth around $1,000. The IRS will find your assumption reasonable. Therefore, Uncle Jesse's farm has 40 more acres than the one selling for $85,000, so you can figure that the value of the farm in 1970 was $125,000 ($85,000 plus $40,000).

The IRS simply won't accept your statement that you looked up this information. Remember, all IRS agents act as if they come from Missouri (the "Show Me" state — in case you were absent from school the day your fifth grade teacher lectured on state mottos). If you go to all the trouble to visit the library, make sure you come away with a copy of the paper's real estate section. The IRS requires documentation, especially if you're using an alternative method to establish a fact.

Local real estate board and broker records

If your trip to the library or local newspaper office comes up short, try the local real estate board or a real estate broker (one may owe you a favor or want to hustle for your business). Both individual brokers or local real estate boards usually keep historical data on property that was sold in their area. Again, you may have to estimate selling prices if you don't find a piece of property exactly like yours.

Assessed value

The assessed-value method very well could uncover the most accurate value of all. Because property taxes are collected on the basis of assessed values, try to obtain the assessed value on the date you're interested in. With this information, along with the percentage of the fair market value that the tax assessor used in determining assessed values, divide that percentage into the assessed value to come up with the market value.

You can obtain assessed values (and the percentage of the fair market value of property assessed in your area) from the office of the receiver or collector of property taxes, usually found in your county courthouse. Don't forget to get a copy of this information.

For example, if the assessed value was $2,700 and the percentage of the fair market value that the property was assessed at was 30 percent, the fair market value would have been $9,000 ($2,700 divided by 30 percent).

Consumer Price Index

It's not three strikes and you're out. When all else fails, use the Consumer Price Index (CPI) method. Because you already know what you sold the property for, another trip or call to the library will enable you to determine the increase in the Consumer Price Index between the acquisition date and the sale date. If your local library doesn't have the CPI data you need, you can obtain them by writing to the U.S. Department of Labor in Washington, D.C.

Securities received by inheritance or gift

Establishing the price of a stock or a bond on a particular date is much easier than having to come up with value of other property, especially if the stock or bond is traded on a major exchange.

When you receive a stock or bond by inheritance or gift, you often have the added task of establishing the date when the donor acquired the security. You can write to the transfer agent in order to find out this information. The transfer agent is the company that keeps track of the shares of stock that a company issues. Your stockbroker will tell you how to locate the transfer agent.

Once you determine the acquisition date, either the back issue of a newspaper or a professional service can provide the value on any particular day for a certain security. A back issue of a newspaper doesn't reveal, however, if there were any stock dividends or splits since the acquisition date. A professional service will.

One service that we recommend in order to obtain the value of stocks and bonds (plus any splits or dividends) is Prudential-American Securities, Inc., 921 East Green Street, Pasadena, CA 91106 (818-795-5831). This company will charge a small fee; typically a couple of bucks for a stock quote.

Also check with the investment firm where the securities were held — it may be able to research this information as well.

Improvements to a residence

How many taxpayers who sold their home ever saved any of the records regarding improvements that they made, even if those expenditures were substantial? Because improvements to a home quite often are made over a 30- to 40-year span, and it's a lot to ask people to save records for that many years. For example, landscaping expenditures — one tree or bush at a time — add up.

 Before you estimate how much you spent, you first have to determine what you spent it on. This step is necessary because, if you can't document the amount spent, you at least can establish that an improvement was made. Your family photo album (which may contain before and after pictures) is probably the best source for obtaining such information.

Using a Certificate of Occupancy

 If you can't get a receipt from the contractor who made any substantial improvement to your home, hike down to the county clerk's office to obtain a copy of the Certificate of Occupancy (the house's birth certificate, so to speak, which shows what your house consisted of when it was built). Records at the county clerk's office also reveal any changes in the house's assessed value as the result of improvements that you made, along with building permits that were issued. Any of these documents will clearly establish whether improvements were made.

Using an estimate

When original invoices, duplicate invoices, or canceled checks aren't available, obtain an estimate of what the improvement would cost now, and then back out the increase in the Consumer Price Index (as explained earlier in this chapter). This procedure establishes a reasonable estimate of what the improvement originally cost.

Casualty losses

A casualty loss is probably the most difficult deduction to establish. No one consistently saves receipts on the purchase of personal items such as jewelry, clothing, furniture, and so on. If the casualty loss occurs from a fire or hurricane, any receipts that you may have had were probably destroyed along with your property. Although a police, a fire, or an insurance company report establishes that a casualty loss was sustained, how do you establish the cost of what was stolen or destroyed? The answer: with a little bit of luck and hard work.

For example, the value of an expensive necklace that was stolen was once established by the use of a photograph showing the taxpayer wearing the necklace, and the taxpayer obtained an appraisal from a jeweler of what a similar necklace would cost. Because most jewelry is acquired as a gift, receipts sometimes don't exist.

Although you can prove to the IRS that you have enough money to afford the lost or stolen item, the IRS also needs proof that shows that you had the item in your possession. For example, say that your $10,000 Rolex is stolen (we feel for you). In order to make the IRS folks happy, you have to do two things:

- ✔ prove that you could afford the Rolex; your total income from your tax return will prove that.
- ✔ prove that you had the Rolex; a statement from a friend, a relative, or an acquaintance establishes that you actually owned the item.

Business records

If business records have been lost or destroyed, you can easily obtain duplicate bills from major vendors. You shouldn't have a great deal of trouble getting copies of the original telephone, utility, rent, American Express, oil company, and other bills. A reasonable determination of business use of an automobile can be made by reconstructing a typical month of automobile use. If that month's use approximates an average month's business use of an auto, the IRS usually accepts such reconstructed records as adequate substantiation.

Using duplicate bank statements

If all your business income was deposited in a checking or savings account, income can be reconstructed from duplicate bank statements. Although banks usually don't charge for copies of bank statements, they do for copies of canceled checks. These charges can be quite expensive — about four to five dollars a check — so be careful before ordering copies of all checks. For example, you should obtain a copy of a lease and a statement from the landlord saying that all rent was paid on time before you request duplicate copies of rent checks.

Using past returns

By ordering copies of past returns with Form 4506 (Request for Copy of Tax Form), you can have a point of reference for determining whether you have accounted for typical business expenses. Past returns not only will reveal gross profit percentages or margins of profit, but also the amounts of recurring expenses.

Lost Tax Returns

Last year's tax return is the starting point for filling out this year's tax return. It serves as a guide to make sure you didn't forget anything. But what if you lost the return from 1993? Or say you need a return from a previous year but can't find it?

 You can request a duplicate return and all attachments (including Form W-2) by using Form 4506. Send the completed form to the Internal Revenue Service Center where you filed the return. You must pay a $14 charge when you file the form, but there is no charge for asking for a copy of Form W-2.

Returns filed six or more years ago may or may not be available for making copies, but tax account information generally is still available for those years. When you request copies of returns that are more than six years old, insert next to Box 5 of Form 4506 `"IF COPIES OF THE ORIGINAL RETURN ARE NO LONGER AVAILABLE, PLEASE SEND TAX ACCOUNT INFORMATION."`

You also can use Form 4506 to request a tax return transcript showing most lines from your original return, including the accompanying forms and schedules. A transcript tells you the amount of penalties, interest, and payments made subsequent to the filing; it also tells you if an amended return was filed.

If you need a statement of your tax account showing any later changes that you or the IRS made to the original return, you need to request tax account information. To get tax account information, you can simply call or write your local IRS office for account information.

The Cohan Rule

Before we end this section on undocumented claims, we must tell you about the case of George M. Cohan and the resulting *Cohan Rule*. It's the story of one person's victory over the IRS, and it may inspire you to defend your own rights as a taxpayer. Even if his victory has been eroded over the past years, Cohan's battle for the right to estimate deductions still has repercussions today.

In 1921 and 1922, George M. Cohan deducted $55,000 in entertainment expenses. The IRS refused to allow him any part of these entertainment deductions on the grounds that it was impossible to tell how much was spent because Mr. Cohan didn't have any receipts to support the deductions he claimed.

Later Mr. Cohan appealed to the Second Circuit Court of Appeals, and the court established the rule of *approximation*. The court instructed the IRS to "make as close an approximation as it can, bearing heavily, if it chooses, upon the taxpayer whose inexactitude is of his own making." (Isn't "inexactitude" a lovely way of saying "no records.")

For over 30 years, the *Cohan Rule* allowed taxpayers to deduct travel and entertainment expenses without having to substantiate what they spent. Taxpayers only had to establish that it was reasonable for them to have incurred travel and entertainment expenses in the amount that they claimed they spent.

But in the early 1960s, Congress changed the law regarding travel and entertainment expenses. Since this change, taxpayers no longer can deduct travel or entertainment expenses without adequate substantiation.

Cohan still applies, however, to other expenses where records are not available. Under the *Cohan Rule,* courts routinely allow deductions based on estimates for the following deductions:

- ✔ petty cash and office expenses
- ✔ delivery and freight charges
- ✔ tips and Christmas gifts
- ✔ cleaning and maintenance expenses
- ✔ small tools and supplies
- ✔ taxi fares
- ✔ casualty losses (fire, flood, and theft losses)

For some expenses, it is impractical, if not downright impossible, to obtain receipts for what was spent. Petty cash and tips are just two examples of such expenses.

Cohan doesn't mean that you can stop keeping receipts and use estimates. You must have a valid reason for relying on *Cohan*, such as impracticability or lost or destroyed records. In fact, taxpayers have had penalties assessed against them for not attempting to obtain duplicate records that were lost when they moved and for periodically destroying all business records immediately upon the filing of their tax return. One court held that the unexplained loss of corporate records carries a strong presumption that they would have prejudiced the taxpayer's position.

Chapter 4

Getting Ready to File: Put on Your Thinking Caps

In This Chapter

▶ Wandering through 1040 abbreviations

▶ Meandering through filing statuses

▶ Walking through joint return issues

▶ Stumbling through exemption decisions

*Y*ou have to make some key decisions before grabbing the good old tax forms and marking them up. So even though we know you're anxious to begin, read this chapter because we spent a lot of time writing it. And besides, we explain some important issues you must resolve each tax year.

What Rendition of 1040 Shall We Play?

If you could get across town by taking one bus rather than having to transfer and take two, you'd do it, right? That is, unless you enjoy riding city buses, are sightseeing, or save time and money by transferring.

Like your transportation options, you have a few choices of tax forms — three to be exact. In order from mind-boggling (read *simplest* in IRS jargon) to mind-numbing (read *complex*), they are Form 1040EZ, Form 1040A, and Form 1040.

The simpler forms are easier to finish because they have fewer lines to complete and therefore far fewer instructions to read. Having to read additional IRS instructions is like having to diagram sentence structures from a Faulkner novel.

Number crunching

Here's a little trivia that will definitely come in handy this Saturday at the neighbor's potluck dinner. The following is a breakdown of the types of returns filed in 1992. The source is the *IRS 1992 Annual Report.*

1040EZ	17 million
1040A	20 million
1040	77 million
Total	114 million

The simpler forms also save you time and maybe a headache or two, but — and this is an important b-u-t — the simpler forms offer you far fewer opportunities and options to take deductions for which you may be entitled. Thus, in a rush to save yourself a little work and time, you could cost yourself hundreds, maybe thousands, in additional tax dollars.

1040EZ

Here's the low-down on this *easy* form. The IRS actually test-marketed this form before they started using it — very much like Procter and Gamble does before they try something new, like purple-colored Crest. Unfortunately, the IRS has a bit of an advantage over Procter and Gamble — if you don't like the forms, you can't switch to Brand X.

1040EZ is the easiest form to fill out and file. All you need to do is insert your name, address, occupation, Social Security number, wages, and taxable interest. To see if you should use this form, see "Who Can File a 1040EZ?" in Chapter 5.

This form is a breeze (see Chapter 5). You don't have to make any computations if you don't want to. If you owe, the IRS bills you. And if you are due a refund, the IRS sends you a check. How EZ! (Just don't forget to attach your W-2s.)

Form 1040A

For those of you who are several rungs up the economic ladder, congratulations! You have just graduated from Form 1040EZ. Your reward is Form 1040A. But there's something you need to know — the best way to be certain you should use Form 1040A is to review Form 1040 before you reach for Form 1040A. Check to make sure there isn't any deduction or tax credit you could use on Form 1040. To see if you qualify for Form 1040A, see "Who Can File a 1040A?" in Chapter 5.

Can I itemize? Should I itemize? And what the heck are itemized deductions?

Deductions are just that: You subtract them from your income before you calculate the tax you owe. To make things more complicated, the IRS gives you two methods for determining your total deductions. The good news is that you get to pick the method that leads to the best solution for you — whichever way offers greater deductions. If you can itemize, you should, because it saves you tax dollars. However, in order to itemize you must use Form 1040.

The first method for deductions — taking the *standard* deduction — requires no thinking or calculations. If you have a relatively uncomplicated financial life, taking the so-called standard deduction is generally the better option. Symptoms of a simple tax life are not earning a high income, renting your house or apartment, and lacking unusually large expenses, such as medical bills, moving expenses, or loss due to theft or catastrophe. Single folks qualify for a $3,800

standard deduction, and married couples filing jointly get a $6,350 standard deduction in 1994. If you're age 65 or older or blind, you get a slightly higher standard deduction.

The other method of determining your allowable deductions is *itemizing* them on your tax return. This method is definitely more of a hassle, but if you can tally up more than the standard amounts above, itemizing saves you money. Use Schedule A of IRS Form 1040 for summing up your itemized deductions.

Many of the categories on Schedule A, such as line 10, "Home mortgage interest and points reported to you on Form 1098," are reasonably self-evident. If you own your home and have a mortgage, early in the new year your bank should send you Form 1098, which tells you to the penny how much deductible interest you paid.

Form 1040 (the Long Form)

Because Forms 1040A and 1040EZ are easier to complete than Form 1040, you should use one of them unless Form 1040 allows you to pay less tax. But if you don't qualify for filing Forms 1040A or 1040EZ, you have to use Form 1040.

This is the form that everybody loves to hate. The *Wall Street Journal* believes that the form was invented by tax professionals because The *Wall Street Journal* editors refer to our tax laws as the *Accountants and Lawyers Full Employment Act.*

If you itemize your deductions, claim a host of tax credits, own rental property, are self-employed, or sell a stock or bond, you're stuck — welcome to the world of the 1040.

If you have the option of using or not using the 1040, a quick review of Schedule A will help you check to see if it's worth your while to itemize. There's lots more about this schedule in Chapter 8.

If you're depressed because you have to use the simpler forms for your 1994 return and you want to be able to deduct more and have more favorable adjustments to your income in the future, all is not lost. At a minimum, you can make things better for 1995 by planning ahead. Be sure to read Part IV, "Training for a Better Race Next Time." There may also be some last-minute maneuvering that you can do before you file your 1994 return.

Filing Status

When filing your return, you must choose the appropriate filing status. There are five filing statuses for 1040A and 1040 users. (1040EZ users are either single or joint filers with no dependents). You select a status by checking the appropriate box directly below your name on Page one of the form:

- ✔ Single
- ✔ Married filing jointly
- ✔ Married filing separately
- ✔ Head of household
- ✔ Qualifying widow(er) with dependent child

Each filing status has its own tax rates. As a general rule, you pay the lowest tax by filing jointly or as a qualifying widow(er), and then comes head of household and single. Those who are married filing separately pay tax at the highest rate. However, like every rule there are a few circumstances in which married filing separately will save couples money, as explained later in this section.

Single taxpayers

Most people who are not married file as *single*. The IRS does not recognize couples living together, regardless of sexual orientation, as being married for filing purposes.

However, if you were widowed, divorced, or legally separated by the end of the tax year (December 31,1994) and provided support to dependents such as children or an elderly parent, you may be able to save yourself some tax dollars by filing as head of household or as a qualifying widow(er).

Married filing jointly

If you're married, you know that you share many things with your spouse. One of the more treasured tasks you get to share is the preparation of your annual tax return. In fact, this may be the one time during the year that you jointly examine and combine your financial information. Let the fireworks begin!

For your 1994 return, you are considered married if you got married by or were still married as of the end of the tax year — December 31, 1994. In some rare instances, married folks can save money by filing their taxes as married filing separately. This somewhat oddball status can be useful with couples who have large differences between their two incomes and can claim more itemizable deductions by filing separately. Refer to the section "Married filing separately" in this chapter to see whether you can save money by filing separately.

If you file a joint return for 1994, you may not, after the due date for filing, amend that return and submit a married filing separately return. You're stuck!

You can file jointly if you meet any of the following criteria:

- You were married as of December 31, 1994, even if you did not live with your spouse at the end of the year.

- Your spouse died in 1994 and you did not remarry in 1994.

  For example, if your spouse died during the year, you are considered married for the entire year, providing you didn't remarry. You report all your income for the year — and your spouse's income — up to the date of death.

- Your spouse died in 1995 before filing a 1994 return.

You and your spouse may file jointly even if only one of you had income or if you didn't live together all year. However, you both must sign the return and you are both responsible for seeing that all taxes are paid. This means that if your spouse doesn't pay the tax due, you may have to.

A couple legally separated under a divorce decree may not file jointly. On the other hand, if one spouse lived away from the home during the entire last six months of the tax year (July 1, 1994, through December 31, 1994), the remaining spouse, if taking care of dependents, may be able to file under the more favorable head of household status (see "Head of household" later in this chapter).

While decidedly unromantic, if you're considering a late-in-the-year wedding, especially in December, you may want to understand the tax impact of tying the knot so soon because a considerable number of couples pay higher total taxes when they are married versus when they were single.

Spouses who are nonresident aliens and dual status aliens

If one spouse is a nonresident alien and does not pay U.S. income taxes on all his or her income, regardless of what country or countries in which it is earned, then the couple may *not* take the married filing jointly tax status.

You may file jointly if:

- You were married as of December 31, 1994, even if you did not live with your spouse at the end of 1994.

- You make a special election to do so. IRS Publication 519 (*U.S. Tax Guide For Aliens*) will guide you on how to make this election.

Some couples have been known to postpone their weddings until January and use the tax savings to pay for the cost of their honeymoons! Others choose not to marry and they cohabitate instead. Although we don't want to criticize or condone such decisions, it is unfortunate that there should be such a high tax cost to getting married for a sizable minority of couples (see "The marriage penalty" later in this chapter).

Married filing separately

The vast majority of married couples would pay more taxes if they chose to file separate returns. The IRS won't stand in your way of doing this. However, by filing separately you may be able to avoid the marriage penalty. To determine whether filing separately is to your benefit, you're going to have to figure your tax both ways (married filing jointly and married filing separately).

Another reason you may file separately is to avoid being responsible for your spouse's share of the joint tax bill if some kind of monkey business is suspected.

If you file separately, the following restrictions may apply:

- ✔ You cannot take the standard deduction if your spouse itemizes deductions.
- ✔ You cannot take the credit for child and dependent care expenses in most cases.
- ✔ You cannot take the earned income credit.
- ✔ You cannot exclude the interest from series EE U.S. savings bonds issued after 1989, even if you paid higher education expenses in 1994.
- ✔ You cannot take the credit for the elderly or the disabled unless you lived apart from your spouse for all of 1994.
- ✔ You may have to include up to 50 or 85 percent of any Social Security benefits you received in 1994 as income.
- ✔ You usually report only your own income, exemptions, deductions, and credits. Different rules apply to people who live in community property states (see "Filing separately in community property states" later in this chapter).

Instead of filing separately, you may be able to file as head of household if you had a child living with you and you lived apart from your spouse during the last six months of 1994. See the head of household rules for more information.

TECHNICAL STUFF

The marriage penalty

Some couples' first year of marriage brings surprises. Others find that the song remains the same. But of all the many things that newlyweds discover about being married, one of the most annoying is the marriage penalty — the additional tax that filing jointly extracts from them.

It's a fact of life for millions of married couples: As single taxpayers, their combined taxes are less than when they're married. The tax law changes enacted in 1993 made the marriage penalty even worse because the tax rates were raised for higher-income earners.

Couples most likely to be hit with the marriage penalty are two-income earning households, especially spouses who have similar individual incomes and/or are higher-income earners. Why? Because our tax brackets are graduated — which simply means that you pay a higher tax rate at higher-income levels (see the discussion in Chapter 1). When a couple gets married, the second person's income is effectively added on top of the first person's income, which can push the couple into higher tax brackets. Not only that, but the couple may lose some of their itemized deductions and personal exemptions as well.

Is there anything you can do about it? In a small number of cases, married couples can cut their tax bills simply by filing separately (explained in this section).

Some people opt for another approach — not marrying or getting a divorce. By living together as unmarrieds, you and your significant other pay taxes at the individual rate. We're not advising this course, but it's simply what we hear and see. You should also know that you can't divorce in December just to save on your taxes and then remarry the next year. Taxpayers have tried this scam in the past and have been slapped with penalties in addition to the extra taxes they would have owed if they had stayed away from divorce court.

If you decide not to stay married for the long haul just to save on your income taxes, be warned that unmarried couples are not eligible for any of the significant survivor Social Security benefits if your partner passes away or splits. People who do not work are particularly vulnerable — if they were married and their spouse passed away or divorced them, the non-working spouse would qualify for Social Security benefits based on the working partner's income history and Social Security taxes paid. If you're not married and you don't work, you get no Social Security coverage if your partner leaves you.

You should also know that not all couples pay higher taxes. In fact, some couples find that their joint tax bill is *less*. This situation usually occurs with couples in which one person doesn't earn any income or has a very low income.

Marriage is a tax issue that can be confounding. Most of the time, you will save taxes if you're married, but because of certain vagaries of the tax law and the way our society is shifting toward more two-income families, you can be hurt from a tax standpoint if you use the married filing jointly status.

To see whether you need to escape the marriage penalty, you have to prepare three returns — two separate and one joint. We know it's a time sink, so you may want to spend $50 and spring for a computerized tax program that can do the number crunching for you.

Couples most likely to save tax dollars filing separately are those who meet both of the following criteria:

- ✔ couples who have two incomes *and*
- ✔ have hefty deductions for medical expenses, miscellaneous itemized deductions, or casualty losses (there were lots of them in L.A. last year).

If you fall under this umbrella, by all means do three returns to see which works best.

Here's how those deductions come into play. To figure out your medical deduction, take your medical expenses and subtract 7.5 percent of your adjusted gross income (AGI). For example, if your AGI is $100,000 and you have medical expenses of $10,000, you perform the following calculation: $10,000 – ($100,000 × 7.5 percent). Your medical deduction comes to $2,500. For miscellaneous deductions, you subtract 2 percent of your income instead of 7.5 percent. And for personal casualty losses, you subtract 10 percent of your income.

Now, as you see in Table 4-1, these deductions may be a lot more valuable if you're filing separately. Let's say your spouse had a $9,000 casualty loss. If your income is $60,000 and your spouse's is $40,000, none of that $9,000 casualty loss is deductible. The math: $9,000 – ($100,000 × 10 percent) equals $1,000. But by filing separately, your spouse gets to deduct $5,000, because 10 percent of your spouse's income amounts to only $4,000. For the purpose of this illustration, the $100.00 nondeductible portion of casualty loss is not being considered.

The potential for savings doesn't stop there. If your combined income is $167,700 or more, a portion of your personal exemptions starts getting whittled away. (Personal exemptions are those $2,450 deductions you get for yourself and each of your dependents.) When one spouse's income is less than half that amount, you may be better off filing separately and piling the personal exemptions onto that person's return, if that spouse was otherwise entitled to the dependency exemption.

Filing separately in community property states

Community property states are Arizona, California, Idaho, Louisiana, Nevada, New Mexico, Texas, Washington, and Wisconsin. If you and your spouse live in one of these states, you have to follow your state's law in determining what is community income and what is separate income if you want to file separately.

In a community property state, each spouse, as a general rule, must report one-half of the joint income. However, this step isn't necessary if you and your spouse lived apart for the entire year and don't file a joint return. To qualify, at least one of you must have salary, wages, or business income — none of which was transferred between you and your spouse. Child support is not considered a transfer. This is an area where you should either read IRS Publication 555 (*Federal Tax Information on Community Property)* or consult a tax advisor.

It's worth doing the numbers. For example in Table 4-1, the sample couple saved a total of $1,703 by filing separately.

If you think you could have saved money in a previous year by filing separately, sorry. There's nothing you can do about it now. After you file a joint return, you can't turn back the clock and change it to separate ones. On the other hand, if you and your spouse filed separately you can, within three years from the due date of your return (or two years from the date the tax was paid), file an amended return and switch to filing jointly. You may want to do this if, on audit, some of the deductions you and your spouse claimed were disallowed or if you get an insurance recovery greater than you expected, reducing the amount of the casualty loss. If you're making estimated tax payments during the year, it doesn't matter whether you file them jointly or separately. You can still file your actual return however you wish.

Table 4-1   Filing Jointly vs. Separately: A Sample Couple

	Jointly	Husband	Wife
Gross income	$130,000	$70,000	$60,000
Casualty loss	$10,000	$0	$10,000
Less 10 percent of income	($13,000)	($0)	($6,000)
Deductible Casualty loss	$0	$0	$4,000
Medical expenses	$6,500	$500	$6,000
Less 7.5 percent of income	(9,750)	($5,250)	($4,500)
Deductible medical	$0	$0	$1,500
Miscellaneous deductions	$3,000	$1,300	$1,700
Less 2 percent of income	($2,600)	($1,400)	($1,200)
Deductible miscellaneous	$400	$0	$500
Taxes	$5,000	$3,000	$2,000
Mortgage interest	$9,500	$9,500	$0
3 percent itemized deduction phaseout	($546)	($423)	($123)
Total itemized deductions	$14,354	$12,077	$7,777
Personal exemptions	$4,900	$2,450	$2,450
Taxable income	$111,746	$55,473	$49,773
Tax	$26,636	$13,350	$11,583

Head of household

You may file as head of household if you maintain a home for one of the following reasons:

✔ You paid more than half the cost of keeping up a home (see Table 4-2 to compute that figure) that was the main home during 1994 for a parent whom you can claim as a dependent. Your parent did not have to live with you in your home.

✔ You paid more than half the cost of keeping up a home in which you lived and in which *one* of the following also lived for more than half of the year:

- Your *unmarried* child, adopted child, grandchild, great-grandchild, or stepchild. This child does not have to be your dependent. But you still enter the child's name in the space provided on line 4 of Form 1040A or Form 1040.

- Your *married* child, adopted child, grandchild, great-grandchild, or step child. This child must be your dependent. But if the married child's other parent claims him or her as a dependent under the IRS rules for children of divorced or separated parents, this child does not have to be your dependent. Enter this child's name on line 4 of Form 1040A or Form 1040.

- Your *foster* child, who must be your dependent.

- Any of the following relatives that you can claim as a dependent: parents, grandparents, siblings, step-relatives, in-laws, and, if related by blood, your uncle, aunt, nephew, or niece.

- One parent may claim head of household if more than 50 percent of maintaining a house is paid by that parent and child lives with parent for over six months.

    You are related by blood to an uncle or aunt if he or she is the brother or sister of your father or mother. You are related by blood to a nephew or niece if he or she is the child of your brother or sister. If you are just living with someone, that won't cut it.

    Note: You *cannot* file as head of household if your child, parent, or relative described in the preceding section is your dependent under a multiple support agreement.

✔ You are married but you did not live with your spouse. Even if you were not divorced or legally separated in 1994, you may be able to file as head of household if you fulfill *all* these requirements:

- You have lived apart from your spouse for the last six months of 1994, and you are filing a separate return.

- You paid more than half the cost of keeping up your home in 1994, and your home was the main residence of your child, adopted child, stepchild, or foster child for more than half of the year. Temporary absences such as for school, vacation, or medical care are counted as time lived in your home.

- You must claim this child as your dependent (or the other parent claims the child under the rules of children of divorced or separated parents). If this child is not your dependent, be sure to enter the child's name on line 4 of Form 1040A or Form 1040.

If all of the above factors apply, you may also be able to take the credit for child and dependent care expenses and the earned income credit. You can take the standard deduction even if your spouse itemizes deductions. More details are forthcoming — in Chapters 5 and 6.

Table 4-2	How to Compute the Cost of Maintaining a Household	
	Amount You Paid	*Total Cost*
Property taxes	$	$
Mortgage interest expense		
Rent		
Utility charges		
Upkeep and repairs		
Property insurance		
Food consumed on the premises		
Other household expenses		
Totals	$(a)	(b)
Amounts others paid (subtract Total (a) from Total (b) and enter here)		( )
Note: If you paid more than the amount in the preceding line, you qualify for head of household status.		

In the case of a birth or death of a dependent, you are considered to have provided more than half his or her support, even for someone who was born on December 31 or died on January 1.

Qualifying widow(er) with dependent child

If you meet *all* five following tests, you can use the tax table for married filing jointly.

- ✔ Your spouse died in 1992 or 1993, and you did not remarry in 1994.

- ✔ You have a child, a stepchild, an adopted child, or a foster child whom you can claim as a dependent.

- ✔ This child lived in your home for all of 1994. Temporary absences, such as for vacation or school, count as time lived in the home.

- ✔ You paid more than half the cost of keeping up your home for this child.

- ✔ You could have filed a joint return with your spouse the year he or she died, even if you didn't actually do so. (But you can't claim an exemption for your deceased spouse.)

If your spouse died in 1994, you may not file as a qualifying widow(er) with dependent child. But see whether you qualify for filing jointly.

And if you can't file as qualifying widow(er) with dependent child, see whether you can qualify as head of household. If you don't meet the rules for a qualifying widow(er) with dependent child, married filing a joint return, or head of household, you're going to have to file as a single.

For example, suppose that a mother with children died in 1992 and the husband has not remarried. In 1993 and 1994, he kept up a home for himself and his dependent children. For 1992, he was entitled to file a joint return for himself and his deceased wife. For 1993 and 1994, he may file as a qualifying widow(er) with dependent children. After 1994 he may file as a head of household, if he qualifies.

Joint Tax Liability & the Innocent Spouse Rule

Many taxpayers not experiencing marital bliss or those in the throes of divorce proceedings continue to file jointly so they cut their current tax bill. This decision may be shortsighted because of the ramifications of one spouse not paying his or her share of the tax bill. Here's why:

When you file jointly, you are separately and jointly liable for any unpaid tax. Forget the legalese for a second — this means that if your spouse is a deadbeat and doesn't pay any tax owed, you may end up paying more than your fair share of the tax, or maybe all of it.

Under limited circumstances — if you didn't know about any omission of income or inflated deductions, for example — the so-called *innocent spouse rule* may protect you (more about this interesting rule in a second). But the IRS may not be very charitable in defining your case.

Consider the real-life example of a couple who filed jointly in the year they sold their residence. The following year they divorced. The wife invested her share of the proceeds of the sale in a new home, thereby deferring the tax on her share of the gain, as allowed by law. But her ex-husband squandered his share. Because the proceeds of the sale weren't reinvested in a new home, the couple owed a bundle of tax. Guess who got stuck for it? Need a hint — let's just say *she* didn't need the extra expense.

Filing separately, however, isn't entirely a one-way street. Certain tax breaks, such as deductions for losses on real estate that you actively manage, can't be claimed on a separate return if you and your spouse live together. Nor can you take an IRA deduction for a nonworking spouse if you file separately. When filing separately, you can't take the earned income credit or claim a deduction for dependent care unless you and your spouse lived apart for the last six months of the tax year.

There's another drawback of filing separately: You can't use one spouse's losses to offset the other's capital gains. For example, if you have a $6,000 capital gain and your spouse has a $9,000 capital loss, on a joint return you can net the two and claim a $3,000 loss. On separate returns, you are required to report your $6,000 gain, while your spouse can only deduct $1,500 of his or her $9,000 loss. Also keep in mind that by filing separately, half of any Social Security payments automatically become taxable — or possibly more under the new tax law. When you file jointly or as a single person, the tax bill on your Social Security will almost always be smaller.

To determine each spouse's share of a joint refund, see "You Haven't Received Your Refund" in Chapter 16. This knowledge can really help if things get sticky in a divorce.

The innocent spouse provision is interesting. The argument that an innocent spouse can't pay or that forcing the innocent spouse to pay is unfair, while a compelling one, is irrelevant when invoking the innocent spouse rule.

The innocent spouse provision of the tax law requires that the spouse pass a test of innocence as well as a mathematical test. This mathematical test is based on the relationship that the innocent spouse's income bears to the amount of additional tax the government claims is due. An innocent spouse will be relieved from paying any additional tax that was due under the following conditions:

✔ A joint return was filed for the year involved.

✔ The substantial understatement of tax is in excess of $500 and is the result of grossly erroneous items of the other spouse.

✔ The innocent spouse didn't know at the time the return was signed that there was a substantial understatement of tax.

✔ After taking into account all the circumstances, it would be inequitable to hold the innocent spouse liable for the understated tax.

When a married couple has separated, the IRS should be informed of each spouse's new address so that all the notices that are received by one spouse are received by the other. You can take care of this by filing Form 8828 (Change of Address).

Personal Exemptions and Exemptions for Dependents

For you 1040A and 1040 filers there is another hurdle to jump: Lines 6a-e of these forms ask you to figure your total number of exemptions. (You 1040EZ filers have Line 4 to contend with, but this line is a breeze. We explain it in Chapter 5 in the section "How to Fill Out a 1040EZ.")

Each exemption that you are entitled to claim reduces your taxable income by $2,450, so exemptions are a *good* thing, right? There are two kinds of exemptions:

Personal exemptions

You can take one for yourself and one for your spouse. Here are the details on personal exemptions:

✔ **Your own.** You may take one exemption for yourself unless you can be claimed as a dependent by someone else. For example, if your parents *could* claim you as a dependent but they choose not to, you still can't claim an exemption for yourself. This situation usually applies to teenagers with a part-time job. If this is the case, check Box 5 on Form 1040EZ, Box 18b on Form 1040A, or Box 33b on Form 1040.

✔ **Your spouse**. If filing jointly, you can take one exemption for your spouse, provided that your spouse can't be claimed on someone else's return.

If you file a separate return, you can claim your spouse as a dependent only if your spouse is not filing a return, had no income, and can't be claimed as a dependent on another person's return.

If by the end of the year you obtain a final decree of divorce or separate maintenance, you can't take an exemption for your former spouse even if you provided all his or her support. If you didn't remarry, you can claim an exemption for your spouse only if you file jointly. For example, Mr. Jones died on August 1. Since the Joneses were married as of the date of Mr. Jones's death, Mrs. Jones can file a joint return and claim an exemption for her husband. Mrs. Jones reports all of her income for 1994 and all of Mr. Jones's income up to August 1.

On a separate return you can take an exemption for your deceased spouse only if this person had no income and couldn't be claimed as someone else's dependent.

Exemptions for dependents

You can claim an exemption for a dependent if you provide more than half his or her support and this person passes the five dependency tests. (Don't forget that if you claim someone, that person can't claim a personal exemption for his or her own tax return.)

Personal and dependency exemption phaseout

Depending on your filing status, each $2,450 exemption you are entitled to is whittled away in $49 increments ($24.50 for married filing separately) as your income rises above these limits:

Married filing separately	$ 83,850
Single	$111,800
Head of household	$139,750
Married filing jointly or qualifying widow(er)	$167,750

We could give you a 4-page (or more) table to help you figure your exemption phaseout, but it would probably be just as easy for you to pick up the wonderful (and free) IRS Publication 17 *(Your Federal Income Tax)* and use the official worksheet. And we can use our pages for more interesting stuff.

Okay, you may open your booklets and begin the tests now. Any person who meets **all five** of the following tests qualifies as your dependent:

Test 1: member of your household or relative

Your dependent must live with you the entire year as a member of your household. But a person related to you by blood or marriage does not have to live with you for the entire year as a member of your household to meet this test. (But a cousin meets this test only if he or she lived with you as a member of your household for the entire year.)

If you file a joint return, you don't need to show that a dependent is related to both you and your spouse.

Temporary absences are ignored. If a person is placed in a nursing home for constant medical care, the absence is also considered temporary.

Here are some more details you may need to consider:

- ✔ **Death or birth.** A person who died during the year, but was a member of your household until death, meets the member of your household test. The same is true for a child who was born during the year and was a member of your household for the rest of the year.

- ✔ **Violation of local law.** A person does not meet the member of your household test if your relationship violates local law.

- ✔ **Adoption.** Before the adoption is legal, a child is considered to be your child if he or she was placed with you for adoption by an authorized adoption agency (and the child must have been a member of your household). Otherwise, the child must be a member of your household for the entire tax year in order to satisfy this test.

- ✔ **Foster care.** A foster child or adult must live with you as a member of your household for the entire year to qualify as your dependent. However, if a government agency makes payments to you as a foster parent, you may not take the child as your dependent.

Test 2: married person

If your dependent is married and files a joint return, you can't take this person as an exemption. However, if the person and the person's spouse file a joint return in order to get a refund of all tax withheld, you may be able to claim this person if the other four tests are met.

Test 3: citizen or resident

The dependent must be one of the following:

- a U.S. citizen or U.S. resident alien
- a resident of Canada or Mexico
- your adopted child who is not a U.S. citizen but who lived with you all year in a foreign country

A child who isn't a U.S. citizen or resident and lives abroad (other than Canada or Mexico) can't be claimed.

Test 4: income

The dependent's gross income must be less than $2,450. Gross income does not include nontaxable income, such as welfare benefits or nontaxable Social Security benefits. Income earned by a permanently and totally disabled person for services performed at a sheltered workshop school is generally not included for purposes of the income test.

Of course there are exceptions. Your child can have gross income of $2,450 or more under one of the following conditions:

- He or she was under the age of 19 at the end of 1994.
- He or she was under the age 24 at the end of 1994 and was a student.

  Your child is a student if enrolled as a full-time student at a school during any five months of 1994. A school includes technical, trade, and mechanical schools. It does not include on-the-job training courses or correspondence schools.

Test 5: support

You provided over half the dependent's total support in 1994. If you file a joint return, support can come from either spouse. If you remarried, the support provided by your new spouse is treated as support coming from you. For exceptions to the support test, see the sidebar "Children of divorced or separated parents and persons supported by two or more taxpayers." (You can't miss it with that title.)

Support includes food, a place to live, clothing, medical and dental care, and education. It also includes items such as a car and furniture, but only if they are for the dependent's own use or benefit. In figuring total support, use the actual cost of these items, but figure the cost of a place to live at its fair rental value. Include money the person used for his or her own support, even if this money wasn't taxable. Examples are gifts, savings, Social Security and welfare benefits, and other public assistance payments. This support is treated as *not* coming from you.

Total support does not include items such as income tax and Social Security taxes, life insurance premiums, or funeral expenses. A person's own funds are not support unless they are actually spent for support.

Children of divorced or separated parents and persons supported by two or more taxpayers

The parent who had custody of the child for most of the year is the one entitled to claim the child as a dependent — provided that both parents together paid over half of the child's support.

A noncustodial parent can claim the child if any of the following apply:

✔ The custodial parent gives up the right to claim the child as a dependent by signing Form 8332 (Release of Claim to Exemption for Child of Divorced or Separated Parents). The form allows for the release of an exemption for a single year, a number of years, or all future years. The noncustodial parent must attach this form to the return.

✔ A decree or separation agreement signed before 1985 provides that the noncustodial parent is entitled to the exemption and not the custodial parent. In addition to listing the child's name, Social Security number, and the number of months the child lived in your home, you must check Box 6d on Form 1040A or Form 1040.

✔ A decree or separation agreement signed after 1985 provides that the noncustodial parent is entitled to the exemption, and that this parent provided $600 or more toward the child's support. You must attach a copy of the cover page of the decree or agreement with: (1) the custodial parent's Social Security number written next to his or her name, along with (2) the page that unconditionally states that you can claim the child as a dependent. (3) And attach a copy of the signature page.

Even if you did not pay over half of a dependent's support, you may still be able to claim this person as a dependent if all five of the following apply:

✔ You and one or more eligible person(s) paid over half of the dependent's support. An eligible person is someone who could have claimed the dependent but didn't pay over half of the dependent's support.

✔ You paid over 10 percent of the dependent's support.

✔ No individual paid over half of the dependent's support.

✔ Tests 1 through 4 of the dependency tests are met.

✔ Each eligible person who paid over 10 percent of support completes Form 2120 (Multiple Support Declaration), and you attach this form to your return. The form states that only you will claim the person as a dependent for 1994.

Social Security Numbers for Dependents

You must list a Social Security number on Line 6c column (3), Form 1040 and 1040A for every dependent over the age of one. To obtain a Social Security number, call 1-800-772-1213. You will be sent a one page form called an "SS-5." Based on your zip code you will be directed to the nearest Social Security office. Take your driver's license, your child's original birth certificate (no duplicates), and another form of ID for your child such as a birth announcement or a doctor's bill together with the SS-5. It takes about two weeks to get a number.

Filing for Children and Other Dependents

If you as the parent can claim a child (or someone else) as a dependent on your return, the dependent must file a return under both of the following circumstances:

- ✔ The dependent had unearned income (interest, dividends, capital gains, and so on) and the total of that income plus earned income exceeds $600.
- ✔ The dependent had no unearned income but had earned income that exceeds $3,800.

For example, suppose that your teenager has interest income of $200 and salary from a summer job of $350. This dependent doesn't need to file because total income was less than $600. If your teenager had no unearned income, but gained $2,000 from a summer job, this dependent wouldn't have to file either.

But here's an important point: The dependent must file to get back the tax that was withheld from the paychecks. This situation can be avoided, however, if a dependent who starts to work claims an exemption from having tax withheld by filing Form W-4 with the employer. That way, the dependent won't have to file a return to get back the tax that was withheld. Once he or she reaches $3,800 in income, withholding will have to start.

Children under the age of 14 with more than $1,200 in investment income are subject to the *Kiddie Tax.* The income is considered earned by their parents at the parents' tax rate (see"Line 38: Tax" in Chapter 13 for more details on this wonderful tax law nuance).

Must I File?

Yes, you must file when your income exceeds the amounts for your age and filing status shown in Table 4-3.

Table 4-3	**When You Must File**		
Marital Status	*Filing Status*	*Age**	*Gross Income*
Single, divorced, legally separated	Single	under 65 65 or older	$6,250 $7,200
	Head of household	under 65 65 or older	$8,050 $9,000
Married with a child and living apart from spouse during last 6 months of 1994	Head of household	under 65 65 or older	$8,050 $9,000
Married and living with spouse at end of 1994 (or on date of spouse's death)	Married (joint return)	under 65 (both spouses) 65 or older (one spouse) 65 or older (both spouses)	$11,250 $12,000 $12,750
	Married (separate return)	any age	$2,450
Married, and not living with spouse at end of 1994 (or on date of spouse's death)	Married (joint or separate return)	any age	$2,450
Widowed before 1994 and not remarried in 1994	Single	under 65 65 or older	$6,250 $7,200
	Head of household	under 65 65 or older	$8,050 $9,000
	Qualifying widow(er) with dependent child	under 65 65 or older	$8,800 $9,550

*If you become 65 on January 1, 1995, you are considered to be age 65 at the end of 1994.

When to file

If you don't file by **April 17, 1995** , you will have to pay penalties and interest. Are you surprised we didn't say April 15? Pull out your old Beetle Bailey calendar — the 15th is a Saturday this year, so the nice people at the IRS have given you until Monday the 17th. If you live or work outside the United States, you have an automatic extension of time to file until June 17, 1995.

If you know that you can't file by April 17, you can get an automatic four-month extension of time to file — until August 15, 1995 — by filing Form 4868 (Application for Automatic Extension of Time to File U.S. Individual Income Tax Return). Keep in mind that this form must be filed by April 17, 1995.

Form 4868 (see Appendix) does not extend the time to pay. You will be charged interest and a late payment penalty of 0.5 percent a month if you don't pay at least 90 percent of your tax by April 17, 1995 (Note: You will be charged interest on outstanding tax owed.) If you still can't file by August 15, 1995, you can obtain an additional two-month extension of time to file until October 16, 1995, by filing Form 2688 (Application for Additional Extension of Time to File U.S. Individual Income Tax Return). This form must be filed by August 15. Extensions of time to file beyond October 16 are not permitted.

If you don't file

You could end up crushing rocks. But it's more likely you will end up being assessed penalties that make crushing rocks seem like a stroll in the park. Annually, the IRS prosecutes only 5,000 individuals (you can't call them taxpayers) for tax evasion. Some 80 percent are members of organized crime or drug dealers, and the balance is made up of high-profile individuals and others. You don't want to be one of the *others*.

If you don't file, based on the information reported to the IRS by your employers, the IRS will either prepare a substitute return and assess a late filing penalty of 25 percent, a late payment penalty of 0.5 percent a month to a maximum of 25 percent plus interest (and possibly a 75 percent fraud penalty) — or issue a summons for you to appear with your tax records so that the IRS can use those records to prepare a more accurate return. Interest and penalties are charged whichever way the IRS decides to proceed.

Where to file

We wouldn't want to leave you with any excuses not to get those tax forms in (sorry), so we have listed all the locations to which you can send your crinkled and tear-stained forms in the Appendix under "Where to File."

How to file

Okay, so this whole book is supposed to be about this subject. But what we mean here is that there are several ways to get the forms — and the check, if necessary — to IRS Central. The most popular way to file is through the U.S. Postal Service. This is the preferred and the simplest way to file. But there are other ways to get it done, such as electronic filing, filing by phone in states that allow you to do so, and computer-generated forms like the 1040PC.

Electronic filing

We better define this one. Your return is filed over telephone lines by a company that offers this service. A computer-generated tax return that you mail in is *not* electronic filing.

Generally, what you do is take your return to a firm like H&R Block that offers electronic filing. A number of tax-preparation software programs can submit returns electronically if you have a modem. What happens is that you send the return to a telephone number of an electronic filing service, and the service sends it on to the IRS.

The advantage of electronic filing is that you get your hands on your hard-earned dough as fast as IRS-ly possible. Also, you can have your refund deposited directly into your bank account. Some firms will not only file your return, they will also loan you money based on the projected amount of the refund — these clever loans are called *refund anticipation loans.*

Electronic filing may be one of the worst ideas to come down the pike in a long time. Our principal objection is that it's too pricey. According to the IRS, the average refund check for electronic filers is $1,300. By filing electronically, you can get your refund around 25 days earlier. But depending on where you live, you'll pay between $25 to $40 for this service. Suppose that you pay someone $35 to have your return filed electronically. The fee is the equivalent of paying a near 40-percent rate of interest to get your refund 25 days earlier. If you're thinking about a refund or anticipation loan, you can expect to pay a $20 fee for a service — that amounts to a 37.4 percent rate of interest!

Filing by phone

Single taxpayers who qualify to use Form 1040EZ can file his or her return by means of a touch-tone telephone. The drawback is that this service is available only to residents of Florida, South Carolina, Indiana, West Virginia, Kentucky, Colorado, Michigan, Southern Texas, Ohio, and Northern California. The IRS sends special 1040EZ tax packages with instructions on filing by phone to those who qualify.

1040PC

Stay clear of this form. It's intended for accountants. This nifty one-page tax return that you prepare on a computer has on-line numbers and amounts. The IRS likes this return because it can be read by a scanner — a data processing clerk does not have to input everything manually.

A Final Bit of Advice

Here's an old saying from a wise man — one of our fathers. He said, "Son, there are two kinds of payments in the world you should avoid: too early and too late." That kind of advice also applies to filing your taxes. Thanks Dad.

Part II
GO!

Reprinted with permission

In this part...

Rituals make the world go round. And what annual ritual is quite so enjoyable as completing one's tax return? Cleaning up an overflowing toilet? Figuring whom to call when you lock your car keys in the trunk? Then there's always the challenge of figuring out what forms you must have and finding all the receipts and other tax documentation needed to plug into those small lines. And just when you're ready to quit, you have to wade knee deep through those dreadful IRS instructions. Thanks to the *...For Dummies* translation of jargon into plain English, here is what you'll need to know to get an A+ on tax return preparation.

Chapter 5

Easy Filing: 1040EZ and 1040A

In This Chapter
▶ The really EZ life
▶ The semi-easy life: the 1040A
▶ The IRS does the math

*I*t's best to start out a challenging part of the book with something EZ. Trust us, things will get much more complicated in a hurry (although if you can file a simplified tax form, you'll be able to bypass much of what's in the rest of Part II of the book).

But for now, let's take a look at the easier forms; they are easier because there are not as many lines to fill out, dreadful schedules to complete and attach, and not as many receipts and records to dig out.

The most difficult decision to make is whether to choose the 1040EZ or 1040A (the infamous *Short Form*). From then on, it's downhill. In fact, the forms are so simple that the IRS will compute the tax for you.

Who Can File a 1040EZ?

With the 1040EZ (see Figure 5-1), all you have to do is fill in the numbers (you don't have to do the math), and the nice folks at the IRS do the rest for you. The IRS likes this form, by the way, because it can be processed by optical scanner. You may use the 1040EZ if you meet all of the following criteria:

✔ You are single or are married filing jointly and do not claim any dependents.

✔ You (and your spouse, if married filing jointly) are not 65 or older or blind.

✔ You have income only from wages, salaries, tips, taxable scholarships, and fellowship grants — and not more than $400 of taxable interest income.

✔ Your taxable income is less than $50,000.

✔ You are not receiving any advance earned income credit (EIC) payments.

✔ You are not itemizing deductions or claiming any adjustments to income or tax credits (such as child care expenses).

If you can't file Form 1040EZ, all is not lost. You may be able to use another simplified form: 1040A (see "Who Can File a 1040A?" later in this chapter).

Form 1040EZ	Department of the Treasury—Internal Revenue Service
	Income Tax Return for Single and Joint Filers With No Dependents (99) **1994**

OMB No. 1545-0675

Use the IRS label (See page 12.) Otherwise, please print.

Print your name (first, initial, last)

If a joint return, print spouse's name (first, initial, last)

Home address (number and street). If you have a P.O. box, see page 12. | Apt. no.

City, town or post office, state and ZIP code. If you have a foreign address, see page 12.

Your social security number

Spouse's social security number

See instructions on back and in Form 1040EZ booklet.

Presidential Election Campaign (See page 12.)

Note: *Checking "Yes" will not change your tax or reduce your refund.*
Do you want $3 to go to this fund? ▶
If a joint return, does your spouse want $3 to go to this fund? ▶

Yes   No

Dollars   Cents

Income

Attach Copy B of Form(s) W-2 here. Enclose, but do not attach, any payment with your return.

Note: *You must check Yes or No.*

1 Total wages, salaries, and tips. This should be shown in box 1 of your W-2 form(s). Attach your W-2 form(s). **1**

2 Taxable interest income of $400 or less. If the total is over $400, you cannot use Form 1040EZ. **2**

3 Add lines 1 and 2. This is your **adjusted gross income.** If less than $9,000, see page 15 to find out if you can claim the earned income credit on line 7. **3**

4 Can your parents (or someone else) claim you on their return?
☐ Yes. Do worksheet on back; enter amount from line G here.   ☐ No. If single, enter 6,250.00. If married, enter 11,250.00. For an explanation of these amounts, see back of form. **4**

5 Subtract line 4 from line 3. If line 4 is larger than line 3, enter 0. This is your **taxable income.** ▶ **5**

Payments and tax

6 Enter your Federal income tax withheld from box 2 of your W-2 form(s). **6**

7 **Earned income credit** (see page 15). Enter type and amount of nontaxable earned income below.
Type | $ **7**

8 Add lines 6 and 7 (don't include nontaxable earned income). These are your **total payments.** **8**

9 **Tax.** Use the amount on **line 5** to find your tax in the tax table on pages 28–32 of the booklet. Then, enter the tax from the table on this line. **9**

Refund or amount you owe

10 If line 8 is larger than line 9, subtract line 9 from line 8. This is your **refund.** **10**

11 If line 9 is larger than line 8, subtract line 8 from line 9. This is the **amount you owe.** See page 20 for details on how to pay and what to write on your payment. **11**

Sign your return

Keep a copy of this form for your records.

I have read this return. Under penalties of perjury, I declare that to the best of my knowledge and belief, the return is true, correct, and accurately lists all amounts and sources of income I received during the tax year.

Your signature | Spouse's signature if joint return

Date | Your occupation | Date | Spouse's occupation

For IRS Use Only — Please do not write in boxes below.

For Privacy Act and Paperwork Reduction Act Notice, see page 4.   Cat. No. 11329W   Form 1040EZ (1994)

1040EZ-1

Figure 5-1: The Form 1040EZ, Page 1.

How to Fill Out a 1040EZ

The IRS has provided nice little boxes where you can put your numbers (but please leave off the dollar signs). What a considerate organization!

Line 1: Total wages, salaries, and tips

Enter your wages (from Box 1 of your W-2). If your employer hasn't provided you with this, go squawk at your payroll and benefits department.

Line 2: Taxable interest income of $400 or less

Enter your interest income on line 2. You can locate this on Boxes 1 and 3 of your 1099-INTs, which your bank and other investment companies should provide. If this amount is over $400, you can't use the 1040EZ. Sorry!

Line 3: Adjusted gross income

Add the amounts of lines 1 and 2 together and enter the total here. This is your adjusted gross income (AGI).

Line 4: Deductions and exemptions

From your AGI, you have to subtract your standard deduction and personal exemption. The amount you are entitled to deduct is indicated to the left of the boxes, but you first have to take the IRS "yes or no" test. Read the question on line 4: "Can your parents (or someone else) claim you on their return?" Mark your answer. (Aren't you at least glad that this isn't an essay test?)

Reprinted with permission

If you checked "yes," you have to use the worksheet on the back of the form to figure your standard deduction. If your parents are entitled to claim you as dependent, you are not entitled to a personal exemption for yourself.

If you checked "no," your life is just that much simpler now. Enter in the boxes the amount for single ($6,250) or married ($11,250), whichever applies. You should feel good about this number that you're deducting from your taxable income. The IRS is effectively saying that this amount of income is tax-free to you.

Line 5: Taxable income

Subtract the amount you entered on line 4 from line 3, and enter the remainder here. Line 5 is your taxable income.

Line 6: Federal income tax withheld

Enter your federal tax withheld (from Box 2 of your W-2) here.

Line 7: Earned income credit

If your adjusted gross income (from line 3) is less than $9,000, you may be eligible for the earned income credit (see "Line 56: Schedule EIC" in Chapter 13 for more details on this credit). The credit can be as high as $306 and is subtracted from your tax. If you don't owe tax, the credit is refunded to you. You don't have to compute the credit. A worksheet in the IRS 1040EZ instruction booklet refers you to the earned income credit table. Just look up the credit for your income and enter the credit here. Before you leave this line, take notice of two boxes to the left of Box 7 called "Type" and "$." Enter in WAGES for Type and the amount from Box 1 of your W-2 in the $ box.

Line 8: Total payments

Add the amounts on lines 6 and 7, and put the sum here.

Line 9: Tax

To figure your tax, look up in the booklet (Pages 28-32) the amount on line 5 in the tax tables for your income bracket and filing status. While you have your finger in the right place, enter that amount here.

Line 10: Refund time!

The last computation that you have to make is quite simple. Now look at lines 8 and 9. If the amount on line 8 is larger than that of line 9, you're going to get a refund. Just subtract line 9 from line 8. The remainder is your refund!

Line 11: Payment due

Yes, you guessed it. If the amount on line 9 is larger than that on line 8, you still owe because not enough tax was withheld from your paycheck or paid by you during the year. Subtract line 8 from line 9. 'Fess up and pay up.

Finishing up

Don't forget to attach your W-2s to your return. Staples are just great! (And staples are preferable to tape and paper clips. You don't want your W-2s going one way at IRS Central while your tax return goes another way.)

If you owe money, make sure to write your Social Security number on the front of the check along with the notation 1994 INCOME TAX — just in case the folks at the IRS think you are trying to make a payment on your new boat but sent them the check by mistake.

Spell out INTERNAL REVENUE SERVICE on the check. If your check goes astray, *IRS* is just too darned easy to alter (such as changing the IRS to MRS, and anyone can fill in her name, such as Mrs. Robinson). Don't try that trick at home.

Sign your return and mail it to the IRS Service Center for the area where you live. Normally, an addressed envelope is provided with your tax form. If you are missing the address, see the addresses provided in the Appendix.

Who Can File a 1040A?

You have the gracious permission of the IRS to use the 1040A if you meet all the following conditions:

 ✔ You have income only from wages, salaries, tips, taxable scholarships, fellowship grants, pensions or annuities, taxable Social Security benefits, withdrawals from your individual retirement account (IRA), unemployment compensation, interest, and dividends.

Let the IRS figure your tax

Instead of struggling with all the math, subtracting this from that, and looking up the tax for your tax bracket, the IRS will figure the tax for you. For 1040EZ and 1040A filers who don't want the hassle of doing the math, letting the IRS compute your tax after you enter your basic information on the forms is headache-free. If you are due a refund, the IRS will send you a check. If you owe money, the IRS will bill you. And if you are entitled to the earned income credit or credit for the elderly or disabled, you don't have to spend hours filling out the forms.

Be careful, though; even the IRS makes mistakes (no kidding). If you are entitled to one of the credits, check the IRS computation (the credits will be itemized on it) when they either bill you or send you your refund check.

Here's how it works for 1040EZ filers. On lines 1 through 7, fill in the lines that apply to you. If your income is under $9,000, you could be entitled to the earned income credit. So you have to enter your wages again in the box to the right of the box marked $ — in the other box write WAGES.

Attach your W-2s. Sign your return and send it to the IRS Service Center for the area where you live. Ignore all the "subtract this line from that and enter it here" on the Form 1040EZ. The IRS does all that fun stuff.

For 1040A filers, fill in the lines 1 through 12 that apply. If you're entitled to a credit for child and dependent care expenses, you must complete Schedule 2 (the child and dependent care form) and attach it to your return. Enter the amount of credit on line 24a.

If you're entitled to claim a credit for the elderly or the disabled, attach Schedule 3, and fill in your filing status on lines 11 or 13, if they apply. In the space to the left of line 24b write CFE. You won't have to tackle this nightmarish form. The IRS will prepare it for you.

If you're entitled to the earned income credit, the IRS will fill in the credit for you. Write EIC in the space to the left of line 28c. Fill in page 1 of Schedule EIC and attach it to your 1040A.

Sign your return. Attach your W-2s and make sure your Schedule 2 or 3 is attached if you are claiming any child care or credit for the elderly and disabled credits. Mail your return to the IRS Service Center for the area where you live.

Here's a warning, however. Although this method sounds EZ, it may lead to a false sense of security because you may overlook something like an important deduction that could work to your tax advantage. Also, the IRS is not infallible and may make an error.

> ✔ Your taxable income is less than $50,000.
>
> ✔ You are not itemizing deductions.

You can also use Form 1040A (see Figure 5-2) to claim the earned income credit, the deduction for contributions to an IRA, nondeductible contributions to an

IRA, the credit for child and dependent care expenses, and the credit for the elderly or the disabled. You may use the 1040A even if you made estimated tax payments for 1994 — or if you can take the exclusion of interest from series EE U.S. savings bonds issued after 1989.

How to Fill Out a 1040A

We hope you have already figured out your filing status and exemptions. If you need help here, see Chapter 4.

Line 6: Exemptions

Make sure to provide Social Security numbers for the youngsters age one and older (see Chapters 4 and 23 to learn how to obtain Social Security numbers for your children). If you don't, the IRS will penalize you $50. You can claim an exemption for yourself, your spouse, and your kids and other dependents on line 6. Enter the information for items a through e. Each exemption is worth $2,450.

Line 7: Wages, salaries, and tips

Enter your wages from Box 1 of your W-2s, which your employer should provide, here.

Line 8a: Taxable interest income

Enter your interest income on line 8a (on your 1099-INT, Box 1 from banks and S&Ls and Box 3 from U.S. savings bonds). Hey, if you are rolling in interest dough (at least over $400), you have to fill out and attach Schedule 1 (Interest and Dividend Income). Just consider it like homework that you must hand in — unless you want the IRS to keep you after school.

To complete Schedule 1, just put down the name of the payer and the amount in the amount column. If you need help with any part of it, call us (only kidding!). Actually, cruise ahead to Chapter 9 which walks you through completion of Schedule B, which is the schedule just like the one that taxpayers use to tally interest and dividend income for the cumbersome 1040.

Form **1040A** (99)

Department of the Treasury—Internal Revenue Service

U.S. Individual Income Tax Return 1994

IRS Use Only—Do not write or staple in this space.

OMB No. 1545-0085

Label
(See page 16.)

Use the IRS label.
Otherwise, please print or type.

L A B E L H E R E		
Your first name and initial	Last name	Your social security number
If a joint return, spouse's first name and initial	Last name	Spouse's social security number
Home address (number and street). If you have a P.O. box, see page 17.	Apt. no.	For Privacy Act and Paperwork Reduction Act Notice, see page 4.
City, town or post office, state, and ZIP code. If you have a foreign address, see page 17.		

Presidential Election Campaign Fund (See page 17.)

Do you want $3 to go to this fund? . . . . Yes No

If a joint return, does your spouse want $3 to go to this fund?

Note: Checking "Yes" will not change your tax or reduce your refund.

Check the box for your filing status
(See page 17.)
Check only one box.

1 ☐ Single

2 ☐ Married filing joint return (even if only one had income)

3 ☐ Married filing separate return. Enter spouse's social security number above and full name here. ►

4 ☐ Head of household (with qualifying person). (See page 18.) If the qualifying person is a child but not your dependent, enter this child's name here. ►

5 ☐ Qualifying widow(er) with dependent child (year spouse died ► 19). (See page 19.)

Figure your exemptions
(See page 20.)

If more than seven dependents, see page 23.

6a ☐ **Yourself.** If your parent (or someone else) can claim you as a dependent on his or her tax return, do not check box 6a. But be sure to check the box on line 18b on page 2.

b ☐ **Spouse**

No. of boxes checked on 6a and 6b

c **Dependents:**

(1) Name (first, initial, and last name)	(2) Check if under age 1	(3) If age 1 or older, dependent's social security number	(4) Dependent's relationship to you	(5) No. of months lived in your home in 1994

No. of your children on 6c who:
• lived with you
• didn't live with you due to divorce or separation (see page 23)

Dependents on 6c not entered above

Add numbers entered on lines above

d If your child didn't live with you but is claimed as your dependent under a pre-1985 agreement, check here . . . . ► ☐

e Total number of exemptions claimed.

Figure your total income

Attach Copy B of your Forms W-2 and 1099-R here.

If you didn't get a W-2, see page 25.

Enclose, but do not attach, any payment with your return.

7 Wages, salaries, tips, etc. This should be shown in box 1 of your W-2 form(s). Attach Form(s) W-2. 7

8a **Taxable** interest income (see page 25). If over $400, attach Schedule 1. 8a

b **Tax-exempt** interest. DO NOT include on line 8a. 8b

9 Dividends. If over $400, attach Schedule 1. 9

10a Total IRA distributions. 10a   10b Taxable amount (see page 26). 10b

11a Total pensions and annuities. 11a   11b Taxable amount (see page 27). 11b

12 Unemployment compensation (see page 30). 12

13a Social security benefits. 13a   13b Taxable amount (see page 31). 13b

14 Add lines 7 through 13b (far right column). This is your **total income.** ► 14

Figure your adjusted gross income

15a Your IRA deduction (see page 34). 15a

b Spouse's IRA deduction (see page 34). 15b

c Add lines 15a and 15b. These are your **total adjustments.** 15c

16 Subtract line 15c from line 14. This is your **adjusted gross income.** If less than $25,296 and a child lived with you (less than $9,000 if a child didn't live with you), see "Earned income credit" on page 44. ► 16

Cat. No. 11327A

1994 Form 1040A page 1

1040A-1

Figure 5-2:
The Form
1040A,
Page 1.

Line 8b: Tax-exempt interest

If you received any tax-exempt interest (such as from a municipal bond), enter this amount on line 8b. This amount does not increase your taxable income unless you are receiving Social Security. If you are on Social Security, tax-exempt interest is used to figure out how much of your Social Security is subject to tax. That's why this tax trap is here. Line 8b is not a harmless little line to some folks.

Line 9: Dividends

Enter on line 9 any dividend income (from Box 1a of your 1099-DIV). Once again, if this amount is over $400, you have homework to do on Schedule 1 (and see Chapter 9 if you get stuck).

Line 10a and 10b: Total IRA distributions

The custodian of your IRA, your bank, or investment company, should send you a 1099-R by January 31 for the prior tax year. The amount in Box 1 of this form is entered on line 10a and the amount in Box 2a is entered on line 10b. Because this is an IRA, the amount in Boxes 1 and 2a will usually be the same. But if you made nondeductible contributions to your IRA, not all the money you withdraw is taxable.

To compute what's taxable in such instances, you're going to have to fill out Form 8606 (see "Line 15a and b: Total IRA distributions" in Chapter 6 for the complete low-down on IRAs). If you elected to have tax withheld on your IRA payments, don't forget to enter the tax withheld from Box 4 of your 1099 on line 28a.

Line 11a and 11b: Total pensions and annuities

If you receive income from a pension or an annuity, the payer will provide you with a 1099-R showing the amount you received in Box 1 and the taxable amount in Box 2a. (See "Line 16a and b: Total pensions and annuities" in Chapter 6 to see if the pension plan computed the right amount). Enter the amount from Box 1 on line 11a and the amount from Box 2a on line 11b. If income tax was withheld, enter the amount from Box 4 on line 28a.

Line 12: Unemployment insurance

Believe it or not, unemployment benefits are taxable. Enter on line 12 the amount from Box 1 of Form 1099-G, which your state will send you (see "Line 19: Unemployment compensation" in Chapter 6 to learn more about this issue).

Line 13a and 13b: Social Security benefits

Yes, you have to pay tax on your Social Security benefits if your income is over the income levels described in "Line 20a and 20b: Social Security benefits" in Chapter 6.

Enter on line 13a your total amount from Box 5 of Form SSA-1099 (which reports the amount of Social Security you received). Also, don't forget to add the amount from your spouse's SSA-1099. These forms are sent by the Social Security Administration by January 31, 1995. To obtain the taxable amount of your Social Security, you have to compute the Social Security worksheet provided in Chapter 6.

Line 14: Total income

Here you put the total of lines 7 through 13b. All those numbers to add!

Line 15a: Your IRA deductions

You're entitled to deduct up to $2,000 for a contribution to IRAs. Do it if you can! However, if you're covered by a retirement plan at work, this deduction may be reduced or eliminated. See Chapters 7 and 19 for more than you care to know on this issue. You have to make this computation based on the IRS rules and enter the amount on this line.

Line 15b: Spouse's IRA deduction

The rules on line 15a also apply to your spouse's IRA. If the spouse isn't employed, you can deduct an extra $250 for a total deduction of $2,250 (see Chapter 7 again). You have to do the math and enter the amount here.

Line 15c: Total adjustments

After you add the amounts from lines 15a and b, enter it here to find out your total adjustments.

Line 16: Adjusted gross income

Now you get to subtract your total adjustments (line 15c) from your total income (line 14) and enter that amount here.

Don't forget that you may be entitled to an earned income credit if your AGI is less than $23,755 and one child lived with you (the cutoff is $25,296 if two children lived with you, and $9,000 if no child lived with you). See "Line 56: Schedule EIC" in Chapter 13 for more details. Your tax is figured on Page 2 of the form, so turn the page over.

Line 17: Successful transcription of adjusted gross income to back of Form 1040A

You enter your adjusted gross income on line 17 (which you already totaled on line 16). Be careful; don't transpose numbers.

Lines 18a, 18b, and 18c: Exemption amount

Check the right box. If you or your spouse is over 65 or blind, you're entitled to an increased standard deduction. To figure the increased amount, refer to the standard deduction chart for people 65 or older in Chapter 8. Enter that amount on line 19.

If your parent or someone else can claim you as a dependent, check Box 18b and use the standard deduction worksheet for dependents in Chapter 8 to compute your standard deduction. Enter that amount (instead of the standard deduction that all others are entitled to) from the worksheet on line 19.

If you are married filing separately and your spouse itemizes deductions, check Box 18c and enter 0 on line 19. You are not entitled to any standard deduction because both you and your spouse must use the same method.

Line 19: Standard deduction

So many choices! Find your filing status and enter the number here.

- ✔ single — $3,800
- ✔ head of household — $5,600
- ✔ married filing jointly or qualifying widow(er) — $6,350
- ✔ married filing separately — $3,175

If you checked Box 18a or 18b, find your standard deduction in Chapter 13. If you checked Box 18c, enter 0 on this line.

Line 20: IRS subtraction quiz

Go ahead and subtract the amount you have on line 19 from your adjusted gross income on line 17. Put the result of this mathematical computation here. If you ended up with a larger number on line 19 than on line 17 (and you started to wonder how you could subtract a larger number from a smaller number), you have to start over from the beginning. No! Just kidding! If line 19 is larger than line 17, you place 0 on line 20.

Line 21: Total number of exemptions times $2,450

Take the number of exemptions you claimed on line 6e and multiply it by $2,450. Enter that amount here.

Line 22: Taxable income

Now subtract the amount on line 21 from line 20, and carefully place that number here. Well done; you have arrived at your taxable income.

Line 23: Find your tax!

Use the tax tables to find your tax. With the tax tables, you don't have to make a mathematical computation to figure your tax. For example, if you are single and your taxable income is $43,610, look up the bracket between $43,600 and $43,650 and read across to the single column. The answer is $9,258.

On line 23 you also notice a box to check if you are using Form 8615. This form is used to compute the tax for a child under the age of 14 who has investment income of more than $1,200. Isn't it nice having a kid who is better off than you are. This tax is commonly referred to as the *Kiddie Tax*. (See "Line 38: Tax" in Chapter 13 for complete details). This form is used when preparing your child's return.

Line 24a: Credit for child and dependent care expenses

Use Schedule 2 to figure this amount. See "Line 41: Credit for child and dependent care expenses" in Chapter 13 for more details.

Line 24b: Credit for the elderly or the disabled

Use Schedule 3 to compute this credit. See "Line 42: Credit for the elderly or the disabled" in Chapter 13 for further explanation.

Line 24c: Total credits

Compute your total credits; add the amounts from lines 24a and 24b!

Line 25: Another IRS subtraction problem

Gee whiz, it never ends, does it? Now subtract your total credits (line 24c) from the amount on line 23. Enter that remainder here. But if your total credits are more than the amount on line 23, you get the easy way out and enter 0.

Line 26: Advance earned income payments

This amount is in Box 9 of your W-2s, which your employer provides for you.

Line 27: Total tax

Add the amounts from lines 25 and 26 to arrive at your total tax.

Line 28a: Total federal income tax withheld

Get this amount from Box 2 of your W-2s and W-2G. And don't forget to add in any tax withheld and listed in Box 2 of 1099-INTs, 1099-DIVs, and 1099-Rs.

Line 28b: 1994 estimated tax payments and amount applied from 1993 return

If you made quarterly tax payments, enter the amount here. You could be penalized for not paying at least 90 percent of your tax by means of withholding and quarterly tax payments. The IRS does not like to wait until April 15 to collect most of the tax you owe. See Form 2210 in "Underestimating tax penalties" in Chapter 13.

If you have income such as interest, dividends, pension, and IRA withdrawals, and the tax you owe after what was withheld will be more than $500 come next April, you have to make quarterly estimated payments on Form 1040ES. If you don't meet one of the exceptions to this rule, you will be penalized (see Chapter 13).

Line 28c: Earned income credit

You may be entitled to an earned income credit if your AGI is less than $25,296 if two children lived with you or $23,755 and one child lived with you (less than $9,000 if no child lived with you). See "Line 56: Schedule EIC" in Chapter 13 for more details.

Line 28d: Total payments

Now you get to *add*. Find the sum of lines 28a, 28b, and 28c — but do not include your nontaxable earned income from the second half of line 28c.

Line 29: We smell refund!

Subtract your total tax (line 27) from your total payments (line 28d) — if line 27 is smaller than line 28d! Here's your refund. Don't spend it all in one place.

 Although refunds are fun, large ones are a sign that you made the IRS an interest-free loan. Ask your employer's payroll department (or call the IRS at 800-TAX-FORM) and request Form W-4 to adjust the amount of tax being withheld.

Lines 30-31: What to do with your refund

If you have a refund, but you think you are going to owe tax in 1995 and cannot trust yourself to hang on to the cash, you may want to apply some or all of the refund toward next year's tax (do this on line 31).

This is an excellent option for people who have to make quarterly estimated payments because they are not making their first quarterly payments on April 15 and then waiting for a refund.

If you want the refund pronto, indicate how much of your refund you actually want to receive on line 30.

Line 32: Amount you owe

Three of the most dreaded words in the English language. If the amount on line 27 is greater than that of line 28d, subtract line 28d from line 27.

Line 33: Estimated tax penalty

If the estimated tax payment that you had previously made does not equal 90 percent of your tax, you will be assessed a penalty — you can turn to Chapter 13 and the compute the penalty on Form 2210.

Final instructions

Put your John Hancock(s) on your form. (Sign it, OK? Don't get funny and write in John Hancock; the IRS does not have our sense of humor.) Attach your W-2s and any 1099s where tax was withheld and check or money order, if required, to the form and mail it to the IRS Service Center for the area where you reside. See the Appendix for the correct address.

Chapter 6

Form 1040 Income Stuff

. . . .

In This Chapter

▶ Your W-2

▶ Where to report different income on your 1040

▶ Your 1099-R

▶ Other income stuff

. . . .

*Y*ou surely remember the old war slogan "Divide and Conquer" (we think Alexander the Great or some other real famous warrior said it). Well, that's our strategy here. We will break down each section and each line of the Form 1040, and pound each into submission.

Note: You're going to be jumping into a deeper section of the pool here. If you're unsure about which Form 1040 to use (EZ, A, or long), you need to take one step back to Chapter 5. Likewise, if you're unsure of your filing status (single, married filing separately, married filing jointly, head of household), take two steps back to Chapter 4.

Now for Chapter 6, which is the guts of the return: the income section (see Figure 6-1). Each heading has the specific line references of the Form 1040 listed first. After you go through the segment, plug the correct number in the line of the 1040 and move on.

Lines 7-22: Income

Income is, in brief, money or something else of value that you receive whether you work for it or not.

Most of us know that wages earned from toiling away at jobs are income. But *income* also includes things such as alimony, certain interest, dividends and profits on your investments, and even your lottery winnings or prizes won on the *Wheel of Fortune*.

Figure 6-1:
It is
enlightening
to see how
much money
you made in
a given year.
This section
of the Form
1040 will
show you
how to get
there.

Income	7	Wages, salaries, tips, etc. Attach Form(s) W-2	7	
	8a	Taxable interest income (see page 15). Attach Schedule B if over $400	8a	
Attach Copy B of your Forms W-2, W-2G, and 1099-R here.	b	Tax-exempt interest (see page 16). DON'T include on line 8a 8b		
	9	Dividend income. Attach Schedule B if over $400	9	
	10	Taxable refunds, credits, or offsets of state and local income taxes (see page 16) . .	10	
If you did not get a W-2, see page 15.	11	Alimony received	11	
	12	Business income or (loss). Attach Schedule C or C-EZ	12	
	13	Capital gain or (loss). If required, attach Schedule D (see page 16)	13	
Enclose, but do not attach, any payment with your return.	14	Other gains or (losses). Attach Form 4797	14	
	15a	Total IRA distributions . 15a b Taxable amount (see page 17)	15b	
	16a	Total pensions and annuities 16a b Taxable amount (see page 17)	16b	
	17	Rental real estate, royalties, partnerships, S corporations, trusts, etc. Attach Schedule E	17	
	18	Farm income or (loss). Attach Schedule F	18	
	19	Unemployment compensation (see page 18)	19	
	20a	Social security benefits 20a b Taxable amount (see page 18)	20b	
	21	Other income. List type and amount—see page 18	21	
	22	Add the amounts in the far right column for lines 7 through 21. This is your **total income** ▶	22	

All people who work for an employer are likely to receive the famous Form W-2 (Wage and Tax Statement), which your employer issues at tax-year's end. That form helps you learn what you earned during the year, as well as what was taken away from you.

In this chapter you discover the meaning of all those various boxes on your W-2 (your regular income stuff). Then we explain all those other line numbers in the big section of the 1040 called "Income," lines 7 through 22. Don't worry, we'll go into more detail for the various schedules that some line numbers ask for.

We must warn you that you may become dejected to see your other non-employment income that you need to report in the lines ahead as taxable income. We will make sure to highlight foolproof ways to keep this tragedy from happening again next year.

Line 7: Wages, salaries, tips

In order to fill in the blank on line 7, scrounge around for your W-2s (see Figure 6-2). You should receive your W-2s from your employer by January 31, 1995. It's a three-part form. Why three parts? Copy B gets nailed to the federal return; copy C is filed with your neat and organized records; and copy A is affixed to your state return. If you look at the lower left-hand corner of your W-2s, you'll see what to do with each copy.

If you're self-employed and you don't receive W-2s, you get to skip this line, but you're going to end up doing tons more work completing Schedule C in order to fill in line 12 of the 1040. Retirees can skip 'em both! If your W-2 is wrong, contact your employer to have it corrected as soon as possible. Otherwise you will pay too much tax or too little — and you wouldn't want to do that.

If you didn't receive your W-2, call your employer. If that step doesn't work, file Form 4852 (Employees' Substitute Wage and Tax Statement), which is a substitute for missing W-2s (as well as missing 1099s). The magnanimous IRS allows you to estimate your salary and the amount of tax withheld on this form. You then attach Form 4852 to your tax return. You can get that form or any other form by calling the IRS toll-free (1-800-829-3676).

What those W-2 boxes mean

Each of the numbered boxes on your W-2 contains either welcome information (like your gross income, which momentarily makes you feel rich) or the type of information that will surely have you shaking your head in disbelief (like the total amount of different types of taxes you paid throughout the year, which effectively makes you feel poor again). If you notice in the discussion ahead that we're skipping over some of those silly little boxes, rest assured that we'll explain them when we need to in the chapters ahead.

Figure 6-2:
Find out how much dough you made and how much you donated to your favorite charity — government.

a Control number	
	OMB No. 1545-0008

	1 Wages, tips, other compensation	2 Federal income tax withheld
b Employer's identification number		
c Employer's name, address, and ZIP code	3 Social security wages	4 Social security tax withheld
	5 Medicare wages and tips	6 Medicare tax withheld
	7 Social security tips	8 Allocated tips
d Employee's social security number	9 Advance EIC payment	10 Dependent care benefits
e Employee's name, address, and ZIP code	11 Nonqualified plans	12 Benefits included in box 1
	13 See Instrs. for box 13	14 Other

15 Statutory employee ☐	Deceased ☐	Pension plan ☐	Legal rep. ☐	942 emp. ☐	Subtotal ☐	Deferred compensation ☐

16 State	Employer's state I.D. No.	17 State wages, tips, etc.	18 State income tax	19 Locality name	20 Local wages, tips, etc.	21 Local income tax

Department of the Treasury—Internal Revenue Service

Form **W-2** Wage and Tax Statement **1994**

Copy B To Be Filed With Employee's FEDERAL Tax Return

This information is being furnished to the Internal Revenue Service.

Box 1: Wages, tips, other compensation

Your taxable wages, tips, other compensation, and taxable fringe benefits are listed here. This is a biggie. Everything but the kitchen sink was thrown into Box 1. Common examples are your salary, your tips, and the taxable portion of any fringe benefits like the personal-use part of that company car. Other stuff that your employer tossed into Box 1 includes back pay, bonuses, commissions, severance or dismissal pay, and vacation pay. That whopping $7 per day you got paid for jury duty is reported in Box 1 as well.

Because Box 1 is a catch-all, the figure in it may be larger than your actual cash salary. Get it over with — fill in the amount on line 7. If you have one or more W-2s, add 'em up and put in the total.

Box 15a: Statutory employee

Full-time life insurance salespeople, agents, commission drivers, traveling salespeople, and certain homeworkers can file as self-employed instead of as employees. This status allows them to deduct their business expenses on Form 1040 with Schedule C (Profit or Loss From Business) or on Schedule C-EZ.

Don't report the amount of your W-2's Box 1 on your Form 1040 if you want to deduct your business expenses. Report it on Schedule C or C-EZ. By doing it this way, you may deduct all your travel, entertainment, auto, and other business-related expenses instead of having to claim them as itemized deductions. (See Chapter 10 for loads of Schedule C stuff.)

Itemized deductions are reduced by 2 percent of your Adjusted Gross Income (AGI) and then shaved a second time if your income is too high. So reporting business expenses on Schedule C is clearly to your advantage. Additionally, deducting these expenses on Schedule C lowers your AGI, which means you pay less tax. You can only do this stuff if the statutory box is checked.

Box 8: Allocated tips

If you worked in a restaurant and didn't report all your tip income, Box 8 includes the difference between your share of at least 8 percent of the restaurant's income and what you reported. **This income is not reported in Box 1. Therefore, you must add this to the amount on Form 1040 (line 7).** You must then also enter this amount on Form 4137 (Social Security and Medicare Tax on Unreported Income). You'll get an earful about this form in the section "Line 50" in Chapter 13.

Box 9: Advance EIC (earned income credit) payment

If your income is less than $25,296 (with two or more qualifying dependents and $23,755 for one dependent), you might be entitled to the earned income credit (see the stuff under "Line 56" in Chapter 13 for more information).

If you're entitled to an EIC you can — instead of waiting until you file your return to have this credit refunded — file Form W-5 (EIC Advance Payment Certificate) with your employer. By filing the W-5, up to 60 percent of the credit you're entitled to can be added to your paycheck. You can obtain this form from your employer or from the IRS at 1-800-829-3676.

The purpose of the EIC is not to penalize low-income workers for working. Rather, it is a way to refund a portion of the Social Security and Medicare tax to them if their income is below $25,296.

Box 10: Dependent care benefits

If your employer has a day-care plan or provides day-care services, the reimbursement from your employer for day-care costs or the value of the day-care services your employer provides is included in this box. The amount in Box 10 above $5,000 is taxable and also included in Box 1. Don't report it again!

To determine if the amount of $5,000 is nontaxable, you have to complete Part III of Form 2441 (Child and Dependent Care Expenses). Enter this amount on Form 1040 (line 7). Next to it write DEPENDENT CARE BENEFITS. The reason you are being directed to Form 2441 is because the portion of the tax-free child care benefits you received reduces the amount of your child care and dependent care expenses eligible for the child care credit.

Box 13: See Instrs. for Box 13

See the instructions on the reverse side of your W-2 for what the symbols in this box mean. This box includes your 401(k) contributions, the premium on group life insurance over $50,000 (that amount will also be included in Box 1), nontaxable sick pay, and uncollected Social Security and Medicare taxes on tips that you reported to your employer (and that your employer wasn't able to collect from you). Uncollected Social Security tax is added to your final tax bill and is reported on Form 1040 (line 53). Next to it write UNCOLLECTED TAX.

Line 8a: Taxable interest income

If your interest income (from Box 1 and 3 of all your 1099-INTs) is $400 or less, enter the amount on this line. If this amount is over $400, you must complete a Schedule B. No biggie! Schedule B is easy to complete. For more information, you have permission to cruise to Chapter 9 to dig further into that schedule. When you get the total, come back and fill it in. With the exception of municipal bonds, all interest you earn is taxable. If you need examples, the IRS publications have pages of them. But be careful and don't report the interest that you earn on your IRA or retirement account; that's only taxed when you withdraw the funds.

Different definitions of what you earned

Many of the boxes on your W-2 include wage information you don't need to include on your Form 1040. Think of these as FYI boxes. They simply show you the different ways that the IRS computes income for assessing different taxes. For example, Box 3, "Social Security wages," reports the amount of your wages for the tax year subject to Social Security taxation. (Not the wages that the Social Security Administration is paying you!) Your Social Security wages may differ from your wages as reported in Box 1 because some types of income are exempt from income tax, but *not* exempt from Social Security tax. For example, if you put $3,000 in a 401(k) retirement plan in 1994, Box 3 is going to be $3,000 higher than Box 1.

Box 5, "Medicare wages and tips," reports the amount of your wages subject to Medicare tax. For most people, their wages subject to Medicare equal their total wages as reported in Box 1, thanks to the tax law changes enacted in 1993. Although the amount of your wages subject to

Social Security tax is 6.2 percent up to $60,600, there is no maximum on wages subject to the 1.45 percent Medicare tax.

Box 7, "Social Security tips," is the amount of tips that you received and reported to your employer. This amount is included in Box 1, so don't count it again!

Box 11, "Nonqualified plans," pertains to retirement plans on which you can't defer the tax. If a portion of a Section 457 (State and Local Government Deferred Compensation Plan) over the deferred limits was contributed to the retirement plan, the taxable portion is included in Box 11 and Box 1.

Box 13, "Benefits," refers to taxable fringe benefits, such as your personal use of a company car, the cost of group life insurance in excess of $50,000 paid for by your employer, and parking and education assistance exceeding $5,250. Benefits in this box are also included in Box 1.

Line 8b: Tax-exempt interest

Because muni-bond interest is not taxable, you are not going to receive a 1099. Your year-end statement from your stockbroker has this information. The IRS wants you to fill in the interest you received on tax-exempt bonds. Plug it in. Just so you know — although this interest is not taxable, the number is used to compute how much of your Social Security benefits may be subject to tax.

Surprisingly, some people who invest money in tax-exempt bonds shouldn't. These people are often not in a high enough income tax bracket to benefit. If your taxable income is not at least $22,750 if you're filing as a single, or $38,000 as married filing jointly, you shouldn't be so heavily into tax-exempt bonds. You'd be better off moving at least some of your money into taxable bonds. (See Chapter 21 to learn more.)

Line 9: Dividend income

Dividends are income you receive from stocks and mutual funds that you own. These are reported on Form 1099-DIV. Dividends come in three flavors: ordinary (taxed at regular rate), capital gains (maximum rate of 28 percent), and nontaxable. If your dividend income is under $400 and you didn't receive any capital gain distributions (Box 1c is 0), enter the amount from Box 1b on line 9.

Once again, we send you to Chapter 9 to unearth this figure. Be careful, though: You don't have to own a $100,000 nest egg to fill in this line; you may own one or two mutual funds and need to put some information here.

Line 10: Taxable refunds, credits, or offsets of state and local income taxes

As a general rule, state and local income tax refunds are taxable because you deducted your state tax payments on last year's federal income tax return. State and local tax refunds that you receive are reported on Form 1099-G, a form that your state department of revenue sends to you. If you chose to apply part or all of your 1993 state tax overpayment to your 1994 estimated state or local tax payments that you have to make (instead of having it refunded), the overpayment is still considered a refund even though a check wasn't sent to you.

But like just about every tax rule there is always an exception. For example, your refund isn't taxable if you claimed the standard deduction in a prior year instead of itemizing your deductions.

Even though you may itemize your deductions, only the part of your refund representing the amount of your itemized deductions in excess of the standard deduction is taxable. But in order to make this computation you're going to do some number crunching. The following worksheet (Table 6-1) gives you the answer. Suppose that your 1993 state refund was $700. You filed jointly and your itemized deductions were $6,550.

Table 6-1 State and Local Income Tax Refund Worksheet

	Sample	Your Computation
1. Enter the income tax refund from Form(s) 1099-G (or similar statement)	1. $700	1. ___
2. Enter your total allowable itemized deductions from your 1993 Schedule A (line 26)	2. $6,550	2. ___
3. Enter on line 3 the amount shown below for the filing status claimed on your 1993 Form 1040: Single — $3,700 Married filing jointly or Qualifying widow(er) — $6,250 Married filing separately — $3,100 Head of household — $5,450	3. $6,250	3. ___
4. If you didn't complete line 33a on your 1993 Form 1040, enter -0- Otherwise, multiply the number on your 1993 Form 1040, line 33a, by $700 ($900 if your 1993 filing status was single or head of household) and enter the result	4. $0	4. ___
5. Add lines 3 and 4	5. $6,250	5. ___
6. Subtract line 5 from line 2. If zero or less, enter -0-	6. $300	6. ___
7. Taxable part of your refund. Enter the smaller of line 1 or line 6 here and on Form 1040, line 10.	7. $300	7. ___

Line 11: Alimony received (by you)

Because the person who pays the alimony can deduct these payments from his or her taxable income (on line 29), the spouse who receives them must include alimony as taxable income. You report alimony received on line 11. You will know the figure to enter from the divorce decree or separation agreement.

You need to know what alimony is before you can report it as income or deduct it as an expense. The alimony rules aren't simple (why should they be?), but we've tried our best to clear them up. We offer a more detailed explanation of alimony under "Line 29" in Chapter 7.

Here's an important tip about alimony and IRAs. You can set up and make deductible contributions to an IRA if you receive taxable alimony and separate maintenance payments. Basically, if you receive taxable alimony, you can set up an IRA and deduct what you contribute to it — 100 percent of your alimony up to $2,000 is deductible. Your deduction may be reduced or eliminated if you are covered by a retirement plan through your work. See Chapters 7 and 19 on how to set up IRAs.

Line 12: Business income (or loss)

If you are self-employed, you must complete a Schedule C to report your business income and expenses. If you just receive an occasional fee and don't have any business expenses, you can report that on line 21 as other income. And remember, if you're a statutory employee (life insurance salespeople, agents, commission drivers, traveling salespeople), you have a choice of reporting your income on line 7 or Schedule C.

The amount you enter on line 12 is the result of the figuring and jumbling that you do on a Schedule C or C-EZ. Check out Chapter 10 to dive into that material.

Line 13: Capital gain or (loss)

You don't have to be Ross Perot to have a capital gain or loss (Ross has mostly gains; how about you?). You have a capital gain or loss when you sell stock or bonds or investment property. When you sell an asset like your house for a profit, you have a taxable gain, but you have a nondeductible loss if you lose money on the sale. Chapter 11 gives you the scoop (and the right amount to enter here) on this heady concept.

Line 14: Other gains or (losses)

You guessed it, grab another form — Form 4797 (Sales of Business Property). Fill that form out and enter the final figure on line 14. Form 4797 is used when you sell property you have been depreciating (such as that two-family house you have been renting out). This form is explained in Chapter 11.

Line 15a and 15b: Total IRA distributions

One of the benefits from all those years of hard work and diligent savings is that someday, hopefully, you'll be able to enjoy and live off the fruits of your labor. Although this line number is for reporting money that you've withdrawn from an Individual Retirement Account (IRA), we must share with you some important information if you haven't yet started withdrawals.

You must start taking out a minimum amount from your IRA by April 1 of the year after you turn 70$^{1}/_{2}$. If you don't, there is a 50 percent penalty. Suppose that you should have taken out $4,000 and you didn't. You will have to pay a $2,000 penalty. You can request that the penalty be excused if your failure to make a minimum distribution was due to a reasonable error, or if you are taking steps to remedy the error. Illness, a computational error, or incorrect advice are three examples of reasonable error. The 50 percent penalty is computed on Form 5329.

If you just discovered you should have been taking out money, do so immediately. Then try to see if one of the preceding reasonable causes will help you avoid the penalty. Part III, line 14 of Form 5329 will help you plead your case; write and attach a statement explaining why you didn't make the required distribution. A math error or illness are some of the valid reasons for having the penalty excused. Say that you have corrected the error and are taking out what the law requires you to withdraw every year. Also, state that you do not feel that you should be penalized because it is the only time that it has happened and you took immediate measures to correct the mistake.

Line 15a is for reporting money that you withdrew from your IRA during the tax year. If you receive a distribution from an IRA, the payer — your bank or broker — will send you Form 1099-R (See Figure 6-3). As a general rule, distributions made from an IRA are fully taxable unless you made nondeductible contributions to the IRA as we explain in the instructions for Box 2a of the 1099-R. Here's a rundown of the important boxes you need to read on your 1099-R in order to report an IRA distribution on Form 1040.

Box 1: Gross distribution

This is the amount of money that you withdrew from your IRA and that was reported to the IRS. Make sure it's correct by checking to see if it matches the amount withdrawn from your IRA account statement. If you've never made a nondeductible contribution to an IRA — that's an IRA contribution where you did not take a tax-deduction and thus filed Form 8606 (Nondeductible IRA Contributions, IRA Basis, and Nontaxable IRA Distributions) — write the number from Box 1 on line 15a of your Form 1040.

Box 2a: Taxable amount

This box contains the taxable amount of the IRA distribution. However, the payer of an IRA distribution doesn't have enough information to compute if your entire IRA distribution is completely taxable or not. Therefore, if you simply enter the amount reported in Box 1 on Form 1040 (line 15b) as being fully taxable, you will overpay on your taxes if you had made nondeductible contributions to your IRA. If you made nondeductible contributions, you compute the nontaxable portion of your distribution on Form 8606. You must attach Form 8606 to your return.

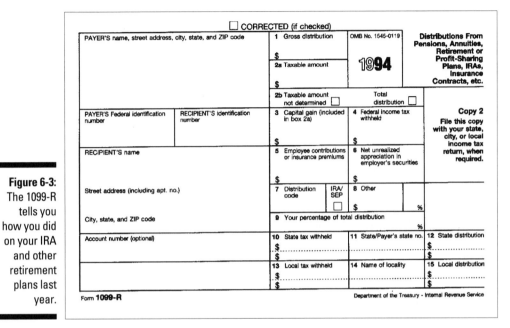

Figure 6-3:
The 1099-R tells you how you did on your IRA and other retirement plans last year.

Box 7: Distribution code

A number code will be entered in this box if one of the exceptions to the 10 percent penalty for distributions before age 59$\frac{1}{2}$ applies.

- ✔ Code 2 — annuity exception
- ✔ Code 3 — disability exception
- ✔ Code 4 — beneficiary exception

Distributions before 59½

If you withdraw money from your IRA before you're 59$\frac{1}{2}$, you not only have to include the amount in your income, you owe a 10 percent penalty on the amount you withdraw. The penalty is computed on Form 5329 (Return for Additional Taxes Attributable to Qualified Retirement Plans). Attach the form to your return and carry over the penalty to Form 1040 (line 51). The penalty doesn't apply to IRA distributions when paid due to death or disability, paid over your life expectancy, or rolled over to another IRA.

Transfers pursuant to divorce

The transfer of an IRA account as a result of a divorce or maintenance decree isn't taxable to you or your former spouse. Nor is it subject to the 10 percent penalty. Here's how you deal with the reality of dividing an IRA in a divorce. If your divorce decrees requires that you transfer all or part of your IRA to the former spouse, the transfer is *not* taxable, nor is it subject to the 10 percent early distribution penalty if you're under 59$^1/_2$.

To make sure that you don't run afoul of the 10 percent penalty, the spouse receiving the money should set up his or her own IRA account. Have the money tranferred to that account.

Withdrawal of nondeductible contributions

If you made nondeductible contributions to your IRA, use Form 8606 (which we just described!) to compute the taxable portion of your withdrawal. You don't have to pay tax on nondeductible contributions that you withdraw. The total of IRS distributions is found on line 7 of Form 8606; enter that on line 15a of Form 1040. The figure from line 13 of Form 8606 is carried over to line 15b of the 1040.

Line 16a and 16b: Total pensions and annuities

Here's where you report your retirement benefits from your pension, profit sharing, 401(k), SEP, or Keogh plan. How they are taxed depends on whether you receive it in the form of an annuity (paid over your lifetime) or lump-sum.

The amount you fill in on line 16a is reported on a 1099-R that you receive from your employer or another custodian of your plan.

Pensions and annuities

If you didn't pay or contribute to your pension or annuity — or if your employer didn't withhold part of the cost from your pay while you worked — then the amount you receive each year is fully taxable. The amount that you contributed, which you received a deduction for, such as contributions to a 401(k), SEP, IRA, or Keogh, isn't considered part of your cost.

If you paid part of the cost (that is to say, if you made nondeductible contributions or contributions that were then added to your taxable income on your W-2) you are not taxed on the part you contributed because this represents a tax-free return of your investment. The rest of the amount that you receive is taxable. To compute this amount, you can use either the *Simplified General Rule* or the *General Rule*.

Simplified General Rule

You can use this method for figuring out the taxable amount of your pension only under the following conditions:

- ✔ Your annuity starting pay-out date is after July 1, 1986.

- ✔ The annuity payments are either for your life, or your life and that of your beneficiary.

- ✔ You were 75 or under, or your payments were guaranteed for fewer than five years at the time the payments begin.

- ✔ The pension or annuity payments are from a qualified employee plan, a qualified employee annuity or a qualified tax shelter annuity.

Under the Simplified General Rule, the IRS allows you to declare as nontaxable part of the money you receive from a certain number of payments made to you or to your beneficiary, based on your age when benefits start. Divide the amount of your contribution to the pension by the number of payments the IRS allows using Table 6-2 to arrive at the nontaxable amount of each payment.

Table 6-2	Simplified General Rule
Age at Annuity Starting Date	*Divide By*
55 and under	300 payments
56-60	260 payments
61-65	240 payments
66-70	170 payments
71 and over	120 payments

Suppose that you retired at age 65 and began receiving $1,000 per month under a joint and survivor annuity with your wife. You contributed $24,000 to the pension. Divide the $24,000 by 240 (the amount for age 65). The resulting $100 is the monthly amount that you receive tax-free. If you live to collect more than the 240 payments, you will have to pay tax on the full amount of your pension that you receive beyond that point. Your cost includes amounts withheld from your paycheck as well as any contributions made by your employer that were reported as additional income.

If you die before you receive 240 payments, your spouse continues to exclude $100 from each payment until the payments received, when added to yours, total 240. If the spouse dies before the 240 payments are made, a miscellaneous itemized deduction on the final return is allowed for the balance of the 240 payments multiplied by $100. This deduction is not subject to the 2 percent adjusted gross income limit. If your spouse dies with 40 payments remaining to be made, a $4,000 deduction would be allowed (40 × $100).

If your annuity starting date was after July 1, 1986, but before January 1, 1987, you can take the $100 exclusion as long as you are receiving payments. You don't stop at 240.

Death-benefit exclusion

If you are a beneficiary of a deceased employee, you may qualify for a death-benefit exclusion up to $5,000. If more than one beneficiary is receiving benefits, the $5,000 exclusion must be allocated proportionately among them.

You are entitled to the $5,000 exclusion if the employee died before receiving the pension. This exclusion is treated as if you had contributed an additional $5,000 to the cost of your pension plan. For example, Jane Smith, age 48, began receiving $1,500 per month because of her husband's death. Mr. Smith contributed $25,000 to his pension. Mrs. Smith is entitled to the $5,000 death-benefit exclusion. The cost of her pension as the survivor is $30,000 (the $25,000 contribution of Mr. Smith plus the $5,000 death-benefit exclusion). To determine the tax-free portion of her pension, divide $30,000 by 300 (the amount for age 48). The result, $100, is the amount of every monthly payment that is received tax-free. If Mrs. Smith lives to receive only 260 payments, $4,000 (40 × $100) is allowed as a deduction on her final return.

The Form 1099-R that Mrs. Smith receives from the payer will have a larger amount as being taxable, because the payer doesn't take the $5,000 death benefit into account when computing the taxable amount. The payer will divide the $25,000 cost by 300 and come up with $83.33 as a monthly tax-free amount. A signed statement must be attached to Mrs. Smith's return explaining that she is entitled to the death-benefit exclusion. And the statement must say that is why the amount she computed as being taxable is less than reported on the 1099-R she received.

General Rule

You must use the General Rule to figure the taxability of your pension or annuity if your annuity starting date is after July 1, 1986, and you do not qualify for — or you do not choose — the Simplified General Rule.

Under the General Rule, a part of each payment is nontaxable because it is considered a return of your cost. The remainder of each payment (including the full amount of any later cost-of-living increases) is taxable. Finding the nontaxable part is very complex and requires you to use actuarial tables. For a full explanation and the tables you need, get IRS Publication 939 (*Pension General Rule — Nonsimplified Method*).

The nontaxable amount remains the same under the General Rule even if the monthly payment increases. If your annuity starting date was before 1987, you continue to exclude the same nontaxable amount from each annuity payment for as long as you receive your annuity. If your annuity starting date is after 1986, your total exclusion over the years cannot be more than your cost of the contract reduced by the value of any refund feature.

If your annuity starting date is after July 1, 1986, and you (or a survivor annuitant) die before the cost is recovered, a miscellaneous itemized deduction is allowed for the unrecovered cost on your (or your survivor's) final income tax return. The deduction is not subject to the 2 percent AGI limit.

Lump-sum distributions

To qualify as a *lump-sum* distribution, the lump-sum must be your entire balance in all your employer's pension plans and it must be paid within a single tax year. The distribution must be paid because of one of the following reasons:

- ✔ you die
- ✔ you reach age 59$^1/_2$
- ✔ you leave the firm
- ✔ you become totally and permanently disabled (if self-employed and under the age of 59$^1/_2$)

A lump-sum distribution from your employer's pension plan can be rolled over to an IRA or to your new employer's retirement plan. Or this distribution can be given capital gain or special averaging treatment if the participant was in the plan for at least five years.

Capital gain treatment

If you reached aged 50 before 1986, you can choose to treat a portion of the taxable part of the lump-sum distribution as a capital gain that is taxable at a 20 percent rate. This treatment applies to the portion you receive for your participation in the plan before 1974. You can select this treatment only once, and you use Form 4972 (Tax on Lump-Sum Distributions) to make this choice.

Special averaging method

If you reached age 50 before 1986 (you were probably born before 1936, right?), you can elect special averaging of the ordinary income portion of the distribution. (This procedure also includes the capital gain portion of the distribution if you do not choose capital gain treatment for it.) To qualify, you must elect to use special averaging on all lump-sum distributions received in the tax year.

To use special averaging, you must have been a participant in the plan for at least five full tax years. You can only make one lifetime election to use this method for any plan participant. If you choose the special averaging method, you generally figure your tax, using Form 4972, as if the distributions were received over five years.

However, you can treat the distribution as though it was received over ten years instead of five years, provided that you apply the 1986 tax rates to it. Form 4972 also computes your tax under the ten-year method. The instructions accompanying Form 4972 contain a 1986 tax rate schedule that must be used in making the ten-year averaging computation. Five- or ten-year averaging can save you a bundle — if you were born before 1936.

Form 1099-R

If you receive a total distribution from a retirement plan, you will receive a Form 1099-R . If the distribution qualifies as a lump-sum distribution, Box 3 shows the capital gain amount, and Box 2a minus Box 3 shows the ordinary income amount. Code A is entered in Box 7 if the lump-sum qualifies for special averaging. If you do not get a Form 1099-R, or if you have questions about it, contact your plan administrator.

Pension distribution on Form 1099-R

Pension distributions are reported on Form 1099-R, which is the same one used to report IRA distributions. The difference between how the information on an IRA distribution is reported to you and the distribution from your pension is as follows:

Box 3: If the distribution is a lump-sum and you were a participant in the plan before 1974, this amount qualifies for capital gain treatment.

Box 5: Your after-tax contribution that you made is entered here.

Box 6: Securities in your employer's company that you received are listed here. This amount is not taxable until the securities are sold.

Box 7: If you are under 59 and your employer knows that you qualify for one of the exceptions to the 10 percent penalty the employer enters:

Code 2 — separation from service after 55

Code 3 — disability

Code 4 — death

Code A — qualifies for lump-sum treatment

Code I — no exception (according to your employer) applies

Code G — direct rollover to an IRA

Code H — direct rollover to another retirement plan

Box 8: If you have an entry here, seek tax advice.

Box 9: Your share of a distribution if there are several beneficiaries.

Tax on early distributions

Distributions that you receive from your employer's retirement plan before the age of 59¹/₂ are subject to a 10 percent penalty as well as being fully taxable. But here are some of the exceptions to the 10 percent penalty, which are more liberal than the exceptions to the 10 percent penalty for taking money out of an IRA before age 59¹/₂.

- ✔ death
- ✔ total and permanent disability
- ✔ distributions (after separation from service) paid over your lifetime or the joint lives of you and your beneficiary
- ✔ distributions made after you stopped working (retirement or termination) during or after the calendar year you reach age 55
- ✔ distributions made under a qualified domestic relations court order
- ✔ distributions made to you (to the extent you have deductible medical expenses in excess of 7.5 percent of your adjusted gross income)

You report the penalty you have to pay on Form 5329 (Additional Taxes Attributable to Qualified Retirement Plans), if none of the exceptions apply. Attach the form to your return and carry over the 10 percent to Form 1040 (line 51).

Minimum distributions

The same rule that applies to IRAs also applies to pension plans for failing to take a minimum distributions by April 1 of the year following the year you turned 70¹/₂.

Disability income

If you retire on disability, your pension is usually taxable. If you are 65, or older (or if you are under 65, and are retired because your disability is total and permanent and you received disability income), you may be able to claim a credit for the elderly or the disabled. However, payments made because of the permanent loss or use of part of the body, or for permanent disfigurement, are exempt from tax.

If you contributed to a plan that paid a disability pension, the part of the pension that you receive that is attributable to your payments isn't subject to tax. You report all your taxable disability on line 7 of your 1040, until you reach the minimum retirement age, and then on line 16a or b. You must use the Simplified General Rule or the General Rule to compute the part of a disability pension that isn't taxable due to your contribution. VA disability benefits are tax-free.

Here is a quick reference list on sickness and injury benefits.

- ✔ **Workers' compensation**. Not taxable if paid under a workers' compensation policy due to a work-related injury or illness.

- ✔ **Federal Employees' Compensation Act (FECA)**. Not taxable if paid because of personal injury or sickness. However, payments received as continuation of pay for up to 45 days while a claim is being decided and pay received for sick leave while a claim is being processed are taxable.

- ✔ **Compensatory damages**. Not taxable if received for injury or sickness.

- ✔ **Accident or health insurance**. Not taxable if you paid the insurance premiums.

- ✔ **Disability benefits**. Not taxable if received for loss of income or earning capacity due to an injury covered by a *no-fault* automobile policy.

- ✔ **Compensation for permanent loss or loss of use of a part or function of your body, or for permanent disfigurement**. Not taxable if paid due to the injury. The payment must be figured without regard to any period of absence from work.

- ✔ **Reimbursements for medical care**. Not taxable; the reimbursement may reduce your medical expense deduction.

Tax on excess withdrawals

Not only is there a penalty for taking your pension too early or too late, there is also a 15 percent penalty for taking too much. If you withdraw more than $150,000 or take a lump-sum distribution of more than $750,000 in any one year from your IRA or pensions accounts, you have to pay a 15 percent penalty on the excess. You use Form 5329 (The form with the really long name! See the Appendix!) to assess this penalty. A rollover isn't considered a lump-sum distribution. Generally, there is a 15 percent penalty if you leave more than $750,000 when you die. The actual amount is based on a very complicated formula.

Line 17: Rental real estate, royalties, partnerships, S Corporations, trusts

This line is an important one for all you self-starters who are landlords, business owners, authors, and honest taxpayers collecting royalties (like us!), and those people lucky enough to have someone set up a trust fund for them. Jump to Chapter 12 to find out more about this and good old Schedule E — the necessary form to wrestle with for this line.

Line 18: Farm income or (loss)

What comes after *E*? You got it. If you have farm income or losses, seek ye old Schedule F, fill it out, and fill in the final number on line 18. It is similar to Schedule C; check out IRS Publication 225 (*Farmer's Tax Guide*).

Line 19: Unemployment compensation

Being down-sized was bad enough. And now you received another nasty surprise — a Form 1099-G, which means the unemployment compensation that you received is taxable! Unemployment compensation is fully taxable, and you enter it on line 19.

If you repaid some or all of the unemployment compensation benefits you received in 1994, you subtract the amount you repaid from the total amount you received and enter the difference on line 19.

Why would you have to give back some of your benefits? Because when you are collecting unemployment insurance, you have to be looking for a job. And if you aren't, the folks at the unemployment office may determine that you owe some money back. If you gave back the benefits in the same year that you received them, no problem; just subtract what you returned from the total you received and enter that amount on line 19.

But if you returned money in 1994 that you paid tax on in 1993, things aren't as easy. Suppose in 1993 you received and paid tax on $10,000 of unemployment benefits. Then during 1994 you had to pay $2,500, as determined by the Unemployment Office. The $2,500 you paid back is deductible on Schedule A (see Chapter 8).

You also enter REPAID and the amount you repaid on the dotted line next to the difference. If you repaid unemployment compensation (that was less than $3,000) in 1994 that you included in gross income in an earlier year, you may deduct the amount repaid with Form 1040, Schedule A (line 22).

If the amount you repaid was more than $3,000, either you can take a deduction for the amount repaid as an itemized deduction, or you can take a credit against your tax for the amount of tax you originally paid by including this amount in your income in a prior year.

For example, in 1994 suppose that you repaid $4,000 of unemployment compensation that you received and paid tax on in 1993. Compute your 1993 tax without the $4,000 being included in your income. If your original tax was $10,000 and your tax without the $4,000 of unemployment was $8,416, you can claim the difference ($1,584) as a credit against your 1994 tax. If this credit is more than what you would save by deducting the $4,000 as an itemized deduction, enter the $1,584 on Form 1040 (line 59), and to the left of the $1,584 credit write IRC 1341. The term IRC comes from Section 1341 of the Internal Revenue Code of 1986.

Line 20a and 20b: Social Security benefits

Politicians don't want to do away with Social Security; they just want to tax more of it. As a result, they have made retirement more complicated. Here's how to figure out what to plug in.

Don't forget that if you are married and file a joint return for 1994, you and your spouse must combine your incomes and your benefits when figuring if any of your combined benefits are taxable. Even if your spouse did not receive any benefits, you must add your spouse's income to yours when figuring if any of your benefits are taxable.

Form SSA-1099

Every person who receives Social Security benefits will receive a Form SSA-1099, even if the benefit is combined with another person's in a single check. If you receive benefits on more than one Social Security record, you may get more than one Form SSA-1099.

Your gross benefits are shown in Box 3 of Form SSA-1099, and your repayments are shown in Box 4. The amount in Box 5 shows your net benefits for 1994 (Box 3 minus Box 4). This is the amount you will use to figure if any of your benefits are taxable.

How much is taxable?

The starting point for determining the taxable portion of your Social Security is your base income, which is your adjusted gross income with a few adjustments. The base income worksheet we give you shows you how to compute this amount. It's an extremely easy computation to make unless you're covered by a pension and decide to make a deductible contribution to an IRA because your income was under $50,000 (for joint filers) or $35,000 (for others).

Here's a suggestion. Unless you want to drive yourself crazy, stay away from making deductible contributions to an IRA if you're covered by a pension and are also receiving Social Security. But in case you want to do the math, here's how to go about it.

Base Income Worksheet

Example: You're married filing jointly and have interest and dividend income of
$10,000, a $20,000 pension, and you received $16,000 from Social Security.

1. AGI (1040 — line 31) before addition of taxable Social Security $30,000

2. Social Security (Box 5, SSA-1099) $16,000

3. 50 percent of line 2 $8,000

4. Tax-exempt interest income   0

5. Foreign earned income exclusion   0

6. Total of lines 3, 4, 5 $8,000

7. Base income (add lines 1 and 6) $38,000

Now use one of the following worksheets to figure the taxable portion of your
Social Security benefits: If line 7 is more than $44,000 (if you are married and
filing jointly) or $34,000 (if unmarried) you have to use Worksheet II.

Worksheet I

1. Base income $38,000

2. Enter the appropriate amount below

    Married filing jointly — $32,000

    Married filing separately and living with spouse
    at any time during year — 0

    All others — $25,000 $32,000

3. Subtract line 2 from line 1 $6,000

4. 50 percent of line 3 $3,000

5. Social Security (Box 5, SSA-1099) $16,000

6. 50 percent of line 5 $8,000

7. Taxable Social Security - smaller of lines 4 and 6 $3,000

    Enter the amount on line 5 ($16,000) on line 20a, Form 1040 and the
    amount on line 7 ($3,000) on line 20b, Form 1040.

Worksheet II

Example: Assume the same facts in the example on Worksheet I, except that your AGI is $36,000, your Social Security is $16,000, and you had $6,000 in tax-exempt interest.

1. AGI	$36,000
2. Tax exempt interest	$6,000
3. 50 percent of Social Security	$8,000
4. Base income	$50,000

tier one adjustment

5. Enter the appropriate below.

       Married filing jointly — $32,000

       Married filing separately and living with spouse at any time during year — 0

       All others — $25,000 $32,000

6. Subtract line 5 from line 4 $18,000

7. 50 percent of line 6 $9,000

8. Enter the appropriate amount below.

       Married filing jointly — $6,000

       Married filing separately and living with spouse at any time during year — 0

       All others — $4,500 $6,000

9. The smaller of lines 3, 7, and 8 $6,000

tier two adjustment

10. Enter the appropriate amount below

       Married filing jointly — $44,000

       Married filing separately and living with spouse at any time during year — 0

       All others — $34,000 $44,000

11. Subtract line 10 from line 4 $6,000

12. 85 percent of line 11 $5,100

TAXABLE PORTION

13. Add lines 9 and 12 $11,100

14. 85 percent of Box 5, SSA-1099 ($16,000) $13,600

15. Taxable Social Security (smaller of lines 13 and 14) $11,100

You would enter the amount in Box 5, SSA-1099 ($16,000) on line 20a of Form 1040 and $11,100 from 15 on line 20a, Form 1040.

Repayment of benefits

In some situations, your Form SSA-1099 will show that the total benefits you repaid (Box 4) are more than the gross benefits you received (Box 3). If this situation occurs, your net benefits in Box 5 will be a negative figure, and none of your benefits will be taxable. If you receive more than one form, a negative figure in Box 5 of one form is used to offset a positive figure in Box 5 of another form. If you have any questions about this negative figure, contact your local Social Security Administration office.

If you and your spouse file a joint return and your SSA-1099s show that your repayments are more than your gross benefits, but your spouse's are not, subtract the amount in Box 5 of your form from the amount in Box 5 of your spouse's form to get your net benefits when figuring if your combined benefits are taxable.

Lump-sum payment

If you receive a lump-sum payment of benefits in 1994 that includes benefits for prior years, you have two choices. You can consider the entire payment as the amount of Social Security received in 1994 and compute the taxable portion by using Worksheet I or II. Or you can allocate the amount that you received for a prior year as being received in that year.

It makes sense to do it this last way because prior to 1994 the maximum amount of Social Security that could be taxed was 50 percent — and if your income was lower in a prior year, even less than 50 percent may be taxable.

If you elect the second way of treating a lump-sum that covers more than one year, you don't file an amended return for that year. Here's what you do. You compute the amount of the lump-sum that would have been taxable had it been received in the prior year. You then add that amount to your income for the current year.

For example, suppose that you receive a lump-sum payment of $20,000 covering benefits for 1993 and 1994. If you report the whole amount in 1994, 85 percent, or $17,000, is taxable. But because $10,000 was for 1993 and $10,000 was for 1994, you only have to report $13,500 as taxable in 1994. That's because the $10,000 attributable to 1993 only increased your income by $5,000, and the $10,000 attributable to 1994 increases your income by $8,500.

Retirees, watch your step

People who retire but continue working a little to supplement their Social Security income may be in for a nasty surprise come April 17,1995.

If you are between 62 and 65, you lose out on $1 of Social Security benefits for every $2 you earn above $8,040. (Remember, this is earned income only; unearned income, such as a pension, doesn't count.) Between 65 and 70, you lose $1 of Social Security for every $3 earned above $11,160. This is known as the Social Security *give back,* though it seems like a *take back* to us.

Starting in 1994, not only do you have this give back to contend with, but more of your Social Security is subject to tax. Married couples with incomes above $44,000 and singles who make more than $34,000 will pay tax on 85 percent of their Social Security income — up from 50 percent in 1993.

The long and short of all of this is that if you're not careful, working a little extra to add to your Social Security income could cost you money. Suppose that you earned $2,000 above that $8,040 threshold and, bad luck, it knocked you from the 15 to the 28 percent tax bracket. First, you pay 7.65 percent Social Security tax on the extra $2,000 of income, which works out to $153. Next you have to pay an extra $1,039 of income tax because you're in a higher bracket now and more of your Social Security is taxable. Then you would have to give back $ 1,000 of your Social Security benefit. Your cost of making that extra two grand: $2,192.

Our advice to retirees under the age of 70: Once you reach either the $8,040 or the $11,160 level, take a vacation until December 31. The 1995 thresholds are $8,160 if you're under 65 and $11,280 if you're 65 to 70.

Repayment of benefits received in an earlier year

If the sum of the amount shown in Box 5 of each of your SSA-1099s is a negative figure and all or part of this negative figure is for benefits you included in gross income in an earlier year, you can take an itemized deduction on Schedule A for the amount of the negative figure — or you can claim credit for the tax that was paid on this in a prior year because you included it in your income.

Line 21: Other income

Line 21 of Form 1040 is a catch-all for reporting income that doesn't fit the income categories listed on page one of Form 1040. Hey, even if you *find* some money, the IRS treats it as income! Just report all this miscellaneous income here. Don't forget to write a description of these earnings on the dotted line next to the amount.

Here are some examples of stuff that goes on line 21.

Bartering

Bartering is the trading of your services for goods or other services. You usually must declare the fair market value of goods you receive. If you participate in a barter exchange, you may get a 1099-B — and the IRS gets a copy, too. For example, suppose that you're a carpenter with a child who needs braces; you agree to make the cabinets in a dentist's office in exchange for your child's braces and treatment. Although no cash changed hands, you have to pay tax on what the dentist would normally charge because that is your income from making the cabinets.

Canceled debt

A canceled debt, or a debt paid for you by another person, is generally income to you and must be reported. A discount offered by a financial institution for the prepaying of your mortgage is income from the cancellation of the debt. However, you have no income from the cancellation of a debt if the cancellation is a gift. For example, suppose that you borrow $10,000 from a relative who tells you that you don't have to repay it. It's a gift! (And be sure to invite *that* relative to Thanksgiving dinner every year.) See IRS Publication 908 *(Bankruptcy and Other Debt Cancellation)* for more information.

If your debt is canceled as the result of bankruptcy or because you are insolvent, the cancellation of the debt negates your having to pay tax on the income. And you do not have income if your student loan is canceled because you agreed to certain conditions to obtain the loan — and then performed the required services.

Fees you snare

Maybe you're a corporate director, a notary public, or an election official. You made some extra cash. Good job!

If these payments are $600 or more you will receive Form 1099-MISC. If you receive a fee or commission from an activity you're not regularly engaged in, it's reported instead on line 12. Fees are considered self-employment income, which means you owe Social Security tax on it. You compute the Social Security tax you owe on Schedule SE (Self-Employment Tax). The amount owed is then reported on line 47 of Form 1040, and half of it is deducted on line 25.

Free tour

The free tour you received from a travel agency or the group organizer is taxable at its fair market value. Bon voyage.

Gambling winnings

Gambling winnings are taxable. And losses to the extent of your winnings are allowed as an itemized deduction on line 28 of Schedule A.

Prizes and awards

If you get lucky and hit the lottery or win a prize in a contest, the winnings are taxable. Sorry! Some employee achievement awards may be nontaxable. Check with your Human Resource department.

Deductions

You also use line 21 to claim two types of deductions: a net-operating loss and the foreign earned income and housing exclusion.

Net operating loss (NOL)

This deduction to your income occurs when your business expenses in a prior year exceed your income for that year. You first carry back the loss 3 years as a deduction and then forward for 15 years — until it is used up. Chapter 17 deals with amended returns and how NOLs are carried back and forward. When you carry a NOL forward from a previous year you enter it as a negative number (for example, $-10,000 on line 21).

Foreign earned income and housing exclusion

U.S. citizens and residents working abroad are entitled to exclude up to $70,000 of their foreign salary or their income if they are self-employed. The portion of their foreign housing costs above an annual threshold ($9,060 for 1994) can also be deducted. The exclusion isn't automatic. You have to file Form 2555 (Foreign Earned Income) to claim the exclusion and the housing deduction, and attach it to your return. There is also a Form 2555-EZ.

To qualify for the exclusion you must either be a resident of a foreign country or be physically present in a foreign country.

To qualify as a resident, you must reside in a foreign country for an uninterrupted period that includes the entire year (January 1 to December 31). So if you start working in London on March 31, 1994 you can't qualify for the exclusion under this rule, but you could possibly under the *physical presence test.* Brief trips back to the U.S. don't disqualify you from being a resident of a foreign country.

Under the physical presence test, you must be in a foreign county for 330 days during a 12-month consecutive period. If you weren't physically present or a bona fide resident for the entire year, the $70,000 exclusion has to be reduced based on the number of days you were out of the country.

To determine if you meet the 330-day test, you may have to apply for an extension of time to file (Form 2350, Application for Extension to File U.S. Income Tax Return). Say you started to work in Paris on July 1, 1994; you won't know until July 1, 1995, if you meet the 330-day test for the twelve month period July 1, 1994, to July 1, 1995.

You enter your foreign earnings on Form 1040 (line 7). Then you enter the amount of those earnings that you can exclude — plus your foreign housing deduction — as a negative number on line 21 and deduct it from your income.

Line 22: Your total income

Whew! Are you ready to do the math? Don't be stubborn or proud; grab the calculator. Add lines 7 through 21 and put the final figure on line 22.

Chapter 7

Adjustments to Income Stuff

- -

In This Chapter

▶ IRA deductions

▶ Moving expenses

▶ One-half of self-employment tax

▶ Keogh and SEP deductions

▶ Penalty on early withdrawal of savings

▶ Alimony paid (that you deduct!)

- -

*C*ongratulations! If you're reading this chapter, you've probably made it through one of the more depressing parts of the tax return. Completing lines 7 through 22 is a bit like trying to count up the number of kindergarten students at the end of a field trip — it's hard to corral everyone, and the total keeps increasing. Despite the IRS calling this last section *Income*, most people just think of their employment earnings as income. If you've done lines 7 through 22, you now know that the IRS definitions include a whole lot more. Ugh!

Although your spirits may be low, keep your chin up — it's (almost) all down-hill from here, tax-wise, that is. However, the reality may be that many of you will not be able to reduce your taxable income by reading this chapter.

Nevertheless, the first step in the tax-slimming process is completing the *adjustments to income* section — adjustments are things that reduce the amount of income that can be taxed. It sure would be easier for you to understand if adjustments to income were simply called deductions from income. But no one ever said the IRS likes to make things simple. When you flip over your Form 1040, you'll soon see that there's another section that allows you to actually deduct things.

Adjustments to Income

So in this section (see Figure 7-1), you'll be summing your adjustments to income (lines 23a through 30) and subtracting these from your total income (line 22). The result of this subtraction is called your *adjusted gross income* (AGI). Your AGI is an important number, because it's used as the benchmark for calculating many allowable deductions such as medical and miscellaneous itemized deductions — as well as the taxable amount of your Social Security income. In fact, if your AGI is too high in the eyes of the IRS, we're sorry to say that you may even lose the one deduction you can always at least try to claim — the one for yourself, the so-called personal exemption.

An important thing to keep in mind is that you don't have to itemize your deductions on Schedule A to claim adjustments to income in this section. Everyone gets to make these adjustments!

Figure 7-1:
Forget about the rest of the gobbledy-gook and focus on this one little section. You can cruise through it in no time.

Adjustments to Income	23a	Your IRA deduction (see page 19)	23a
	b	Spouse's IRA deduction (see page 19)	23b
	24	Moving expenses. Attach Form 3903 or 3903-F . . .	24
Caution: See instructions . . ▶	25	One-half of self-employment tax	25
	26	Self-employed health insurance deduction (see page 21)	26
	27	Keogh retirement plan and self-employed SEP deduction	27
	28	Penalty on early withdrawal of savings	28
	29	Alimony paid. Recipient's SSN ▶	29
	30	Add lines 23a through 29. These are your total adjustments . . . . ▶	30

Here's the line-by-line rundown of the adjustments you may be able to make. The headings refer to line numbers where you plug your data into your 1040.

Line 23a: Your IRA deduction

IRAs were established by Congress to allow taxpayers to establish a retirement plan on their own when they weren't covered by one at work. In the 1980s, Congress changed their collective minds and the law was changed so that everyone could put away and deduct $2,000 even if he or she was covered by a retirement plan. Then — you guessed it — Congress did a backflip in 1986 and the law was modified again.

Now if our elected officials were serious about wanting people to contribute to retirement accounts, they would make the IRA tax laws easy to understand. Well, they didn't. Your ability to take an *adjustment* or a tax-deductible IRA contribution is based not only on your income level, but also on whether you (and your spouse, if you're married) are already covered by some sort of retirement plan. We'll get to these issues in a minute. Before we do, you need first to determine if you even have income that qualifies you for a contribution. Read on.

Compensation needed to qualify for an IRA

If you don't earn employment income or receive alimony and just have income from something like investments, you are *not* allowed to contribute to an IRA. As explained in the next section, limits exist on the size of the IRA contribution that you can make.

You may contribute to an IRA if you have at least some of the following types of compensation:

- ✔ salary and wages
- ✔ commissions and tips
- ✔ self-employed earnings from your business — reduced by your contribution to your other retirement plan (Keogh or SEP) and the deduction allowed for one-half of your Social Security tax
- ✔ alimony received

Covered by an employer's plan

If you have income that qualifies you to contribute to an IRA, you've made it over the first hurdle. If you're filing as single and have total income listed on line 22 of $25,000 or less, or $40,000 or less for married filing jointly, you're eligible to make a fully deductible IRA contribution. You may skip this section on IRAs (see you later).

If your income is above these thresholds — pause to catch your breath — here comes another big hurdle. If you (or your spouse if you're married) are covered by a retirement plan, your ability to deduct an IRA contribution is reduced or eliminated completely if your income exceeds threshold amounts that we'll get to in a minute. So how do you know if you're *covered?* And what the heck is a *retirement plan?*

The simplest way to determine if you are covered by an employer's retirement plan is to look at Box 15 (the pension plan box) on your W-2. If it's marked with an "X," you are considered covered by some type of retirement plan. One of these boxes will be checked by your employer if your employer offers you any of the following:

✔ pension, profit-sharing, stock bonus, or Keogh plans

✔ 401(k) plans

✔ union retirement plans — 501(c)(18) plans for you Trivial Pursuit players!

✔ qualified annuity plans

✔ tax-sheltered annuity — also known as a 403(b) plans

✔ simplified employee pension plan (SEP-IRA) plans

✔ retirement plans established by a federal, state, or local government

You are considered covered, or an active participant, even if you haven't earned the full right (known as *vesting*) to the benefits under your plan. If you switch employers during the year and one of the employers has a plan and the other doesn't, you're considered covered.

If your employer offers you a retirement plan that you can contribute to, such as a 401(k) or 403(b), and you and your employer did not add any money to your account and no forfeitures were allocated during the tax year, you are *not* considered covered during the year. Thus, you could make a tax-deductible IRA contribution if your spouse also is not covered.

If you're currently completing your tax return for 1994, the IRA represents your last chance to make retirement contributions for 1994 (unless you had self-employment income that enables you to contribute to a SEP-IRA — see "Line 27: Keogh retirement plan and self-employed SEP deduction" later in this chapter). Unfortunately, you can't go back now and make contributions to your employer's plan for last year.

If you have plenty of cash around, go ahead and make the IRA contribution. If you're tight on cash, it may be better to forego making the IRA contribution for the last tax year. Looking forward, if you can contribute through your employer's plan, odds are quite high that you may make a higher tax-deductible contribution through that plan than through an IRA. Get signed up for your employer's retirement plan and start funneling money into it now! If you have self-employment income, be sure to read Chapter 19 to learn all about retirement plans that you may establish.

Don't bother contributing to an IRA account if you're already receiving Social Security benefits and are still earning employment income and are covered (or considered covered) by an employer's retirement plan. Why? Because the paperwork is a nightmare. You need to complete the worksheets in Appendix B of Publication 590 (*Individual Retirement Arrangements*) to figure your IRA deduction as well as the taxable portion, if any, of your Social Security benefits. It is just too much of a hassle. If you're receiving Social Security, you're pretty close to the age when you have to start withdrawing money from your IRA anyway. If you want to try to figure this out, good luck. The small tax savings won't be worth paying a tax advisor to figure it out for you.

Income limitations

If you or your spouse is covered by a retirement plan where you work, all is not lost. You may still be able to take the tax deduction for an IRA contribution. However, *if* what's called your *modified adjusted gross income* (explained in the "How to figure partial IRA deductions" sidebar) *exceeds* the following thresholds (also pay attention to the filing status), you may not take the IRA deduction:

- $35,000 and above, no deduction allowed if you are single or a head of household. At $25,000 or less, you may take a full deduction for an IRA. If your modified AGI is between $25,000 and $35,000 you're entitled to a partial deduction.

- $50,000 and above, no deduction allowed if you're filing jointly or as a qualifying widow(er). At $40,000 or less, you may take a full deduction for an IRA. If your income is between $40,000 and $50,000, you are entitled to a partial deduction.

- $10,000 and above, no deduction allowed if you're married filing separately. Below $10,000, a partial deduction is allowed.

If you can't take any IRA deduction or can take only a partial one, you can still make a nondeductible contribution to an IRA, as discussed later in this chapter. Although you don't get a deduction, the earnings on your contribution aren't subject to tax until the money is withdrawn.

Contribution limits

The most that you can contribute for any year to your IRA is the *smaller* of the following:

- your compensation (as we just defined in the section "Compensation needed to qualify for an IRA"), which you must include in income for the year, or
- $2,000

How to figure partial IRA deductions

If your modified adjusted gross income falls between $25,000 to $35,000 (if you're single) or between $40,000 to $50,000 (if you're married filing jointly or qualifying widow(er)) or below $10,000 for married filing separately, you get a partial deduction. If it's above the phaseout limits, you are not entitled to a deduction.

First you have to determine your modified AGI, which is your AGI from Form 1040 (line 31), **but the following deductions must be added back:**

✔ your IRA deduction

✔ foreign earned income and housing deductions; this only applies to taxpayers who live and work abroad

✔ the exclusion for Series EE U.S. Savings Bond Interest (shown on Form 8815)

If you did not live with your spouse at any time during the year and you file a separate return, your filing status is considered, for this purpose, as single.

1. Fill in your modified AGI   1._____

2. Subtract one of the following, depending on your filing status:

     $25,000 — single or head of household

     $40,000 — joint or qualifying widow(er)

     $10,000 — married filing separately   2._____

3. Subtract line 2 from line 1   3._____

4. Phase-out Amount ($10,000)   4._____

5. Subtract line 4 from line 3   5._____

6. Multiply line 5 by 20%   6._____

7. Your deductible contribution   7._____

If you're married, your spouse may be able to contribute to an IRA as well. See the instructions for the next line in "Line 23b: Spouse's IRA deduction."

Peter is a real person who read his IRS instruction booklet and learned that he could contribute $2,000 to an IRA. He liked investing in mutual funds, so he set up three IRA accounts at three different mutual funds and contributed $2,000 to each one, for a total contribution of $6,000 for the year! The IRS computers discovered this glitch when the three mutual funds each reported under Peter's Social Security number that he had made this many contributions for the same tax year. Remember that the $2,000 limit is the maximum you can contribute regardless of whether your contributions are to one or more IRAs, or whether all or part of your contributions is deductible. (See the discussion of "Nondeductible IRA contributions" in the next section.)

You should receive Form 5498 (Individual Retirement Arrangement Information) — it's like a little 1099 — or a similar statement from the custodian of your IRA by May 31, 1995. This form shows all the contributions you made to your IRA for 1994.

Nondeductible IRA contributions

Although your deduction for an IRA contribution may be reduced or eliminated because of the adjusted gross income limitation, you may make nondeductible IRA contributions of up to $2,000 or 100 percent of your compensation, whichever is less. The difference between your allowable deductible contribution, which is entered on line 23a, and your total contributions made, if any, is your nondeductible contribution.

If you can't deduct an IRA contribution, you might be wondering why or how you would still contribute to an IRA. An astonishing number of taxpayers don't realize that you may still contribute to an IRA even if your contribution isn't deductible. And you may want to make nondeductible contributions, because the *growth* (from interest, dividends, and appreciation) on your contribution is sheltered from taxation inside the tax-friendly confines of an IRA, and the growth dollars will not be taxed until they are distributed to you years from now in retirement.

For example, Alex is single. In 1994 he is covered by a retirement plan at work. His salary is $42,000 and his modified AGI is $45,000. Alex makes a $2,000 IRA contribution for that year. Because he is covered by a retirement plan and his modified AGI is over $35,000, he can't deduct his IRA contribution.

Because Alex cannot deduct the $2,000 he contributed to the IRA, he can choose between two courses of action. He can designate his contribution as a nondeductible contribution by completing Form 8606 (Nondeductible IRAs — Contributions, Distributions, and Basis), or he can withdraw his $2,000 tax-free by April 15, 1995. But he also has to withdraw his earnings on the $2,000, which are taxable. The April 15 date can be extended if Alex files for an extension.

You must report nondeductible contributions to the IRS. You must file Form 8606 to report nondeductible contributions even if you do not have to file a tax return for the year. If you are filing a 1040, you must attach Form 8606 to your 1040. There is a $50 penalty for not filing your 8606!

Where to set up an IRA

Mutual fund companies, particularly no-load (commission-free) firms, are ideal choices. See Chapter 21 for more information.

Line 23b: Spouse's IRA deduction

If your spouse is employed, the deductible amount of your spouse's IRA contribution goes on this line.

If your spouse is not employed, you can set up a spousal IRA and contribute an extra $250 beyond the $2,000 limit and put that amount on this line.

If your spouse works

If your spouse is employed during the year — and each of you is under $70^1/_2$ at the end of the year — you can both have an IRA. Each of you can contribute up to the $2,000 limit, unless your taxable compensation (or your spouse's) is less than $2,000. Qualifying income is the same as explained earlier in the section, "Compensation needed to qualify for an IRA."

You or your spouse can choose to be treated as having no compensation for the year and use the rules for spousal IRAs. Generally, if one spouse has compensation of less than $250 for the year, a spousal IRA is more advantageous than a regular IRA.

For example, Bill and Linda file a joint return for 1994. Bill earned $27,000 and Linda earned $190. Linda chose to be treated as having no compensation. Bill thus set up a spousal IRA for her. Because he contributed $1,800 to his IRA, the most that can be contributed to the spousal IRA is $450 ($2,250 minus his $1,800 contribution).

Nonworking spouses

If you decide to set up a spousal IRA, the most that you can contribute is 100 percent of your taxable compensation up to $2,250. If your salary is $1,500, you can contribute $1,500. If your salary is over $2,250, the most you can contribute is $2,250.

You can divide your IRA contributions between your IRA and your spouse's IRA any way you choose, but you cannot contribute more than $2,000 to either IRA.

If your spouse is younger than you and you are close to retirement age (70 1/2), it would make sense to contribute $250 to your IRA and the balance of $2,000 to the spousal IRA. That way the money contributed will continue to grow tax-free for a longer period before it has to be withdrawn.

To contribute to a spousal IRA you need to fulfill the following requirements:

- ✔ You must be married at the end of the tax year.
- ✔ Your spouse must not have reached 70 1/2 by the end of the year.
- ✔ You must file a joint return.
- ✔ You must have taxable compensation for the year.
- ✔ Your spouse must have no compensation — or must choose to be treated as having no compensation for the year.

Spouse under age 70 1/2

You can't make contributions to your own IRA for the year in which you reach age 70 1/2 or in any later year. However, for any year you have compensation, you can continue to make contributions of up to $2,000 to a spousal IRA. You can contribute to a spousal IRA until the year your spouse reaches 70 1/2.

Line 24: Moving expenses

If you incur moving expenses because you have to relocate, you can deduct moving expenses for which your employer didn't reimburse you. Self-employed individuals may also deduct their moving expenses and plug the total on this line.

And unlike other deductible expenses, this deduction isn't subject to varying interpretations. It's subject to two mathematical tests. The first one: The distance between your new job location and your former home must be at least 50 miles more than the distance between your former home and your former job location. What? You reread that last sentence three times and still don't get it? You're not the only one. Try it this way.

Distance in miles between:

A. Your former residence and new job location .... _____

B. Your former residence and old job location .... _____

C. Subtract line B from line A .... _____

If line C is 50 miles or more, you may have a deduction, provided you pass the second math test: You must remain employed on a full-time basis at your new job location for at least 39 weeks during the 12-month period immediately following your arrival. In other words, you cannot make a deduction unless you pass the distance test and satisfy the employment duration requirement.

The rule is even tougher on the self-employed. To get the deduction, you must work in the same new job for 78 weeks during the 24 months after your arrival. To save you this bit of math, a part-time job won't satisfy the 39- or 78-week test.

If you work outside the U.S., there is a special exemption: You can deduct expenses for a move to a new home in the U.S. when you permanently retire. The move doesn't have to be related to a new job. This exemption also applies to a survivor of someone who worked outside the U.S.

Now for some bad news. 1993's tax bill drastically scaled back the number and kinds of moving expenses that can be deducted. Meals, temporary living expenses, and expenses incurred in the sale or lease of a residence are no longer deductible. As of January 1994, you may deduct only the cost of moving your household goods and personal effects from your former residence to your new one, plus your own travel costs for lodging but not for meals. These are the federal rules. Some states allow a deduction for moving expenses — your state rules may or may not be similar to the federal rules.

Form 3903

The place to deduct moving expenses is Form 3903 (Moving Expenses). For a move to a foreign location, you have to use Form 3903-F. If you haven't met the 39- or 78-week test by the time you have to file your return, don't worry. You're still allowed to claim the deduction if you expect to meet the test. However, if it turns out that you fail the 39- or 78-week test, you've got to report the deduction as income on next year's tax return. No fun at all.

But you've lucked out with Form 3903 because it's only eight lines to get through! Here's what you do:

Line 1: Enter the number of miles from your old home to your *new* workplace.

Line 2: Enter the number of miles from your old home to your *old* workplace.

Line 3: Subtract line 2 from line 1.

If line 3 is less than 50 miles, you can't deduct any of your moving expenses.

Line 4: Enter the cost of transporting and storing your household goods and personal effects.

Line 5: Enter the travel and lodging expenses for you and members of your household from your old home to your new home.

Line 6: Add lines 4 and 5 (your total moving expenses).

Line 7: Enter the amount your employer reimbursed you for your moving expenses.

This amount is entered in Box 13 of your Form W-2 with a code P next to it. If you weren't reimbursed by your employer, there won't be anything in Box 13, so put 0 on line 7 of Form 3903.

Line 8: Subtract line 7 from line 6.

This is the amount of your deductible 1994 moving expenses. Now enter this amount on your Form 1040 (line 24).

Reimbursement of 1993 expenses

If you incurred moving expenses in 1993 but weren't reimbursed by your employer until 1994, you have to report the reimbursement as part of your salary income. If you didn't deduct your moving expenses in 1993 (because you weren't reimbursed until 1994), you can deduct them in 1994 by filling out Page 2 of Form 3903. This deduction isn't subject to the new 1994 moving expense limitations. It's subject to the 1993 limitations, and it's not deducted as an adjustment to your income on line 24. It's deducted as an itemized deduction on Schedule A (line 27). It's not subject to the 2 percent limitation of your AGI.

Line 25: One-half of self-employment tax

If you're self-employed, you have to pay your own Social Security tax. It's a little confusing because this tax is called a self-employment tax (not a Social Security tax) — don't you wish the IRS would use English?

If you're self-employed and file Schedule C or Schedule C-EZ, or are a working partner in a partnership, or if you earned income for services you provided that you reported on line 21 of Form 1040 as miscellaneous income and you didn't incur any expenses in earning it, you have to file Schedule SE (Self-Employment Tax). That's the form you use to compute the Social Security tax you owe. See Chapter 10 to learn how to complete Schedule SE.

Now for some good news. Half of your self-employment tax that you have to pay is deductible. Complete Schedule SE and note the following: The amount on line 5 of Schedule SE is the amount of tax you have to pay, and it is carried over to Form 1040 (line 47) and added to your income tax that's due; half of what you have to pay is entered on Form 1040 (line 25).

Line 26: Self-employed health insurance deduction

Although the line for claiming this deduction is listed on Form 1040, as it now stands, it can't be claimed in 1994 because this deduction expired on December 31, 1993. It has expired before — and Congress always reinstates it. (We guess that's why the IRS listed it on this year's tax form!)

In case Congress decides to reinstate this deduction retroactive to 1994 — and there is a good chance it will — you can deduct 25 percent of your health insurance premiums from your income. A general partner (but not a limited partner), an independent contractor, or a shareholder in an S Corporation can also claim this deduction. For example, if the health insurance premiums for you and your dependents are $4,000, you can deduct $1,000 on line 26. The $3,000 balance is deducted on Schedule A (line 1) as a medical expense if you are itemizing your deductions.

But some married couples don't have to wait to have this deduction restored. If your spouse is employed by you, even for a nominal salary, you may be able to deduct 100 percent of your family's medical expenses and not just 25 percent of your medical insurance premiums.

That's because self-employed people can pay and deduct an employee's family health insurance premiums as a business expense, even if the health insurance policy covers the owner as well; and if you set up a medical reimbursement plan you may be able to deduct your family's other medical costs. A tax advisor can show you how to do this stuff.

Two things make all this unattractive, however. You have to provide all employees with this coverage, and the payroll tax expense is on your spouse's salary.

In order to find out the latest and greatest about our tax code, including information on the now-it-is-now-it-isn't deductible health insurance premium, you may call the IRS by using the appropriate number you find in the Appendix.

Line 27: Keogh retirement plan and self-employed SEP deduction

You can still open a self-employment retirement plan called a SEP in 1995 and deduct your contribution to it on your 1994 return. You have until August 15 or October 15, 1995, to do this if you have an extension of time to file until then.

As a self-employed person, you can set up a Keogh Plan. Your contributions to the plan are not only deductible, but are also exempt from tax until you start receiving benefits. But in order to make a Keogh contribution in 1995 that's deductible on your 1994 return, the plan must have been set up by December 31, 1994. (See Chapter 19 to learn about Keoghs.) If you already have a Keogh set up by the end of the tax year, see "Keogh contributions" later in this chapter.

As a general rule, employees who work less than 1,000 hours per year don't have to be included in the plan, as well as employees that have been with you less than two years. Check your plan document to see who needs to be covered in your plan. If you and your spouse are the only ones covered by the plan, you don't have to file an annual information return with the IRS until the plan's assets exceed $100,000. If you're subject to the filing requirements, you file Form 5500EZ; if you have employees, you use Form 5500.

If you forgot to set up a Keogh by December 31, 1994, you can't make a deductible contribution to it for 1994 because the plan wasn't in existence in 1994. But with a SEP you can take a deduction for 1994 as long as you set one up and contribute to it by the due date for filing your 1994 return (which can be extended to October 15, 1995).

Keogh contributions

With a Keogh pension plan you can contribute up to 25 percent of your earnings after deducting one-half of your self-employment tax and your Keogh contribution. With a profit-sharing Keogh plan you can only contribute up to 15 percent. Although 25 percent of $150,000 is $37,500, you're limited to a maximum deduction of $30,000. So once your earnings reach $186,460, the maximum you can contribute to a Keogh is 20 percent, because 20 percent multiplied by the maximum earnings base of $150,000 is $30,000.

Example 1

Earnings	$186,460
Less 50% of self-employment tax	$6,460
Balance	$180,000
Less 25% of $180,000 to a maximum of $30,000	$30,000
Maximum earnings base	$150,000

Example 2

Earnings	$60,000
50% of self-employment tax	$4,590
Balance	$55,410
Keogh contribution (20% of $55,410)	$11,082
Maximum earnings base	$44,328

25% of $44,328 equals $11,082.

Use Table 7-1 to determine your effective contribution rate based on the actual plan percentage that you choose to contribute.

SEP contributions

The most you can contribute to a SEP is 15 percent of your net earnings from self-employment less one-half of your self-employment tax and your contribution to the SEP. This amount works out to be 13.0435 percent of your net earnings after the deduction for one-half of self-employment tax. You don't have to make a contribution every year. Some years, you can skip making a contribution entirely or you can choose any contribution percentage up to 15 percent. The maximum amount of earnings that can be used to figure your SEP contribution after deducting one-half of your self-employment tax and your SEP contribution is $150,000, and the maximum SEP contribution is $22,500.

Example 1

Earnings	$178,850
Less 50% of self-employment tax	$6,350
Balance	$172,500
Less SEP contribution (13.0435% of $172,500)	$22,500
Maximum earnings base	$150,000

Fifteen percent of $150,000 amounts to $22,500, the maximum deductible SEP contribution that can be made. Therefore, once your earnings reach $178,850, you're at the $22,500 limit. If you have employees, you simply multiply their salary by 15 percent, if that's the percentage you selected. You don't have to do this calculation.

Example 2

Earnings	$60,000
Less 50% of self-employment tax	$4,590
Balance	$55,410
Less SEP contribution (13.0435% of $55,410)	$7,227
Maximum earnings base	$48,183

15% of $48,183 equals your SEP contribution of $7,227.

Table 7-1	Keogh and SEP Conversion Table
Actual Plan Rate	*Effective Rate That You Contribute*
1%	.009901
2	.019608
3	.029126
4	.038462
5	.047619
6	.056604
7	.065421
8	.074074
9	.082569
10	.090909
11	.099099
12	.107143
13	.115044
14	.122007
15	.130435
16	.137931
17	.145299
18	.152542
19	.159664
20	.166667
21	.173554
22	.180328
23	.186992
24	.193548
25	.200000

If you choose to put away 10 percent, subtract half of your Social Security tax from your earnings and multiply that by the effective rate — .090909.

Line 28: Penalty on early withdrawal of savings

If you withdraw funds from a savings account before maturity or redeem a certificate of deposit before it's due and you are charged a penalty, you can deduct it on your 1040 (line 28). You don't have to itemize your deductions to claim this deduction. You can deduct the entire penalty, even if it exceeds the interest income reported on the Form 1099-INT that you received. The penalty amount, if any, is shown in Box 2 of the 1099, which the bank will send you by January 31, 1995.

Line 29: Alimony paid

The alimony you paid is deducted on line 29, and to the left of the line you have to enter your former spouse's Social Security number. If you don't enter the number, you can expect to hear from the IRS because there is a $50 penalty for making this boo-boo. If you paid alimony to more than one person, enter the total amount of alimony you paid on line 29, and enter the amount and Social Security number for each recipient on a separate schedule and attach it to your return.

You need to know what alimony is before you can deduct it as an expense. The alimony rules aren't simple, so hang in there.

This is alimony

Payments count as alimony only if *all* the following conditions are met:

- ✔ Payments are required by the divorce decree. Or maybe there is a separation decree.

- ✔ The payer of alimony and its recipient don't file a joint return.

- ✔ The payment is in cash, which includes checks or money orders.

- ✔ The spouses who are separated or divorced are not members of the same household.

- ✔ The payments are not required after the death of the spouse who receives the alimony.

- ✔ The payment is not designated as child support.

This is not alimony

Payments do not count as alimony if *any* of the following conditions is true:

- ✔ The payment is a noncash property settlement.

- ✔ The payments are a spouse's part of community income.

- ✔ The payments are destined to keep up the payer's property.

- ✔ The payments are not required as part of the separation or divorce settlement.

Rules and exceptions to alimony

Looks simple, you say? Sorry. The rules on alimony are one of the most complex areas of the law. The reason for this absurd complexity is that each party to a divorce is trying to achieve opposite goals. The payer usually wants to deduct every payment and the recipient wants to pay as little tax as possible. So to keep everyone honest, more regulations breed more regulations and so on! Here's some more information that will help you plug in the right amount on line 11 for income or line 29 for alimony paid.

Cash payments

A cash payment must be in cash. (Makes sense, doesn't it?) Property settlements don't qualify. The transfer of a home or business are considered property settlements.

Payments to a third party

Payments to a third party qualify as alimony if they are used in place of alimony and are requested in writing by your former spouse. These payments can be for medical expenses, housing costs, taxes, tuition, and so on.

Life insurance premiums

Life insurance premiums on your life insurance qualify as deductible alimony if the payment is required by the divorce or separation agreement and your former spouse owns the policy.

Mortgage payments

Mortgage payments are alimony if you must make mortgage payments (principal and interest) on a home jointly owned with your former spouse — and the terms of the decree or agreement call for such payments. You can deduct half of the total of these payments as alimony. Your spouse reports the other half as income.

Members of the same household

You can't be members of the same household even if you and your spouse separate yourselves physically in your home (or in your tropical hut, just like Gilligan and the Skipper did once after they had a fight). However, payments made within one month of departure qualify as alimony. For example, suppose that on June 1, while you are still residing in the same residence with your spouse, you make a support payment. If you move out by July 1, this payment is deductible. Any payments made prior to June 1st do not qualify, however. A technical exception exists, however. If you are not legally separated or divorced, payments made under a separation agreement or a support decree qualify as alimony even if you are members of the same household.

Taxes and insurance

Tax and insurance payments qualify as alimony if you must make them on a home you hold as *tenants in common* — which means that your heirs get your share when you die. (The person you own the property with doesn't get your share.) You can deduct half of tax and insurance payments as alimony, and your spouse reports the other half as income from alimony. If the property is held as *tenants by the entirety* or as *joint tenants* (where the survivor gets it all), none of your payments for taxes and insurance qualifies as alimony.

Minimum payment period

For alimony agreements executed in 1985 and 1986, annual payments in excess of $10,000 had to continue for at least six years. For agreements made after 1986, no minimum payment period exists.

Recapture

To keep people from disguising large divorce settlements as alimony, a *recapture* provision was enacted for agreements executed after 1986. Recapture means that you have to report as income part of what you deducted during the first two years that you started paying alimony. The recapture rule applies if your average payments decline in the first three years by more than $15,000.

For example, suppose that in year one and year two you paid and deducted $25,000 in alimony, but in year three you paid only $5,000. You triggered the recapture rules because your payment decreased by more than $15,000. See a tax expert. This is one area you shouldn't fool around with. However, recapture doesn't apply if your spouse dies or remarries, or if your alimony payments are geared to a fixed percentage of your income and your income decreases.

Payments after death

Alimony payments must stop at your spouse's death. If you must continue to make payments after your spouse's death — because of the legalese included in the agreement — none of the payments that you made before or after death qualifies as alimony that you can deduct.

Child support

A required payment that is specifically designated as child support under your divorce decree isn't deductible as alimony. Even if a payment *isn't* specially designated as child support, part of it will be considered child support if the payment is to be reduced when your child reaches a specified age, dies, marries, leaves school, or becomes employed.

For example, suppose that you are required to pay your spouse $2,000 a month. However, when your child reaches age 21, your payment will be reduced to $1,250. Only $1,250 of your $2,000 monthly payment is considered alimony, and the $750 is considered nondeductible child support.

For *pre*-1985 divorce decrees, combined spouse and child support payments that are reduced when the child comes of age are treated as alimony. The IRS deemed this deal too good (of course) and thus changed the rules for agreements executed after 1984.

Payments to nonresident aliens

Alimony paid to nonresident aliens is considered U.S. source income. This stipulation means that you have to withhold 30 percent for tax and send it to the IRS, just like your employer does with the tax withheld from your salary. Find out if the U.S. has a tax treaty with the country of your former spouse — under a number of tax treaties, alimony is exempt from withholding. See IRS Publication 901 (*U.S. Tax Treaties*) for some really interesting reading!

Line 30: Total adjustments

Go ahead, make your day. Add all the figures you have on lines 23a to 29. The total is your total adjustments — we hope it's a big one. But alas, it may be zero. Don't despair, there are more deductions to come on the backside of Form 1040.

The next step is taking away — please savor that expression because it is not often you get to take away taxable income — the amount in line 30 from line 22 (the total income). The result is the adjusted gross income, which is one of those big tax terms that you hear a good deal about. Now you even know what it means.

The IRS must think that this is a pretty important amount because the good people at the Department of the Treasury have designed an easy-to-find adjusted gross income line at the bottom of the 1040 (line 31) where you enter this amount before you turn to the backside of the form. Congrats! You're halfway there! (But be sure to read the fine print on line 31 to see if you may qualify for earned income credit.)

Chapter 8

Itemized Deductions: Schedule A

*1*f Hamlet were to be written today, we wonder if Shakespeare would have him lamenting, "To itemize or to take the standard deduction, that is the question." Forgive the Shakespearean reference, but that is indeed the question that must be answered.

The Decision

You've reached that point in preparing your return where this decision has to be made. You totaled your income and subtracted your allowable adjustments to income. Now to arrive at your taxable income you have to subtract your standard deduction and exemptions — or take the more difficult road and subtract your itemized deductions.

The Standard Deduction

If you're under 65, the standard deductions are as follows:

▶ $6,350 — Married filing jointly or a qualifying widow(er)

▶ $5,600 — Head of household

▶ $3,800 — Single

▶ $3,175 — Married filing separately.

If you are married filing separately, you may claim the standard deduction only if your spouse also claims the standard deduction. If your spouse itemizes, you must also itemize. So if you decide not to itemize your deductions, enter the standard deduction for your filing status on line 34.

Over 65 or blind

If you are blind or over 65, the standard deduction is increased by $950 if you are single or a head of household, and $750 if you are married filing jointly or a qualifying widow(er).

So instead of having to add this extra deduction to your regular standard deduction, just check the appropriate blanks in the chart (see Table 8-1).

If you are claiming an increased standard deduction, you can't use Form 1040EZ; you must use Form 1040A or Form 1040.

Table 8-1   Standard Deduction Chart for People Age 65 or Older or Blind

Check the number of blanks below. Then go to the chart.

You	65 or older _____	Blind _____
Your spouse, if claiming spouse's exemption	65 or older _____	Blind _____
Total number of blanks you checked		_____

If Your Filing Status Is:	*And the Number in the Blank Above Is:*	*Your Standard Deduction Is:*
Single	1	$4,750
	2	$5,700
Married filing joint return or qualifying widow(er) with dependent child	1	$7,100
	2	$7,850
	3	$8,600
	4	$9,350
Married filing separate return	1	$3,925
	2	$4,675
	3	$5,425
	4	$6,175
Head of household	1	$6,550
	2	$7,500

Standard deduction for dependents

If you can claim your child or dependent on your or on another person's tax return, their standard deduction is limited to either $600 or to the individual's earned income for the year (whichever amount is larger) — but not more than their regular standard deduction amount of $3,800. So if you're helping your son or daughter prepare their return, they have to use this worksheet to compute their standard deduction.

However, if your dependent is 65 or older or blind, this standard deduction may be higher (see Table 8-2).

Table 8-2	**Standard Deduction Worksheet for Dependents**

If you were 65 or older or blind, check the blanks below. Then go to the worksheet.

You   65 or older ____   Blind _____

Your spouse, if claiming spouse's exemption   65 or older ____   Blind _____

Total number of blanks you checked   _____

1. Enter your **earned income** (defined at the end). If none, go on to line 3.   **1.** _____

2. Minimum amount   **2. $600**

3. Compare the amounts on lines 1 and 2   **3.** _____

Enter the larger of the two amounts here.

4. Enter on line 4 the amount shown below for your filing status.   **4.** _____

    Single, enter $3,800

    Married filing separate return, enter $3,175

    Married filling jointly or qualifying widow(er) with dependent child, enter $6,350

    Head of household, enter $5,600

5. Standard deduction.

a. Compare the amounts on lines 3 and 4.   **5a.** _____

Enter the smaller of the two amounts here.

If under 65 and not blind, stop here. This is your standard deduction. Otherwise, go on to line 5b.

b. If 65 or older or blind, multiply $950 by the total number of blanks checked ($750 if married or qualifying widow(er) with dependent child).   **5b.** _____

Enter the result here.

c. Add lines 5a and 5b. This is your standard deduction for 1994.   **5c.** _____

Earned income includes wages, salaries, tips, professional fees, and other compensation that you got for services performed. It also includes anything received as a scholarship that counts as income.

Itemized Deductions

Often taxpayers will quickly compute their tax using the standard deduction and don't like the results. In those cases where you are unhappy, try itemizing and then use the higher of the two amounts. Does this advice make sense or what?

Here's your itemized deduction shopping list:

- medical and dental expenses that exceed 7.5 percent of your adjusted gross income (AGI)

- taxes you paid

- interest you paid

- gifts to charity

- casualty and theft losses

- moving expenses incurred in 1993 but paid in 1994 (1994 moving expenses are deducted as a reduction of your AGI)

- job-related, investment, and tax-preparation expenses that exceed 2 percent of your AGI

- other miscellaneous itemized deductions not subject to the 2 percent limit

You claim these deductions on Form 1040 with Schedule A. You carry the total on line 29 over to Form 1040 (line 34) where you subtract it from your AGI.

In case you looked at the above list and said "Hey that's easy," there are two rules you have to be aware of. Read on.

Separate returns and limits on deductions

If you are married and filing separately, both spouses have to itemize the deductions. One spouse can't use the standard deduction while the other itemizes. If you are divorced or legally separated, you are considered single and you can itemize your deductions or claim the standard deduction no matter what your former spouse does. However, in itemizing your separate expenses, you can claim only those expenses for which you or your spouse are personally liable. For example, if a residence is in your spouse's name and you paid the property taxes and the mortgage interest, you can't deduct them. But neither can your spouse, because your ex-spouse didn't pay them.

If you and your spouse are separated but don't have a decree of divorce or separate maintenance, you may be able to itemize or use the standard deduction and file as head of household. You can do this if you didn't live with your spouse during the last six months of 1994, and if you maintained a home for more than half of 1994 for yourself and a child that you are entitled to claim as a dependent.

But if you change your mind

Oops! Suppose that you discover you should have itemized after you already filed. Or even worse, suppose that you went to all the trouble to itemize but shouldn't have done so. Just amend your return by filing Form 1040X (Amended U.S. Individual Income Tax return).

But if you're married and you filed separately, you can't change your mind unless both you and your spouse make the same change. And if either of you must pay additional tax as a result of the change, you both need to file a consent. (Sorry, dear!) Remember that if one of you itemizes, the other no longer qualifies for the standard deduction.

Lines 1-4: Medical and Dental Expenses

Your total medical and dental expenses (after what you were reimbursed by your health insurance policy) must exceed 7.5 percent of your adjusted gross income (line 31 or 32 of your Form 1040). This detail knocks many people out of contention for this deduction. For example, if your adjusted gross income equals $30,000, you'd need to have at least $2,250 in medical and dental expenses. If you don't, you can cruise past these lines.

You can deduct medical and dental expenses for you, your spouse, and your dependents. You can also deduct the medical expenses of any person who is your dependent even if you can't claim an exemption for this person because he or she had income of $2,450 or more or filed a joint return. You fill in the amounts on lines 1-4 on the Schedule A (see Figure 8-1).

Medical and dental expense checklist

The following is a list of things that are deductible, so remember to save all those bills:

- medical services (doctors, dentists, opticians, podiatrists, registered nurses practical nurses, psychiatrists, and so on)

- hospital bills

- medical, hospital, and dental insurance premiums that you pay (but you cannot deduct premiums paid by your employer)

- guide dog

- Social Security tax paid for worker providing medical care as well as the wages for a worker providing medical care

- birth control pills

- legal abortion

- special items (artificial limbs, contact lenses, and so on)

- wages for nursing service

- oxygen equipment and oxygen

- part of life-care fee paid to a retirement home designated for medical care

- treatment at a drug or alcohol clinic

- special school or home for a mentally or physically handicapped person

- ambulance service

- transportation for medical care

- drugs and medicines prescribed by a doctor

- costs for medical equipment or modifications to your home for needed medical care

- laboratory fees and tests

- childbirth classes (but if your husband attends the classes as your coach, his portion of the fee isn't deductible)

Be aware that many medical- and dental-related expenses can't be deducted. Suprisingly, a number of expenses that you make to improve your health, such as fees paid for a stop-smoking class, which should reduce your medical expenses, are not deductible.

You can't deduct these things:

- diaper service

- funeral expenses

- health club dues

- household help (even if recommended by a doctor)

- life insurance premiums

SCHEDULES A&B (Form 1040)
Department of the Treasury Internal Revenue Service (99)

Schedule A—Itemized Deductions

(Schedule B is on back)

▶ Attach to Form 1040. ▶ See Instructions for Schedules A and B (Form 1040).

OMB No. 1545-0074 **1994** Attachment Sequence No. 07

Name(s) shown on Form 1040 | Your social security number

Medical and Dental Expenses		Caution: *Do not include expenses reimbursed or paid by others.*		
	1	Medical and dental expenses (see page A-1)	1	
	2	Enter amount from Form 1040, line 32. 2		
	3	Multiply line 2 above by 7.5% (.075)	3	
	4	Subtract line 3 from line 1. If line 3 is more than line 1, enter -0-		4
Taxes You Paid (See page A-1.)	5	State and local income taxes	5	
	6	Real estate taxes (see page A-2)	6	
	7	Personal property taxes	7	
	8	Other taxes. List type and amount ▶	8	
	9	Add lines 5 through 8		9
Interest You Paid (See page A-2.)	10	Home mortgage interest and points reported to you on Form 1098	10	
	11	Home mortgage interest not reported to you on Form 1098. If paid to the person from whom you bought the home, see page A-3 and show that person's name, identifying no., and address ▶	11	
Note: Personal interest is not deductible.	12	Points not reported to you on Form 1098. See page A-3 for special rules	12	
	13	Investment interest. If required, attach Form 4952. (See page A-3.)	13	
	14	Add lines 10 through 13		14
Gifts to Charity If you made a gift and got a benefit for it, see page A-3.	15	Gifts by cash or check. If any gift of $250 or more, see page A-3	15	
	16	Other than by cash or check. If any gift of $250 or more, see page A-3. If over $500, you **MUST** attach Form 8283	16	
	17	Carryover from prior year	17	
	18	Add lines 15 through 17		18
Casualty and Theft Losses	19	Casualty or theft loss(es). Attach Form 4684. (See page A-4.)		19
Job Expenses and Most Other Miscellaneous Deductions	20	Unreimbursed employee expenses—job travel, union dues, job education, etc. If required, you **MUST** attach Form 2106 or 2106-EZ. (See page A-5.) ▶	20	
	21	Tax preparation fees	21	
(See page A-5 for expenses to deduct here.)	22	Other expenses—investment, safe deposit box, etc. List type and amount ▶	22	
	23	Add lines 20 through 22	23	
	24	Enter amount from Form 1040, line 32. 24		
	25	Multiply line 24 above by 2% (.02)	25	
	26	Subtract line 25 from line 23. If line 25 is more than line 23, enter -0-		26
Other Miscellaneous Deductions	27	Moving expenses incurred before 1994. Attach Form 3903 or 3903-F. (See page A-5.) . .		27
	28	Other—from list on page A-5. List type and amount ▶		28
Total Itemized Deductions	29	Is Form 1040, line 32, over $111,800 (over $55,900 if married filing separately)? **NO.** Your deduction is not limited. Add the amounts in the far right column for lines 4 through 28. Also, enter on Form 1040, line 34, the **larger** of this amount or your standard deduction. **YES.** Your deduction may be limited. See page A-5 for the amount to enter.	▶	29

For Paperwork Reduction Act Notice, see Form 1040 instructions. Cat. No. 11330X **Schedule A (Form 1040) 1994**

1040:3

Figure 8-1: Schedule A goes through the itemized deductions that you can claim.

✔ maternity clothes

✔ stop-smoking programs

✔ medical insurance included in a car insurance policy covering all persons injured in or by the car

✔ social activities (such as swimming or dancing lessons)

✔ trips for general health improvement

✔ nursing care for a healthy baby

✔ weight-loss programs

✔ over-the-counter medicines, toothpaste, toiletries, cosmetics

✔ surgery for purely cosmetic reasons (such as face lifts, tummy tucks, and so on)

Deductible travel costs

The cost of traveling to your doctor or a medical facility for treatment is deductible. If you use your car, you can deduct a flat rate of 9 cents a mile, or you can deduct your actual out-of-pocket expenses for gas, oil, and repairs. You can also deduct parking and tolls. You can't deduct depreciation, insurance, or general repairs.

Special cases — who gets the deduction?

Sometimes when two or more people are supporting someone, special rules apply to determine who can claim the medical expenses that were paid.

One tricky case is that of divorced and separated parents. A divorced and separated parent can deduct the medical expenses he or she paid for a child's medical costs — even if the child's other parent is entitled to claim the child as a dependent.

For the purposes of claiming medical expenses, a child is considered the dependent of both parents if all of the following conditions are met:

✔ they were legally separated or divorced or were married and living apart for the last six months of 1994

✔ both parents provided more than half the child's support in 1994

✔ either spouse had custody of the child for more than half of 1994

Another complicated case is that of a *multiple-support agreement* where two or more people together provide more than half of a person's total support — but no one on his or her own provides more than half. Such an agreement allows *one* and only one of the individuals to claim the exemption for the person (even without providing more than half the support). If you are the person entitled to claim the exemption under the agreement, you can deduct the medical expenses you pay. But any other taxpayers who also paid medical expenses can't deduct them!

Deductible travel costs to seek medical treatment aren't limited to just local auto and cab trips — a trip to see a specialist in another city also qualifies for the deduction. Unfortunately, transportation costs incurred when you're not going to and from a doctor's office or a hospital is a deduction the IRS likes to challenge (maybe because a lot of taxpayers tried to deduct as a medical expense travel to a warm climate for health reasons!) The cost of transportation to a mild climate to relieve a specific condition is deductible — but the airfare to Arizona, say for general health reasons, isn't.

Trips to visit an institutionalized child have been allowed where the visits were prescribed by a doctor.

Meals and lodging

Your bill at a hospital is fully deductible. You may be able to deduct as a medical expense the cost of lodging not provided in a hospital while you are away from your home if you meet all the following requirements:

- ✔ The lodging is necessary for your medical care.
- ✔ The medical care is provided by a doctor in a medical facility.
- ✔ The lodging is not extravagant.
- ✔ There is no significant element of personal pleasure, recreation, or vacation involved in the travel.

The amount you can deduct as a medical expense cannot exceed $50 a night for you and $50 a night for anyone accompanying you.

Insurance premiums

You can deduct the premiums you pay for hospitalization, surgical, and other medical and dental coverage. Premiums for prescription drugs and damage to contact lenses are also deductible.

The Medicare tax you pay isn't deductible, but the premium for the Supplemental Part B Medicare Coverage that you signed up for at 65 is deductible. This premium is usually deducted from your Social Security benefit and is listed on Form SSA-1099 (which lists the total amount of Social Security you received during the year). Don't forget to deduct the health insurance premiums that were subtracted from your paycheck.

Reimbursements and damages

You must reduce your medical expenses by what you were reimbursed under your health insurance policy and from Medicare. Payments that you received for loss of earnings or damages for personal injury or sickness aren't considered reimbursement under a health insurance policy and don't have to be deducted from your medical expenses.

If the total reimbursement you received during the year is the same as or more than your total medical expenses for the year, you cannot claim a medical deduction.

If you are reimbursed in a later year for medical expenses you deducted in an earlier year, you must report as income the amount you received up to the amount you previously deducted as a medical expense. If you didn't deduct the expense in the year you paid it because you didn't itemize your deductions or because your medical expenses weren't more than 7.5 percent of your adjusted gross income, the reimbursement isn't taxable.

If you receive an amount in settlement of a personal injury suit, the part that is for medical expenses deducted in an earlier year is taxable if your medical deduction in the earlier year reduced your income tax.

Special schooling

You can deduct as a medical expense the cost of sending a mentally or physically handicapped child or dependent to a special school in order to help him or her overcome a handicap. The school must have a special program geared to the child's specific needs. The total cost, transportation, meals, and lodgings, as well as tuition, qualifies. The types of school that qualify are ones that do the following things:

- ✔ teach Braille or lip reading
- ✔ help cure dyslexia
- ✔ treat and care for the mentally handicapped
- ✔ treat individuals with similar handicaps

Nursing home

You can include in medical expenses the cost of medical care in a nursing home or home for the aged for yourself, your spouse, or your dependents. This deduction includes the cost of meals and lodging in the home if the main reason for being there is to get medical care.

You can't deduct the cost of meals and lodging if the reason for being in the home is personal (such as taking up residence in a retirement home). You can, however, include in medical expenses the part of the cost that is for medical or nursing care.

Improvements to your home

You can deduct as a medical expense the cost of installing equipment and making improvements to your home in order to help treat a disease or ailment. For example, you can deduct the cost of an air conditioner because your suffer from allergies or asthma. But if the equipment or improvement increases the value of your home your deduction is limited to the cost of the equipment or improvement minus the increase in the value to your home.

Be prepared to have a battle when making a large improvement to your home for medical reasons. Unless you go to the audit in a wheel chair with tears streaming down your cheeks, don't expect an overly sympathetic IRS. On the other hand, deductions for swimming pools have been allowed as a form of therapy in treating a severe ailment or disease. But improvements such as a spa or health club that merely help improve someone's general health aren't deductible.

The increase in value test to a home doesn't apply to handicapped persons. Modifying stairs and doorways, building ramps, railings and support bars, and accommodating a home to the special needs of the handicapped are allowed. Chair lifts, but not elevators, are also part of the no-increase-in-value category.

Figuring your medical and dental deduction

Your deductible medical and dental expenses equal the total expenses that you've paid minus what you were reimbursed by your insurance policy. The result is then reduced by 7.5 percent of your adjusted gross income (AGI).

For example, suppose that your medical and dental expenses for the tax year were $4,500 and that your health insurance company reimbursed $500 of this. Thus, you had $4,000 of unreimbursed medical expenses — enter this amount on line 1 of Schedule A. On line 2 you enter your AGI from Form 1040 (line 32). On line 3 you enter 7.5 percent of your AGI (suppose that your AGI is $40,000, you would enter $3,000 — $40,000 × 7.5). Subtract this amount from the medical expenses that you reported on line 1 of Schedule A and stick the remainder on line 4.

Lines 5-9: Taxes You Paid

It may seem odd that the IRS allows you to deduct other taxes you've paid — but not the federal income and Social Security taxes you're paying to them. How nice.

As a general rule, you may deduct only the following tax payments you made during the tax year:

- state and local income taxes
- local real estate taxes
- state and local personal property taxes
- other taxes (such as foreign income taxes)

Line 5: State and local income taxes

This deduction consists of two elements, the amount of state and local taxes withheld from your salary, and what you paid in 1994 when you filed your 1993 state tax return. You'll find this information on your W-2s. If you made estimated state and local income tax payments in 1994, they are also deductible.

If you applied your 1993 refund on your state return as a payment against next year's state tax, that's also considered a deductible tax payment. However, you also have to report the amount as taxable income on Form 1040 (line 10).

Enter the total of your state and local tax payments from Boxes 18 and 21 of your W-2 on line 5 of Schedule A. Also enter on this line your estimated state and local income tax payments that you made in 1994. And don't forget to add in the balance that you paid on your 1993 return. Mandatory payments that you have to make to your state's disability fund are also deductible.

These payments are deducted from your salary, but your employer may or may not be reporting them in Box 13 on your W-2. If your employer reported it, enter the amount on line 8 of Schedule A. If the amount isn't entered on your W-2 or on your pay stub, check with your employer.

Line 6: Real estate taxes

You can deduct real estate taxes you paid during the year. If your monthly mortgage payment also includes an amount that's placed in escrow by the bank, you can't claim a deduction for that amount until the bank actually pays the local tax authorities. At the end of the year, the bank will send you a statement — probably called your Annual Mortgage Statement — indicating the amount that was paid to the local property tax collector. The statement usually lists the dates of the payments.

If you don't have a mortgage, you won't be making payments to the bank. You'll be making payments to the tax collector. So add up your canceled checks to figure the amount of tax you paid and enter the amount on this line. (And if you don't have canceled checks, your problems are more serious than filling out Schedule A.)

Cooperative apartment

Tenants or stockholders of a cooperative housing corporation may deduct their share of the real estate taxes paid by the corporation. The corporation will furnish you with a statement at the end of the year indicating the amount of the deduction you are entitled to claim.

Special assessments

Water, sewer, and garbage pick-up aren't deductible because they are considered nondeductible personal charges — and so are charges by a homeowner's association. Assessments by the local tax authorities to put in a new street, sewer system, or sidewalks aren't deductible. These types of assessments are added to the tax basis of your home. Either your annual mortgage statement from your bank or the tax collector's bill will indicate if you are paying a special assessment or a real estate tax.

When you buy or sell real estate

When real estate is bought or sold, the buyer and the seller must apportion the real estate taxes between them. This stuff is done at the closing where the buyer and seller are furnished a settlement statement. For example, suppose that you paid $1,000 in real estate taxes for the year on January 1. On June 30 you sell the property. So at the time of settlement on your home sale, your settlement statement should reflect a payment or credit from the buyer for the property taxes you already paid for the remainder of the year. It's easier for the buyer to simply pay you for the taxes you've effectively paid on his or her behalf for the remainder of the year when he'll be in the home. Therefore, you can only deduct the taxes you paid ($1,000) minus what the buyer reimbursed you ($500). Thus, you only deduct $500 in real estate taxes for the year on line 6 of Schedule A.

You can find this information on your settlement statement as well as in Box 5 of Form 1099-S (Proceeds from Real Estate Transactions). The 1099-S should be issued to you when you sell your home.

If the buyer pays back taxes (in other words, taxes that the property seller owed from the time he or she actually owned the home) at the closing or at a later date, they can't be deducted. They are added to the cost of the property. The seller can deduct back taxes paid by the buyer from the sales price when submitting the sales information on his or her tax return with Form 2119 (Sale of Home).

The downside of property tax refunds and rebates

If you receive a refund or rebate in 1994 for real estate taxes you paid in 1994, you must reduce your itemized deductions that you're claiming for real estate taxes by the amount refunded to you. For example, if you paid $2,000 in property taxes during the year and also received a $300 refund because of a reduction in your tax that was retroactively granted, you may claim only $1,700 as the deduction for real estate taxes.

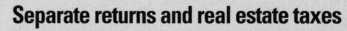

Separate returns and real estate taxes

When a couple decides to file separate returns, deducting real estate taxes becomes a complicated matter. That's because the deduction is based on how title to the property is held. If the title is in your spouse's name and you paid the real estate taxes, neither of you can claim a deduction. If your payment is required as a result of your divorce or separation decree the payment may qualify as an alimony deduction (see Chapter 7).

If property is owned by a husband or wife as *tenants by the entirety* or as *joint tenants* (which means the survivor inherits the other's share) either spouse can deduct the amount of taxes paid. If the property is held as *tenants in common* (each owner's share goes to their heirs at his or her death) each spouse may deduct his or her share of the taxes paid. However the rules are somewhat different in community property states; see IRS Publications 555 *(Federal Tax Information on Community Property)*.

If you receive a refund or rebate in 1994 for real estate taxes that you took as an itemized deduction on Schedule A in an earlier year, you must include the refund or rebate in income in the year you receive it. Enter this amount on your 1040 (line 21).

In the unlikely event that your refund exceeds what you paid in taxes during the year, you need to include only the portion of the refund up to the amount of the deduction you took in the earlier year. For example, if you claimed a $500 deduction in 1993 and received a $600 rebate in 1994, only $500 of the rebate is taxable.

Line 7: Personal property taxes

Personal property taxes, both state and local, are deductible if the tax charged is based on the value of the personal property. Usually, you pay personal property taxes based on the value of your car and motor boat.

In most states, a registration fee is assessed on cars. These fees are not deductible unless the fees are based on the value of the car. The state organization that invoices you for this fee should state what portion, if any, of the fee, is based on the car's value.

Don't get confused. This section doesn't cover business taxes; they belong on Schedule C. And if you pay sales tax on the purchase of equipment, you can't deduct the sales tax separately. It's added to the cost of the asset, which is depreciated on Schedule C and E. And finally, as much as you'd like to deduct your Social Security tax here, you can't.

If you are self-employed, one-half of your Social Security tax may be deducted — see "Line 25: One-half of self-employment tax" in Chapter 7 for details.

Line 8: Other taxes (foreign income taxes)

You can deduct foreign taxes you paid (along with your state or local income taxes) as an itemized deduction on Schedule A, or you can claim a credit for foreign taxes by filing Form 1116 (Foreign Taxes). **Note:** If your foreign income wasn't subject to U.S. tax (because it was excluded under the $70,000 foreign earned income allowance), you can't claim a deduction or a credit for any foreign taxes paid on the income that you didn't pay U.S. tax on.

In case you're asking yourself what foreign taxes have to do with you, the answer is that if you invested in a mutual fund that invests overseas, the fund may end up paying foreign taxes on some of your dividends. It seems more people are investing in these types of funds than ever before. If your mutual fund paid any foreign taxes, you'll find that information in Box 3 of Form 1099-DIV that you were received.

You can either deduct the foreign tax you paid on this line of Schedule A or claim a credit on Form 1040 (line 43). A deduction reduces your taxable income. A credit reduces the actual tax you owe. So if you're in the 28 percent tax bracket, claiming a deduction for $100 of foreign taxes will reduce your tax bill by $28. On the other hand, if you claim the $100 you paid as a foreign tax credit, you reduce your tax liability by $100, because credits are subtracted directly from the tax you owe.

So to the unsuspecting, claiming a foreign tax payment as an itemized deduction would appear to be a poor choice, because claiming the payment as a credit produces a greater tax savings. But have you ever tried to tackle Form 1116? The IRS estimates that it should take you over six hours to read the instructions and fill out the form.

If you have a tax software program, claim the payment as a credit. But if you don't have a software program and the amount of your foreign tax deduction is small, don't bother claiming it as a credit — simply write off the amount as a state and local tax deduction. If the amount is significant, you can tackle Form 1116 on your own, see a tax advisor, or buy a software program.

Lines 10-14: Interest You Paid

The IRS allows you to deduct interest on certain types of loans. Acceptable loans to the IRS include some (but not all) mortgage loans and investment loans. Interest incurred for consumer debt, such as on credit cards and auto loans — so called *personal interest* — is no longer deductible. The IRS wants you to borrow money for purposes they consider productive. So they'll help you to go into hock to buy a home — but not a car to drive you from your home to the job necessary to help pay for the home. Business interest isn't deducted as an itemized deduction, it's deducted from your business income on Schedule C (see Chapter 10).

Lines 10-11: Home mortgage interest and points

You can deduct mortgage interest on your main home as well as a second or vacation home. Why two? We think it's because most representatives in Congress own two homes — one in Washington and one in their district! It doesn't matter if the loan you are paying interest on is a mortgage, a second mortgage, a line of credit, or a home equity loan. The interest is deductible as long as your homes serve as collateral for the loan.

Where's the data?

If you paid mortgage interest of $600 or more during the year on any one mortgage, you receive a Form 1098 (Mortgage Interest Statement) from your mortgage lender showing the total interest you paid during the year. Enter this on line 10 of your Schedule A. Enter mortgage interest not reported on a 1098 on line 11. If you purchased a main home during 1994, Form 1098 reports the deductible points you paid that you claim on line 12.

You can deduct late payment charges as home mortgage interest. You will find these charges on your annual mortgage statement.

If you have the ability to pay down your mortgage more quickly than required, don't assume that doing so is not in your best financial interests just because of the deductions allowed for it (see Chapter 22).

Limitations on deductions

In most cases, you will be able to deduct all your home mortgage interest. Whether all of it is deductible depends on the date you took out the mortgage, the amount of the mortgage, and how the mortgage loan was used.

Interest on mortgage loans of up to $1 million taken out after October 13, 1987, to buy, build, or improve a first or second home are deductible. Your main home is the home you live in most of the time. It can be a house, a condominium, a cooperative apartment, a mobile home, a boat, or similar property. It must provide basic living accommodations including sleeping space, toilet facilities, and cooking facilities. Your second or vacation home is similar property that you select to be your second home.

In addition, interest on a home-equity loan of up to $100,000 taken out after October 13, 1987, is also deductible regardless of how the money is used. (Cut these amounts in half if you are married and file a separate return.) The proceeds of a home-equity loan don't have to be used to buy, build, or improve your home. They can be used to pay off bills, pay college tuition, or take a vacation.

Interest on a home-improvement loan isn't deductible if it isn't a mortgage loan. The rule is simple: no mortgage, no interest deduction. So if a relative lends you money to buy a home, any interest that you pay isn't deductible unless the relative obtains a mortgage on the house.

Mortgages of any size are tax deductible if you took out your mortgage before October 14, 1987, and you still retain that mortgage. If you've refinanced into a new mortgage since this magical date, you could be out of luck if you refinanced the mortage for more than you owed prior to refinancing.

Interest on refinanced loans

If you refinanced a mortgage on your first or second mortgage for the remaining balance of the old mortgage, you're safe. If the interest on the old mortgage was fully deductible, the interest on the new mortgage is also fully deductible.

But if you refinanced your old mortgage for more than its remaining balance, the rules on whether you can deduct all the interest on your new mortgage are crazy — the deductibility of the mortgage interest on the new loan depends on how you use the excess funds and the amount you refinanced. If the excess is used to improve, build, or buy a first or second home, and the excess plus all other mortgage loans are under $1 million, the interest or the new loan is fully deductible. If any of the excess of a new mortgage loan isn't used to build, buy, or improve your home, the excess is applied to your $100,000 home equity limit. If the excess is under $100,000, you're safe and it's fully deductible. The interest on the part that exceeds $100,000 is not deductible.

Points

The term *points* is used to describe certain up-front charges (pre-paid interest) that a borrower pays to obtain a mortgage. One point equals one percent of the loan amount financed. For example, if the loan is for $200,000, 2 points equals a $4,000 charge. You can deduct the amount you pay in points in 1994 if the loan was used to buy or improve your *main* residence.

Points on refinances

The points paid to refinance a mortgage on a main home aren't usually deductible in full in the year you pay them — even if the new mortgage is secured by your main home. However, if you use part of the refinanced mortgage to improve your main home and you pay the points instead of paying them from the proceeds of the new loan, you can deduct in full (in the year paid) the part of the points related to the improvement. But you must deduct the remainder of the points over the life of the loan. The points you pay on a second mortgage have to be deducted over the term of the loan.

For example, suppose that the remaining balance of your mortgage is $100,000. You take out a new mortgage for $150,000 and use $25,000 for improvements, $25,000 for personal purposes, and $100,000 to payoff the old loan. The points on the $25,000 used for improvements are deductible in 1994. The points on the remaining $125,000 balance of the new mortgage have to be written off over the term of the loan.

But here's a tip. Say that you refinanced your home three years ago and are writing off the points you paid over the 25-year term of the mortgage. If you refinance your mortgage again in 1994, the points remaining to be written off on your old mortgage can be written off in full in 1994. The points on your new refinanced loan have to be deducted over the term of the new mortgage.

Seller paid points

Sometimes desperate times call for desperate measures. So if the seller pays the points that the buyer normally does, the buyer gets a double windfall. The buyer not only gets the seller to pay the points, but the buyer also gets to deduct them. The buyer also has to subtract the points deducted from the tax basis of the home. Although the seller paid the points, the seller can't deduct them. The points the seller paid are deducted from the selling price.

This crazy twist is retroactive to 1991. So if you are a buyer who had the seller pay the points on the purchase of your home but didn't deduct them, you can still do so by filing a Form 1040X (Amended Return). But you have to do take this step before the three-year statute of limitations expires or you can kiss any refund good-bye. When you file Form 1040X, write SELLER PAID POINTS on the upper right-hand corner of the form.

Line 12: Points not reported to you on Form 1098

If the points you paid, for some reason, were not reported on the 1098, based on the rules above, you will have to compute this amount on your own. If the points were for your main house, you can deduct the amount for 1994. If it was refinancing for your second home, you have to deduct it over the term of the mortgage. Hunting for this information isn't all that difficult. When the loan was made, you were given a closing statement with the points you paid on it. Sometimes it's referred to as an *origination fee*.

Line 13: Investment interest

When you borrow against the value of securities held in a brokerage account, the interest paid on this so-called *margin loan* is deductible. This deduction, however, can't exceed your total investment income. If it does, the excess is carried forward and deducted from next year's investment income — or carried over to future years until it can be deducted. You use Form 4952 (Investment Interest) to compute the deduction and carry over the result to Schedule A (line 13).

Remember that investment income is income from interest, dividends, annuities, and royalties. It doesn't include income from rental real estate or from a *passive activity* (a passive activity is IRS jargon for a business deal or venture where you are a silent partner).

If you borrow money to buy or carry tax-exempt bonds, you can't deduct any interest on the loan as investment-interest expense. If 20 percent of your portfolio consists of tax-exempt bonds, 20 percent of your margin interest on your security account isn't deductible.

Capital gains aren't usually considered investment income, but you can choose to treat capital gains as investment income. There is a trade-off. You have to reduce the amount of your capital gains eligible for the 28 percent maximum long-term capital gain rate by the amount of your capital gains you are treating as investment income. Did you follow that?

For example, suppose that you have dividend income of $5,000, investment interest expense of $10,000, and a $20,000 long-term capital gain. You can deduct only $5,000 of your investment interest expense. The balance is carried over to 1995. However, if you treat $5,000 of your capital gain as investment income, you can deduct your entire investment interest expense of $10,000. But the amount of your $20,000 capital gain that is eligible for the 28 percent maximum rate on long-term capital gains is reduced to $15,000.

Interest expense incurred in a passive activity such as rental real estate, an S Corporation, or as a limited partnership isn't considered investment-interest expense. It can be deducted only from your passive-activity income.

Lines 15-18: Gifts to Charity

You can deduct your charitable contributions, but the amount of your deduction may be limited and you must follow a number of strict rules. One good turn doesn't always deserve another!

After you understand the types of things you can and cannot deduct, completing this section is a snap. Qualifying contributions that you make by cash and check get totaled and entered on line 15, and those made other than by cash and check (for example, you donate your old *Taxes For Dummies* books to charity when new editions come out) are entered on line 16.

If you make out a check at the end of the year and mail it by December 31, you can deduct your contribution even if the charity doesn't receive the check until January. If you charge a contribution on your credit card, you get to deduct it in the year you charged it — even if you don't pay off the charge till the following year.

Qualifying charities

You can deduct your contribution only if you make them to a *qualified* organization. To become a qualified organization, most organizations (other than churches) must apply to the IRS. To find out whether an organization qualifies, just ask the organization for their tax exemption certificate.

Don't overlook your out-of-pocket expenditures

A commonly overlooked deductible charitable expense is your out-of-pocket expenses (money spent) incurred while doing volunteer work for a charity.

For example, you can deduct out-of-pocket expenses (such as gas and oil, but probably not rest-stop candy bars!) that are directly related to the use of your car in charitable work. You can't deduct anything like general repair or maintenance expenses, tires, insurance, depreciation, and so on. If you don't want to track and deduct your actual expenses, you can use a standard rate of 12 cents a mile to figure your contribution. You can deduct parking fees and tolls with any method you choose — actual expenses or the standard rate.

If you must travel away from home in order to perform a real and substantial service, such as attending a convention for a qualified charitable organization, you can claim a deduction for your unreimbursed travel and transportation expenses, including for meals and lodging. If you get a daily allowance (*per diem*) for travel expenses while providing services for a charitable organization, you must include in income the amount that is more than your travel expenses. Of course, you can deduct your travel expenses that are more than the allowance.

One restriction on these deductions — they are allowed only if there is *no significant amount* of personal pleasure derived from your travel. What is the limit the IRS sets on personal pleasure? Well, we can't find an IRS chart, but we can at least assure you that the IRS allows you to enjoy your service without automatically disqualifying you from this deduction. The IRS does not mind if you decide to do some sightseeing, but you can't deduct expenses for your spouse or children who may accompany you. If you go to a church convention as a church member rather than as a representative of the church, you can't deduct your expenses.

You can deduct the cost and upkeep of uniforms that you must wear while doing volunteer work — as long as these uniforms are unsuitable for everyday use. A Boy or Girl Scout uniform, for example, would not be the type of clothing you would just wear anywhere!

If for some reason you doubt that an organization qualifies, you could also check IRS Publication 78 (*Cumulative List of Organizations*). Most libraries have Publication 78, or you can call the IRS toll-free tax help telephone number in your area.

Contributions that you make to the following charitable organizations are generally deductible:

- ✔ religious organizations, along with churches, synagogues, mosques, and so on

- ✔ public park and recreational facilities

- ✔ nonprofit schools

- ✔ organizations such as CARE, the Red Cross, the Salvation Army, Goodwill Industries, the Girl and Boy Scouts, and so on

- ✔ war veteran's groups

- ✔ our federal, state, and local government — if your charitable contribution is only for public purposes

Nonqualifying charities

Generally speaking, contributions or donations made to causes or organizations that just benefit the organization as opposed to the greater society are not deductible. The following are examples of organizations or groups that you can't deduct contributions to:

- ✔ individuals

  Big surprise here! So don't try to deduct what you gave to your brother-in-law because he doesn't count in the eyes of the IRS! The contribution can be to a qualified organization that helps needy and worthy individuals — like your brother-in-law.

- ✔ social and sport clubs

- ✔ members of the clergy who can spend the money as they wish

- ✔ labor unions

- ✔ groups that lobby for law changes (such as changes to the Tax Code!)

  The IRS does not want you to deduct contributions to organizations from which you may benefit — so include bingo and raffle tickets in this forbidden group.

- ✔ political groups or candidates running for public office

✔ foreign organizations

But you can deduct contributions to a U.S. charity that transfers funds to a foreign charity — if the U.S. charity controls the use of the funds.

✔ homeowner's associations

✔ lottery ticket costs (gee, we wonder why not?)

✔ dues paid to country clubs, lodges, orders, and so on

But union dues are deductible as an itemized deduction subject to the 2 percent AGI limit on Schedule A.

✔ tuition to attend private or parochial schools

This list can go on and on (didn't you suspect that it was longer than the list of deductible charitable contributions?), but we think you get the idea — so don't try to deduct the value of your blood donated at a blood bank, and don't even think about trying to deduct your contribution to the Communist Party!

Contributions that are some of both

If you receive a benefit from making a valid deductible contribution, you can deduct only the amount of your contribution that is more than the value of the benefit. For example, if you pay to attend a charity function such as a ball or banquet, you can deduct only the amount that is more than the fair market value of your ticket. Or suppose that you pay $25 for a dinner-dance at a church, and the church gets all the proceeds. The tasty shrimp dinner has a fair market value of $10. You can also deduct unreimbursed expenses such as uniforms and actual automobile expenses or use a standard rate of twelve cents per mile. Just subtract the value of the benefit you received from your total payment.

To save yourself the hassle of a survey of seafood restaurant dinner prices, just ask the charity for a receipt that details what the actual amount you contributed is. Most charities will be happy to provide this information. In fact, if the value of your contribution is $75 or more that is partly for goods and services, the charity must give you a written statement informing you of the amount you can deduct. If you can't easily obtain a receipt, use an estimate based on something the IRS can't disagree with — common sense!

Contributions of property

Generally you can deduct the *fair market value* of property given to a charity. FMV is the price at which property would change hands between a willing buyer and a willing seller. So if you bought a painting for $2,000 that's worth $10,000 when you donate it to a museum, you can deduct $10,000.

You can only use the FMV if — on the date of the contribution — the property would have produced a long-term capital gain or loss (property held one year or more) if it had been sold. If you donate property you held for less than a year, or you donate *ordinary income property*, your deduction is limited to your cost. Ordinary income property is inventory from a business, works of art created by the donor, manuscripts prepared by the donor, and capital assets held one year or less.

If you contribute property with a fair market value that is less than your cost or depreciated value, your deduction is limited to fair market value. You can't claim a deduction for the property's decline in value since you acquired it.

If you have an asset that has declined in value, sell that asset to lock in the capital loss deduction (see Chapter 11), and donate the cash for an additional deduction. For example, suppose that you paid $9,500 for 100 shares of IBM that are worth $6,000 today. If you donate the shares, all you can claim is a $6,000 charitable deduction. But by selling the shares and donating the cash, not only will you be entitled to a $6,000 deduction, you will have a $3,500 capital loss that you can deduct as well.

If you have an asset that has appreciated substantially in value, don't sell the asset and get stuck for the tax and then make a donation of the cash you have left. Rather, give the asset to the charity. That way, you get the deduction for the full value of the asset, thereby escaping the tax.

Used clothing and household goods

Clean out those closets for next year so that you can save on your taxes! Hey, even Bill and Hillary Clinton took a deduction for this one! Used clothing and household goods usually have a fair market value that is much less than the original cost. For used clothing, you claim the price that buyers of used items pay in used-clothing stores. See IRS Publication 561 (*Household Goods*) for information on the value of items such as furniture and appliances and other items you want to donate.

Cars, boats, and aircraft

If you contribute a car, a boat, or an aircraft, you may be able to determine its fair market value by using guides such as *blue books* that contain dealer sale or average prices for recent model years. These guides also give estimates for adjusting because of mileage and physical condition. The prices are not official, however, and you can't consider a blue book as an appraisal of any specific donated property. But the guides are a good place to start.

The records you need: Part I

For contributions of $250 or more, you need a receipt from the charity — otherwise you could have your deduction tossed out in the event of an audit. The receipt should indicate either the amount of cash you contributed or a description (but not the value) of any property you donated. The receipt must also indicate the value of any gift or services you might have received.

For cash contributions, a canceled check will suffice. But remember, if you donate cash or property valued at $250 or more, you also need a receipt. If you donate property, you need a receipt from the charity listing the date of your contribution and a detailed description of the property.

If you contribute property worth more than $500, you have to attach Form 8283 (Noncash Charitable Contributions). On the form you list the name of the charity, date of gift, your cost, the FMV, and how you arrived at that value. If the value of the property you contributed exceeds $5,000, you not only need a written appraisal, the appraiser also has to sign-off on Part III in Section B of Form 8283. The charity has to complete and sign Part IV of the Form. A written appraisal isn't needed for publicly traded stock or nonpublicly traded stock of $10,000 or less.

Charitable deduction limits

All cash and noncash gifts are subject to some limits. Depending on whether you contributed cash or property, the amount of your deduction may be limited to either 30 or 50 percent of your adjusted gross income. Contributing cash to churches, associations of churches, synagogues, and all public charities such as the Red Cross, for example, are deductible up to 50 percent of your AGI. Gifts of ordinary income property qualify for this 50 percent limit.

A 30 percent limit applies to gifts of capital gain property that has appreciated in value. In such instances, you can use the 50 percent limit — if you limit your deduction to your cost instead of using the FMV. For example, suppose that you donate a painting to a museum, a painting that cost you $10,000. It's currently worth $20,000. If you use the $20,000 value, your deduction for 1994 can't exceed 30 percent of your AGI. If you use the $10,000 value, you can deduct up to 50 percent of your AGI. The contribution has to be to a church or public charity, and you have to have owned the gift for at least one year.

Line 17 (for the great humanitarians of the world)

Line 17 is a pretty obscure line. The general rule for cash contributions is that it cannot exceed 50 percent of your AGI. For gifts of property like stocks, bonds, and artwork, the amount cannot exceed 30 percent of your AGI. So if you contribute more than the IRS permits as a deduction in one year, you can carry over the amount you couldn't deduct and deduct it within the next five years. Enter on line 17 the amount that you couldn't deduct from the last five years and want to deduct this year.

Line 19: Casualty and Theft Losses

We hope that you don't need to use this one. But if you do, and if you've come to view the Internal Revenue Service as heartless, we would like to correct that impression. It's not — well, not completely. If you have suffered a casualty or theft loss, you will find the IRS can be somewhat charitable. Unfortunately, as is the case to claim many an unusual deduction, you've got to jump through quite a few hoops to nail it down.

After you have determined whether your loss is deductible, get a copy of IRS Form 4684 (Casualties and Thefts), on which you list each item that was stolen or destroyed. If your deduction ends up being more than your income — and it does happen — you may have what's known as a *net operating loss*. You can use this type of loss to lower your tax in an earlier or in a later year. This rule is an exception (of course!) to the normal rule that you must be in business to have a net operating loss.

Do you have a deductible loss?

Strange as it might seem, there has been extensive Tax Court haggling over what is and isn't a casualty. The phrase to remember is *sudden, unexpected, and unusual.* If property you own is damaged, destroyed, or lost as the result of a specific event that is sudden, unexpected and unusual, you have a deductible casualty. Earthquakes, fires, floods, and storms meet this strict legal test.

But if you dropped a piece of the good china, if Rover bit a hole in the sofa, if moths ate your entire wardrobe, or if termites gobbled up your brand-new backyard deck, you're doubly out of luck. You've suffered a nondeductible loss. These incidents don't meet the sudden-unexpected-unusual test.

Casualty losses? You be the judge

Listen to this. A loss as the result of water damage to wallpaper and plaster seems like it ought to be deductible. Not according to the Tax Court, which ruled on such a case in the 1960s. The homeowner failed to prove that the damage came after a sudden, identifiable event. The water had entered the house through the window frames and the damage could have been caused by progressive deterioration. Now suppose that a car door is accidentally slammed on your hand, breaking your diamond ring. The diamond falls from the ring and is never found. That lost diamond qualifies as a casualty. On the other hand, if your diamond merely falls out of its setting and is lost, there is no deduction. The number of cases like this is endless.

Proving a theft loss can be just as complex. The mere disappearance of cash or property doesn't cut it. You have to prove there was an actual theft. The best evidence is a police report — and your failure to file one could be interpreted as your not being sure something was stolen.

You should know that theft losses aren't limited to robbery — they also include theft by swindle, larceny, and false pretense. This very broad definition includes fraudulent sales offers or embezzlement. In one case, a New Yorker was even able to get a theft-loss deduction after handing over a bundle of money to fortune tellers. The reason? The fortune tellers were operating illegally.

Figuring the loss

Unfortunately, the amount of your deduction isn't going to equal the amount of your loss because the IRS makes you apply a deductible just as your auto insurer does. The IRS makes you reduce each individual loss by $100 and your total losses by 10 percent of your adjusted gross income. So if your adjusted gross income is $100,000 and you lost $11,000 when the roof caved in, your deduction is only $900. (That's $11,000 minus $100 minus 10 percent of your adjusted gross, or $10,000.)

That stipulation effectively wipes out a deduction for plenty of people. For those whose losses are big enough to warrant a deduction, though, the fun is just beginning. That's because your deduction is limited to either the decrease in the fair market value of your property as a result of the casualty, or the original cost of the property — whichever is lower.

Suppose that you bought a painting for $1,000 that was worth $100,000 when damaged by fire. Sorry. Your loss is limited to the $1,000 you paid for it. Now reverse it. You paid $100,000 for the painting, and thanks to the downturn in the market for black-velvet portraits of Elvis, it's worth only $1,000 right before it's destroyed. Your deductible loss is limited to $1,000. And you must apply this rule to each item before combining them to figure your total loss. (One exception is real estate. The entire property, including buildings, trees, and shrubs, is treated as one item.)

TECHNICAL STUFF

The insurance effects

You've got casualty insurance? Great. But there are a couple of things you need to watch out for. First, if you expect to be reimbursed by your insurer but haven't seen any cash by tax-filing time, you've got to subtract an estimate of the expected reimbursement from your deductible loss. Second — and this sounds strange — you must reduce the amount of your loss by your insurance coverage even if you don't file a claim. Suppose that your loss is 100 percent covered by insurance but you decide not to ask for a reimbursement for fear of losing your coverage. You can't claim a deduction for the loss. Only the amount of your loss that's above the insurance coverage would be deductible in that case.

If you're reimbursed by insurance and decide not to repair or replace your property, you could have a taxable gain on your hands. That's because the taxable gain is calculated by subtracting your cost from the insurance proceeds and not the property's fair market value. For example, imagine that your home, which cost $150,000 (the cost here refers to the value of the building and excludes the land value), burned to the ground.

You get $190,000 in insurance money (the house's current FMV), giving you a fully taxable $40,000 gain.

To postpone the gain, you have to replace the property with a similar one, and it must be worth at least as much as the insurance money you received. If the new place is worth less than that, you must report the difference as a capital gain. In addition, you've got to replace the property within two years. The two-year period begins on Dec. 31 of the year you realize the gain. If your home is located in a federally declared disaster area, you have four years, and you can generally get a one-year extension beyond that, if necessary.

Disaster-area losses are subject to another special rule that can be a big help to your cash flow. You can choose to deduct the loss in either the current year or the preceding year. Turning back the clock with an amended return means that you can get a refund within 45 days — instead of waiting until the next year. This maneuver may also help if you were in a higher tax bracket last year.

Because your loss is the difference between the fair market value of your property immediately before and after the casualty, an appraisal is usually the best way to calculate your loss. The only problem is that the appraiser can't see your property before the casualty, and any photographs or records you might have had probably went up in smoke or floated away. You're not totally out of luck if you don't have before-and-after photos, though. A picture after the casualty and one showing the property once it was repaired will come in very handy when trying to prove the dollar value of your loss.

Normally you can't deduct the cost of repairing your property because the cost of fixing something isn't really a measure of its deflated fair market value. As with every IRS rule, however, this one has exceptions. You can use the cost of cleaning up or making a repair under the following conditions:

✔ The repairs are necessary to bring the property back to its condition before the casualty, and the cost of the repairs aren't excessive.

✔ The repairs take care only of the damage.

✔ The value of the property after the repairs is not — due to the repairs — more than the value of the property before the casualty.

Another point is worth knowing. With leased property, such as a car, the amount of your loss is in fact the amount you must spend to repair it. And while appraisal fees aren't considered part of your loss, they count as miscellaneous itemized deductions.

Lines 20-26: Job Expenses and Most Other Miscellaneous Deductions

Everybody likes to see a deduction that says something about "other." Oh goody, you think, here's my opportunity to get some easy deductions. Unfortunately, if you're like the vast majority of taxpayers, you won't get any mileage out of these deductions. Why? Because the allowable items in this category tend to be small-dollar items. And you have to clear a major hurdle: you get a deduction only for the amount that your total deductions in this category exceed 2 percent of your adjusted gross income. Here's how it works: If your adjusted gross is $50,000 and you have $1,500 of job-related expenses, only $500 is deductible. That's $1,500 minus 2 percent of $50,000. Please note that if you are deducting 1993 moving expenses that you paid in 1994, they are not subject to the 2 percent limit because they get deducted on line 27 of Schedule A. 1994 moving expenses that you pay are deducted as an adjustment to income (see Chapter 7).

Line 20: Unreimbursed employee expenses

Even if you're not employed by Scrooge International — famous for offering few fringe benefits and not reimbursing job-related expenses — there's a good chance you are spending at least some out-of-pocket money on your job. Ever take an educational course that helped you get ahead in your career? How about that home fax machine you bought so customers could reach you after hours? If your employer didn't pick up the tab, all is not lost. You can deduct those expenses — or at least a portion of them — from your taxes.

One word of caution. Just about every IRS rule regarding job-related expenses is subject to varying interpretations, which has made the IRS extremely inflexible as to what is and isn't deductible. On the other hand, the Tax Court, which ultimately decides disputes of deductibility, has a tendency to be more liberal than the IRS.

Job search expenses

Job search expenses are deductible even if your job search isn't successful. The critical rule is that the expenses must be incurred in trying to find a new job in the same line of work. So if you're looking to make a career change or seeking your first job, you can forget about this deduction. A taxpayer who retired from the Air Force after doing public relations for the service was denied travel expenses while seeking other employment in PR. The way the IRS sees the world, any job he sought in the private sector would be considered a new trade or business.

Here are job search expenses that are considered deductible:

- ✔ employment-agency and career-counseling fees
- ✔ the cost for placing situation wanted ads
- ✔ telephone calls
- ✔ printing, typing, and mailing of resumes
- ✔ travel, meals, and entertaining

Another time, the IRS held that because a taxpayer had incurred a "substantial break" of more than a year between his previous job and his hunt for a new one, there was a lack of continuity in the person's line of work. No deduction. The IRS is unyielding when it comes to interpreting this rule. Fortunately, the Tax Court sees things differently. It tends to consider such gaps as temporary.

If you're away from home overnight looking for work, you can deduct travel and transportation costs, as well as hotels and meals. The purpose of the trip must be primarily related to searching for a job, though. A job interview while on a golf outing to Palm Springs won't cut it. The IRS looks at the amount of time spent seeking new employment in relationship to the amount of time you are away.

Normally, you deduct job-related expenses on Form 2106 (Employee Business Expenses). However, unless you are claiming job-related travel, local transportation, meal, or entertainment expenses, save yourself some trouble. You can enter the most basic job-hunting expenses directly onto Schedule A (line 20) instead of having to fill out Form 2106.

Job education expenses

If you find that your employer demands greater technical skills, or the fear of being downsized has sent you back to the classroom, the cost of those courses is deductible (even if they lead to a degree) under the following conditions:

- ✔ You are employed or self-employed.
- ✔ The course doesn't qualify you for a new line of work.
- ✔ You already have met the minimum educational requirements of your job or profession.
- ✔ The course is required by your employer or state law or the course maintains or improves your job skills.

Like many other tax terms, "maintains or improves job skills" has consistently placed the IRS and taxpayers at odds. The intent of the law was to allow a deduction for refresher courses, such as the continuing education classes tax advisers have to take every year.

For example, an IRS agent was denied a deduction for the cost of obtaining an MBA, while an engineer was allowed to deduct the cost of his degree. The rationale: A significant portion of the engineer's duties involved management, interpersonal, and administrative skills. The court felt the engineer's MBA didn't qualify him for a new line of work and was directly related to his job. The IRS agent flunked this test. (There's something strangely satisfying about seeing the IRS turn on its own, isn't there?)

The general rule is that you must be able to prove by clear and convincing evidence how the course is helpful or necessary in maintaining or improving your job skills. So if you can clear that hurdle, here's what's deductible:

- ✔ tuition and books
- ✔ local transportation
- ✔ travel and living expenses while away from home

Travel expenses are allowable if you must go abroad to do research that can only be done there. Travel and living expenses are also deductible when taking a course at a school in a foreign country or away from your home, even if you could have taken the same course locally. Unfortunately, you can't claim a deduction for *educational* trips. Let's say you are a French teacher who decided to spend the summer traveling in the south of France to brush up on your language skills. Nice try, says the IRS, but no deduction.

Miscellaneous job expenses

Just because your job requires you to incur certain expenses, it doesn't mean they are automatically deductible. So here's a rundown on what is generally deductible:

- ✔ professional and trade-association dues
- ✔ books, subscriptions, and periodicals
- ✔ union dues
- ✔ unreimbursed travel and entertainment (covered in detail in the next section)
- ✔ uniforms and special clothing
- ✔ medical exams to establish fitness
- ✔ commuting expenses to a second job (moonlighting, are you?)
- ✔ small tools and equipment
- ✔ computers and phones

Deductions for computers and cellular phones are hardest to nail down. You must prove you need the equipment to do your job *because* your employer doesn't provide you with it or because the equipment at work isn't adequate or available. A letter from your employer stating that a computer is a basic requirement for your job isn't good enough. You must also establish that its use is for your employer's convenience and not yours.

For example, suppose that you are an engineer who, rather than staying late at the office, takes work home. You have a computer at home that is similar to the one in the office. Because the use of your computer isn't for the convenience of your employer, you cannot claim a deduction. On the other hand, if you need a computer to use while traveling on business, it would be deductible because you now meet the convenience-of-your-employer requirement.

Fax machines, copiers, adding machines, calculators, and typewriters aren't subject to this rigid rule. You must, however, be able to prove that this equipment is job-related and not merely for your own convenience. Although the law requires that you keep a diary or record that clearly shows the computer's or cellular phone's percentage of business use, you don't have to keep a similar record for other office equipment. Be prepared, however, to prove that it is used mainly for business. With a fax machine, for example, it's worth keeping those printouts showing where your calls have been going and where they've been coming from.

We know, this is a crazy thing to ask; after all, are you going to write down every time you use a copier if the copies are for work or personal reasons? But that behavior is exactly what the law requires. Write your representative in Congress and tell him or her what you think. (You'll probably get a reply that says: "Really? When was that law passed?")

Just because your employer requires that you be neatly groomed doesn't mean the cost of doing so is deductible. An airline pilot couldn't deduct the cost of his haircuts, even though airline regulations required pilots to have haircuts on a regular basis. Nor could a secretary deduct the cost of coiffures because her employer demanded that she maintain a special appearance.

Meeting the requirements and keeping the necessary records to deduct job-related expenses can become a part-time job. Unpleasant as it is, though, it will almost certainly slash your taxes and save you in the event you're audited.

Job travel (and entertainment!)

There is probably no other group of expenses that has created more paper-work than travel and entertainment expenses. Taxpayers spend more time on the paperwork accounting for a business trip than they do planning for it. Unfortunately, this situation can't be changed. But at least we can help you deduct every possible expense in this area. So let's begin with the three basic rules regarding travel and entertainment expenses:

- ✔ You have to be away from your business home to deduct travel expenses. (Makes sense, doesn't it?)
- ✔ You can deduct only 50 percent of your meal and entertainment expenses.
- ✔ You need good records.

Travel expenses that are deductible include taxi, commuter bus, and limousine fares to and from the airport or station — and between your hotel and business meetings or job site. You can also deduct auto expenses, whether you use your own car or lease, the cost of hotels, meals, telephone calls, and laundry while you're away. Don't forget about tips and baggage handling. Finally, take advantage of the obvious deductions on airplane, train, and bus fares between your *tax home* and business destination.

TIP

The records you need: Part II

For every travel and entertainment expense that exceeds $25, you need a receipt. No receipt, no deduction if you're audited. And a canceled check just won't cut it anymore. The receipt — or a separate diary entry — must also show the business purpose.

For entertainment you need the name and location of the restaurant or the place where you did the entertaining; the number of people served or in attendance; the date and amount; and the business purpose, such as "Bill Smith, buyer for Company Z."

A hotel receipt has to show the name and location of the hotel; the dates you stayed there; and the separately stated charges for the room, meals, telephone calls, and so on.

Your tax home and travel expenses

Yes, we said tax home. This is where the situation gets a little tricky because, in order to be able to deduct travel expenses, you must be traveling away from your tax home on business. You are considered to be traveling away from your tax home if the business purpose of your trip requires that you be away longer than an ordinary working day — and you need to sleep or rest so you can be ready for the next day's business. Wouldn't it be nice if the law simply stated that you have to be away overnight?

Your tax home isn't where you or your family reside. Of course not. It's the entire city or general area in which you work, or where your business is located. For example, suppose that you work in Manhattan but live in the suburbs. You decide to stay in Manhattan overnight because you have an early breakfast meeting the next morning. You are not away from your tax home overnight and therefore you can't deduct the cost of the hotel. The only meal expense you can deduct is the next morning's breakfast — if it qualifies as an entertainment expense.

At this point you probably want to know how far away from your tax home you have to be. Unfortunately, there isn't a mileage count. When it comes to determining if you are away from home overnight, the IRS uses that famous U.S. Supreme Court definition: "I can't define it, but I know it when I see it."

Also, your tax home may not be near where you live. For example, if you move from job to job without a fixed base of operation, each place you work becomes your tax home. And travel expenses are not deductible. And if you accept a temporary assignment that lasts for more than a year, you have moved your tax home to the place of the temporary assignment. So sorry, no deduction.

Trips that mix business with pleasure

For travel within the U.S., the transportation part of your travel expenses is fully deductible even if part of it is for pleasure. For example, perhaps the airfare and cabs to and from the airport cost $700 for you to attend a business convention in Florida. You spend two days at the end of the convention playing poker with some old friends. Your transportation costs of $700 are fully deductible, but your meals and lodging for the two vacation days aren't.

Transportation costs for travel outside the U.S. have to be prorated based on the amount of time you spend on business and vacation. Suppose that you spend four out of eight days in London on business. You can deduct only 50 percent of your airfare and four days of lodgings and meals. Any other travel costs (such as taxis and telephone while you were conducting business) are deductible.

But this general rule on travel abroad doesn't apply if you meet any of the following conditions:

- ✔ The trip lasts a week or less.

- ✔ More than 75 percent of your time outside the U.S. was spent on business. (The day you start and end your trip are considered business days.)

- ✔ You don't have substantial control in arranging the trip.

You are considered not to have substantial control over your trip if you are an employee who was reimbursed or paid a travel expense allowance, are not related to your employer, and are not a managing executive. Oh well, *c'est la vie.*

Weekends, holidays, and other necessary standby days are counted as business days if they fall between business days. Great! But if these days follow your business activities and you remain at your business destination for personal reasons, they are not business days.

For example, suppose that your tax home is in Kansas City. You travel to St. Louis where you have a business appointment on Friday and another business meeting on the following Monday. The days in between are considered tax-deductible business-expense days — you had a business activity on Friday and had another business activity on Monday. This case is true even if you use that time for sightseeing (going up in the arch!) or other personal activities.

Trips primarily for personal reasons

If your trip was primarily for personal reasons (such as that vacation to Disney World), some of the trip may be deductible — you can deduct any expenses at your destination that are directly related to your business. For example, calls into work are deductible, as well as a 15-minute customer call in Fantasyland. But spending an hour on business does *not* turn a personal trip into a business trip to be deducted.

Convention expenses

You can deduct your convention-travel expenses if you can prove that your attendance benefits your work. A convention for investment, political, social, or other purposes that are unrelated to your business isn't deductible. Non-business expenses (such as social or sightseeing costs) are personal expenses and are not deductible. And you can't deduct the travel expenses for your family!

Your selection as a delegate to a convention does not automatically entitle you to a deduction. You must prove that your attendance is connected to your business. For conventions held outside North America, you must establish that the convention could be held only at that site. For example, an international seminar on tofu research held in Japan would qualify if that seminar were unique.

Entertainment

You may deduct business-related expenses for entertaining a client, customer, or employee. For example, suppose that you purchase two tickets to a concert and give them to a client — it's deductible. Goodwill entertaining — to obtain new business — is deductible if it is directly before or after a business discussion. If you give two tickets to a prospective client, these tickets are deductible only if you have a business discussion before or after the event. To deduct an entertainment-related meal, you or your employee must be present when the food is provided. Meal expenses include the cost of food, beverages, taxes, and tips.

Entertainment includes any activity generally considered to provide amusement or recreation (a broad definition!). Examples include entertaining guests at night clubs (and social, athletic, and sporting clubs), at theaters, at sporting events, on yachts, and on hunting or fishing vacations. If you buy a scalped ticket to an entertainment event for a client, you usually can't deduct more than the face value of the ticket.

And you can't claim the cost of a meal as an entertainment expense that you are also claiming as a travel expense (this activity is known as *double-deducting*). Expenses are also not deductible when a group of business acquaintances takes turns paying for each other's checks without conducting any business.

With regards to gifts, you can't deduct more than $25 for a business gift to any one person during the year. A husband and wife are considered one person. So if a business customer is getting married, you can't give a $25 gift to each newlywed-to-be and expect to deduct $50.

Standard meal and hotel allowance — hi-low method

Instead of keeping records for your actual meal and incidental expenses (tips and cleaning), you can deduct a flat amount of $26 a day. You don't need to keep receipts with this method. But you do have to establish that you were away from home on business. If you travel to what the IRS considers a high-cost area, you can use $30, $34, or $38 a day (see IRS Publication 463 for high-cost areas and IRS Publication 1542 for city-by-city per diem rates. Employees as well as self-employed taxpayers can use the standard meal allowance.) Taxpayers in the transportation industry (those involved in moving people and goods) can use a flat rate of $32 a day in the U.S. and $36 outside the U.S.

Instead of keeping records for your hotel and meal expenses, you can use a flat rate of $95 a day. You need only to show that the trip was for business. If you are traveling in what the IRS considers the high-cost location area, you can use $152 per day. Both rates are in addition to your transportation expenses, of course. IRS Publication 463 has the high-cost locations and IRS Publication 1542 has the city-by city per diem rates.

The standard meal and hotel allowances don't apply to Alaska, Hawaii, Puerto Rico, or foreign locations, however. You can find the standard allowances for those locations in "The Maximum Travel per Diem Allowances for Foreign Areas" (published monthly), which can be ordered from the Government Printing Office (202-783-3238) — or you can call the State Department (703-875-7910) for the rate in a specific location.

And you can't use the standard meal and hotel allowances if you are traveling for medical, charitable, or moving expense purposes. The rate also can't be used if your employer is your brother or sister, or half-brother or half-sister, ancestor, or lineal descendent. Finally, you can't use the standard allowance if your employer is a corporation in which you own ten percent or more. So many details!

What IRS form to use

What other form you attach to your Form 1040 depends on whether your are an employee or self-employed. If you are self-employed, you deduct travel and entertainment expenses on Schedule C (line 24). If you are employed, you must use Form 2106 (Employee Business Expenses).

For example, if you are paid a salary with the understanding that you will pay your own expenses, you claim these expenses on Form 2106, and then carry over the amount from line 11 of the 2106 to Schedule A (line 20) of your Form 1040 where the amount is claimed as an itemized deduction. Form 2106 also allows you to claim travel and entertaining costs that exceed your travel allowance or the amount for which you were reimbursed.

If you received a travel allowance, your employer adds the amount of the allowance to your salary, and it will be included in Box 1 of your W-2. So if you received a travel allowance of $10,000 and spent $10,000, the $10,000 is not completely deductible because it's reduced by 2 percent of the AGI. For example, if your income is $100,000, you can only deduct $8,000 ($10,000 minus 2 percent of $100,000) of your travel expenses. If your income exceeds $111,800, or $55,900 and you are married filing separately, a portion of these deductions is reduced again.

But here's a neat hint. Instead of an allowance, have your employer reimburse you for your actual expenses that you submit on an expense report. You won't have to file Form 2106, and you won't have to pay tax on the money that you never earned and lose part of your deductions due to silly rules like the 2 percent rule. Neat, huh?

Line 21: Tax preparation fees

You can deduct the fees paid to a tax preparer or advisor! You may also deduct the cost of being represented at a tax audit, and the cost of tax preparation software programs, tax publications, books like this one, and any fee you paid for the electronic filing of your return.

Fees paid to prepare tax schedules relating to business income (Schedule C), rentals or royalties (Schedule E), or farm income and expenses (Schedule F) are deductible on each one of those forms. The expenses for preparing the remainder of the return are deductible on Schedule A.

Line 22: Other expenses — investment, safe deposit box, and so on

You may be scratching your head as to how the IRS can throw in a line item here called "other expenses" when we're within the miscellaneous deduction category. The expenses that are most likely to help you on this line to build up to that 2 percent hurdle are fees you incur in managing your investments. Here's a run-down of deductible investment expenses:

- ✔ financial periodicals

- ✔ accounting fees to keep track of investment income

- ✔ investment fees, custodial fees, trust administration fees, and other expenses you paid for managing your investments

- ✔ investment fees shown in Box 1e of Form 1099-DIV

- ✔ safe deposit box rentals

- ✔ trustee's fees for your IRA, if separately billed and paid

- ✔ investment expenses of partnerships, S Corporations, and mutual funds (You will receive a Schedule K-1 that will tell you where to deduct those expenses.)

You can't deduct expenses incurred in connection with investing in tax-exempt bonds. If you have expenses related to both taxable and tax-exempt income but cannot identify the expenses that relate to each, you must prorate the expenses to determine the amount that you can deduct.

One of the benefits of all the lawyers we have in America is that when you hire one for a variety of personal purposes, you may qualify to write off the cost. For example, you can deduct a legal fee in connection with collecting taxable alimony and for tax advice related to a divorce if the bill specifies how much is for tax advice, and it's determined in a reasonable way.

Part of an estate tax planning fee may be deductible. That's because estate planning involves tax as well as nontax advice. A reasonable division of the bill between the two will usually support a deduction for the portion attributable for tax advice. Legal costs in connection with contesting a will or suing for wrongful death aren't deductible. The same goes for financial planner fees you pay. The part that applies to tax advice is deductible.

You may deduct legal fees directly related to your job, such as fees incurred in connection with an employment contract or defending yourself from being wrongfully dismissed. You can deduct legal expenses that you incurred if they are business related or in connection with income-producing property.

A legal fee paid to collect a disputed Social Security claim is also deductible to the extent that your benefit is taxable. For example, you paid a $2,000 fee to help collect your Social Security benefits. If 50 percent of the your Social Security is taxable, you can deduct $1,000 (50 percent of the fee).

Lines 23-26: Miscellaneous math

Congratulations! You've slogged through one of the parts of the tax return that clearly highlights how politicians and years of little changes adds up to complicated tax laws. We know you've spent a lot of the time to identify and detail expenses that fit into these ridiculous categories. As we warned you in the beginning of this section on job expenses and other miscellaneous deductions, you can deduct only these expenses to the extent that they exceed 2 percent of your adjusted gross income. Lines 23-26 walk you through this arithmetic.

Lines 27-28: Other Miscellaneous Deductions

More miscellaneous deductions? You bet. These "other miscellaneous deductions" are different from those on lines 20-26 in that they are not subject to the 2 percent adjusted gross income limit. Hooray, no convoluted math! These are 100 percent Grade A, no-fat deductions!

- ✔ **Moving expenses.** You enter your 1994 moving expenses on Form 3903 (see Chapter 7 for how to complete it) or 3903-F (foreign) and deduct them as an adjustment to your income on Form 1040 (line 24). You don't have to itemize your deductions to claim this deduction. But expenses incurred in 1993 and not paid until 1994 (because you were not reimbursed until 1994) are claimed on Page 2 of Form 3903, and the amount of the deduction on Form 3903 is carried over to Schedule A (line 27).

- ✔ **Gambling losses to the extent of gambling winnings.** Enter on line 28 of Schedule A.

- ✔ **Estate tax on income you received as an heir.** Enter on line 28 of Schedule A. You can deduct the estate tax attributable to income you received from an estate that you paid tax on. For example, suppose that you received $10,000 from an IRA account when the owner died. You included this amount in your income. The owner's estate paid $2,000 of estate tax on the IRA. You can deduct the $2,000 on line 27. Its called an *IRD deduction.* That's IRS lingo for "income in respect of a decedent," which means the IRA owner never paid income tax on the money in the IRA.

✔ **Repayment of income.** If you had to repay more than $3,000 of income that was included in your income in an earlier year, you may be able to deduct the amount you repaid or take a credit against your tax.

✔ **Unrecovered investment in a pension.** If a retiree contributed to the cost of pension or annuity, a part of each payment received can be excluded from income as a tax-free return of the retiree's investment. If the retiree dies before the entire investment is returned tax free, the unrecovered investment is allowed as a deduction on the retiree's final return.

✔ **Work expenses for the disabled.** If you have a physical or mental disability that limits your being employed or that substantially limits one or more of your activities (such as performing manual tasks, walking, speaking, breathing, learning, and working), your impairment-related work expenses are deductible.

✔ **Impairment-related work expenses.** These expenses are allowable business expenses of attendant care services at your place of work and expenses in connection with your place of work that are necessary for you to be able to work. See IRS Publication 907 (*Information for Persons with Disabilities*) for more information.

If you are an employee, enter your impairment-related work expenses on Form 2106. You enter the amount on line 11 of Form 2106, (the amount related to your impairment). This amount is entered on line 28 of Schedule A. And the amount that is unrelated to your impairment is entered on line 20 of Schedule A.

Line 29: Total Itemized Deductions

You've (thankfully) reached the end of Schedule A. Warm up that calculator again because we need to do some adding. Sum up the totals that you've written on the far right hand column on the schedule. You should be adding the amounts on lines 4, 9, 14, 18, 19, 26, 27, and 28.

But wait! You can't just go ahead and enter that total on line 29. Why would the IRS allow you to do that after plowing through this difficult schedule? If your adjusted gross income (listed on line 32, which is the same as line 31 of your Form 1040) exceeded $111,800 for the year (or above $55,900 if you're married filing separately), you're going to have to jump through more hoops because the IRS wants to limit your itemized deductions if you make this much money.

If your adjusted gross income is $111,800 or less for the year ($55,900 or less if married filing separately), you can call it quits now and simply write the total you calculated on line 29 of your Schedule A. Then you can enter this amount on line 34 of your Form 1040. Just make sure that the total of your itemized deductions is greater than the standard deduction (see amounts next to line 34 of your Form 1040).

If your income is above these limits, you've got more work to do. Read on.

Limit on itemized deductions

If your adjusted gross income exceeds $111,800 or ($55,900 if you are married filing separately), you have to reduce your total itemized deductions by 3 percent of your income above $111,800. Here's how it works. Say that your income is $131,800 and your total itemized deductions are $30,000. Because your income exceeds $111,800 by $20,000, you have to reduce your itemized deductions by $600 ($20,000 × 3 percent). So although you started with itemized deductions of $30,000, you can deduct only $29,400.

The 3 percent rule won't completely eliminate your itemized deductions because your deductions cannot be reduced by more than 80 percent. So in the preceding example, if your income was $1 million, you would still get to deduct $6,000 because your $30,000 in deductions cannot be reduced by more than $24,000 ($30,000 × 80 percent).

So let's put this on paper in order to make it easier to do the math: Use the following worksheet in Table 8-3 if your AGI exceeds $111,800 (married filing jointly) or $55,900 (married filing separately) to figure your allowable deductions.

Table 8-3	Itemized Deduction Worksheet

Example: AGI is $150,000 and your investment interest deduction is $10,000; you made charitable gifts of $2,000, and paid taxes of $8,000

	Sample	Your Computation
1. AGI line 31 (1040)	$150,000	1. _____
2. Enter $111,800 ($55,900 if filing separately)	$111,800	2. _____
3. Subtract line 2 from line 1	$33,200	3. _____
4. Total itemized deductions (Schedule A)	$20,000	4. _____
5. From Schedule A enter:		
Medical (line 4)		5. _____
Investment interest (line 13)	$10,000	_____
Casualty loss (line 19)		_____
Gambling losses (line 28)		_____
6. Subtract line 5 entries from line 4	$10,000	6. _____
7. Multiply line 6 by 80%	$8,000	7. _____
8. Multiply line 3 by 3%	$1,014	8. _____
9. The smaller of line 7 and 8	$1,014	9. _____
10. Your reduced itemized deductions: line 4 less line 9	$18,986*	10. _____ *

This is the amount you are allowed to deduct. Now you can enter this amount on line 29 of Schedule A and carry it over to line 34 of your Form 1040. Just make sure that the total of your itemized deductions is greater than the standard deduction (see amounts next to line 34 of your Form 1040).

You may be wondering why you subtracted your medical and dental expenses, investment interest, casualty and theft losses, and gambling losses. The IRS doesn't limit or reduce your ability to write off these expenses so that they aren't subject to the 3 percent reduction rule. The IRS *does* want to limit your ability to deduct too much in the way of state and local taxes (including property taxes paid on your home), home mortgage interest, gifts to charity, job expenses, and miscellaneous deductions.

The net effect of the IRS tossing out some of these write-offs is that it raises the effective tax rate that you're paying on your income higher than what the IRS tables indicate. This may encourage you, for example, to spend less on a home, or to pay off your mortgage faster (see Chapter 22) because you don't merit a full deduction.

What your neighbors are deducting

Table 8-4 shows the IRS statistics of the average deductions taken by taxpayers on their 1992 tax returns. But you can't simply go ahead and claim the amounts listed in the chart — the IRS imposes penalties for doing that! And if your deductions exceed these amounts, you stand a greater chance of being audited.

Table 8-4	Average Itemized Deductions (1992)				
AGI ($000)	Medical	Taxes	Contributions	Interest	Misc. Itemized Deductions
$25-30	$ 4,247	$ 2,216	$ 1,273	$ 5,422	$ 2,613
$30-40	2,991	2,627	1,401	5,435	2,743
$40-50	3,641	3,263	1,450	5,811	3,154
$50-75	4,588	4,379	1,734	6,856	3,103
$75-100	5,239	6,214	2,368	8,867	3,925
$100-200	6,088	9,854	3,776	12,174	6,384
Over $200	15,600	37,679	9,906	22,114	11,887

Source: Statistics of Income Bulletin, The Internal Revenue Service

Chapter 9

Interest and Dividend Income: Schedule B

In This Chapter

▶ Interest income stuff

▶ Your 1099-INT

▶ Dividend income stuff

▶ Your 1099-DIV

▶ Foreign accounts and trusts

A h! More income — bring it on, you say? Remember that you're going to add it to the taxable income section. We are going to go through Schedule B in this chapter (see Figure 9-1). Can you find the form? It's a little IRS trick — Schedule B is on the back of Schedule A. After we get done doing the math on Schedule B, we'll put the total on line 9 of the trusty Form 1040.

Year after year, many taxpayers dutifully complete Schedule B, file it with the rest of their return, and forget about it until they need to complete their next return. This particular schedule is a potential goldmine for reducing your future taxes. Why? Because you report on this schedule all the *taxable* interest and dividend income that you received during the year. If you complete this schedule and are in the higher tax brackets, we feel obliged to tell you there are many investments that are tax-friendly. Be sure to check out Chapter 21 to learn all about them.

What you'll need to complete Schedule B are those 1099s (1099-INT and 1099-DIV) that bank, brokerage firm, and mutual fund companies send you in the late winter and early spring. Make sure that you have one of these forms for each and every nonretirement account that you held money in during the tax year. If you're missing any, get on the horn to the responsible financial institution and request it.

If you don't report all your interest or dividend income (or don't furnish the payer with your Social Security number), your future interest and dividend income is subject to backup withholding of 31 percent! To add insult to injury, about 18 months after filing your taxes, you will receive a nasty notice called a CP-2000 listing the interest and dividends you didn't report. You'll end up owing interest and penalties.

While getting ensnared in backup withholding is unpleasant, don't worry that the amounts withheld by financial institutions from your accounts and sent to the IRS are for naught. They simply represent a forced payment of your expected tax on your interest and dividends. You get "credit" for it on line 54, "Federal income tax withheld," on your Form 1040 (see Chapter 13 for more details).

Part I, Lines 1-4: Interest Income

In this first part of the schedule, you need to declare interest income that you earned during the tax year. While this income can come from a variety of sources, as you'll soon learn, most of it is reported by large, impersonal financial institutions that will send you a computer-generated form, the 1099-INT. So before we get to completing the lines on Schedule B, we'd like to explain how to read your 1099-INT forms.

Understanding Form 1099-INT

You receive a Form 1099-INT from the financial institution, such as a bank, that pays you interest. These forms aren't too difficult to read. The following are brief descriptions of little boxes and other stuff you find on your 1099-INT (see Figure 9-2).

Don't assume that your 1099-INT forms are all correct. Big companies make mistakes and they often cause you to pay more tax. Check your 1099-INT forms against your statements that you received throughout the year from the financial firm where you had the account paying the interest. If you receive an incorrect 1099-INT, ask the payer to issue a corrected one on the double!

Boxes 1 and 3: Taxable interest income

The amount in Boxes 1 and Box 3 is the taxable interest that you have to report on line 1 of this schedule. But if you don't have more than $400 of total interest income for the tax year, you need not complete this part of Schedule B (you have to complete Part II, "Dividend Income," if you had more than $400 in dividend income). Don't concern yourself with the rest of the boxes on your 1099 right now. When you have to use those numbers on other chapters in this part, we'll let you know.

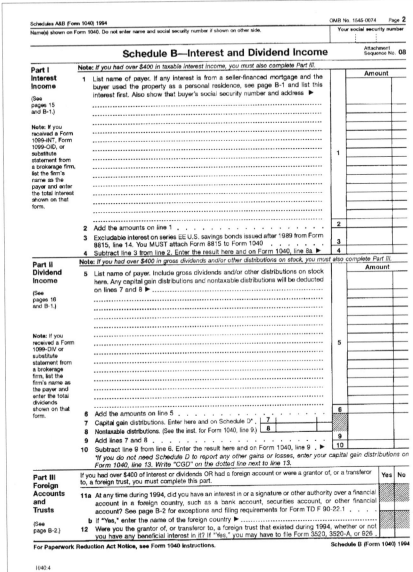

Figure 9-1:
Schedule
B — Interest
and
Dividend
Income.

Completing lines 1-4

Now that you've located and understand Form 1099-INT, we're ready to complete Part I of Schedule B.

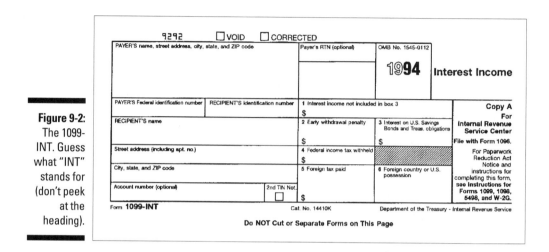

Line 1: Taxable interest

Taxable interest includes interest you receive from bank accounts, interest on loans you made to others, and interest on loans from most other sources (anything except municipal bond interest).

Taxable interest does not include interest on insurance dividends you leave on deposit with the Department of Veterans Affairs (for people who were in the armed services).

Joint returns, minors, and interest stuff

If your Social Security number (SSN) is the one that's reported on the 1099-INT, the computers at the IRS check to see if this number is on your return. Those diligent computers also check to make sure you put the interest from the 1099 on your return. On a joint return, either your SSN or your spouse's number can be on the account because you are filing jointly.

But what about an account owned by you and someone other than your spouse (or if you are merely holding the money for someone else)? Suppose that only 50 percent of the $1,200

reported under your SSN is yours. Report the $1,200 on Schedule B and on the line below subtract the $600 belonging to the other person. In the space for the name of the payer, write `BELONGING TO NOMINEE`.

When minors have an account, make sure that their Social Security number is on the account. If they have more than $600 in interest, they have to file a return. If they're under the age of 14 and their interest and investment income exceeds $1,200, the excess is taxed at their parent's tax rate (see more about the Kiddie Tax in Chapter 13).

Dividends that are actually interest

Often Savings and Loans, credit unions, savings banks, and money market funds report the interest you earned as *dividends*. Report such interest as dividends; and instead of receiving a 1099-INT, you will receive a 1099-DIV. Don't you think, sometimes, that everyone out there is trying to confuse you?

Gifts for opening an account

The value of that toaster you received will be reported as interest on Form 1099-INT. Enjoy your toast!

Interest on life insurance dividends

This interest is taxable, but the dividends you receive aren't taxable until the total of all dividends received exceeds the total of all the premiums paid. Keep your annual dividend statements from your company in a file so that you can track that amount versus the premiums you paid.

Interest on EE U.S. savings bonds

If you don't have EE bonds, you may happily skip this line. (If you want to learn about them, be sure to read Chapter 23). You report the interest on EE bonds when you cash in the bonds. You can choose to report the interest every year.

Reporting the interest every year may make sense if you have a child who has little or no income because the first $600 of interest is exempt from tax (see Chapter 23). Attach a statement to your child's return saying that you elect to report the interest annually. If the interest is under $600, you're going to have to file a return even if one isn't required in order to make this election for the initial year. After that, as long as the interest is under $600, you don't have to file.

Series E bonds stop earning interest after 40 years, and it's after 30 years for EE bonds. (Series E was issued before 1980 and Series EE after that time.) You can avoid paying the tax on the accumulated interest at or before maturity by exchanging these bonds for HH bonds.

When the owner of an E or EE bond dies, the heir pays the tax when the bond is cashed in — unless the interest was reported on the decedent's final return. This choice makes sense if the owner of the bond died at the beginning of the year and had little or no income (and was in a lower tax bracket than the heir).

For example, if the owner died on January 10 and filed a return reporting the accumulated EE bond interest of, say, $5,000, no tax would be added because the decedent would be entitled to a standard deduction of $3,800 (if single) and a personal exemption of $2,450. On the other hand, if the heir is in the 31 percent tax bracket and had to report the $5,000 of accumulated interest when the heir cashed in the bond, the tax would be $1,550.

U.S. H and HH bonds

H and HH bonds are issued only in exchange for E and EE bonds. Interest is paid semi-annually, and you receive a Form 1099-INT from the government with the amount of interest you have to report. H bonds have a 30-year maturity and HH bonds have a 20-year maturity. (In case you really want to know, H bonds were issued before 1980 and HH after this time.)

The amount of interest earned on the E or EE bonds that you exchanged is stated on the H or HH bonds, and you report this amount when you cash in the H or HH bonds.

U.S. Treasury bills

U.S. Treasury bills are short-term obligations of the U.S. government issued at a discount. These bills mature in 1, 2, 3, 6, or 12 months. You report the interest in the year the bill matures, not when you purchase it.

For example, suppose that you purchase a $10,000 6-month t-bill for $9,700 in December 1994. You report the $300 of interest you earned when the bill matures in 1995. This maneuver is an excellent way to defer income into the next year.

Zero coupon bonds

Zero coupon bonds don't pay annual interest, but they are issued at a discount very similar to U.S. savings bonds. Each year the bond increases in value equal to the amount of interest it is considered to have earned. In tax lingo this is referred to as *original issue discount* (OID). Each year the issuer or your broker will compute the amount of interest you have to report and sends you a Form 1099-OID.

Interest on bonds bought or sold

When you buy a bond between the interest payment dates, you pay the seller the interest that was earned up to the sale date.

For example, suppose that on April 30 you buy a bond that makes semi-annual interest payments of $600 on June 30. You must pay the seller $400 for the interest earned up to April 30. You report the $600 in interest that you received for the bond on Schedule B. On the line below, subtract the $400 of interest you paid the seller, and to the left of the $400 amount write ACCRUED INTEREST PAID.

Tax refunds

Interest on tax refunds is taxable. This is shown in Box 1 of your 1099.

Tax-exempt bonds

Interest on city and state bonds are exempt from tax. But you still must report it on Form 1040A (line 8b) or on Form 1040 (line 8b). Although the entry on line 8b is not added to your taxable income, it is used to determine the amount of your Social Security that may be subject to tax.

Most states have a provision that tax-exempt bonds are exempt from state income tax only if these bonds are issued by the state. For example, a New York State resident will pay tax on a tax-exempt bond issued by Ohio.

Line 3: U.S. savings bonds — education program

This is one tax shelter that most people are unaware of. Uncle Sam wants you to put money aside for your children's education and will provide you with a tax exemption to boot. All or part of the interest on U.S. savings bonds used to pay college tuition is exempt from tax under the following conditions:

- Any U.S. savings bonds (Series EE) issued after December 31, 1989.

- You are 24 years old when you buy the bonds.

- The total redemption proceeds — interest and principal — don't exceed the tuition and fees paid for the year. (Room and board aren't considered tuition.)

- The tuition is for you, for your spouse, or for your dependents.

The amount of interest that can be excluded is reduced if your 1994 adjusted gross income meets the requirements spelled out in the following:

- Unmarried taxpayers with income of $41,200 or less are entitled to a full interest exclusion. Between $41,200 and $56,200, the exclusion is gradually phased out, and if your income exceeds $56,200, there is no exclusion.

- For married people filing jointly, there is a complete interest exclusion if your income is under $61,850 with a phaseout range between $61,850 and $91,850.

The amount of interest that you can exclude is computed on Form 8815 (Exclusion of Interest from Series EE U.S. Savings Bonds Issued after 1989). The amount of excludable interest is entered on Schedule B, line 3, and the total interest is listed on line 1.

Congress is considering raising the phaseout range to $46,900 to $61,900 for unmarried taxpayers and $70,350 to $100,350 for married taxpayers as of our publication date.

Part II, Lines 5-10: Dividend Income

Well, we hope you made a good bit of extra dough in Part I. Part II provides another opportunity to count your silver coins, er, we mean dividends. You find out about your dividends from another version of a 1099. You will receive Form 1099-DIV (see Figure 9-3) from the payer by January 31, 1995. If your 1099-DIV is incorrect, get the payer to correct it; otherwise you may pay tax on income you never earned. You have to report all your dividend income on your taxes or you'll be in big trouble. We'll explain some of those nice boxes just for you.

On how to report the income from jointly owned stock, follow the rules as explained for reporting interest on a joint bank account in the sidebar entitled "Joint returns, minors, and interest stuff." (Hint: You already passed it.)

Box 1a: Gross dividends

If the total amount of all the dividends in Box 1a of all your 1099s is less than $400, enter it on Form 1040 (line 9). If the amount is more than $400, enter it on Schedule B (line 5).

Schedule B, Part II has a column for the name of the payer and a column for the amount of the dividend you received. Enter the name of the payer in the column that says list the name of the payer. Enter the amount of the dividend you received in the column that says amount. For each 1099-DIV you received, enter the name of the payer and the amount received.

Box 1b: Ordinary dividends

The amount in this box is for information purposes only. Don't enter it anyplace on your returns or schedules. It only informs you that this portion of your

Figure 9-3: The 1099-DIV tells you how much money you made from our wonderful world of capitalism.

PAYER'S name, street address, city, state, and ZIP code		1a Gross dividends and other distributions on stock (Total of 1b, 1c, 1d, and 1e) $	OMB No. 1545-0110 1994	Dividends and Distributions
		1b Ordinary dividends $		
PAYER'S Federal identification number	RECIPIENT'S identification number	1c Capital gain distributions $	2 Federal income tax withheld $	Copy A For Internal Revenue Service Center
RECIPIENT'S name		1d Nontaxable distributions $	3 Foreign tax paid $	File with Form 1096.
Street address (including apt. no.)		1e Investment expenses $	4 Foreign country or U.S. possession $	For Paperwork Reduction Act Notice and instructions for completing this form, see Instructions for Forms 1099, 1098, 5498, and W-2G.
City, state, and ZIP code		Liquidation Distributions		
Account number (optional)	2nd TIN Not. ☐	5 Cash $	6 Noncash (Fair market value) $	

9191 ☐ VOID ☐ CORRECTED

Form **1099-DIV**   Cat. No. 14415N   Department of the Treasury - Internal Revenue Service

Do NOT Cut or Separate Forms on This Page

dividend is subject to tax at ordinary tax rates and doesn't qualify for the special capital gain tax rate that can't exceed 28 percent.

Box 1c: Capital gain distributions

If you are filing a Form 1040, you enter capital gain distributions on Schedule B (line 7) and then on Schedule D (line 14) as a long-term capital gain. If you have no other capital gains or losses, don't enter this amount on Schedule D. Enter it instead on Form 1040 (line 13).

The maximum tax on long-term capital gains is 28 percent. So if your taxable income on Form 1040 (line 37) is more than the following amounts, you are going to have to use the Schedule D tax worksheet to compute your tax in order to make sure you don't pay more tax:

- Single — $55,100
- Married filing jointly or qualifying widow(er) — $91,850
- Married filing separately — $45,925
- Head of household — $78,700

So if your taxable income on Form 1040 (line 37) places you in the 36 percent tax bracket and you have $1,000 of long-term capital gain distributions, you will pay $360 in tax on the $1,000 instead of $280 (28 percent) if you don't use the Schedule D tax worksheet.

Box 1d: Nontaxable distributions

For Form 1040 filers, enter nontaxable distributions on Schedule B (line 8). These distributions reduce the taxable amount of your shares when figuring your gain or loss when the shares are sold. For example, suppose that you purchased shares in a company or a mutual fund for $10,000 and you received $500 in nontaxable dividends. Your basis for determining gain or loss when you sell the shares is $9,500.

Box 1e: Investment expenses

This box refers to shares you own in publicly or nonpublicly offered funds — which doesn't apply to most people. We have yet to see a 1099-DIV with an entry in this box! (But it must be there for a reason!)

Box 2: Federal tax withheld

Report your federal tax withheld on Form 1040 (line 54).

Boxes 5 and 6: Liquidating distributions

You report these amounts (cash and noncash) on Schedule D (Capital Gains and Losses). If you have entries in these two boxes, see a tax advisor. And check out Chapter 11 to find out more about Schedule D.

Part III, Lines 11a–12: Foreign Accounts and Trusts

If you have a foreign bank or security account, you have to check "yes" on line 11a of Schedule B and enter the name of the foreign country. However, if the average balance in the account in 1994 was under $10,000, you can check "no." But if you had more than $10,000 in a foreign bank or security account during the year, you have to file Form TDF 90-22.1 by June 30, 1995. On this form, you have to list where your account(s) are located, including the name of the bank, security firm, or brokerage firm, their address, and the account number.

If you are unique enough to have to deal with line 12, it means that you have a foreign trust. You have to check "yes" and complete Form 3520, 3520-A, or 926. Good luck! (These forms are complicated; consider using a tax advisor.)

When a dividend isn't a dividend

Stock dividends and splits

Stock dividends and splits are not taxable. You now own more shares! For example, suppose that you own 100 shares. If the stock is split two for one, you now own 200 shares. If you receive a 10 percent stock dividend, you now own

110 shares. How you treat the shares you received when they are sold is explained in Chapter 11.

Life insurance dividends

Life insurance dividends are not taxable until the total dividends received exceeds the total premiums paid.

Chapter 10

Profit or Loss from Business: Schedule C

*R*unning your own firm really can be the American dream. In fact, the only thing better than working for yourself is knowing how to keep more of what you earn. It's like giving yourself an immediate raise at tax time.

If you are self-employed, you must report your income on a Schedule C (or C-EZ). All your business expenses are also listed on this form. Your expenses are subtracted from your income to arrive at your profit on which you have to pay tax.

Schedule C-EZ

If your income is less than $25,000 and your expenses don't exceed $2,000, you're a candidate for Schedule C-EZ — a three-line form that's relatively EZ to complete. You can't use the C-EZ if you have a net loss from your business, and you can't deduct any expenses for the business use of your home. If you qualify, have a go at it. After you fill in the easy background information in Part I, figure your net profit.

  ✔ Line 1: Fill in your income.

  ✔ Line 2: Fill in your expenses.

  ✔ Line 3: Subtract line 2 from line 1; this amount is your net profit.

You're done. Carry the profit over to Form 1040 (line 12).

Okay, you caught us. If you are deducting automobile expenses on line 2, you have to fill out Part III and answer five (maybe six) more questions so that the IRS can be sure your expenses are legitimate. Four of those questions are yes/no questions. Don't you wish all IRS forms were like this?

Schedule C

This schedule is not so EZ, but it is not as bad as it looks. Here are the line-by-line instructions.

Basic Information (F-J): Accounting Method Stuff

The two methods to report income are *cash* and *accrual*. With the cash method, you report income when it is actually received, and you deduct expenses when they are actually paid. However, if you charge an expense on a credit card, you deduct this expense in the year charged, even if you pay the charge in a later year. (So don't leave home without it!)

You must use the accrual method if you operate a business that has an inventory of merchandise, such as a clothing store. Under this method, you report income in the year sales are made — even if the sales are billed or collected in a later year. You deduct expenses in the year they are incurred, even if these expenses aren't paid until later. Under both cash and accrual methods, you report all income and expenses for the calendar year ending December 31.

Part I, Lines 1-7: Income

Time to tally. This section wants you to find some *gross* things: gross sales, gross profits, and gross income.

Line 1: Gross receipts or sales

If you're operating a service business, enter the income from fees you actually collected (because you're reporting income under the cash method).

If you're selling merchandise, you're required to use the accrual method, so enter here the total of all the sales you billed your customers.

Line 2: Returns and allowances

If you had to return a fee, enter the amount here. If a customer returned merchandise, that amount also goes on this line, along with any discount a customer took.

Line 3: Subtraction quiz

All this line wants you to do is subtract your returns and allowances (line 2) from your gross receipts and sales (line 1).

Line 4: Cost of goods sold

The IRS must think that you're a CPA, otherwise the Agency would simply say to subtract the cost of the merchandise you sold from your sales to arrive at this figure. Service and other businesses that don't sell products don't have to put an amount on this line.

But because you aren't a CPA, you have to compute the cost of the merchandise you sold on Part III (on the back of Schedule C). Part III is an eight-line schedule where you enter your beginning inventory, the merchandise you purchased, the salary you paid your production workers (if you are manufacturing the product you are selling) and production supplies. You total all these expenses on line 38. From this total you subtract your ending inventory to arrive at the cost of the goods you sold. This amount goes back to line 4 (where you are right now!).

Remember, you can't deduct all the merchandise you purchase during the year. You can deduct only the merchandise you sold. That's why you have to subtract your ending inventory, which is the stuff you didn't sell.

Line 5: Gross profit

Hey, here's where you put your profit you made on the merchandise you sold.

Line 6: Other income

Just do what the Schedule orders you to do — see Page C-2 of the 1040 Booklet if you have any questions about other income (which includes federal and state gasoline or fuel tax credit).

Line 7: Gross income

This amount is usually the same as the amount on line 5. But if you had other items of income such as a refund of a prior year's expense, enter that amount on line 6 and add it to the amount on line 5 to arrive at your gross income.

Part II, Lines 8-27: Expenses

Take a breath and get ready for all those wonderful lines split into two columns (so they would all fit on one page!).

Line 8: Advertising

For example, you would enter here the cost of your ad in the Yellow Pages.

Line 9: Bad debts from sales or services

If you use the accrual method for reporting income, you can write off losses when a customer goes bust. But if you use the cash method, you can't — because you never paid tax on the money your client owes. The rules regarding when a cash-method taxpayer can write off a bad debt are similar to those regarding when you can write off a personal loan that went bad. We explain such things in "Nonbusiness bad debts" in Chapter 11.

Line 10: Car and truck expenses

If you plan to make an entry on this line, be sure to answer the questions (41-45b) in Part IV on the other side of the Schedule C, commonly referred to as Page 2.

When you use your car for business, the expenses of operating the car are deductible. But remember that *using it for business* is the key phrase. You can compute this deduction by using either a flat rate of 29 cents per business mile, or you can keep track of actual expenses (gas, oil, repair, insurance, depreciation, and so on).

Regardless of the method you use, you need to keep a log or diary so you can record the business purpose of your trips as well as the mileage (Dear Diary ...). You also have to record the odometer reading at the beginning and end of the year. You need this information in order to divide your expenses between personal and business use. But here's a word of caution. Whether you use the flat rate or tabulate your actual expenses, it's just about impossible to prove that your car is used 100 percent for business. Unfortunately, there is always some personal use!

You don't have to write down in your diary the miles traveled every time you get in and out of your car. Making entries in your diary on a weekly basis meets the IRS requirement that you keep a record of your car's business use near or at the time of its use.

Commuting expenses

Commuting expenses between your home and office are not deductible. These expenses are considered personal commuting expenses, no matter how far your home is from your office or place of work. And making telephone calls from your car while commuting or having a business discussion with a business associate who accompanies you doesn't turn the ride into a deductible expense (besides, you ought to be watching the road). And the use of your car to display advertising material does not count as a deduction, either. Finally, parking at your place of business isn't deductible — but parking when visiting a customer or client is.

If you use your car to call on clients or customers and don't have a regular office to go to, the mileage between your home and the first customer you call on — as well as the mileage between the location of the last customer that you call on and your home — is considered commuting. If your office is in your home (which is a tough nut to crack), you can deduct all your auto expenses for calling on clients or customers. Line 42 on the back of your Schedule C inquires about the first-and-last-customer-of-the-day rule, only the IRS refers to it as commuting. The IRS wants you to enter on this line (42) the number of miles you use your car commuting.

Second job

If you moonlight after work, you can deduct the cost of getting from one job to the other. But transportation expenses going from your home to a part-time job on a day off from your main job aren't deductible. A meeting of an Armed Forces Reserve unit is considered travel to a second job, however. If the meeting is held on the same day as your regular job, it's deductible.

Temporary job site

If you have a regular place of business and commute to a temporary work location, you can deduct the cost of the daily round trip between your home and the temporary job site.

If you don't have a regular place of work (but ordinarily work at different locations in the general area where you live), you can't deduct the daily round trip between your home and your temporary job site. But if you travel to a job site outside your general area, your daily transportation would be deductible. Sounds like a distinction without a difference, right? But if this exception applies to you, don't look a gift horse in the mouth.

You can deduct the business portion of the following: depreciation, leasing and rental fees, garage rent, licenses, repairs, gas, oil, and tires, insurance, parking, and tolls.

If you are self-employed, you can deduct the business portion of interest on a car loan — but if you are an employee, you can't. Fines for traffic violations aren't deductible, either (so slow down!).

Sales taxes can't be deducted separately — they are added to the car's tax basis for the purposes of determining the amount of depreciation you are entitled to claim. But personal property taxes on your car can be deducted if you itemize your deductions on Schedule A.

Standard Mileage Rate or Actual Expenses

You can either deduct the business portion of your actual expenses or use the standard rate of 29¢ per mile for your your business miles (see sidebar). But if you decide to use your actual expenses, you start off by deducting the amount of depreciation on your car that you are entitled to claim.

Standard mileage rate

Instead of figuring your actual expenses with those maddening depreciation computations, you can use a flat rate of 29 cents for every business mile. If you used your car 15,000 miles for business, you would be entitled to a $4,350 deduction. You claim this deduction on page 2 of Form 2106. You multiply the business miles on line 14 by 29 cents and enter the result on line 22. This amount is carried over to line 1 of Form 2106. If you were reimbursed for any of your car expenses that weren't included in Box 1 of your W-2 as taxable wages, a code L will appear next to the amount of the reimbursement in box 13 of your W-2. You must deduct this amount from your auto expenses and enter it on line 7 of Form 2106.

If you choose the flat-rate method, you can't claim any of your actual expenses such as depreciation, gas, oil, insurance, and so on. If you want to use this method, you must choose it in the first year you start using your car for business. If you didn't use the standard mileage rate in the first year you started using your car for business, you can't use the standard mileage rate in a subsequent year. If you started using the standard mileage rate, you can switch to deducting your actual expenses but you probably won't want to do this once you take a look at the rules in the IRS Publication 917 (*Business Use of a Car*).

If you trade in your car, you can use the flat rate for both cars because you owned them at different times.

If you sell your car, you have to reduce its tax basis by the amount of depreciation built into the flat rate so you can determine if you made a taxable profit or loss. There is a table (of course!) in IRS Publication 917 that shows you how to make this computation.

Depreciation

Computing the amount of depreciation on your car is mind-numbing. Unfortunately, the only way around this exercise in frustration is if you use the 29 cents flat rate.

Automobiles are lumped into the _listed property_ category of assets by the IRS (they are subject to the 50-percent business use test), and the IRS has given cars a whole bunch of rules and regulations. Listed property is an IRS term for autos, telephones, computers, boats, and airplanes — items that the IRS suspects you might be using more for pleasure than for business. The IRS lists cars as 5-year property (which means that the IRS deems them to have a useful life of five years.) Ready for the computation? Here goes.

If the business use of your car is thus 50 percent or more, your depreciation is computed (under MACRS — Modified Accelerated Cost Recovery System) according to what is known as the _half-year convention_ (see Table 10-1).

Table 10-1	Half-Year Convention for Auto Depreciation		
Year	_Yearly percent_	_For a $30,000 car_	_Maximum yearly limit_
1-1994	20.00%	$ 6,000	$2,960
2-1995	32.00	9,000	4,700
3-1996	19.20	5,760	2,850
4-1997	11.52	3,456	1,675
5-1998	11.52	3,456	1,675
6-1999	5.76	1,728	1,675
	100%	$30,000	1,675 in each succeeding year

So for a car purchased in 1994, the maximum amount of depreciation that can be claimed is $2,960, and then $4,700 in 1995, $2,850 in 1996, and $1,675 a year until the $30,000 if fully depreciated (which will take $14^1/_2$ years). This formula, however, assumes that the car is being used 100 percent for business. So if business use is less, the maximum yearly limits have to be reduced.

If you thought all this rigmarole was bad enough, Congress — in its infinite wisdom — enacted the 40-percent rule. If more than 40 percent of all your business assets (including your auto) were purchased in the last quarter of 1994 (October to December), you don't use the depreciation percentages in Table 10-1. Instead, you must use the depreciation percentages known as the _mid-quarter convention_ (See Table 10-2).

Table 10-2   Mid-Quarter Convention for Auto Depreciation

Year	First quarter	Second quarter	Third quarter	Fourth quarter
1	35.00%	25.00%	15.00%	5.00%
2	26.00	30.00	34.00	38.00
3	15.60	18.00	20.40	22.80
4	11.01	11.37	12.24	13.68
5	11.01	11.37	11.30	10.94
6	1.38	4.26	7.06	9.58

For example, suppose that you purchase a car for $20,000 in December (fourth quarter) and a computer for $10,000 in May (second quarter). The percentage that you would use to depreciate the computer in 1994 would be 25 percent. Your auto depreciation schedule, however, would look like something else (see Table 10-3).

Table 10-3   Mid-Quarter Convention for Auto Depreciation

Year	Yearly % per the 4th quarter chart above	For a $20,000 car	Maximum yearly limit
1-1994	5.00%	$1,000	$2,960
2-1995	38.00	7,600	4,700
3-1996	22.80	4,560	2,850
4-1997	13.68	2,736	1,675
5-1998	10.94	2,188	1,675
6-1999	9.58	1,916	1,675
	100%	$20,000	1,675 in each succeeding year

As the result of the 40-percent rule, your depreciation only comes to $1,000 ($20,000 × 5 percent) because you started using the car in the fourth quarter. In 1994, you would use 38 percent. But remember that 38 percent comes to $7,600, and you're limited to $4,700. However, you can increase your depreciation deduction for 1994 by electing to write off as a current expense part of the cost of the car the first year the car was placed in service. This procedure is known as *section 179 depreciation*.

Section 179 allows you to write off up to $17,500 a year in the first year an asset is placed in service. However, because this is a car, you cannot expense more than the yearly maximum depreciation limits for autos (listed property). That is to say, regular depreciation plus section 179 expensing can't exceed whatever the yearly maximum limit for depreciation is for an auto. Because in the preceding example you are forced to use the 5-percent mid-quarter convention (the car was placed into service in the fourth quarter of the year), your depreciation deduction works out to be $1,000. However, you can kick this up to the $2,960 maximum by electing to expense part of the cost of the auto under the section 179 expensing allowance. Phew! But on we go.

You must then reduce the basis of the car by the expensed amount ($20,000 - $2,960 = $17,040). The $17,040 becomes your new basis for depreciation in the coming years. Calculate depreciation from there on using $17,040 as your basis. Next year, thus, you will be allowed to deduct the maximum amount of depreciation for an auto placed in service in 1994, $4,700 in 1995, $2,850 in 1996, and $1,675 thereafter. If you started depreciating your car prior to 1994, Table 10-4 shows you the maximum yearly depreciation limits:

To compute your annual depreciation deduction, first figure the maximum depreciation you are allowed assuming the car was used 100 percent for business. Then multiply that amount by the business-use percentage. As an example, on a car you started using in 1994, the maximum depreciation amount is $2,960. If you used your car 75 percent of the time for business, you can deduct $2,220 ($2,960 × 75 percent).

Table 10-4		**Annual Depreciation Ceiling for Cars Placed in Service after 1986**						
Year	*1987*	*1988*	*1989*	*1990*	*1991*	*1992*	*1993*
1987	$2,560						
1988	4,100	$2,560					
1989	2,450	4,100	$2,660				
1990	1,475	2,450	4,200	$2,660			
1991	1,475	1,475	2,550	4,200	$2,660		
1992	1,475	1,475	1,475	2,550	4,300	$2,760	
1993	1,475	1,475	1,475	1,475	2,550	4,400	$2,860
1994	1,475	1,475	1,475	1,475	1,575	2,650	4,600
1995	1,475	1,475	1,475	1,475	1,575	1,575	2,750
1996*	1,475	1,475	1,475	1,475	1,575	1,575	1,675

* and later years

If the business use of your car is less than 50 percent, you must depreciate your car using the *straight-line method* under the *alternative depreciation system* (ADS). Straight-line depreciation is relatively easy, right? Wrong, in this case. Remember, this is for a car with business use of less than 50 percent, so the IRS makes you reduce the amount of depreciation you would be allowed under the straight-line method by the percentage of personal use.

So if you use the car for business 40 percent of the time, the maximum depreciation allowed by law in the first year is $1,184 ($2,960 × 40 percent).

Table 10-5   Straight-Line Method (ADS) for Auto Depreciation

Year	5-year property	Maximum yearly limit*
1	10%	$2,960
2	20	4,700
3	20	2,850
4	20	1,675
5	20	and each succeeding year
6	10	and each succeeding year

* Remember to reduce to the same percentage as your business usage.

In the coming years, you calculate your depreciation deduction in the same way. In years 2, 3, 4, and 5 you would use a depreciation rate of 20 percent per the above chart, and then 10 percent for year 6. Any depreciation you couldn't claim in years 1-6 because of the yearly maximum limits are deducted in subsequent years at $1,675 a year less your personal use, until the car is fully depreciated.

Leased autos

If you lease a car instead of purchasing it, you're probably asking yourself why we waited so long to discuss how leased autos are deducted. The reason is that a special rule applies. This is your lucky day!

If you lease a car, you can deduct the rental payments. If the rental payments are, for example, $700 a month, enter $8,400 on line 24a of Form 2106. This sounds like a great deal. Why buy a car if the most you can deduct in depreciation for a car purchased in 1994 is $2,960 — when you can deduct $8,400 in rental payments? Don't celebrate yet.

Here's how the IRS gets back at you. Look at the line directly below line 24a. Yes, you see line 24b of Form 2106 — inclusion amount. Based on the value of the car you are leasing, you have to reduce your rental payment by this inclusion. For a car that you lease that's worth $50,000, you have to reduce your lease payments by $252. Every year of the lease, this amount increases. IRS Publication 917 (*Business Use of Your Car*) has a chart of the annual lease-inclusion amounts that are adjusted for inflation each year. The IRS thinks of everything.

As you have probably realized, even with the reduction of your rental payments by the lease-inclusion amount, leasing provides you with a larger deduction than purchasing. But lease payments that are payments towards the purchase price of the car aren't deductible. If you have such a lease agreement, you have to depreciate the car based on its value. As a result, you're back to the annual limit that you can claim for auto depreciation.

Line 11: Commissions and fees

The fee you paid to sell your merchandise or to bring in a new client goes on this line. But remember that if you pay someone who isn't your employee more than $600 in a year, you have to file Form 1099-MISC with the IRS and send the person you paid a copy of the form by January 31. IRS Publication 334 (*Tax Guide for Small Business*) explains how to comply with this requirement.

Line 12: Depletion

This line applies if your business deals with properties such as mines, oil and gas wells, timber, and exhaustible natural deposits. There are two ways to compute depletion, and of course you want to use the one that produces the larger deduction. To be on the safe side, see IRS Publication 535 (*Business Expenses*).

Line 13: Depreciation

Depreciation is the annual deduction that allows you to recover the cost of your investment (that has a useful life of more than one year) in business equipment or in income-producing real estate. The word *depreciation* is itself enough to send most readers to the next chapter, we know, but just think of depreciation as a way of increasing your income! Now are you more excited about depreciation possibilities?

Unless you elect the special provision that allows you to deduct the first $17,500 of equipment or furniture used in your business (we explain this provision later in the chapter in "Your first-year bonanza, the $17,500 deduction"), you have to write off your purchase of these assets over their useful life — as established by the IRS (see Table 10-6). Land and works of art can't be depreciated. (So you can't depreciate your Van Goghs!) See Chapter 20 for a discussion of the pros and cons of depreciating versus taking an outright deduction.

To file (or not to file) Form 4562

You compute your depreciation deduction on Form 4562 (Depreciation and Amortization) for business property you started using in 1994. Carry the amount of depreciation you calculated on this form over to line 13 of Schedule C.

For property you started using prior to 1994, Form 4562 isn't required. Just enter the amount on line 13 of Schedule C. However, if you are depreciating cars, computers, or cellular phones, you must use Form 4562 because only the business portion of these items can be depreciated.

Table 10-6	Useful Life	
Type of property		*Useful life (years)*
Computers and similar equipment		5
Office machinery (typewriters, calculators, copiers)		5
Autos and light trucks		5
Office furniture (desks, files)		7
Appliances (stoves, refrigerators)		7
Shrubbery		15
Residential buildings		27.5
Nonresidential buildings after 5/12/93		39
Nonresidential buildings before 5/12/93		31.5
Goodwill, customer lists, franchise costs, and convenants not to compete		15

If you are an employee claiming auto expenses, you claim the depreciation for the auto on Form 2106 (Employee Business Expenses). Form 4562 isn't required. For rental income reported on Schedule E, you use Form 4562 for property you started renting in 1994. For property you started renting before 1994, you don't need to file Form 4562.

IRS depreciation percentages

To figure the amount of depreciation you are entitled to claim, glance at the IRS depreciation tables (Tables 10-7 through 10-10). For business property other than real estate, you will notice that each table has two categories: *half-year convention* and *mid-quarter convention*. You usually use the half-year convention because the mid-quarter convention applies to stuff you placed in service during the last three months of the year (and which exceeds 40 percent of all your business property that you placed in service during the year). Got that? Read on and follow the example for both types of depreciation conventions.

Half-year convention depreciation

Suppose that you are depreciating a computer that you purchased for $5,000 in 1994; you first look up its useful life. Computers have a useful life of five years, so you use the depreciation percentages for 5-year property. OK, easy enough so far.

Under the half-year convention for 5-year property you find 20 percent as the amount. For 1994 you are entitled to a $1,000 depreciation deduction ($5000 × 20 percent). In 1995 you would multiply the $5,000 cost by 32 percent for a deduction of $1,600. And then you use 19.20, 11.52, 11.52, and 5.76 percent in each of the succeeding years. Fun calculations, right? Based on the convention rules, you will note that the write-off period for stuff is one year longer than its useful life. That's because in the first year you're entitled to only a half-year's worth of depreciation. The half-year convention rule means that all assets are considered to have been purchased on July 1 — which entitles you to only half the normal amount of depreciation.

Mid-quarter convention depreciation

Remember that you must use this convention if the business property you placed in service during the last three months of the year exceeds 40 percent of all your business property placed in service during the year.

For example, suppose that you bought a calculator on February 1, 1994, for $500 and a copier for $1,000 on October 1, 1994. Under the half-year convention you would be entitled to a depreciation deduction of $300 ($1500 × 20 percent). But because more than 40 percent of all your business property was bought and placed into service the last three months of the year, you have to switch to the mid-quarter convention. So here's how you now compute the depreciation for these two pieces of equipment.

Under the mid-quarter convention, for 5-year property for an asset purchased in the first quarter, the depreciation rate is 35 percent. Therefore, you're entitled to a $175 depreciation deduction ($500 × 35 percent) for the calculator. For the copier, you have to use the 5- percent rate for property bought during the fourth quarter ($1,000 × 5 percent), which entitles you to a $50 deduction.

The long and the short of all this is that by using the mid-quarter convention, you can claim only half the depreciation you normally would. At this point you're probably scratching the back of your head and wondering who thinks of these things. We must confess that we don't know either. Just play along.

Table 10-7 MACRS (Modified Accelerated Cost Recovery System): 5-Year Property

Year	Half-year convention	Mid-quarter convention			
		First quarter	Second quarter	Third quarter	Fourth quarter
1	20.00%	35.00%	25.00%	15.00%	5.00%
2	32.00	26.00	30.00	34.00	38.00
3	19.20	15.60	18.00	20.40	22.80
4	11.52	11.01	11.37	12.24	13.68
5	11.52	11.01	11.37	11.30	10.94
6	5.76	1.38	4.26	7.06	9.58

Table 10-8 — MACRS: 7-Year Property

Year	Half-year convention	Mid-quarter convention First quarter	Second quarter	Third quarter	Fourth quarter
1	14.29%	25.00%	17.85%	10.71%	3.57%
2	24.49	21.43	23.47	25.51	27.55
3	17.49	15.31	16.76	18.22	19.68
4	12.49	10.93	11.97	13.02	14.06
5	8.93	8.75	8.87	9.30	10.04
6	8.92	8.74	8.87	8.85	8.73

Table 10-9 — MACRS: 15-Year Property

Year	Half-year convention	Mid-quarter convention First quarter	Second quarter	Third quarter	Fourth quarter
1	5.00%	8.75%	6.25%	3.75%	1.25%
2	9.50	9.13	9.38	9.63	9.88
3	8.55	8.21	8.44	8.66	8.89
4	7.70	7.39	7.59	7.80	8.00
5	6.93	6.65	6.83	7.02	7.20
6	6.23	5.99	6.15	6.31	6.48

Additions or improvements to property

The addition or improvement that you made to property is treated as a separate item for the purposes of depreciation — regardless of how you were depreciating the original asset. For example, suppose that you own a house that you have been renting since 1984 and have been depreciating over 19 years (you were allowed to use that short of a useful life back then). And in 1994 you added a new roof. The roof has to be depreciated over 27.5 years and at the rate in the tables. The depreciation tables reproduced here only go up to six years. For the tables that go beyond six years, send for IRS Publication 534 (*Depreciation*).

Table 10-10   Residential Rental Property (27.5-year)

Use the row of the month of the taxable year placed in service.

	Year 1	Year 2	Year 3	Year 4	Year 5	Year 6
Jan.	3.485%	3.636%	3.636%	3.636%	3.636%	3.636%
Feb.	3.182	3.636	3.636	3.636	3.636	3.636
Mar.	2.879	3.636	3.636	3.636	3.636	3.636
Apr.	2.576	3.636	3.636	3.636	3.636	3.636
May	2.273	3.636	3.636	3.636	3.636	3.636
June	1.970	3.636	3.636	3.636	3.636	3.636
July	1.667	3.636	3.636	3.636	3.636	3.636
Aug.	1.364	3.636	3.636	3.636	3.636	3.636
Sept.	1.061	3.636	3.636	3.636	3.636	3.636
Oct.	0.758	3.636	3.636	3.636	3.636	3.636
Nov.	0.455	3.636	3.636	3.636	3.636	3.636
Dec.	0.152	3.636	3.636	3.636	3.636	3.636

Your first-year bonanza: the $17,500 deduction

Instead of computing depreciation by using the standard depreciation tables, you can elect to deduct up to $17,500 of the cost of business equipment that you purchased and placed into service in 1994.

For a car, the maximum that you can expense in 1994 is $2,960. Real estate doesn't qualify for this deduction. But furniture and refrigerators used in apartment buildings do. So if you bought office machinery, equipment, furniture, or a computer, reach for Form 4562, and write off the whole thing on line 2 of Part I — provided it didn't cost more than $17,500 — instead of hassling with those darn IRS depreciation percentage tables and their convention rules. Unlike the mid-quarter convention rule that you are forced to use if you purchase most of your equipment in the last quarter of the year, you can write off the whole $17,500 (as long as everything was placed in service by December 31).

If you buy a few items, you can pick and choose which ones you want to write off completely and which ones you don't. If perhaps you spend $27,500 for office equipment, you can write off $17,500 and depreciate the $10,000 balance using the 20-percent rate for a total depreciation deduction of $19,500 ($17,500 + $2,000).

Now for the fine print (there always has to be some — this is a tax book, after all). If you are married filing separately, you can deduct only $8,750. If you buy equipment costing more than $200,000, the $17,500 you are entitled to deduct is reduced dollar for dollar by the amount over $200,000. So if the total cost is $217,500 or more, you can kiss your $17,500 write-off good-bye and you have to wade through the depreciation tables to compute your depreciation. Have a nice time. The second rule regarding the $17,500 expensing is that this deduction can't produce a loss from all your business activities. Suppose that your consulting income — after all other expenses — is $10,000 and you bought $17,500 worth of equipment. You can expense only $10,000. The $7,500 balance is carried over to the next year. If you have enough consulting income after your other expenses, you can deduct it then. If you don't, keep carrying it over until you do.

But there is a pleasant surprise. You can count all your earned income in applying the *no-loss test*. So by the preceding example, if you or your spouse had at least $7,500 in wages, you could deduct the whole $17,500.

Line 14: Employee benefit programs

Enter here the premiums you paid for your employee's accident, health, and group term life insurance coverage — but don't put your own here. See "Line 26" in Chapter 7 for how an employee may be able to deduct 25 percent of his or her health insurance premiums.

Line 15: Insurance (other than health)

Enter on this line the premiums you paid for business insurance such as fire, theft, robbery, and general liability coverage on your business property.

Line 16: Interest

Here you can deduct interest on business loans. If you took out a mortgage on your house and used the proceeds of the loan to finance your business, deduct the interest here — and not on Schedule A.

Line 17: Legal and professional services

In addition to legal fees regarding business matters, include also on this line the fees you paid for tax advice and for preparing the tax forms related to your business.

Line 18: Office expense

Enter your costs for stationery, paper supplies, postage, and so on.

Line 19: Pension or profit-sharing plan

Enter your contribution to your employees' Keogh or SEP. As for your own Keogh or SEP, enter that amount on the 1040 (line 27).

Line 20a and b: Rent or lease

If you rented or leased an auto, machinery, or equipment, enter the business portion of the rental payments on line 20a. But if you leased a car for more than 30 days, you may have to reduce your deduction by an amount called the *inclusion amount* if the value of the car you leased exceeded:

Year lease began	Amount
1994	$14,700
1993	14,300
1992	13,700
1991	13,400
1986-91	12,800

See the section on auto expenses in order to compile the inclusion amount. As of this books publication, the IRS hadn't released the 1994 actual amount. See IRS Publication 917 (*Business Use of a Car*).

On line 20b, you enter the rent you paid your landlord.

Line 21: Repairs and maintenance

Enter the cost of routine repairs, such as the cost to repair your computer, on this line. But adding a new hard disk isn't a repair — the cost has to be depreciated over five years unless it qualifies for the special election to write off the first $17,500 of business assets.

Line 22: Supplies

Does your laser printer run on water? If not, enter here the cost of toner that you use, for example.

Line 23: Taxes and licenses

Here you deduct your business taxes such as Social Security and unemployment insurance taxes for your employees. You also enter here the costs of permits and business licenses.

Line 24a-c: Travel, meals, and entertainment

For what you can deduct on travel, meals, and entertainment, see the long explanation in Chapter 8 (in the "Lines 20-26" section). We just couldn't squeeze it into this small space!

Line 25: Utilities

Can you imagine what this line is for? If you are thinking of electric and telephone bills, for example, you've hit the nail on the head.

Line 26: Wages

Enter here the wages you paid your employees.

Line 27: Other expenses

On the reverse side of the Schedule C is Part V, a schedule where you list your expenses whose descriptions defies the neat categories of lines 8-26. Here you can enter dues, subscriptions, messenger services, Christmas expenses, and so on.

Line 30: Form 8829 (Expenses for Business Use of your Home)

Yes, you can deduct home office expenses — but the rules are tough. You must use Form 8829 (Expenses for Business Use of Your Home) to claim this deduction.

You may also be able to derive some nice tax-savings from your home. If you use part of your residence for business, you can deduct the mortgage interest, real estate taxes, deprecation, insurance, utilities, and repairs related to that part of your house. The same applies to renters as well. It sounds simple, but here comes the fine print. To claim a home office deduction, it must be used on a regular and exclusive basis as either a place where you meet with customers or clients or the principal place where you carry on your business.

As if this requirement wasn't bad enough, in 1993 the U.S. Supreme Court added an additional pair of tests — *relative importance* and *time spent*. Now you must compare the relative importance of the work done at all business locations — and that includes yours as well as that of your customers.

Suppose that you're a sales representative who spends 40 hours a week calling on customers and 10 hours in your home office scheduling appointments and maintaining business records. Your home office is not your principal place of business. That's because calling on customers is of primary importance and your home office, although essential, is less important. If the relative importance comparison doesn't identify a principal place of business, you then compare the time spent at each location. You spend most of your time outside your home office providing a service or calling on customers? You can kiss this deduction good-bye.

This deduction can't produce a loss. For example, suppose that your business income is $6,000. You have $5,000 in business expenses and home office expenses of $1,500 (of which $1,000 is for the percentage of your mortgage interest and real estate allocated to the use of the office). First you deduct the interest and taxes of $1,000, which leaves a balance of $5,000 for possible deductions. Then you deduct $5,000 of business expenses, which brings your business income to zero. The remaining $500 of your home office expenses can't be deducted, but it is carried over to the next year. If you don't have sufficient income to deduct the $500 next year, it is carried over again.

In order to fill out Form 8829 correctly, you first have to determine your total rent — including insurance, cleaning, and utilities. Then you deduct the portion used for business. If you rent four rooms and one room is used for business, you're entitled to deduct 25 percent of the total. (If the rooms are the same size you can use this method. If not, you're going have to figure out the percentage on a square-footage basis).

For homeowners, you compute your total cost of maintaining your home, depreciation, mortgage interest, taxes, insurance, repairs, and so on. Then deduct the percentage used for business. Gardening can't be deducted!

Line 31: Net profit

Once you arrive at this amount, copy it onto Form 1040 (line 12) and then on Schedule SE (line 2) so that you can compute the amount of Social Security tax you have to pay. See "Line 47: Self-employment tax" in Chapter 13 in order to learn how to complete Schedule SE.

Line 32a and b

The at-risk rules limit the losses you can deduct on your investment and money you borrowed that you are personally liable to repay. See Chapter 12 ("Line 27a") for more details on the at-risk rules.

Operating loss

Suppose you start a business and it produces an operating loss. In other words, your costs — not just equipment, but rent, salaries, and other expenses — exceed your income. You may write off that loss against any other income you and your spouse made that year.

And get this. If the loss is greater than your combined income in the current year, you can carry it back over each of the past three years and obtain a refund on the tax you paid at the time. The loss still isn't used up by carrying it back? You can carry it forward to offset your income in the next 15 years. See Chapter 16 for amending a prior year's return and for carrying back losses.

Nothing but losses

Keep in mind, however, that you can't operate a part-time business that continually loses money. This situation is known as *hobby losses*. If you don't show a profit in at least three of every five consecutive years, you could have a fight with the IRS on your hands. You've got a show a profit in at least three of every five consecutive years or the IRS will term your business a hobby and disallow your losses. The IRS does not consider your enterprise a business if you have continuing losses. No business, no business deductions.

Now that you've slaved through Schedule C, you know one of the big costs of being self-employed — filling out the darned form. But don't let all that hard work be for naught. Looking ahead to next year, there are probably a number of things you can do to reduce your tax bill. You should definitely read Chapter 20, which deals with such issues as whether you should incorporate, how to maximize your deductions with some advance planning, how to hire employees and keep current on your taxes with the IRS and other tax authorities, how to get and stay organized — and a whole lot more. Also, be sure to check out Chapter 19 where we detail the terrific tax-deductible retirement accounts available to the self-employed.

Chapter 11:

Capital Gains and Losses: Schedule D

. . . .

In This Chapter

▶ Tax basis background stuff

▶ Your introduction to Schedule D

▶ Short-term capital gains and losses

▶ Long-term capital gains and losses

▶ How to handle Form 4797 (if you need to)

▶ Worthless securities and bad debts

. . . .

*1*f you sell a security, such as a stock, bond, or mutual fund (or another investment held outside of a tax-sheltered retirement account), and you sell it for more than you paid for it, you owe capital gains tax on the profit. Conversely, when you sell an investment at a loss, it is tax deductible. Although it may seem unfair, for example, a loss on the sale of your home, auto, jewelry, art, and furniture isn't deductible.

Schedule D is the place where you plug in your profit or loss on the following examples:

- ✔ your coin or stamp collection
- ✔ jewelry and art
- ✔ stocks and bonds
- ✔ your home (if you don't roll over your gain)
- ✔ household furnishings

Although the sale of these assets end up on Schedule D, on some occasions you're going to complete other forms first and then bring your taxable profit or tax-deductible loss to the appropriate line on Schedule D. For example, you report the gain on the sale of your home on Form 2119. Don't worry, we'll point you in the right direction and provide lots of tips on the way.

Tax Basis Background

Before we jump into completing Schedule D, a little background is necessary on gains and losses and how to figure them. When you understand these concepts, Schedule D shouldn't be too difficult. If you already understand these key concepts, you can cruise on ahead to the instructions for completing Schedule D.

If you sold something at a taxable gain or deductible loss, you have to compute its tax basis. *Basis* is the tax system's way of measuring what you paid for your investment in stocks, bonds, or real estate, for example. In addition to helping you to calculate your capital gains and capital losses, your basis is also used to figure deductions for deprecation, casualty losses, and charitable gifts.

For example, if you purchase 100 shares of the Informed Investor's Mutual Fund at $40 per share, your cost basis is considered to be $4,000, or $40 per share. Simple enough. Now suppose that this fund pays a dividend of $2 per share (so you get $200 for your 100 shares) and that you choose to reinvest this dividend into purchasing more shares of the mutual fund. If, at the time of the dividend payment, the fund has increased to $50 per share, your $200 dividend will purchase four more shares. Now you own 104 shares. At $50 per share your 104 shares are worth $5,200. But what's your basis now? Your basis is your original investment ($4,000) plus subsequent investments ($200) for a total of $4,200. Thus, if you sold all your shares now, you'd have a taxable profit of $1,000 (current value of $5,200 less amount invested).

With a home, your basis works the same way. The basis on your home is increased for improvements you make or costs connected in purchasing the property — such as the commission you paid your broker. If you own rental real estate, your basis is reduced by depreciation and any casualty losses you may have deducted (see Chapter 22 for more details).

Property defined

Definitions are the spice of life for IRS agents. Here's an important one.

When most people refer to property as real estate, they mean real estate. But when the IRS talks about property, it could be anything you own such as a stock, bond, car, boat, or computer. So when you see the term *property* on a form, the government is talking about more than the old homestead.

Property you purchased

This tax basis is usually your cost increased by improvements or decreased by depreciation and casualty losses.

Property received as a gift

To figure the basis of property you received as a gift, you must know the donor's basis at the time the gift was made, its *fair market value* (FMV) at the time the gift was made, and any gift tax that the donor paid.

If the FMV at the time of the gift was more than the donor's basis, then your basis for figuring a gain or loss is the donor's basis. For example, suppose that you received as a gift stock that cost your father $5,000, which was worth $12,000 when he gave it you. Your basis for figuring gain or loss is $5,000.

If the FMV at the time of the gift was less than the donor's basis, your basis for figuring a gain is the donor's basis, and your basis for figuring a loss is the fair market value at the time of the gift. In other words the IRS says, "Heads we win, tails we win." For example, say that your father gave you stock that cost him (basis is) $10,000 — but was worth (FMV) $8,000 when he gave it to you. If you sell the stock for $12,000, you have a $2,000 gain (sale price of stock $12,000 - $10,000 donor's basis). If you sell the stock for $7,000, you have a $1,000 loss (sale price of stock $7,000 - $8,000 FMV). If the sale price is between the FMV and the donor's cost ($8,000 and $10,000 in the example), you have neither a gain nor a loss. If your father paid gift tax when he made the gift, a portion of the gift tax he paid is added to your basis.

Property you inherited

Your basis for figuring gain or loss is usually the fair market value on the decedent's date of death. Sometimes — to save on taxes — the executor of an estate is allowed to use an alternative valuation date, which is six months after the date of death. When you inherit something, make sure the executor gives you the estate tax valuation, because when you sell the asset, that figure will be your tax basis.

Property received for services

The amount you are required to include in your income becomes your basis. Suppose that, for putting a deal together, you receive 100 shares of stock valued at $10,000. Because you had to pay tax on the value of the shares, your tax basis for the 100 shares is $10,000.

Property received in a divorce

You use your spouse's basis. Generally, neither spouse is required to pay tax on property transferred as part of a divorce settlement.

What Part Schedule D?

Schedule D is structured into two major parts. Part I is for reporting short-term gains and losses. Part II is for reporting long-term gains and losses. (Parts IV and V on the back page of Schedule D simply replicate Parts I and II, respectively, for those of you with lots of gains and losses.)

If you hold property for one year or less, the gain or loss is *short-term.* If you hold property for more than a year, the gain or loss is *long-term.* You are going to list all your individual capital gains and losses on lines 1 or 9. Line 1 is for the short-term gains and losses, and line 9 is for long-term gains and losses.

Why the distinction? Because the IRS wants to make life complicated. The tax rates for long-term and short-term gains and losses differ. If your net capital gain is a long-term gain, the tax on it can't exceed 28 percent. If the capital gain is short term, the tax on it can be as high as the income tax brackets go (currently 39.6 percent at the federal level).

Schedule D Columns

After you've determined whether the security you sold goes in the short-term (Part I) or long-term (Part II) section, you're ready to work your way across the page. We must say that this is one of the least attractive IRS schedules. For each asset sold, we'll work our way across the page. We'll walk you through an example and then explain how to complete the remaining line numbers.

Details for figuring short-term or long-term

In most cases, whether you've held a security or other asset for 12 months or more or less is obvious. Here are some details that may help in less clear cases.

For securities traded on an established securities market, your holding period begins the day after the trading date you bought the securities and ends on the trading date you sold them. For holding period purposes, ignore the settlement date — which is when you actually pay cash to the broker for a purchase or receive cash from the broker for a sale.

For property you received as a gift, you are considered to have purchased the property on the same day the donor did — and not on the date of the gift if you are using the donor's tax basis as your basis. However, the holding period starts on the date of the gift if you are required to use the fair market value of the property when it was given to you. Property inherited via someone's estate is treated as a sale of a long-term capital asset even if you sold the shares or property the day after you received them. The one-year rule is ignored.

When you purchase an asset such as stocks or bonds by the exercise of an option, the holding period starts the day after the option is exercised — and not on the day you received or purchased the option.

Suppose that you sold 100 shares of General Motors for $4,000 on November 16, 1994. You had paid $6,000 for the shares on November 16, 1992. You have a capital loss of $2,000, and because you held the shares for over a year, it is a long-term loss. Now plug it into Schedule D.

Column (a): Description of the property

100 shares of General Motors

Column (b): Date acquired

11-16-92

Column (c): Date sold

11-16-94

Column (d): Sales price

$4,000

Column (e): Cost or other basis

$6,000

Column (f): Loss

$2,000

Column (g): Gain

[leave blank; sorry you had no gains this time]

Figuring Your Profit or Loss

Now that you understand where the numbers go on the form, where the heck do you get the numbers? The following list tells you where.

✔ **Stocks and bonds.** If you sold a stock or bond, you will receive a Form 1099-B (Proceeds from Broker and Barter Exchange Transactions) or an equivalent from your broker by January 31, 1995. The IRS also gets a copy of this form. Form 1099-B lists the date of every sale and the amount after the broker's commission has been deducted. You enter this information on Form 1040 with Schedule D. The IRS checks to see if it is correct. Just another friendly service by the folks at the IRS.

A redemption or retirement of bonds or notes at their maturity is also considered a sale or trade and also must be reported on Schedule D, whether or not you realized a gain or loss on the redemption.

The tax basis is generally your purchase price plus the broker's commission. If you acquired the shares by gift, your tax basis is that of the donor's basis if sold at a gain and the lower of the donor's basis or the FMV on the date of the gift if sold at a loss, plus any gift tax that was paid. If acquired by inheritance, it is the FMV on the decedent's date of death. If acquired in exchange for services, it is the value that you had to pay tax on when you received the shares.

✔ **Stock dividends and splits.** If you receive additional stock as part of a nontaxable stock dividend or stock split, you must reduce the basis of your original stock. You do this step by dividing the cost of the stock by the total number of shares you now have. You must also reduce your basis when you receive nontaxable cash distributions, because this transaction is considered a return of your investment.

For example, suppose that in 1991 you bought 100 shares of ABC stock for $500, or $5 a share. In 1992 you bought 100 shares of ABC stock for $800, or $8 a share. In 1993 ABC declared a 2-for-1 stock split. You now have 200 shares of stock with a basis of $2.50 a share (200 shares ÷ $500 cost) and 200 shares with a basis of $4 a share (200 shares ÷ $800 cost).

Or suppose that you purchase shares for $10,000 and received a $500 nontaxable dividend. Your tax basis is now $9,500 ($10,000 − $500).

✔ **Identifying shares.** If you buy and sell securities at different times in varying quantities and you cannot definitely identify the securities you sell, the basis of those sold is figured under the *first-in first-out method* — the first securities you acquired are considered the first ones sold.

If you bought 100 shares of GM at $30 and 100 at $50 and then sold 100 shares at $60, you would pay less tax if you used the shares you purchased for $50 as your cost. You can only do this stuff if you specifically tell your broker to sell the shares purchased for $50, otherwise you are deemed to have sold the 100 shares at $30 per share.

✔ **Mutual fund shares.** When you sell shares of a fund, you can average the cost of the shares sold if they were bought at different times — or you can specifically identify the shares that you sold. Remember that the dividends used to purchase additional shares on which you paid tax every year increase your tax basis for determining gain or loss when the shares are sold.

For example, suppose that you bought 1000 shares of a fund for $10,000. Through the years, you received $5,000 in dividends that you used to buy additional shares. Your tax basis is $15,000 ($10,000 original cost plus the $5,000 of dividends received) for the shares you now own.

Now you have all the information you need to tackle your 1994 Schedule D.

Part I, Lines 1-8: Short-Term Capital Gains and Losses

Line 1 is a breeze because you fine-tuned your form skills in the the preceding General Motors example. Now use your very own short-term financial gains and losses as the examples and complete the columns for line 1. If you have more than three items, you can list more on the backside of the schedule.

Line 4: Short-term gain from Forms 2119 and 6252, and short-term gain or (loss) from Forms 4684, 6781, and 8824

All these form numbers! Because they rarely apply to most people, you may as well use them to play the lottery.

Seriously, most people are going to deal with only these forms at some point in their life:

- 2119 (Sale of Your Home); we cover this form later in this chapter under long-term gains or losses, because it is unusual to have a short-term gain or loss on your home.
- 4684 (Casualties and Theft); we cover this form in Chapter 8.

For those of you who are curious, Form 6252 is for installment sales, Form 8824 is for like-kind exchanges, and Form 6781 is for commodity straddles. Enter the short-term gains or losses from these forms on line 4 of Schedule D.

Line 5: Net short-term gain or (loss) from partnerships, S Corporations, and trusts from Schedule(s) K-1

Short-term gains or losses from mutual funds are reported on Form 1099-DIV. And short-term gains or losses from a partnership, an S Corporation, an estate, or a trust are reported on a schedule called a K-1. Enter the short-term gain or loss as indicated on these forms on Schedule B (lines 5 and 7) and then carry this amount over to line 5 of Schedule D (short-term gains and losses only; long-term gains and losses go to line 13).

Line 6: Short-term capital loss carryover

If you had more short-term losses than gains in previous years, the balance is called a *carryover*. If your short-term losses exceeded your long-term gains, you're allowed to deduct up to $3,000 of those losses against your other income and carry over the balance to future years. If you don't have any gains next year, you may deduct $3,000 on next year's Schedule D. You can keep carryover stuff until it is used up. For example, you had a $10,000 short-term loss in 1993 and no long-term gains or losses. You were allowed to write off $3,000 last year, and the $7,000 that you carried over to 1994 is entered on line 6.

Part II, Lines 9-17: Long-Term Capital Gains and Losses

As you did Part I, fill in the columns for your long-term gains and losses. Don't forget, you can use the back if you need room for more than three gains or losses.

Line 12: Gain from Form 4797; long-term gain from Forms 2119, 2439, and 6252; and long-term gain or (loss) from Forms 4684, 6781, and 8824

Here are some more lottery numbers. Everything we said in line 4 applies here — plus Forms 2439 (Notice to Shareholder of Undistributed Capital Gains) and 4797 (Sales of Business Property).

It's worth repeating; you'll probably encounter only the following in your lifetime: 2119 (Sale of Your Home), which is explained later in this chapter, and 4684 (Casualties and Theft), which is described in Chapter 8.

Form 4797

The odds of having to complete any of those other nasty forms are thankfully rare. But just in case you sell a business property, such as a building or office copiers, and have to deal with Form 4797, here are some tips to getting through that form.

First of all, you should know that the reason for a separate form is because the tax treatment of this type of sale is extremely complex. So what's new? Long-term gains are taxed at a maximum rate of 28 percent instead of at the regular rates, which can be as high as 39.6 percent. The government believes that the 28 percent maximum rate is too good a deal — many taxpayers were claiming a depreciation deduction as well as a preferred tax rate.

So Form 4797 was invented. Generally, if you sell a business asset at a profit, the part of the gain that equals the depreciation deductions you took through the years isn't taxed as a capital gain; it's taxed at your regular tax rate. To make this calculation, first you must figure out your tax basis of the property. Your basis is the price you paid minus the total depreciation you've taken over the years.

For example, suppose that you purchased machinery for $10,000 and that you used it in your business. In the three years you owned it, you took depreciation deductions totaling $7,120. This step reduces your tax basis to $2,880 ($10,000 cost – $7,120 depreciation).

Then you figure your profit. Your profit is the price that you sold the property for minus your tax basis. The next step is to figure out what part of that profit is to be taxed at regular rates and what part is to be taxed at the capital gains tax rates. This procedure is known as *depreciation recapture* — you are taxed at regular tax rates (as opposed to the special long-term capital-gain tax rate) on the part of the profit that equals the depreciation deductions you have taken in previous years. Any amount of profit left over is taxed at the capital gains tax rates.

Perhaps you sold that same machinery (in the preceding example) for $5,880. Your profit is $3,000 ($5,880 sale price – $2,880 tax basis). You then subtract the depreciation deductions you have taken, $3,000 – $7,120 = $-4120. If you come up with a negative number, the full profit ($3,000) is taxed at your regular tax rate.

On the other hand, if you sold the machinery for $11,000, your profit would be $8,120 ($11,000 sale price – $2,880 tax basis). Subtract the amount of depreciation you claimed: $8,120 profit – $7,120 depreciation = $1,000. $7,120 (the amount of depreciation you claimed) is taxed at your regular tax rate and the $1,000 that is left over is taxed as a long-term capital gain (if you owned the machinery for more than one year).

For the purposes of depreciation, business property is divided into two types:

✔ auto, business equipment, and machinery

✔ real estate

All the deprecation deducted in the first category is recaptured if the property is sold at a gain. For real estate, depreciation is recaptured if there is a profit when it is sold, depending on if you started to depreciate it before 1981 or between 1982 and 1986. Real estate that you started to depreciate after 1986 isn't subject to the recapture rules.

The depreciation recapture rules don't apply to business property sold at a loss. The loss is deductible from your income without limitation. The part of the profit that is recaptured and taxed at your regular tax rate is carried over from Form 4797 to Form 1040 (line 14). The long-term capital gain portion is carried over from Form 4797 to Schedule D (line 12). Use the long-term capital gain worksheet in Chapter 13 (in "Line 38: Tax") to make sure you don't pay more than 28 percent tax on long-term capital gains!

This stuff may probably be more than you care to know about the sale of business property. But before you even contemplate the sale of business property, seek advice. If the amount involved is large, make sure you're getting the best advice possible.

Form 6252

Here's the story on Form 6252 (Installment Sale Income). Suppose that you sold a parcel of land for $60,000 in 1994. You paid $15,000 for it and will receive $10,000 in 1994 — and $10,000 a year for the next five years. You don't report the $45,000 profit you made in 1994. You report a percentage of the profit as each installment is made.

You report the $10,000 you receive every year on Form 6252, but you only pay tax on 75 percent of what you received, or $7,500. The $2,500 you don't pay tax on is the recovery of your cost. The $7,500 profit you owe tax on is transferred to Schedule D.

Additionally, you can elect out of the installment method and report the entire gain in the year of sale. You may want to go this way if you have a great deal of itemized deductions that would be wasted because they are more than your income (or if you are in an Alternative Minimum Tax situation).

If you have more deductions than income, those excees deductions are going to waste. Don't throw them out like garbage. For example, say you have $10,000 in salary income and personal exemptions and itemized deductions come to $55,000. You could report another $45,000 of income before you have to pay a dime in tax. So reporting all the income from an installment sale in the year of the sale would make sense in this example.

Line 13: Net long-term gain or (loss) from partnerships, S Corporations, estates, and trusts from Schedule (s) K-1

This is similar to the information for line 5. You report long-term gains and losses as indicated on Form 1099-DIV and Schedule K-1 from the partnerships, S Corporations, estates, and trusts on line 13.

Line 14: Capital gain distributions

Mutual fund distributions are reported on Form 1099-DIV. Capital distribution received from a partnership, an S Corporation, or an estate or trust are reported on a schedule called a K-1. You enter these distributions on Schedule B (lines 5 and 7) and then carry this amount over to line 14 on Schedule D.

Line 15: Long-term capital loss carryover

Your long-term capital losses that couldn't be deducted in previous years because you didn't have any capital gains in those years are entered here.

Part III, Lines 18-19b: Summary of Parts I and II

Hey, this part should be easy, right?

Line 18: Combine lines 8 and 17 (capital losses)

If your capital losses exceed your capital gains as reported on line 18 of Schedule D, you can deduct up to $3,000 of that loss ($1,500 if married and filing separately) from your other income. Any remaining loss after deducting the $3,000 is carried over to the next year and applied to capital gains. If there aren't any gains, you can deduct $3,000 in 1995 with any remaining balance carried over to future years until the loss is used up.

For example, suppose that you and your spouse sold securities in 1994 that resulted in a capital loss of $7,000. You had no other capital transactions. On your joint 1994 return you can deduct $3,000. The unused part of the loss, $4,000 ($7,000 – $ 3,000) can be carried over to 1995. If your capital loss had been $2,000, your capital loss deduction would have been $2,000. You would have no carryover to 1995.

Note: Capital losses can't be carried over after a taxpayer's death. They are deductible only on the final income tax return. The capital loss limits ($3,000 a year) apply in this situation, too. An unused capital loss of someone who died can't be deducted by the decedent's estate or by the heirs.

Don't overpay your capital gains tax

The maximum tax rate for long-term capital gains is 28 percent. However, you can end up paying more if you aren't careful. If this occurs, your only defense is if the computer at the IRS service picks this up and recomputes your tax and sends you a refund. But if the computer is lazy, this may not happen.

So if you don't want to pay more than 28 percent on your long-term gains, check to see if your taxable income for your filing status is over the amounts shown in Table 11-1. You find your taxable income on Form 1040 (line 37), of course!

Table 11-1 Maximum Tax on Long-Term Capital Gains

Filing Status	Taxable Income
Single	$55,100
Married filing jointly or qualifying widow(er)	$91,850
Married filing separately	$45,925
Head of household	$78,700

If your taxable income exceeds the amounts for your filing status in Table 11-2, you are going to have to fill out the long-term capital gains worksheet in Chapter 13 (in "Line 38: Tax") to make sure that you don't pay more than 28 percent. Many taxpayers struggle with this worksheet. Others pay someone to do it, or they buy a tax software program to make the calculation. You paid good money for this book, so that's why we put in the schedule. Have a go at Chapter 13!

Important Stuff to Know about Schedule D

If you sold your home, made an investment that went sour, or lent money to a friend, here's what to do to reduce your tax bill.

Sale of your home

Homes are selling again, and it's about time. But if you're itching to unload your place and move on to something a little more palatial, beware of the tax man.

The basic rules when selling a house are simple. You can put off paying capital gains taxes on any profit from the sale of your house as long as you buy a new one for the same price or more. Then when you hit age 55 — a time when many people trade down to smaller homes — you get an important one-time tax break: If you're buying a less expensive home, the first $125,000 of your profit is automatically free from Uncle Sam's clutches.

But you have to know more than these basic rules if you really want to cut your tax bill. Like other parts of the tax law, there are traps you must steer clear of. Otherwise, what you thought was a tax shelter can quickly turn into a tax nightmare.

Nightmare on Elm Street

First of all, you must understand that there's no time for dawdling. When you sell your principal residence, you've got two years to buy or build a new one and move in. That's the crucial part. Not only must you buy another home, you've got to occupy it if you want to roll over your profit. Unlike a penalty for filing a late tax return (which can be excused for reasonable causes such as illness), there are no exceptions to the occupancy rule. The Tax Court is full of cases where hapless taxpayers found out that merely moving their furniture and personal belongings into their new home didn't cut it.

Even George Bush flubbed this one. Back when he was elected Vice-President, he sold his Texas home and bought the Kennebunkport estate, thinking he could roll over his profit. Nothing doing, said the IRS. His permanent residence, officially at least, was the Vice-Presidential mansion, not Maine.

If you buy before you sell

The two-year rule is also in effect when you buy a home before selling your current one. The day you close on the second place, the meter starts running: You've got 24 months to sell the first house or face capital gains taxes on your profit from it.

But there is one exception to the two-year rule. If you're living abroad before the two-year period expires, you get a time-out. For example, let's say you sell your home on June 1, 1994. Your employer transfers you to France a year later, and you still haven't bought another home. You return to the States on June 1, 1996. Luckily for you, that year overseas is wiped from your IRS slate (*magnifique!*). Now you've got until June 1, 1997 to buy a new place. Careful, though. The maximum time-out is two years. If you're going to stay abroad for longer than that, you'd better think about buying a place over there. After all, there's no requirement that your new home be located in the U.S.

Although there is no limit on the number of times you can roll over profits from the sale of your home, keep in mind this important detail: You're allowed only one rollover in any two-year period. If you buy and sell principal residences more than once in two years, the IRS views the last house purchased as the replacement for the first one. The second sale stands on its own, and if there's a profit, you've got to pay tax on it. The only exception to this rule is if you've been transferred to a new location for your job.

Hey, IRS, I sold my house!

To let the IRS know you've sold your house, use Form 2119 when you file your 1040. The form asks whether you plan to replace your home within the two-year replacement period. The natural response is to say yes. But if the replacement period expires and you haven't bought a new home, you should know that you'll have to file an amended return for the year of the sale, paying tax on the profit — plus interest.

Some important things to know about filling out this form:

- ✔ In Part II, you report the gain on the sale of your house.

- ✔ On line 9, you have to check yes or no if you haven't replaced your house but plan to do so in the two-year replacement period.

- ✔ You use Part III to elect the one-time $125,000 exclusion for people over 55.

- ✔ You use Part IV to compute the tax basis of your new home if you deferred part of the gain on your old home. For example, if you are deferring a $50,000 gain and the cost of your new home is $200,000, its tax basis is reduced to $150,000. And that's the figure you are going to use for determining profit or loss when you sell the new house.

You'll also have to amend your state return when the two-year period expires and you haven't replaced your home. This procedure can be especially painful for the unsuspecting. Suppose that you paid $200,000 for a home in Texas, a state that has no income tax, and you sold it for $500,000. You postponed paying taxes on that $300,000 profit when you bought a home in New York City for $500,000. But then you sell the house in New York for $500,000 and move to Florida, which also has no income tax. If you don't buy a home there within two years, you'll get socked with around $40,000 in New York taxes on the $300,000 profit — even though not a cent of it was earned in the Empire State.

How the IRS judges your profit

Here's how the rollover system normally works: When you sell a house and buy another, the profit you made on the first house goes to reduce the cost basis of your second house. Suppose that you make $100,000 selling your house and buy another one for $400,000. The government views your cost basis on the $400,000 home as only $300,000. Fine. That consideration has no effect on you for now. But several years later, when you're ready to sell that second house for $500,000 and buy a smaller home, the IRS will calculate your profit from the sale as $200,000 — that is, the difference between your selling price and your cost basis.

In recent years, with real estate prices falling, many people have sold their homes at a loss. Many of them wonder if they can use that loss to increase the cost basis of their next home, thus reducing their profit when they sell it. Unfortunately, the answer is no.

However, any improvements you make to your house increase the cost basis. What constitutes an improvement? Anything that adds to the value of your house or prolongs its life. Drapery rods, venetian blinds, termite-proofing, and shrubbery all fit the bill. If you own a condo or co-op, your cost basis also includes special assessments to improve the building, such as renovating the lobby or installing a new heating system. Co-op owners get an additional boost, because the part of their maintenance charges that goes to paying off the co-op's mortgage can also be added to their cost basis.

What happens when you sell your place for a profit and buy a less expensive home? If you're under 55, two years later you'll probably have to get out your checkbook and pay some capital gains tax. But don't give up all hope. Within the first two years of selling your old place, any renovations and improvements you make on the new home will directly cut your capital gains taxes. Assume that you sold your house for $400,000, at a $150,000 profit, and bought a $200,000 fix-up special. If you sunk $150,000 into improving it within the first two years of moving in, that move would cut your capital gains on the first place by $100,000. You'd owe taxes on only $50,000 of your profit, plus interest because of the two-year delay.

55 is a special birthday

You can completely escape the tax on up to $125,000 of profit when you're 55 or older on the date of sale. This is a once-in a-lifetime opportunity. But remember, a contract to sell your home is not a sale. A sale occurs when the title to your home has been transferred to its new owners. Missing the age requirement by one day is as bad as missing it by ten years. So if you're about to turn 55, go ahead and enter into a contract to sell your home, but postpone the closing until after your birthday. It'll give you something extra to celebrate. One more tip: On the date of sale, the house you're selling must have been your principal residence for three of the past five years. Otherwise, you don't get that $125,000 exclusion.

Married couples get only one exclusion, unfortunately. And if one spouse used the exclusion before he or she married, it's gone. If you weren't married, you both would get a $125,000 exclusion. (And only one spouse has to be 55, not both.)

Renting before you sell

As a general rule, if you convert your home to rental property and later sell it for profit, you can't roll over the gain or take advantage of the one-time exclusion. But that's not always the case. If you've been forced to rent out your home because you can't find a buyer, you're covered. In one case, the U.S. Tax Court allowed an owner to postpone his gain on a place he'd been renting out for 13 years.

Becoming a landlord isn't the only way out of a jam. If you've bought a new house and can't find a buyer for your old place, you should know that the IRS allowed one taxpayer to form a Sub-Chapter S Corporation — an entity that doesn't pay federal taxes — and sell the home to the corporation before the two years were up. Even though you are in effect selling the home to yourself, the gain will be postponed if you sell it for a price the IRS deems reasonable. True, incorporating will cost you anywhere from a few hundred to a couple of thousand dollars in legal fees. But think of all the money you'll save in capital gains taxes. However, check with your tax advisor.

Home office rule

If you use your home partly for business, you can't postpone the entire profit. Only the portion of your home used as your personal residence qualifies. In the year of the sale, tax must be paid on the profit from the portion used for your business. However, like just about every other section of the tax law, there is one exception: If in the year of the sale you didn't use any part of your home for business, you can postpone the entire profit. But be careful. If you plan to use the $125,000 exclusion, remember that your home must have been your principal residence for three of the past five years. If you used part of your home for business for more than two of those five years, you're snagged: Only the residential part of your profit qualifies for the exclusion.

Worthless securities

You felt certain company X was going to make a comeback, so you invested $15,000. But you were wrong. Not only has company X failed to make this comeback, but its shares are no longer even being quoted in the morning's paper.

Great, so at least $15,000 is a write-off, right? No. The problem with this scenario is that you must be able to prove with an identifiable event that your investment is in fact *completely* worthless. Being partially worthless won't cut it. In one case, bondholders in a company canceled 30 percent of the face value of their bonds to keep the company afloat. But they couldn't deduct the portion of the debt they canceled because their investment hadn't become completely worthless. Likewise, the fact that the shares of company are no longer being quoted does not make them worthless.

We wish we could tell you that convincing the IRS that you are entitled to write off your $15,000 investment is as easy as losing it. It's not — and this is an area of the law that's more confusing than most. You may think that bankruptcy, going out of business, liquidation, the appointment of a receiver, or insolvency would indicate that your investment no longer had any value. But these events only prove that the company is in financial trouble, not that its shareholders won't receive anything in liquidation. In order to claim a deduction for worthless securities, your investment must be completely worthless.

When is an investment worthless?

As a general rule, you can say that an investment is worthless when a company is so hopelessly insolvent that it ceases doing business or it goes into receivership, leaving nothing for its stockholders. If you are not sure, one source worth checking is Commerce Clearing House. This outfit publishes an annual list of worthless securities as part of its "Capital Changes Reports." Most major brokerage firms and public libraries subscribe to this service, or you can reach the company directly at 800-TELL-CCH. Recent high-profile listings include Continental Airline Holdings, Ames Department Stores, and the late Robert Maxwell's media empire, Maxwell Communication Corp.

If proving when unmarketable shares in a company actually became worthless is so difficult, why not lock in a loss by finding some accomplice — the broker who sold them to you, for example — to take the shares off your hands for a penny apiece? Nice try, but no go. A number of taxpayers have attempted to structure "sales" in this fashion, but both the IRS and the Tax Court have denied the losses because these sales weren't considered legitimate. Instead, the taxpayers were told to hang on to their investments and deduct them only when they became certifiably worthless. In other words, they were back to square one.

Nonbusiness bad debts

Suppose that you lent your best friend $2,500 on New Year's Eve and you haven't seen him since New Year's Day. All is not lost. You can deduct the $2,500. This news comes as a surprise to many people, because usually you can deduct losses only on investment and business transactions. But you must be able to prove that there was a valid debt, that the debt is worthless, and that you previously paid tax on the money you lent.

What is worthless? As with securities, there must be some identifiable event — such as bankruptcy, legal action, or the disappearance of the debtor — to prove you can't collect what you're owed. You don't necessarily have to sue the debtor or even threaten to take legal action. This is one of the few instances where the IRS is on your side, not your lawyer's! The IRS realizes that taking someone hopelessly in debt to court would only result in your lawyer being paid, not you.

The right to sue

But to prove you've got valid debt, you should be able to show that you've got a right to sue. This situation creates a special problem for loans to family members. The IRS tends to view such loans as gifts. So if you had your brother sign a promissory note and put up collateral when you lent him money, you would be able to prevail if the IRS ever questioned whether it was a valid debt. Yet, as you probably know, most dealings between family members are done a little more casually than that.

Is the debt deductible?

Finally, to establish that a debt is deductible, you must have paid tax on what you lent. Suppose that you worked in a local bookstore in anticipation of being paid later. The bookstore went out of business and you weren't paid. Sorry. Because you never received this income and didn't report it on your tax return, you're not entitled to a deduction if it's not paid.

You deduct nonbusiness bad debts on good old Schedule D as short-term losses, regardless of how long the money was owed. If you don't have capital gains to offset the deduction, you can deduct $3,000 of the loss and carry the balance over to next year, just like with other investment losses. Additionally, you must attach a statement to your return explaining the following details:

- ✔ the nature of the debt
- ✔ the name of the debtor and if there is any business or family relationship
- ✔ the date that the debt became due
- ✔ the efforts made to collect the debt
- ✔ the reason for determining that the debt is worthless

Wash sales

Suppose that you own a stock that has declined in value. You think it will recover, but you want to deduct the money you lost. If you sell the stock and buy back the shares within 30 days of the sale, you can't deduct the loss. The loss is deducted when you sell the new shares.

Chapter 12

Supplemental Income and Losses: Schedule E

In This Chapter

▶ Defining supplemental income

▶ Completing Schedule E

▶ Discussing tax shelters

Don't let the heading "Supplemental Income" throw you. That's just IRS-speak for the income you receive from rental property or royalties or through partnerships, S Corporations, trusts, and estates. To report your rental or royalty income, you use Schedule E, which is laid out in the form of a profit or loss statement (income and expenses). From your income you subtract your expenses. The remainder is your *net income*, the income that you have to pay taxes on. If you have a loss, the rules get a little sticky as to whether you can deduct it.

Remember that if you're a self-employed taxpayer receiving royalties, such as a musician, you use Schedule C. The information in this chapter applies to people who receive royalties and are not self-employed. For example, George Gershwin received royalties from "Porgy and Bess." But he has passed away, and now his heirs receive royalties that must be reported on Schedule E.

You can input the income and expenses for up to three rental properties or royalty incomes (in columns A, B, and C) on Schedule E. If you have more than three entries, you can use as many Schedule Es as you need — but fill in the total for all the properties on only one Schedule E.

Part I, Lines 3-4: Income

If you receive rent or royalties, you should receive Form 1099-MISC. Box 1 is for rent and Box 2 is for royalties.

As a landlord, you might wonder how some unusual cases of rent are handled regarding whether you count them as income or not. Rent paid in advance, for example, is counted as rent. If you sign a lease in December 1994 and collect January's rent of $1,000, this amount is included in 1994 rent income on this schedule even though it applies to 1995's rent. Security deposits that you must return are not rental income. And if your tenant pays you to cancel the lease, the amount you receive is rent. It's not considered a tax-free payment for damages. Although expenses paid by the tenant are considered rental income, you are entitled to deduct those expenses. Finally, if you are a good Samaritan and charge a relative or friend less than the fair rental value, your deductions for depreciation and expenses can't exceed the rent you collect.

Lines 5-18: Expenses

On these lines you can tabulate the amounts you are allowed to deduct. Now, don't you wish that you were a better bookkeeper? If you have good records, you can save a tidy sum. The expense lines apply to both royalties and rents.

Line 5: Advertising

You are allowed to deduct newspaper ads, for example, if you had to run ads for your property. Same goes if you had building signs made.

Line 6: Auto and travel

Travel to inspect your rental property is deductible. But if you live in Buffalo and go to Florida in January to inspect a vacation home that you rent out part of the time, be prepared for a battle with the IRS. See the guidelines for deducting travel in Chapter 8 ("Line 20") and your auto in Chapter 10 ("Line 10").

Line 7: Cleaning and maintenance

You can deduct your costs for cleaning and maintenance, such as your monthly fee for the window washer and the guy who tunes up your furnace before the cold weather sets in.

Line 8: Commissions

You can deduct commissions paid to a real estate broker to find a tenant. The norm is 5 to 10 percent.

Line 9: Insurance

We hope that you carry insurance to protect against your building burning down, lawsuits, and other perils such as floods and earthquakes. You get to deduct the cost of such policies. One tricky area to be aware of is if you pay for an insurance premium that covers more than one year. In this case, you deduct the portion of the premium that applies to each year's Schedule E. For example, suppose that in 1994 you pay a $900 premium that covers a three-year period. You deduct $300 in 1994, 1995, and 1996.

Line 10: Legal and other professional fees

Legal fees incurred in the purchase of the property must be added to the cost of the building and deducted as part of your depreciation deduction (coming later). Legal fees for preparing a lease are deductible. And the part of your tax-preparation fee used to prepare this Schedule E is deductible.

Line 11: Management fees

You can deduct the costs of managing the property — collecting the rent, seeing to all the repairs, paying a management company (if you have one), and so on.

Line 12: Mortgage interest paid to banks

This amount comes right off of Form 1098 (Mortgage Interest Statement), which you get from the bank that holds the mortgage. The bank will send you this statement by January 31.

Line 13: Other interest

If the person you purchased the property from provided the financing and holds a mortgage on the property, the interest is entered here because this is where the interest that wasn't paid to financial institutions goes. All the fees you paid when you took out the mortgage are deducted over the duration of the loan. You also put the interest on a second mortgage here, as well as the interest on short-term installment loans for the purchase of appliances.

Unlike with a personal residence, points and fees to obtain a mortgage on rental property aren't deductible in the year you pay them. You must write off these amounts over the term of the loan and deduct them on this line. If you didn't receive a Form 1098, enter the interest you paid on this line.

Line 14: Repairs

Repairs are deductible in full. Improvements may be deducted over 27.5 years (see Chapter 10 to obtain the rate of depreciation you can claim every year). A repair — such as fixing a leak in the roof — keeps your property in good operating condition. It doesn't materially add to the value of the property or prolong its life. An improvement such as adding an entire new roof, on the other hand, adds to the value or prolongs its life.

Line 15: Supplies

You can deduct things such as cleaning supplies, light bulbs, and small items that you buy at a hardware store.

Line 16: Taxes

This line includes real estate taxes on the property. If you employ a superintendent or a janitor, enter here the Social Security and unemployment taxes that you have to pay. The bank holding the mortgage will send you an annual mortgage statement that gives you the tax information. The Social Security and unemployment taxes will be listed on your quarterly payroll tax return.

Line 17: Utilities

Why don't you just go ahead and enter your electric, gas, fuel, water, and sewer charges, and phone costs for your property here? We would.

Line 18: Other

This is one of those catch-all lines for things whose description doesn't fit on the preceding lines. For example, you can enter costs such as gardening permits, and any other expenses that you cannot find a home for on lines 5-17.

Line 20: Depreciation expense or depletion

The tax law allows you to claim a yearly tax deduction for depreciation. You can't depreciate land. So for example, you can depreciate only 85 percent of your cost (because at least fifteen percent of a building's purchase price has to be allocated to land). You can make this allocation based on the assessed value for the land and the building or on a real estate appraisal. You compute your depreciation deduction on Form 4562 (Depreciation and Amortization), and you attach this form to your 1040 only if you first started to claim a deduction in 1994. The depreciation rates are available in Chapter 10.

Line 22: Income or loss from rental real estate or royalty properties

The first part is just basic arithmetic. Go ahead and subtract line 21 from your income from line 3 or 4. If you have a positive number, you have supplemental income; if your total is negative, you have a loss. On this line you'll notice a reference to Form 6198. This refers to the wonderful at-risk rules; don't concern yourself with these rules unless you were lucky enough to get a mortgage where you are not personally liable for the payments.

Line 23: Deductible rental real estate loss

If your real estate property showed a loss for the year (line 22), you may not actually be able to claim that entire loss on your tax return. If you didn't show a loss, skip ahead to the next line.

Line 23 is where you enter how much of the loss on line 22 can be deducted. Rental real estate is considered a passive activity and normally you have to complete Form 8582 (Passive Activity Loss Limitations) to determine the portion, if any, that you are allowed to deduct. However, if you meet *all* the following conditions, you're spared from Form 8582 (keep your fingers crossed):

- ✔ Rental real estate is the only passive activity you're involved in. (Remember that *passive activity* is a business or investment where you act as a silent partner — you're not actively involved.)

- ✔ You actively participated in making management decisions or arranged for others to provide services such as repairs.

- ✔ Your rental real estate loss did not exceed $25,000 — or $12,500 if you are married and filing separately.

- ✔ You didn't have rental or passive activity losses that you could not deduct in a prior year.

- ✔ If you are married and filing separately, you must have lived apart from your spouse for the entire year.

- ✔ Your modified AGI (see the following worksheet) is less than $100,000 (or $50,000 if you are married and filing separately).

If you meet all of the above six criteria, congratulations — you can skip the dreaded form 8582 and write your deductible real estate loss right here on line 23.

If you have to fill out Form 8582 in order to compute your rental loss(es) on Schedule E (line 22) because your Modified AGI is over the limit (or you were involved in other passive activities), you have to be familiar with tax shelter rules and other rules that allow you to deduct up to $25,000 of losses from rental real estate that you actively manage.

If Form 8582 applies to you, O taxpayer you do need a tax advisor!

Worksheet to determine if you need to use Form 8582

This little worksheet will get you to your modified AGI so that you can determine if it's over the limits we just mentioned. If it is, off you go to Form 8582.

1. AGI from Form 1040 (line 31) $ _____
2. Less: taxable portion of Social Security (line 20b)   _____
           passive activity income (line 17)   _____
3. Subtract line 2 from line 1   _____
4. Your IRA deductions (lines 23a and b)   _____
5. One-half of self-employment tax (line 25)   _____
6. Passive activity losses (line 17)   _____
7. Interest on Form 8815   _____
8. Add lines 4-7   _____
9. Add line 8 to line 3 = Modified AGI   _____

(If this line is under $100,000, or $50,000 if you are married and filing separately, you don't have to go to Form 8582.)

If you have only rental or royalty income or losses, you don't need to turn the page of your Schedule E. You're done! After you follow all those little instructions about what lines to add, take the amount from line 26 over to your 1040 (line 17).

But, if you must continue, bear up. You're halfway there.

The $25,000 exemption

Here's why that $100,000 modified AGI figure is so important. You can deduct up to $25,000 of the losses you incurred in rental real estate if you actively participate in the management of the property and own at least 10 percent — which means you have to make management decisions regarding the approval of new tenants and rental terms, approving expenditures, and similar decisions. So if you turn an apartment or home that you own over to a real estate agent to rent and manage, the $25,000 loss deduction rule doesn't apply. You might be able to pull off this deduction, though, if you reserve the right to approve all expenditures and improvements that have to be made.

Now for the ever-present exception to the general rule. If your income exceeds $100,000, the $25,000 limit is reduced by 50 cents for every dollar of income over $100,000. When your income reaches $150,000, the $25,000 allowance is completely phased out.

The $25,000 figure is reduced to $12,500 if you are married filing separately and living apart from your spouse for the entire year; the phaseout begins at $50,000 of your AGI (not $100,000) and is completely phased out at $75,000.

If you lived with your spouse at any time during the year and are filing separate returns, you can't use the $12,500 exception (half of $25,000). Please don't ask us about the reason for this one. You compute on Form 8582 the portion of the $25,000 allowance you are entitled to.

Two other points are worth making. First, you must own at least ten percent of the property. And second, to see if your income exceeds $100,000 ($50,000 if you are married and filing separately), take your adjusted gross income from Form 1040 (line 31) but don't include

- ✔ any passive activity losses or income
- ✔ the taxable portion of your Social Security
- ✔ deductible IRA contributions
- ✔ the deduction for one half of your self-employment tax from Form 1040 (line 25)

Interest on U.S savings bonds that you used to pay excludable tuition is included for purposes of determining the $100,000 amount.

The Tax Shelter Rules

If you rent your vacation home or part of a two-family house, you are operating a tax shelter — and you always thought that tax shelters were something that only movie stars and high-income athletes got involved in!

In 1986 Congress decided to kill tax shelters and passed an anti-tax shelter law. As a result, a loss from a *passive activity* (that's what a tax shelter is now called in IRS jargon) can be deducted only if you have income from another passive activity. If you don't, the loss is *disallowed*. Disallowed losses are suspended and carried over to future years. If you have passive income (that's income from a shelter) next year, you can deduct the loss. If you don't have passive income next year, you keep carrying over the loss until you do, or until you sell the property or your interest in the tax shelter.

TIP

Vacation homes

Determining the expenses you can deduct on a vacation home is no fun in the sun because you have to allocate the operating expenses depending on how many days you rent your home and on how many days you use it. What is deductible and what's not is based on the following three mind-numbing rules:

Rule 1. If you rent your home for fewer than 15 days, you don't have to report the rent you collected and none of the operating expenses are deductible. Your mortgage interest and real estate taxes are deducted as itemized deductions.

Rule 2. If your personal use of your home is more than the greater of 14 days or 10 percent of the total days it is rented, then the property isn't considered rental property and the expenses allocated to the rental period can't exceed the rental income. The expenses that are allocated to the rental period, but which cannot be deducted, are carried forward to future years and can be deducted to the extent of your rental income or until you sell the property. If you have a profit on the rental of a vacation home, this rule doesn't apply.

In figuring the rental days, count only the days the home was actually rented. The days you held the property out for rent but it was not rented do not count as a rental day. After making this computation, you allocate your rental expenses based on the total number of days rented divided by the total number of rented days plus the days you used it. For example, suppose that your beach cottage was rented for 36 days and you used it for 36 days. In such a case, 50 percent of the operating expenses for the year would be allocated to the rental period, 36 days rented ÷ 72 days (36 rented and 36 personal days). Don't count any days you work in effect full-time to repair the property as personal days.

The Tax Court is on your side when it comes to deducting mortgage interest and taxes, which don't have to be allocated under the preceding formula. You can allocate this stuff on a daily basis. So, in the example, ten percent (36 rental days ÷ 365) of your taxes and mortgage interest would have to be allocated to the rental period. This process means that a larger amount of your other rental expenses can be deducted from your rental income and (better yet) you get to deduct 90 percent of your mortgage interest and taxes as an itemized deduction instead of 50 percent.

Rule 3. If the personal use of your residence doesn't exceed 14 days or 10 percent of the rental days it is rented, then your vacation home is treated as rental property, and if your rental expenses exceed your rental income they are deductible if you have other passive income (or if the $25,000 special deduction allowance permits). You still have to allocate the expenses of running the property between personal and rental days.

For example, suppose that you have a rental loss of $5,000 in 1994 and no other passive income. The loss is carried over to 1995. If in 1995 the property generates a $4,000 profit, you can deduct $4,000 of the suspended loss and carry over the $1,000 balance to 1996. If you sell the property in 1996, the $1,000 can be deducted — even if you don't have a rental income in 1996.

If you have two or more passive activities, you combine them to determine if a loss in one can be used to offset a profit in another. For example, suppose that you own one building that you rent out at a $6,000 loss and another building which produces a $5,000 profit. You can use $5,000 of the $6,000 loss to offset the $5,000 profit from the second building, and the $1,000 balance is carried over to 1995.

If you have a passive activity loss, you compute the amount of the loss that can be deducted or that has to be carried over to future years on Form 8582 (Passive Activity Loss Limitations). On this form, you combine your passive activity losses and income. If income exceeds losses, you have a deduction. If it doesn't, you have a suspended loss. But remember: If you sell the property, the loss, together with any suspended losses, is deductible.

Part II, Lines 27-31: Income or Loss From Partnerships and S Corporations

The average taxpayer finds Page 2 of the Schedule E the most daunting. On this page you report income and losses from partnerships, S Corporations, estates, and trusts. Instead of the nice, long, symmetrical columns of Page 1, Schedule E's flipside looks as if it had been designed to confuse rather than clarify.

Partnerships and S Corporations are not taxable entities. The income, gains, losses, and deductions of a partnership or an S Corporation are passed through to each partner or shareholder based on the ownership percentage. Instead of a 1099, each partner or shareholder receives a form called a K-1 that reflects the income, loss, or deduction that belongs on the return. For a partnership, it's Form 1065 K-1, while for an S Corporation it's Form 1120S K-1.

Line 27a: Name . . . and so on!

Now you have to deal not only with line numbers, but also letters! So here's what you enter in the following columns:

(a) Enter the name of the Partnership or S Corporation.

(b) Enter "P" for Partnership or "S" for S Corporation.

(c) Put a check here if it's a foreign partnership.

(d) Scribble in the identification number for the partnership or S Corporation. (Hey, this is pretty easy so far!)

(e) and (f) Oops, we spoke too soon. Did you notice the question "Investment At Risk"? Here you have to check if "all is at risk" (e) or "some is not at risk" (f). The purpose of the at-risk rules is to prevent investors from deducting losses in excess of what they actually stand to lose.

This rule prevents you from investing $10,000 and deducting $30,000 if the partnership lost an additional $20,000 that you're not personally responsible for. The K-1 that you receive indicates what you're at risk for (see Item F). The at-risk rules are extremely complex. This is one area where we recommend that you see a tax advisor for help.

Passive income and loss

(g) The K-1 indicates a passive activity with a little check in the box — limited partner or publicly-tracked partnership. If you have a passive activity loss, enter the loss on Form 8582. On this form you compute your allowable passive loss and then enter that amount in this column.

(h) Enter the income from the passive activity in this lovely column.

Nonpassive income and loss

(i) If you're a working partner in the partnership or a shareholder in an S Corporation, line 1 of the K-1 shows your share of the loss you're entitled to deduct. Enter that amount here.

(j) The wonderful K-1 also shows the amount of the partnership's or S Corporation's special depreciation that you get to deduct — line 9 of the K-1 for Partnerships and line 8 for S Corporations. Enter it here.

(k) Enter the amount of income from Schedule K-1 in this column — it's the amount on line 1.

Part III, Lines 32-36: Income or Loss from Estates and Trusts

In this part you enter your income or loss from an estate or trust that you're a beneficiary of. You should receive a K-1 from either the estate or trust, and the K-1 also indicates income such as dividend, interest, and capital gains. Interest and dividends go to Schedule B (see Chapter 9), and capital gains go to Schedule D (see Chapter 11). It's the ordinary income or loss on the K-1 that goes on Schedule E. Maybe that's why the IRS gives us only two lines to work with in this part of the form (and last year there were *three* lines!). But all those columns once again!

Line 32a: Name . . . and so on!

(a) Carefully inscribe the name of the estate or trust.

(b) Enter the identification number.

Passive income and loss

(c) Here you put the passive loss from Form 8582.

(d) Enter the passive income from the K-1s.

Nonpassive income and loss

(e) and (f) Because most heirs or beneficiaries don't participate in the management of the estate or trust, it is very rare for an heir or beneficiary to have nonpassive income or loss.

Part IV, line 37: Income or Loss from Real Estate Mortgage Investment Conduits

If you've invested in a REMIC, which is a company that holds a pool of mortgages, you'll most likely receive interest on Form 1099-INT or Form 1099-OID (Original Issue Discount). But if you received Form 1066, Schedule Q, enter the amounts on that form on line 37.

Part V: Summary

Unless you're a farmer and file Form 4835, everything on Schedule E is pulled together on line 40. Do the math and transfer the amount to Form 1040 (line 17), and take a break or something. You deserve it.

The Rest of the 1040 and Other Yucky Forms

*W*hen you turned your 1040 over you probably had that same sickening feeling you often had as a student when you turned over an exam … just to find so much more junk that you thought you would never finish before the bell rang! But we think you can beat the bell this time if you take it line-by-line, relax, and let us help you. For some of you, the worst is over, for others, well, you've still got some nasty schedules ahead of you.

The first line on this page is a piece of cake. To complete line 32 at the top of the back page, turn your return back over and copy the entry you made on line 31 — they are both your adjusted gross income!

Tax Computation

You might think that because this section is entitled tax computation, you're going to calculate how much tax you owe or will be refunded and be on your merry way (see Figure 13-1). Wrong! What you're going to do here is to calculate your taxable income — that is, the income that you actually owe tax on for the year. This won't be the finish line, however, because there may be some "other credits" (these are good because they reduce your tax bill) and some "other taxes" (these are obviously bad). Then you'll have to settle up with the IRS and figure in the "payments" section whether you paid too much, too little, or just the right amount of tax during the year (yeah, that part will be a little like Goldilocks, the three bears and the porridge tasting stuff!)

Line 33a

On line 33a, check the box if either you or your spouse is over 65 or blind. If you check one of those boxes and you are not itemizing your deductions, see the work-sheet in Chapter 8 ("Over 65 or blind") to compute your increased itemized deductions.

If you check box 33b (your parent or someone else can claim you as a dependent), the standard deduction you are entitled to is limited. You're going to have to use the worksheet for dependents in Chapter 8 ("Standard deduction for dependents") to figure your allowable standard deduction.

Lines 34-35: the big choice

This section can be a complicated line so don't make a quick decision between the two choices the IRS offers for "deductions." Either choice is good in the sense that the result will reduce your taxable income — the income that you owe tax on. HOWEVER, and this a big however, you may be cheating yourself if you automatically jump into the easier of the two choices to take the so-called "standard deduction."

Form 1040 (1994) Page 2

Tax Computation

(See page 23.)

32 Amount from line 31 (adjusted gross income) 32

33a Check if: ☐ You were 65 or older, ☐ Blind; ☐ Spouse was 65 or older, ☐ Blind.
Add the number of boxes checked above and enter the total here . . . . ▶ 33a

b If your parent (or someone else) can claim you as a dependent, check here . ▶ 33b ☐

c If you are married filing separately and your spouse itemizes deductions or you are a dual-status alien, see page 23 and check here. . . . ▶ 33c ☐

34 Enter the larger of your:
Itemized deductions from Schedule A, line 29, OR
Standard deduction shown below for your filing status. **But if you checked any box on line 33a or b,** go to page 23 to find your standard deduction. If you checked **box 33c,** your standard deduction is zero.
- Single—$3,800
- Head of household—$5,600
- Married filing jointly or Qualifying widow(er)—$6,350
- Married filing separately—$3,175

34

35 Subtract line 34 from line 32 35

36 If line 32 is $83,850 or less, multiply $2,450 by the total number of exemptions claimed on line 6e. If line 32 is over $83,850, see the worksheet on page 24 for the amount to enter . 36

If you want the IRS to figure your tax, see page 24.

37 **Taxable income.** Subtract line 36 from line 35. If line 36 is more than line 35, enter -0- . 37

38 Tax. Check if from a ☐ Tax Table, b ☐ Tax Rate Schedules, c ☐ Capital Gain Tax Work-sheet, or d ☐ Form 8615 (see page 24). Amount from Form(s) 8814 ▶ e ______ 38

39 Additional taxes. Check if from a ☐ Form 4970 b ☐ Form 4972 39

40 Add lines 38 and 39. . . . . ▶ 40

Figure 13-1: The tax computation section of Form 1040.

The standard deduction is tempting because without any complicated figuring, you simply take the deduction that corresponds to your filing status. For example, if you're filing as a single, you get to take a standard deduction of $3,800.

The other option for taking deductions, itemizing on Schedule A, takes a lot more work. Think of this path as the grass-roots deduction process because you must identify and tabulate numerous items to build enough deductions to exceed the standard one the IRS grants you. Otherwise, why would you make more work for yourself?

If you're in doubt about whether itemizing will save you money or what expenses you may actually itemize, jump over to Chapter 8 right now. Even if itemizing can't save you money for this year's return, you should educate yourself for the future about the deductions that are available. The major expenses that you may itemize include some homeownership expenses (mortgage interest and property taxes), state income taxes, medical and dental expenses (that exceed 7.5 percent of your adjusted gross income), gifts to charity, casualty and theft losses, moving expenses (that's 1993 moving expenses paid in 1994, but remember 1994 moving expenses are an adjustment to income), job expenses, and other miscellaneous things (that exceed 2 percent of your adjusted gross income).

Once you've either completed Schedule A or elected to take the standard deduction, enter the result on line 34, and then subtract it from line 32 and enter the result on line 35. If your adjusted gross income is over $111,800 ($55,900 if married filing separately) your itemized deductions have to be reduced. See the worksheet at the end of Chapter 8 to reduce your itemized deductions if this situation applies to you.

Line 36: Exemptions

Multiply by $2,450 the number of exemptions you claimed on line 6e. You already filled out line 6e by now (didn't you?), but in case you need to go back to make sure you grabbed all the exemptions that you are allowed, return to the section "Personal exemptions and exemptions for dependents" in Chapter 4.

Enter the amount of your multiplication on line 36. For example, if you claimed 4 exemptions on line 6e, enter $9,800 on line 36.

Don't forget that if your income exceeds certain amounts, your deduction for personal exemptions is limited. If you have more questions about exemptions, check out Chapter 4 again.

Line 37: Taxable income

Hey, you get an easy math problem. Subtract line 36 from line 35 and enter the result on line 37. But if line 36 is more than line 35, you get to place 0 on line 37. If this occurs, you could possibly have a NOL (see Chapter 17). Now you've arrived at another tax landmark, your taxable income, which is your adjusted gross income minus your deductions (either standard or itemized) and minus your personal exemptions.

Line 38: Tax

Here's where you finally calculate the total federal tax that you should pay based on your taxable income. If your taxable income is under $100,000, you figure your tax by finding the income bracket for your taxable income and filing status in the tax tables on Pages 41-52 of your 1040 instruction booklet. If your income is over $100,000, you must use the tax rates for your filing status in the tax-rate schedules on Page 53 of the 1040 booklet.

Capital gain tax worksheet

This is another way to figure your tax. If your tax rate is in excess of 28 percent, you must use this capital gain tax worksheet to make sure you don't pay more than 28 percent on your capital gains, which you are not required to do. If your taxable income exceeds these amounts, you get to fill out a worksheet!

- ✔ single — $55,100
- ✔ married filing jointly or qualifying widow(er) — $91,850
- ✔ married filing separately — $45,925
- ✔ head of household — $78,700

Yes, we know we are repeating this information from Chapter 11 (and in a different form), but we think it's important. So here's the worksheet.

Table 13-1	Capital Gain Tax Worksheet	
1. Enter the amount from line 37 of your 1040		1.
2. Enter the smaller amount of your net capital gain from Schedule D, line 17 or 18		2.
3. If you are filing form 4952, enter the amount from line 4e of this form		3.
4. Subtract line 3 from line 2. If the amount is zero or less, stop here. Use the Tax table or Tax Rate Schedule, instead.		4.

5. Subtract line 4 from line 1	5.
6. Enter the appropriate amount: $22,750 (single), $38,000 (married filing jointly or qualifying widow(er), $19,000 (married filing separately), or $30,500 (head of household)	6.
7. Enter the larger amount from line 5 or line 6.	7.
8. Subtract line 5 from line 1	8.
9. Figure the tax on the amount of line 7. Use the Tax Table or Tax Rate Schedule (for your particular case)	9.
10. Multiply line 8 by 28% (.28)	10.
11. Add lines 9 and 10.	11.
12. Figure the tax on the amount on line 1. Yes, use the Tax Table or the Tax Rate Schedules.	12.
13. Enter the smaller amount from line 11 or line 12 here. Then enter this amount also on Form 1040 (line 38, in case you lost your place!). Don't forget to check that little Box c on line 38.	13.

The Kiddie Tax

Don't jump over to the next line quite yet. If you have children under age 14 who have investment income, you may need to complete some additional forms (see the following section on Forms 8615 and 8814).

Why your three-year-old may be in the 39.6 percent tax bracket

Notice to the left of line 38 the two boxes indicating Form 8615 and Form 8814. You use Form 8615 to compute the tax for children under the age of 14 who have investment income of more than $1,200. You file this form with the child's tax return. Form 8615 is commonly referred to as the *Kiddie Tax*.

Once upon a time, if you were in the 70 percent tax bracket (rates were that high before 1981), it made sense to make a gift of investment property to your children because the income it produced would be taxed at the child's tax rate — which could have been as low as 11 percent. But that was in the good old days (if you think there's something nostalgic about 70-percent tax rates.)

Since 1986, this tax savings scheme no longer works. Nowadays, if a child is under the age of 14, all their investment income over $1,200 is taxed at their parent's tax rate — which could be as high as 39.6 percent. This nasty state of affairs is known as the *Kiddie Tax*. Why they call it that is a mystery because there is nothing small about it. Just think about it. You're trying to save for your youngster's college education and your kid (maybe still in diapers) is in the 39.6 percent tax bracket.

Here's how the Kiddie Tax works. If a child has $2,200 in interest income, for example, the first $600 is exempt from tax. The next $600 is taxed at the child's tax rate (15 percent) for a tax of $90, and the remaining $1,000 at the parent's rate. So if the parent is in the 31 percent tax bracket, the Kiddie Tax will amount to $310 ($1,000 × 31 percent) for a total tax bill of $400.

Children whose investment income is over $600 must file, but if it's under $1,200 they can file their return using the less complicated Form 1040A. If they don't have any taxable investment income (you invested the money their grandparents gave them in tax-exempt bonds), they don't have to file a return until their earned income, such as income from a part-time job, exceeds $3,800.

Unless your child was 14 by the end of 1994, here's how to compute the Kiddie Tax. Your Social Security number and taxable income are entered on Form 8615. Your child's investment income in excess of $1,200 is added to your taxable income. You recompute your tax and the difference between the tax on your return and the recomputed figure is the Kiddie Tax. A good tax software program will save you all this math.

But if all you have is a calculator and your child's investment income in excess of $1,200 is $1,000, you add the $1,000 to your taxable income. Now you compute your tax on this amount. For example, if the tax on this amount is $9,310 and the tax on your return is $9,000, the $310 difference is the Kiddie Tax. That amount plus $90 (the $600 that isn't exempt from tax that's taxed at the child's rate of 15 percent) is entered on your child's return. Depending on which form you are using, it goes on Form 1040A (line 23) or Form 1040 (line 38), and check the box marked 8615. The computation of the Kiddie Tax Form on Form 8615 doesn't effect your children's tax liability. Your taxable income is used only to compute the Kiddie Tax. It only feels like you're being taxed twice.

But there's more. If you and your spouse are filing separate returns, the larger of either your or your spouse's taxable income goes on Form 8615. If you are separated or divorced, the parent who has custody of the child for the greater part of the year uses their taxable income in completing Form 8615. But if you and your spouse are living apart and qualify to file as unmarried (single or head of household), the custodial parent's taxable income is used on Form 8615.

And it gets worse! If you have two or more kids, the total of all their investment income above $1,200 is entered on Form 8615. The Kiddie Tax is computed and allocated among them. For example, suppose that your daughter's investment income in excess of $1,200 is $3,000, and your son's is $2,000. $5,000 is entered on each one's Form 8615. Then each one's share of the total Kiddie Tax is allocated. Your daughter's share would be $3/5$ of the tax and your son's is $2/5$.

By now you're looking for a way to avoid having to file a separate tax return because your child has $1 over $600. Is there one, you ask? Yes. If your child only has investment income of $5,000 or less and it's all from interest and dividends, you can report the income on your return by filing 8814. That's $5,000 per each child. **But we do not recommend this course of action because if you pick this income, the Kiddie Tax will be higher than it would be on the child's return.** To learn more about investing in your child's name, read Chapter 23.

Line 39: Additional taxes: Forms 4970 and 4972

Form 4970 (Tax on Accumulation Distribution of Trusts) is a rather esoteric form. Suppose you turned 30 in 1994. If you were fortunate enough to have someone set up a trust for you, where all the income it earned was being saved until your 30th birthday, happy birthday! Form 4970 is your birthday present.

Form 4972 (Tax on Lump-Sum Distributions), however, is more common. If you decide to take all your money out of your employer's retirement plan in a lump-sum, use this form to compute your tax under the 5- or 10-year averaging method. Using one of these methods could save you a bunch of dough. See Chapter 6 ("Line 16a and 16b: Total pensions and annuities") for a complete discussion of this issue.

Line 40: IRS addition test

Add lines 38 and 39 and put the sum here. If you make a mistake, your grade will suffer.

Credits

Now it's time for your credits — and each one has a nice form for you to fill out (see Figure 13-2).

Line 41: Credit for child and dependent care expenses

If you hire someone to take care of your children so you can work, you're entitled to the credit you figure on Form 2441. This credit may save you several hundred dollars. To be eligible for the credit, your child must be under the age of 13 or a dependent of any age who is physically or mentally handicapped.

Line 1 of the form requires that you report the name, address, Social Security number of the person providing the care, and the amount you paid to the provider. Therefore, if your nanny or baby sitter is off the books, no credit. However, if your annual payment to any one individual is less than $1,000, you're not liable for the payment of Social Security taxes for your child care provider.

Enter what you paid your nanny or babysitter on line 4 of this form. However, you can't enter more than $2,400 for one child or $4,800 for two or more children. On line 5, enter your earned income, and enter your spouse's earned income on line 6. On line 8, enter your adjusted gross income (AGI). Based on your AGI, use the chart right below line 8 to find the percentage of what you paid that can be claimed as a credit.

For example, if your amount on line 8 was over $28,000, you are entitled to a credit equal to 20 percent of the amount entered on line 4. Enter the percentage on line 9 and do the math to get the figure on line 10. Copy that number over to line 41 on the 1040.

Many states also allow a credit. New York, for example, allows a credit equal to 20 percent of the federal credit.

Looking ahead, check to see if your employer offers you the ability to have money deducted from your paycheck — before taxes — into a dependent-care spending account. You may be able to do this in the future instead of taking this credit (you can't do both). See Chapter 23.

Line 42: Credit for the elderly or the disabled

You use (and attach!) Schedule R for this credit. You are entitled to claim this credit (which could amount to as much as $1,125) if you are married and both you and your spouse are over 65 — or both of you are disabled (at any age). For single taxpayers the maximum credit is $750. But wait, there are requirements that make most people ineligible for this credit.

The reason many are ineligible is that you have to reduce the amount of the income that is eligible for the credit by the nontaxable portion of your Social Security and other pension and disability benefits. Also, if your income is over $7,500 (if you're single) or $10,000 (if you're married), the amount of your income that is eligible for this credit is reduced further. Yup.

Figure 13-2:
The credits section of Form 1040.

Credits				
(See page 24.)	41	Credit for child and dependent care expenses. Attach Form 2441	41	
	42	Credit for the elderly or the disabled. Attach Schedule R . .	42	
	43	Foreign tax credit. Attach Form 1116	43	
	44	Other credits (see page 25). Check if from **a** ☐ Form 3800 **b** ☐ Form 8396 **c** ☐ Form 8801 **d** ☐ Form (specify)_____	44	
	45	Add lines 41 through 44		45
	46	Subtract line 45 from line 40. If line 45 is more than line 40, enter -0- . . . . ▶		46

The long and short of all this interesting information is that after completing this two-page form, most people will discover that the credit is zero. But try this step: Instead of struggling with the form, you can have the IRS figure the credit for you. Fill out Page 1 of the form — which asks questions about your age, filing status, and whether you're disabled. Attach the form to your return and on Form 1040 (line 42) write `CFE`. Remember: Always check the IRS computation for a form you have asked them to calculate to make sure they've got it right. The IRS isn't infallible.

The amount of the credit is 15 percent of the following base amounts.

- ✓ $5,000 if you are single, head of household, or a qualifying widow(er)

- ✓ $5,000 if you are filing jointly and only one of you is over 65 or disabled

- ✓ $7,500 if you are filing jointly and both of you are over 65 or disabled, or one of you is over 65 and the other is under 65 and disabled

- ✓ $3,750, if you are married filing separately and are 65 or older (or disabled) and didn't live with your spouse in 1994

Additionally, the base amount is reduced by the amount of your Social Security income that isn't subject to tax and one-half of the excess of your adjusted gross income that exceeds:

- ✓ $7,500 if you are single, head of household, or a qualifying widow(er)

- ✓ $10,000 if you are married filing jointly

- ✓ $5,000 if you are married filing separately, and lived apart from your spouse for all of 1994

For example, suppose that your AGI is $20,000, you have nontaxable Social Security of $2,000, and you and your spouse are over 65.

Base amount	$ 7,500
Nontaxable portion of Social Security	$ 2,000
AGI	$ 20,000
Reduction limit	$ 10,000
Excess	$ 10,000
One-half of excess	$ 5,000
Reduced base amount ($7,500 — $5,000 — $2,000)	$ 500
Credit 15% of $500	$ 75

The $75 credit is entered on line 42. The credit can't exceed your tax. So if your tax is $60 and the credit is $75, the $15 difference isn't refundable. If you're claiming the credit because your are under 65 and disabled, your doctor has to complete and sign Part II on Page 1 of Form Schedule R.

Line 43: Foreign tax credit

Use Form 1116 to figure this credit. If you are not itemizing your deductions, you have to claim the foreign tax you paid as a credit if you want to use it to reduce your tax.

Unfortunately, the computation of this credit is a killer — and even the IRS agrees. The instructions say that it should take you about $6^1/2$ hours to read the instructions, assemble the data, and fill in the form. Give it a whirl. If you hate number-crunching, a computer tax software program can help (see Chapter 2). If using a computer isn't your thing, see a tax advisor. Attach this form to your return and bid it good riddance! For more on foreign taxes, see "Line 8: Other taxes (foreign income taxes)" in Chapter 8.

Line 44: Other credits

The application of these credits is extremely limited and few people are eligible for them. Nevertheless, we probably piqued your interest. If you want to explore them further, we are forced to refer you to IRS publications. Call the IRS (1-800-829-3676) and ask for the form and instructions. Sorry!

Here's the list: Form 8801 (Credit for Prior Year Minimum Tax — Individuals and Fiduciaries) — on this form, you list some of the following: Form 8834 (Qualified Electric Vehicle Credit) — for all you environmentalists, Form 3468 (Investment Credit), Form 5884 (Jobs Credit), Form 6478 (Credit for Alcohol Used for Fuel), Form 6765 (Credit for Increasing Research Activities, Or for Claiming the Orphan Drug Credit), Form 8586 (Low-Income Housing Credit), Form 8830 (Enhanced Oil Recovery Credit), Form 8826 (Disabled Access Credit), Form 8835 (Renewable Electricity Production Credit), Form 8845 (Indian Employment Credit), Form 8846 (Credit for Employer Social Security and Medicare Taxes Paid on Certain Employees' Tips), and Form 8847 (Credit for Contributions to Certain Community Development Corporations).

We wanted to say something about Form 8396 (see the box on your 1040 by line 44). This is called the Mortgage Interest Credit and you may be eligible for this credit if you were issued a mortgage credit certificate by a state or local government agency.

Other Taxes

What! More taxes? Could be. Read the following to see if any apply to you (see Figure 13-3).

Line 47: Self-employment tax

If you earn income from being self-employed as well as other sources, Schedule SE is used to figure another tax that you owe — the Social Security Tax and Medicare Tax. The first $60,600 of your self-employment earnings is taxed at 12.4 percent. There isn't any limit for the Medicare tax. It's 2.9 percent of your total self-employment earnings. For amounts $60,600 or less the combined rate is 15.3 percent, and above $60,600 the rate is 2.9 percent.

Your self-employment earnings may be your earnings reported on:

- ✔ Schedule C (line 31)
- ✔ Schedule C-EZ (line 3)
- ✔ Schedule K-1 (line 15a), Form 1065 if you are a partner in a firm
- ✔ Schedule F (line 36)
- ✔ Form 1040 (line 21) — your self-employment income that you reported as miscellaneous income

You can use Section A of Schedule SE, called the *short worksheet,* if you only have self-employment income. If you are self-employed and also are employed, you have to use the long form, otherwise you will pay more Social Security than you are required to, because Social Security tax has already been withheld from your salary. To prevent this disaster, enter the amount from Boxes 3 and 7 of your W-2 on line 8a of Page 2 of Schedule SE. And if you file Form 4137 on unreported tips, enter the amount from line 9 of that form on line 8b of Schedule SE.

The short worksheet

On line 1 enter your self-employment income from Schedule F (line 36).

On line 2 enter the amount from Schedule C (line 31) or Schedule C-EZ (line 3) and Schedule K-1 (line 15a) — Form 1065 from partnerships.

Combine the amounts of lines 1 and 2 on line 3.

Now turn on your calculator, because you have to multiply the amount on line 3 by .9235. So if your self-employment income is $100,000, your self-employment tax is computed on $92,350 — not $100,000. The reason for this reduction is that because 50 percent of your self-employment tax is deducted from your income on Form 1040 (line 25), your income subject to the self-employment tax must also be reduced by this deduction. If all this stuff sounds confusing, it's the IRS way of putting the way self-employed people pay their Social Security tax on a par with the way taxpayers who are employed pay their Social Security tax. This computation is another reason we suggest a tax software program.

Line 48: Alternative Minimum Tax

You would think with all of the schedules and forms we've slogged through that you'd almost be done. Well, this line can prove to be a real bummer for some. This line refers you to yet another whole tax system — the Alternative Minimum Tax (AMT). The AMT is designed to snare people who reduce their taxable income by claiming too many deductions. You need to figure your tax under the AMT system and compare it to the regular system on Form 1040. Guess what? You pay whichever one is higher.

Figure 13-3:
The other taxes portion of the Form 1040.

Other Taxes (See page 25.)	47	Self-employment tax. Attach Schedule SE	47	
	48	Alternative minimum tax. Attach Form 6251	48	
	49	Recapture taxes. Check if from a ☐ Form 4255 b ☐ Form 8611 c ☐ Form 8828 . .	49	
	50	Social security and Medicare tax on tip income not reported to employer. Attach Form 4137 .	50	
	51	Tax on qualified retirement plans, including IRAs. If required, attach Form 5329	51	
	52	Advance earned income credit payments from Form W-2	52	
	53	Add lines 46 through 52. This is your **total tax**. . . . . ▶	53	

If you have any of the following types of deductions or income, you could have the AMT. So get out your Form 6251 (Alternative Minimum Tax — Individuals) and start calculating. The starting point is line 35 of your Form 1040 — your AGI after deducting your itemized deductions or standard deduction, but before you subtract your deductions for exemption in arriving at your taxable income. Enter the amount from line 35 on line 16 of Form 6251. Enter the amount from line 35 on line 16 of Form 6251. From this amount you have to add back the following items to arrive at your AMT income:

- ✔ medical and dental expenses in excess of 10 percent of your income

- ✔ deductions for taxes (line 9 of Schedule A and line 26 of Form 1040)

- ✔ home equity mortgage interest not used to buy, build, or improve your home

- ✔ incentive stock options — the difference that you paid for the stock and what it was worth when you exercised the option

- ✔ depreciation in excess of the straight-line method

- ✔ tax-exempt interest from private activity bonds — issued after August 7, 1986

The preceding amounts are entered on lines 1-14. Although the AMT was designed to make sure that the wealthy didn't escape paying a minimum amount by using loopholes and tax deductions, the Clinton tax plan gave it more teeth. Nobody can say for certain, but our best estimate is that it could grab people with incomes as low as $75,000. And while the preceding items are most likely the ones that the average taxpayer will use in computing their AMT, there are a number of way-out items that also go into figuring the AMT, such as intangible drilling expenses, circulation expenses, depletion, certain installment sales, passive activities and research, and experimental costs.

Is there any way of avoiding the Alternative Minimum Tax? Defer those deductions and tax incentives that trigger the AMT or accelerate income so your deductions will be within the AMT limits. Unfortunately this maneuver requires checking your income and deductible expenses periodically throughout the year. Investing in a tax software program or a tax advisor may help ease the burden.

The only thing that we can say with certainty is that if your income is below the exemption level for your filing status, you don't have to worry about Form 6251. Here are the exemptions:

- ✔ married filing jointly and qualifying widow(er)s — $45,000
- ✔ single or head of household — $33,750
- ✔ married filing separately — $22,500

Line 49: Recapture taxes

If you claimed an Investment Tax Credit, Low Income Housing Credit, or Federal Mortgage Subsidy Credit in a prior year and didn't fulfill all the requirements under the law, now it's payback time. If you need to complete these forms: Form 4255 (Tax from Recomputing a Prior Year's Investment Tax Credit), Form 8611 (Recapture of Low-Income Housing Credit), and Form 8828 (Recapture of Federal Mortgage Subsidy), you can obtain them and the accompanying instruction booklets at 1-800-829-3676.

Line 50: Social Security and Medicare tax on unreported tip income

If you worked in a restaurant that employed at least ten people and didn't report your share of 8 percent of the restaurant's income as tip income, your employer will do it for you. This amount (the difference between what you reported as tip income to your employer and your share of 8 percent of the restaurant's income), your allocated tips, is entered on Box 8 of your W-2. The amount in Box 8 isn't included in Box 1 of your W-2 and has to be added to your total wages on Form 1040 (line 7). The Social Security tax you owe on the amount in Box 8 is computed on Form 4137 and is entered on line 50.

If your employer wasn't able to collect from you all the Social Security and Medicare Tax you owe on your reported tip income, Box 13 of your W-2 will show that amount. Code A next to the amount in Box 13 is for Social Security Tax and Code B next to the amount in Box 13 is for Medicare Tax. Enter the amounts in Box 13 on Form 1040 (line 53) and to the left of the amount write UNCOLLECTED TAX ON TIPS.

Line 51: Tax on qualified retirement plans

The IRS should simply list Form 5329 by the name *IRA and Pension Penalties*. Remember, if you take money out of an IRA or pension before you're $59\frac{1}{2}$ you owe a 10 percent penalty in addition to the tax on the amount you withdraw. If you took out too little after reaching $70\frac{1}{2}$, the penalty is 50 percent of the amount you should have taken, based on your life expectancy, and what you actually withdrew or failed to withdraw. The penalty as computed on the Form 5329 is entered here for "other taxes." See Chapter 6, "Line 15a and 15b: Total IRA distributions," for more details.

If you take out more than $150,000 in any one year, there is a 15 percent penalty on the amount above $150,000. There is also a 6 percent penalty for contributing more money than you are allowed to by law.

Line 52: Advance earned income credits

Enter the amount from Box 9 of your W-2. If you're entitled to an EIC, you can file Form W-5 with your employer, and up to 60 percent of the credit can be added to your paycheck. This way you don't have to wait until the end of the year to get a refund (see Chapter 6, "Box 9: Advance EIC payment" and the following section on "Line 56").

Line 53: IRS pop quiz

Find your total tax by adding lines 46 through 52 and placing the amounts here.

Payments

This is the section of the return where you finally, thankfully, get to tally up how much actual federal tax you paid during the year.

Line 54: Federal income tax withheld

Enter the amount from Box 2 of your W-2 and your W-2G, 1099-DIV, and 1099-INT — as well as Box 4 of your Form 1099-R — on line 54 (see Figure 13-4).

Line 55: 1994 estimated tax payments

If you made estimated tax payments, fill in the total amount of the payments here. If you applied last year's overpayment — don't forget that!

Remember, the IRS doesn't want to wait till April 15, 1996 to collect your 1995 tax. So, if you will owe money come next April 15, you're going to have to file quarterly estimates if 90 percent of your tax isn't being withheld from your income.

For example, suppose that you're self-employed. Your 1994 tax is $7,000 and your self-employment tax is $3,000, for a total of $10,000. The law requires that you make estimated tax payments of 90 percent of your 1995 tax or 100 percent of your 1994 tax. So if you expect that your 1995 total tax will be the same $10,000 that it was in 1994, you must make quarterly estimates of $2,250 (90 percent of $10,000 ÷ 4). However, if you make quarterly estimates of $2,500 (100 percent of your 1994 tax) and your actual 1995 tax comes to $25,000, no penalty will be assessed. Because you paid 100 percent of your 1994 tax ($10,000), you can wait till April 15, 1996 to pay the $15,000 balance.

Caution: If your 1994 income is more than $150,000, you have to make estimated tax payments equal to 110 percent of your 1994 tax to escape a 1995 underestimating penalty if your 1995 tax turns out to be substantially more than your 1994 tax. For example, suppose that your 1994 tax is $200,000. Because your income is more than $150,000, you have to make estimated payments of at least $110,000. So if you expect your 1995 tax to be $200,000, you only have to make estimated payments of $110,000 and you can wait until April 15, 1996, to pay the $90,000 balance without incurring any penalty.

Line 56: Earned income credit

The earned income credit is a special credit for lower-income workers. The credit is refundable — which means that if it exceeds your tax or if you don't owe tax, the IRS will send you a check for the amount of the EIC.

Unlike other credits, the EIC is no small piece of change. The credit can be as high $2,528. To qualify for the credit, your earned income must be less than the following amounts:

✔ $23,755 if you have one child

✔ $25,296 if you have two or more children

✔ $9,000 if you don't have any children and you are at least 25 (but under 65) and are not being claimed as a dependent by anyone else

Figure 13-4:
Here is what you have already paid in taxes.

Payments	54	Federal income tax withheld. If any is from Form(s) 1099, check ▶ ☐	54	
	55	1994 estimated tax payments and amount applied from 1993 return .	55	
Attach Forms W-2, W-2G, and 1099-R on the front.	56	Earned income credit. If required, attach Schedule EIC (see page 27). Nontaxable earned income: amount ▶ [ ] and type ▶	56	
	57	Amount paid with Form 4868 (extension request)	57	
	58	Excess social security and RRTA tax withheld (see page 32)	58	
	59	Other payments. Check if from a ☐ Form 2439 b ☐ Form 4136	59	
	60	Add lines 54 through 59. These are your total payments . . . . ▶	60	

Net self-employment income for the purposes of the EIC is your net earnings reduced by one-half of your self-employment tax on Schedule SE that you deducted on Form 1040 (line 25). If you lost money in your business as reported on Schedule C, you can deduct your loss from your other earned income.

Earned income doesn't include:

✔ interest and dividends

✔ Social Security benefits

✔ pensions or annuities

Figuring the earned income credit

If you meet all of the requirements, figuring the credit is easy. No math is required. Just look up the credit you're entitled to for your earned income bracket in the Earned Income Credit Table. Read across to the appropriate column: no qualifying child, one child, or two children. For example, if your earned income is $12,000 and you have one qualifying child, you're entitled to an EIC of $1,874. Attach the EIC Schedule to your return and enter the credit on Form 1040 (line 56).

A nice feature of this credit is that you don't have to wait till you file your return to claim it. If you're eligible for the credit, you can file Form W-5, EIC (Advance Payment Certificate) with your employer and a portion of the credit will be added to your weekly paycheck. The advanced credit you received during the year is entered on Box 9 of your W-2. You must enter the amount in Box 9 on Form 1040 (line 52) where it's subtracted from the EIC you're entitled to — because part of the credit was added to your paycheck during the year. For example, if you're entitled to an EIC of $1,200 and you received $500 throughout the year from your employer, $500 will be entered in Box 9 of your W-2. The $500 is subtracted from your EIC of $1,200, and $700 will be refunded.

- veterans' benefits
- alimony or child support
- unemployment insurance
- welfare benefits
- taxable scholarships or fellowship that were not reported on your W-2

In addition to your having to meet the earned income test, your child must meet the following tests:

1. Relationship test

Your child must be your, son, daughter, adopted child, stepchild, or foster child.

2. Residency Test

Your child must have lived with you in your main home in the U.S. for more than six months. A foster child has to live in your home for the entire year. For a child who was born or died, the residency test is met if the child lived with you for the part of the year.

3. Age Test

Your child must be under 19 (or under 24 if a full-time student), or any age if permanently and totally disabled.

For individuals without children qualifying for the credit, you must, in addition to the income limit, have had a main home in the U.S. for more than six months, file a joint return if you are married, not be a dependent of another, and be at least 25 but under 65. You 1040 filers need to fill out and attach Schedule EIC.

Line 57: Extension Request

If you requested a four-month extension of time to file with Form 4868, enter the amount you paid when you requested the extension (see the Appendix for a sample form).

Line 58: Excess Social Security and RRTA tax withheld

Line 58 applies only if you worked for two employers and your total wages were $60,600 or more. The maximum Social Security tax you are required to pay for 1994 is $3,757.20. So if $4,057.20 was withheld, $300 is entered on line 58. Box 4 of your W-2s contains the amount of Social Security tax that was withheld from your salary.

Line 59: Other payments

Here are some more obscure forms to wonder about:

- ✔ **Form 2439 (Notice to Shareholders of Undistributable Long-Term Capital Gain).** Investors in mutual funds where the company didn't distribute your share of the long-term capital gains will receive this form. Enter the amount from line 2 of this form on line 59 and attach a copy of the form to your 1040.

- ✔ **Form 4136 (Credit for Federal Tax Paid on Fuels).** This form is for claiming credit for diesel fuels. If you bought a diesel powered car or truck in 1994 that weighs less than 10,000 pounds, you're entitled to a one-time credit of $102 for a car and $198 for a van or light truck. There is also a refundable credit for fuel used in non-highway vehicles. Bulldozers, fork-lifts, generators, and compressors used in your business qualify for the credit. Fuel used in motor boats doesn't qualify.

Line 60: Total payments

You enter the total of the payments (lines 54 through 59) on line 60 and hold your breath (or your nose).

Refund or Amount You Owe

OK, this is it. Now comes the moment you've worked so hard for. Do you get money back? Do you pay? Read on and find out.

Line 61: The amount you overpaid

If the amount of your total payments (line 60) is more than your total tax (line 53), subtract line 53 from line 60 (see Figure 13-5). The remainder is the amount you overpaid. Do you like that word "overpaid?"

Line 62: Amount you want refunded to you

Just do what the nice line says and enter that amount here — provided you have a refund coming!

Line 63: 1995 estimated tax

Here you indicate what amount of your refund you want applied to your 1995 (next year's) estimated tax.

Refund or Amount You Owe	61	If line 60 is more than line 53, subtract line 53 from line 60. This is the amount you OVERPAID. ▶	61
	62	Amount of line 61 you want REFUNDED TO YOU. . . . . ▶	62
	63	Amount of line 61 you want APPLIED TO YOUR 1995 ESTIMATED TAX ▶ 63	
	64	If line 53 is more than line 60, subtract line 60 from line 53. This is the AMOUNT YOU OWE. For details on how to pay, including what to write on your payment, see page 32 . . .	64
	65	Estimated tax penalty (see page 33). Also include on line 64 65	

Sign Here Keep a copy of this return for your records.	Under penalties of perjury, I declare that I have examined this return and accompanying schedules and statements, and to the best of my knowledge and belief, they are true, correct, and complete. Declaration of preparer (other than taxpayer) is based on all information of which preparer has any knowledge.		
	Your signature ▶	Date	Your occupation
	Spouse's signature. If a joint return, BOTH must sign.	Date	Spouse's occupation

Paid Preparer's Use Only	Preparer's signature ▶	Date	Check if self-employed ☐	Preparer's social security no.
	Firm's name (or yours if self-employed) and address ▶		E.I. No.	
			ZIP code	

♲ *Printed on recycled paper*

Figure 13-5:
The rest of the Form 1040 backside. Fill it in and you're done!

Line 64: The gosh darn "AMOUNT YOU OWE" line

If your total tax (line 53) is larger than your total payments (line 60), subtract line 60 from line 53. This is the amount you owe. Sorry.

Line 65: Estimated tax penalty

Unless you have already paid 90 percent of your tax liability in either quarterly estimates or in withholding, you will be assessed an underestimating penalty. There are a number of exceptions that will excuse or reduce this penalty. You calculate this penalty on Form 2210 (Underpayment of Estimated Tax by Individuals and Fiduciaries). See Chapter 17 on penalties to see if one of the exceptions applies to you.

The IRS doesn't want to wait till April 15, 1995, when you file your return, to collect your 1994 tax. You must pay at least 90 percent of your tax by having tax withheld from your salary, pension, or IRA distributions — or by making estimated quarterly tax payments.

If you don't calculate this penalty yourself, the IRS will and bill you for it. You don't want the IRS to prepare this form because the IRS will prepare it on the basis of you paying the maximum! A good tax software program will breeze through this form to see if you are eligible to have the penalty reduced or eliminated by one of the exceptions. The ability to calculate this form alone is worth the price of the software package.

Finishing Up

Attach your W-2s, W-2Gs, 1099s where federal tax was withheld, and all schedules. If you owe money, make sure to write your Social Security number on the front of the check along with the notation `1994 Form 1040`. Sign your return and mail it to the IRS Service Center for the area in which you live. (See the Appendix for the correct address). If you have to send a check, make it out to the Internal Revenue Service and not the IRS. If your check gets lost, it's too easy to alter — "IRS" can easily be changed to "Mrs. Smith."

Ten last-minute tax tips

1. Double-check your return for mistakes that cost money, time, and audits. Put your name and Social Security number on every page, check arithmetic, attach W-2s, W-2Gs, and any 1099s where federal tax was withheld, and sign and date the return. Verify that you've transferred over from last year's return items you need for this year's.

2. Scavenge for overlooked deductions, especially if you're self-employed. Determine if you could save money by electing the filing status of married filing separately or head of household.

3. Check to see that data on forms sent to you by financial institutions and your employer(s) that you use in preparing your return have correct information.

4. If you're self-employed, contribute to a tax-deductible SEP-IRA retirement account. If you work for an employer that does not offer a retirement plan, contribute to an IRA.

5. File extension(s) (Forms 4868, 2688), if necessary, to allow yourself more time to do the forms correctly and ensure you're taking the deductions you're legally entitled to. Don't make the mistake of not filing until you have the money to pay. The penalty for doing so is 25 percent.

6. Organize and complete as much of your return as you can. If you get stuck and are uncomfortable with part of the return, get a second opinion from a tax advisor.

7. Keep copies of everything that you file with the IRS and your state, and obtain a mailing receipt if you file at the last minute and there's a lot of money (or a big issue) at stake.

8. After all the time, trouble, and expense you put into completing your tax return, make use of the information that's tabulated on it to plan for the year ahead. If you received a large refund, change your tax withholding payments so you won't have an overpayment next year.

9. For the year ahead, make sure you're taking advantage of directing your employment earnings into retirement accounts (see Chapter 19).

10. Regardless of your income, assets, and goals, educate yourself about the tax system and tax ramifications of financial decisions you make.

Part III
About Face! Dealing with the IRS

Reprinted with permission

In this part...

You'd think and hope that because you've proved your superhuman status by getting your return filed and taxes paid, Uncle Sam would leave you alone. Have you taken leave of your senses? Sooner or later — without advance warning — you may get an official-looking envelope from the IRS. You could choose to ignore it, but we don't recommend making the IRS angry. Here you'll learn how to deal with just about everything the IRS can throw at you during the year. If you didn't file in time or couldn't pay all your taxes, we'll provide a shoulder to cry on as well as sound counsel for how to make things better.

Chapter 14

The Dreaded Envelope I: IRS Notices

reetings!

With the end of the draft, Americans no longer receive notices from their government bearing such a salutation — a different government agency, the Internal Revenue Service, now provides you with equally unpleasant news. Did you know that you have a 35 percent chance of receiving a notice from the IRS stating that you failed to report all your income, filed late, didn't pay what you owed, or made an error in preparing your return? Maybe you even committed a combination of these infractions!

Getting an envelope in the mail from the IRS strikes fear into the hearts and souls of even the most confident and honest taxpayers. In some cases, the mistakes taxpayers make are easily fixed. An IRS computer, in one of the IRS's ten regional service centers, automatically generates a notice when it spots an inaccuracy. The good news is that this system is cost-effective for the IRS because it brings in billions more tax dollars. The bad news for you is that these notices are often ambiguous, intimidating, and (in some cases) wrong!

You're Not Alone

If you think that you received an IRS notice simply because you're unlucky, you may be mistaken. Winning the IRS notice lottery is easy and you're hardly in exclusive company! Each year, the Internal Revenue Service issues the following items:

- 34 million penalty notices

- 3.5 million notices informing taxpayers that they didn't report all their income

- 3 million notices to taxpayers stating that they failed to file a tax return

- tens of millions of notices to taxpayers, the exact number not being quantifiable, that they either failed to pay what they owed or made a mistake in preparing their tax returns

Every year, approximately 12 million beleaguered taxpayers write back saying that the notices they received are either incorrect or unclear.

In a 1988 report to Congress, the General Accounting Office (GAO) revealed that taxpayers who inquired about a notice stood an astounding 37 percent chance of receiving a response that was either unclear, unresponsive, or incorrect.

The GAO now says that things are getting better. It recently checked nearly 2,000 letters from taxpayers at two of the IRS service centers and found that only 15 percent of the IRS responses were wrong or unclear. So things are looking up — but erring one in seven times is hardly cause for taxpayer celebration. And let's not forget that this is the government's own assessment about how often one of its divisions leads taxpayers down the wrong path!

Not surprisingly, members of Congress receive more requests from their constituents for help with IRS problems than for any other problem.

What You Need Is a Compass

In dealing with the IRS, or with any large bureaucracy, persistence and patience count. The importance of this strategy can't be stressed enough. The only thing that you must not do is give up or become discouraged. "You shall overcome" should be your motto.

If dealing with the IRS appears more like an unsolved mystery, don't be intimidated. You're not alone. Senator David Pryor, Chairman of the Senate Finance

Subcommittee on Oversight of the IRS, is fond of saying, "As a United States Senator, I probably know more about the inner workings of the KGB than I do about the IRS."

One of the biggest headaches in dealing with the IRS is that the agency can be big and impersonal. That's why this part of the book provides you with suggested strategies and sample response letters developed from the decades of experience that have helped our clients deal with those yucky IRS notices. These strategies and letters work. When an IRS form can work better and faster than a letter, we include that form and suggest using it.

All the letters and IRS forms contained in this book may be copied for your personal use. On the sample letters, items that you must fill in are enclosed in brackets [ ] .

The IRS Notice Process

If you never had a pen-pal, you have one now. And you don't even have to write back — the letters just keep coming. However, this pen-pal doesn't like being ignored. The pen-pal doesn't get mad — this pal (the IRS) just takes your money.

Receiving your typical notice

The notice system usually starts with the issuance of a notice of adjustment, a CP-2000, or a 30-day letter. If you fail to respond to this notice, or if the IRS isn't satisfied with your reply, or if you fail to exercise your appeal rights, a Statutory Notice of Deficiency is issued. Remember that adjustments merely correcting a math or processing error — or assessing a penalty — don't require the issuance of a Statutory Notice.

When the IRS makes an assessment, the amount of that assessment — plus penalties — is entered into the service center's computer under your Social Security number. The service center will then send four notices at approximately five-week intervals. All four notices ask for payment within ten days.

The first notice — Form 8488 (Notice and Demand) — states the amount of additional tax due, plus any interest or penalty that is due. The second and third notices are Form 8125 (Reminder of Unpaid Tax Due). The fourth and final notice — Form 8126 (Final Notice) — is sent by certified mail (the law requires that it be sent this way before the IRS starts seizing property or salary). This notice informs you that if payment isn't received within 30 days, the IRS has the right to seize your property and attach your salary. Ouch!

If you receive a Final Notice and can't pay what you owe, see the section "When You Can't Pay Your Taxes" in Chapter 17. If you haven't paid the balance or contacted the IRS to arrange payment within ten days, the contact section of the Automated Collections System (ACS) takes over unless the IRS has what's known as levy source information. In that case, a Notice of Levy will be issued. The contact section handles cases where the payment of tax can't be satisfied by levy. The ACS contacts you by telephone, and if it can't get you to pay, the ACS turns the case over to a revenue officer.

Deciphering a notice

Don't panic! If you're like most taxpayers, you'll look at the notice, see a dollar figure, and decide it's too painful to look at the notice again. The dollar figure might be a refund — but it's not likely.

One critical bit of advice: The computers at the service centers won't tolerate being ignored. Maybe they hooked you by error, but there is no satisfying them until they reel you in, or you convince the IRS that the computers are in error. To do so, you must respond quickly to a notice. Otherwise, you severely prejudice your appeal rights and end up with no recourse but to pay the tax and forget the whole thing — or to pay the tax and then try to get your money back. Good luck!

Every notice contains the following:

- ✔ the date of the notice
- ✔ Taxpayer Identification Number — your Social Security or Employer ID number (Make sure it's yours.)
- ✔ type of tax form
- ✔ tax period — the year
- ✔ Document Locator Number (DLN) at the upper right-hand corner (Every notice and payment that you make to the IRS is assigned a DLN. This number allows the IRS to trace every transaction.)
- ✔ penalties charged
- ✔ interest charged
- ✔ amount owed
- ✔ tax payments you made

Both you and the IRS are able to track any missing tax payment by a long series of numbers printed on the back of your check. The first fourteen numbers make up the DLN; the next ten are your Social Security number, followed by a four-letter abbreviation of your name. The next four numbers are the year the payment was applied (9412 means the year ending December 1994) and the last six digits record the date the payment was received.

Be careful about making a payment with a check drawn on a money market or bank account. These checks may not be returned in your monthly statement, so you wouldn't have it as proof of tax payment. To get a copy from the bank is usually a federal case.

Unfortunately, not every notice provides all the information necessary to precisely determine what went wrong — IRS notices are famous for their lack of clarity. Our favorite one is a client's notice that indicated either that an error was made, or that an outstanding balance existed, or that not all the payments listed on the return were made, or that a penalty was being asserted. The notice went on to promise that a separate notice (which, by the way, never came) would explain which explanation applied.

All is not lost if you receive an IRS notice that, after careful inspection, is not understandable. Call the IRS at the telephone number indicated on the notice and request a transcript of your tax account (which takes two weeks to arrive). This printout lists every transaction posted to your account. With this additional information, you should be able to understand why you were sent the notice.

If the transcript of your tax account fails to clarify why you received the notice in the first place, you need to write to the IRS and ask them to provide a better or more exact explanation. To learn how to do this, see Chapter 16.

Assessment Notices

Assessment notices usually inform you of one of the following situations:

- ✔ You weren't given credit for all the tax payments you made.
- ✔ You made a math error or used the wrong tax table or form.
- ✔ You filed a return but neglected to pay what you owed.
- ✔ You agreed to the results of a tax examination.
- ✔ You owe a penalty.

General assessment notices (Form 8488/8489)

The IRS uses Form 8488/8489 to inform you that your refund is being reduced or eliminated (or that it's being applied against an outstanding balance), because of one of the reasons from the preceding list. The IRS also intercepts refunds to pay nontax governmental debts such as defaults on student loans and nonpayment of child support. The IRS refund interception program is discussed in greater detail in "You Haven't Received Your Refund" in Chapter 16.

The IRS also sends Form 8488/8489 to assess a penalty for filing or paying late, failing to make timely estimated tax payments, failing to report all your income, or overstating credits or deductions on your return. Watch out!

Income verification notice (Form CP-2000)

A few years ago, a convict serving prison time sent the IRS 1099s stating that the prosecutor and judge who sentenced him received $900,000 in income. Can you imagine the face of the prosecutor when he found out the IRS wanted another $200,000 in taxes?

The rule is: Don't believe that the IRS is automatically correct in its assessment of your income.

Income verification notices ask you to explain differences between the income and deductions you claimed on your return — such as mortgage interest — and the income and deductions reported to the IRS by banks, your employer, and brokerage firms. Your salary is reported to the IRS on Form W-2, and all other income is reported to the IRS by the payer on Form 1099. The IRS *assumes* that the information reported to it on these forms is correct and that you made a mistake on your return. A CP-2000 notice thus bills for penalties, interest, and additional tax. If income tax was withheld, the CP-2000 reflects that situation.

The quickest way we know to become separated from your money is to ignore one of these nice little notices. If the notice you receive is wrong or unclear, you need to notify the IRS. On how to do this, see Chapter 16.

In 1992, CP-2000 notices picked up a cool $4.3 billion from 4 million taxpayers. If you fail to report all your income, you can expect to receive a CP-2000 within 18 to 24 months after filing your return.

There are many other reasons why an IRS notice can be wrong:

- ✔ The income that the IRS says you didn't report is exempt from tax.

- ✔ The income that the IRS says you failed to report is not yours. For example, you opened a bank account for your child or for a relative and you inadvertently gave the bank your Social Security number.

- ✔ The IRS counted the income twice. You perhaps reported interest income on a schedule other than the proper one. Or your broker reported your total dividends to the IRS as having been paid by the broker, while you reported those dividends on your return according to the names of the corporations that paid them.

- ✔ You reported income in the wrong year. Maybe someone paid you at the end of the year, but you didn't receive this income until the beginning of the next year — and you reported it in that year.

Backup withholding notice

As a trade-off for repeal of the short-lived mandatory withholding on interest and dividends, Congress enacted a system of backup withholding if you fail to furnish a payer of taxable income with your Social Security number. The IRS also notifies the payer that backup withholding should bestarted if you failed to report interest and dividend income on your tax return.

If the IRS determines that backup withholding is required, some types of income are subject to a 31 percent withholding tax. These incomes include interest and dividends, payments of more than $600 per year in the course of business, gross proceeds that a broker reports in a barter exchange, and annual royalties in excess of $10.

Backup withholding usually applies only to interest and dividend income. Other payments, however, are subject to withholding if you fail to provide the payer with your Social Security number. The IRS doesn't notify you that you are subject to backup withholding — it instead notifies the payer who is required by law to notify you.

By notifying the IRS Problem Resolution Office (see "When the IRS Ignores You" in Chapter 16), you can stop backup withholding under certain circumstances:

- ✔ You did not underreport your income.

- ✔ You did underreport — but you paid the tax, interest, and penalties on the unreported income.

- ✔ The backup withholding will cause you undue hardship — and the underreporting probably will not happen again.

Hardship, IRS style

IRS regulations state that undue hardship exists in several forms. For example, you are under hardship if backup withholding — when combined with other withholding and estimated tax payments — produces a substantial overpayment of tax. Or perhaps your ability to pay medical expenses would be affected. Maybe you rely upon the interest and dividend income to meet living expenses, or your income is fixed. You are also a hardship case if you have filed a bankruptcy petition or if you are an innocent spouse who had no knowledge of your mate's failure to report all income. See Chapter 4 ("Joint Tax Liability & the Innocent Spouse Rule") for more information on this last topic. Every October 15, the IRS makes a determination on hardship cases. *If* it decides in your favor, backup withholding stops on January 1, of the following year. There are two exceptions to the January 1 rule, how-ever. If the IRS determines that there was no underreporting or that you would suffer undue hardship, the IRS notifies you and the payer either not to start backup withholding or to stop back-up withholding within 45 days of their determination.

Withholding allowances notice (Form 6355)

Watch out below; we're going to have to be a little technical here. Please stay with us through this bit of IRS paperwork. If you claimed more than ten withholding exemptions on your Form W-4 (Withholding Allowance Certificate), or if you earned more than $200 per week and you claimed an exemption from all withholding, the W-4 your employer must submit to the IRS. If the IRS determines that you overstated the number of exemptions you are entitled to, it will either notify your employer that your withholding certificate is inaccurate or ask you for written verification of why you believe you are entitled to the extra exemptions you claim.

If the IRS asks you for this information, it will send you Form 6355 (Worksheet to Determine Withholding Allowances). Form 6355 is three pages long and is more detailed than the W-4 that you completed.

If the IRS reviews Form 6355 and determines that you are not entitled to the number of exemptions claimed, it will notify your employer to disregard your W-4 and to withhold tax based on the number of exemptions you're entitled to. This edict remains in effect until the IRS approves a new W-4. To get approval to change the number of your exemptions, you must file a new W-4 with your employer, who again submits the W-4 to the IRS. You also must attach a written statement explaining the reason for requesting a change.

If you don't have a reasonable basis for the number of exemptions claimed, you will be assessed a $500 penalty. A simple error or an honest mistake will not result in a penalty. Phew!

Annually, the IRS receives about 600,000 W-4s either claiming more than ten exemptions or a complete exemption from withholding. All these W-4s get screened, of course. The IRS contacts about 42 percent of the taxpayers submitting these W-4s and sends them a Form 6355 or Form 6450 (Question-naire to Determine Exemption From Withholding).

Are you still with us? To bring you back to life after that stuff, here's the story of why we have all these forms for withholding. A few years back, all the workers from an assembly line in a Michigan auto plant claimed an exemption from withholding; they didn't file returns for that year. It took some time, but the IRS put a stop to those shenanigans!

Federal tax lien notice (Form 668)

A *statutory lien* automatically goes into effect when you neglect or refuse to pay the tax the IRS demands. This type of lien attaches to all property that you own. A statutory lien is sometimes referred to as a *secret lien* because its validity doesn't depend on its being filed as a matter of public record.

Because a statutory lien places the rights only of the IRS ahead of yours, the IRS will usually file a Notice of Lien in order to place itself first in line before your other creditors. (No cutting in line, please!) A federal tax lien covers all of a taxpayer's property, including real estate, cars, bank accounts, and personal property. These liens are filed in accordance with state law, usually with the county clerk, town hall, or court where the taxpayer lives.

You should be aware that credit agencies routinely pick up liens. Once a credit agency has this information, your credit is marked lousy. Even if paid, a lien stays on your credit history for seven years.

Although the law requires that the IRS release a lien within 30 days after it has been paid, the IRS doesn't always comply. Upon paying the tax, you should secure a Form 668 — Part 4 (Certificate of Release of Federal Tax Lien) — from the revenue officer who filed the lien.

The Taxpayer Bill of Rights (discussed in Chapter 17) tells you what to do when the IRS fails to release a lien. The IRS is liable for damages if it fails to release an erroneous lien or a lien that has been paid.

Property levy notice (Form 668A)

A Notice of Levy is used to garnish your wages, as well as to seize bank accounts. You can kiss your money good-bye 30 days after such a levy is served. A Notice of Levy is usually not issued until after the IRS has exhausted all other possible collection procedures, however. The IRS does make an effort to contact you in order to try to arrange a payment schedule, and they usually send at least four notices. Remember, you filed a tax return indicating where you work, where you bank, and where you have other assets!

You may be interested to know that some assets are exempt from levy:

- ✔ a taxpayer's principal residence — unless personally ordered in writing by a district director or an assistant district director, or where the collection of tax is in jeopardy

- ✔ unemployment benefits

- ✔ tools and books of a taxpayer's trade, business, or profession whose total value exceeds $1,100

- ✔ school books (The IRS doesn't want you to stop studying!)

- ✔ court-ordered child support payments

- ✔ wearing apparel

- ✔ $1,650 worth of furniture and personal effects

- ✔ undelivered mail

- ✔ death benefits from Social Security, Medicare, welfare, and worker's compensation, as well as death benefits from any state program

- ✔ military service disability payments

Although pension, Keogh, and IRA benefits are not exempt from levy, it is IRS policy that they will be levied upon judiciously — these plans were established for a taxpayer's future welfare. This policy statement also mandates that pension benefits totaling less than $6,000 annually will not be levied upon.

Wage levy notice (Form 668W)

Form 668W (Notice of Levy on Wages, Salary and Other Income) is used to seize wages. It is a six-part form served on your employer. Whereas a Notice of Levy attaches only to property held by a third party (such as a bank) at the time the levy is issued, a wage levy is a continuing one — it applies to all wages, salaries, and commissions owed, as well as to future wages, salaries, and commissions.

But part of every taxpayer's wages is exempt from levy. This exemption is equal to a taxpayer's standard deduction plus the number of personal exemptions he or she is entitled to, divided by 52. Therefore, in 1994, a married taxpayer entitled to four exemptions (husband, wife, and two children) would be entitled to a weekly exemption of $310.58, computed as follows:

Standard deduction		$6,350
Personal exemptions	(4 × $2,450)	9,800
		$16,150

$16,150 ÷ 52 = $310.58 per week

The taxpayer claims the exemption on Form 668W, Part 6 (Statement of Exemptions). If you don't fill out Part 6 and return it to your employer so it can be sent to the IRS, your employer is required to compute your exemption as married filing separately with one exemption. The amount of wages that can be exempted can be increased for the amount of court-ordered child support payments.

But I never got Part 6 of Form 668W!

If your employer fails to furnish you with Part 6 of Form 668W, send the following statement to the IRS revenue officer (you can find the agent's name, address, and telephone number on the notice, or your employer can tell you):

[date]
Re: [your name]
[Social Security number]

Dear [name]:

In connection with the Notice of Levy that was served on my employer, please be advised that I am married and entitled to claim the following personal exemptions on my tax return:

1. Myself
2. My spouse, [his or her name and Social Security number]
3. My children, [their names, ages, and Social Security numbers]
4. My court-ordered child support payments amount to [$] weekly

Very truly yours,

[your name]

Nonassessment Notices

The IRS usually issues a nonassessment notice to inform you of one of the following situations:

- ✔ You forgot to sign a return.
- ✔ You failed to attach a W-2.
- ✔ You omitted a form or schedule.
- ✔ You didn't indicate filing status.

If you receive such a notice, simply write across the notice in bold lettering: INFORMATION REQUESTED IS ATTACHED. Then attach the requested information to the notice and return it to the IRS in the envelope provided. Once you provide the IRS with the requested information, the matter is usually closed — unless the information submitted conflicts with information previously reported on the return. If this situation occurs, the IRS will send a notice that assesses additional tax, interest, and possibly a penalty, or that instructs you to contact a particular person at the IRS.

A notice correcting a refund due to you (usually made on Form 8488 or 8489) shouldn't be viewed as a nonassessment notice, however. Just because a notice doesn't demand that you write a check, don't think that the IRS isn't billing you for something. Quite often, the IRS reduces a refund when it assesses additional tax or penalties.

Delinquent tax return notice

A word of caution: You should take a delinquent tax return notice as seriously as it sounds. If your tax return is delinquent, you may be contacted either by mail, telephone, or in person. Remember that the IRS has the right to issue a summons commanding you to appear with your tax records and explain why you didn't file a tax return.

Failure to file a tax return or returns could involve possible criminal violation of the Internal Revenue Code. Usually, the IRS isn't terribly interested in prosecuting individuals who haven't filed and who don't owe a substantial amount of tax. The IRS is, however, very interested in prosecuting prominent individuals because such prosecutions make good headlines. Extra! Extra! Read all about it!

If you file late returns — even in response to an IRS inquiry — and don't owe a substantial amount of tax (what is considered substantial is known only to the IRS), the IRS probably will accept the return and assess a penalty for late payment and possibly fraud.

If you don't reply to a delinquent return notice, the IRS can take one of the following steps:

✔ refer the case to the Criminal Investigation Unit

✔ issue a summons to appear

✔ refer you to the Audit Division

✔ prepare a "substitute" return

If the IRS decides to prepare a "substitute" return for you, it will use the information that it has on you in its master file. The IRS prepares a substitute return using the married filing separately tax table, the standard deduction, and one exemption.

Having the IRS prepare your return is the quickest way we know of for you become separated from your money. Unlike having a tax return prepared by a tax advisor, there isn't any fee involved when the IRS prepares a substitute return. The only charge is the amount of tax that you will unnecessarily pay. Remember, the IRS isn't interested in saving you money.

Although you may have a valid reason for not filing (such as illness or insufficient income), or the IRS may have lost or misplaced your return — notwithstanding the fact that this type of error is something that the IRS is reluctant to admit — any taxpayer who receives a delinquent return notice should consider seeking the services of a *qualified* tax advisor (see Chapter 2).

Why not beat the IRS to the punch? The IRS has an official policy of not prosecuting anyone who files a return prior to being contacted. Penalties and interest, however, will be assessed.

Results of an audit notice (Form 4549/1902-B)

The IRS issues Form 4549 (Income Tax Changes) and Form 1902-B (Report of Individual Tax Examination Changes) after an audit has been completed. Forms 4549 and 1902-B spell out any adjustments to income and expenses that have been made, as well as any penalties and interest that are due. The difference between the two forms is that Form 4549 is for field audits and Form 1902B is for office audits. (See " Types of Audits" in Chapter 15 for more details.)

These notices are often referred to as *30-day letters*. Within 30 days after receipt of an audit notice, you must agree to the adjustment, submit additional information explaining why an adjustment shouldn't be made, or request a hearing before the Appeals Division.

If you disagree with the proposed adjustment and the amount of tax is more than $25,000, a written protest must be filed. You will find IRS Publication 556 (*Examination of Returns, Appeal Rights, and Claims for Refund*) extremely helpful in preparing a protest. Consider retaining a tax advisor when protesting large sums.

Taxpayers can make appeals to the Appeals Office, whose purpose is to settle disputes. The IRS agent who examined your return has no authority to take into account the time and expense to the IRS, as well as the possibility that the IRS may lose in court. An appeals officer can. Approximately 85 percent of all cases referred to the Appeals Office are settled.

If the amount involved is less than $2,500, the IRS does not require a written statement. You merely tell the IRS agent that you want to appeal. For amounts between $2,500 and $25,000, you have to submit a brief written statement of the disputed issues and why you feel your deduction should be allowed.

The IRS also issues a 30-day letter if you fail to show up for an audit. In such an instance, the examining agent will review your return and make adjustments to both income and deductions that he or she deems warranted.

If you receive a 30-day letter because you failed to show — even if you missed the audit because you never received the original notice scheduling it — contact the agent at the number given on the letter and schedule an audit appointment. If you make a new appointment within 30 days, the examining agent or appointment clerk will hold your adjusted return in abeyance pending the outcome of the rescheduled audit.

After completion of the audit, the IRS issues a new notice of income tax changes that supersedes the preceding one. If you agree to the audit changes and sign off on the changes, you can pay what you owe at that time or you can wait to be billed.

Statutory Notice of Deficiency

Although a notice (such as one proposing income tax changes, or a CP-2000) informs a taxpayer that additional tax is due, the IRS can't legally enforce the collection of additional tax until a Statutory Notice of Deficiency — often referred to as a *90-day letter* — is sent to a taxpayer by certified mail at the last known address.

A Statutory Notice of Deficiency is not required where additional tax is due because of a math error. Statutory notices are generally required only where additional tax is due as the result of the IRS adjusting a taxpayer's income, deductions, or credits from what was originally reported on the tax return. Unless a petition is filed with the U.S. Tax Court in Washington within 90 days of receipt of a Statutory Notice, the IRS can initiate collection action at the end of the 90-day period. If you file a petition with the Tax Court, you can delay all collection action until 60 days after the court renders its decision. If you live outside the United States, the 90-day period is extended to 150 days. (*Wunderbar!*)

Chapter 15

The Dreaded Envelope II: Audits

*O*n a list of real-life nightmares, most people would rank tax audits right up there with having a tooth pulled without novocaine. The primary trauma of an audit is that it makes many people feel like they're on trial and are being accused of a crime. Don't panic.

First of all, you may be one of the tens of thousands of taxpayers whose returns are audited at random. No, the IRS isn't headed by sadists. Random audits help the IRS identify common areas on tax forms where taxpayers make mistakes or fail to report income. Second, you may be getting audited simply because a business that reports tax information on you, or someone at the IRS, made an error regarding the data on your return.

About 12 percent of audited returns are left unchanged by the audit — that is, you don't end up owing more money. In fact, if you're the lucky sort, you may be one of the rare individuals who actually gets a refund because the audit finds a mistake in your favor!

Unfortunately, it's more likely that you'll be one of the roughly 88 percent of audit survivors who end up owing more tax money. The amount of additional tax that you owe in interest and penalties hinges on how your audit goes.

Types of Audits

Thankfully, only four types of audits exist — office audits, field audits, correspondence audits, and statistical audits. The key to survival is good records. But if you don't have that, we supply a chapter on what to do if you're audited and cannot produce the needed evidence (Chapter 3). An enrolled agent, CPA, or tax attorney can represent you at an audit without you having to be there.

Office audits

An office audit is held at the IRS. The IRS informs a taxpayer that it is scheduling an office audit by sending a notice numbered 904. The front of this notice lists the date of the audit, while the back lists the items the IRS wants to examine.

The audit date isn't chiseled in granite. If you can't gather the information necessary to substantiate the items the IRS is questioning, you can request a postponement. As a general rule, the IRS grants you only two postponements, unless you can demonstrate a compelling reason for an additional delay, such as illness or the unavailability of certain tax records.

If you need more time but can't get an additional postponement, here's what you do: Go to the audit with the records you have, put on your most confident face, and calmly inform the tax examiner that you need more time to secure the documents you need in order to substantiate the remaining items the IRS is questioning. The tax examiner then prepares a list of the additional items the IRS needs to complete the audit, together with a mailing envelope so that you can mail copies of the requested documents to the IRS.

Never mail originals. If the additional documents don't lend themselves to easy explanation through correspondence, then schedule a second appointment to complete the audit.

Most office audits are concerned with employee business expenses, itemized deductions such as medical expenses, charitable contributions, tax and interest-expense deductions, miscellaneous itemized deductions, deductions for personal exemptions, and moving expense deductions. Lately, the IRS has expanded office audits to include small business returns, income from rental property, and income from tips and capital gains.

One of the by-products of tax reform has been that fewer taxpayers itemize deductions. And one of the by-products of fewer itemized deductions is that office audits now focus on income verification as well as deductions. (Thus, office audits are also known as "What did you live on?" audits.) Statistical research has revealed that the IRS can collect more tax by examining sources of income than by examining deductions. If you operate a small business or have rental income, be prepared to explain where every deposit into your bank account came from.

Deciding where your audit happens

Both field and office audits are conducted in the district where a return was filed. This practice may create a burden if you live in one district and are employed or have your businesses located in another. For example, if you work or your business is located in Manhattan and you live in Connecticut, you normally would be contacted by the examination branch in Connecticut. If your tax records are in Manhattan or you spend most of your time there, you can request that the examination be transferred to the Manhattan District.

Besides gaining the convenience of having the audit conducted where either your records, your advisor, or your business is located, you will also have a little time to pull your tax data together.

To transfer an audit from one district to another, first call the examining agent and tell him or her why you want to transfer the audit to a different district. The transfer usually takes two to three months. The IRS also requires that you request the transfer in writing.

The following note will suffice when requesting that a tax examination be transferred from one IRS district to another:

[date]

District Director
[address of district that issued exam notice]

Re: [your name and your social security #]
[exam year]

Dear District Director:

Because my tax records are located in
[ex. Manhattan] and I spend most of my time
there, I respectfully request that the audit
you have scheduled be transferred to the
[ex. Manhattan] District.

You may contact me during business hours at
[telephone number].
May I thank you in advance for your prompt
attention to this request.

Very truly yours,
[your name]

Enclosed: Copy of exam notice

Field audits

Field audits are conducted at a taxpayer's place of business. They focus on audits of business returns and complex individual returns. If you file Form 1040, Schedule C, you're a likely candidate for a field audit.

Again, be prepared to verify the source of every deposit into your bank account. Field agents are required to survey both your preceding and subsequent years' tax returns to determine whether similar items are treated in a consistent manner. If an audit results in a significant increase in tax, you are now suspect, and the revenue agent will audit your subsequent years' tax returns (which normally are only surveyed).

An office audit specifies what items will be examined from the very beginning of the process. Not so with a field audit — revenue agents have a great deal of discretion as to what items they will review and to what depth they will review the items. Count on having to verify gross income, travel and entertainment expenses, gifts, automobile expenses, commissions, payments to independent contractors, and any expenses that appear large in relation to the size of your business.

Revenue agents may examine each and every deduction or merely select a month or two of expenses and examine them on a sample basis. If they turn up no discrepancies, an agent will accept the rest of the expenses for that category as correct.

Correspondence audits

Correspondence audits are exactly what the name suggests; what you see is what you get. The IRS conducts correspondence audits completely by mail and limits such audits to a few key areas of individual returns, such as itemized deductions, casualty or theft losses of less than $2,000, employee business expenses of less than $1,000, IRA and Keogh plan payments, dependency exemptions, child care and low-income credits, deductions for forfeited interest on early withdrawals from savings accounts, and exclusion from income of disability payments. Income items may also be examined by a correspondence audit.

If you're ever the proud subject of a correspondence audit, the IRS gives you a return envelope to submit your documents, canceled checks, bills, and statements to substantiate the items the IRS questions. Again, *never* send original documents — only copies. It is crucial that you retain the originals in case you have to stare down further inquiries. Remember: when it comes to substantiating any deduction, the burden of proof is on you. If what you must substantiate is complex or requires a detailed explanation, you can request an interview to explain yourself in person.

How the IRS selects returns for audit

A computer program called the Discriminant Function System (DIF) selects returns for audits. This program scores each return for potential error based on IRS criteria. IRS personnel then screen the returns and select those most likely to have mistakes. They also look for returns that — when audited — will result in significant additional taxes being assessed.

Some returns are selected at random under the Taxpayer Compliance Measurement Program (TCMP). These examination results are used to measure and evaluate taxpayer compliance and to update and improve the DIF selection process.

Returns are also selected by examining claims for refunds and by matching information documents, such as Forms W-2 and 1099, with returns.

Statistical audits

These are commonly known as TCMP audits, an acronym for Taxpayer Compliance Measurement Program. The IRS conducts them to gather statistical information that can be used to determine pockets of noncompliance.

For example, your friends at the IRS randomly select 1,000 freelance writers (or any other group of individuals or businesses) to measure the degree of tax compliance for that industry, trade, or profession. On the basis of these audits, the IRS National Office determines which areas require stricter or greater enforcement efforts.

Although TCMP audits account for only $\frac{1}{2}$ of 1 percent of all audits in any year, they also are the most detailed. The IRS might even request birth certificates of your children to prove the dependent exemptions you claimed!

Two tax audit myths debunked

#1. If you file at the last minute or get an extension of time to file, you won't be audited because your return will get lost in the crowd.

Wrong! The audit selection, unseen by human eyes, is done by computer.

#2. Don't use the gummed mailing label showing your name and address that the IRS sends. If you do, you will increase your chances of being audited.

Wrong! The weird numbers on this label are used by the IRS for data processing purposes only and not for deciding whether your return should be audited.

Repetitive audits

It is IRS policy *not* to examine an individual's tax return where the taxpayer has been examined for the same issue(s) in either of the two preceding years and the audit resulted in no (or only a small) tax change. However, this policy doesn't apply to business returns or individual returns that include a Schedule C (Profit or Loss from Business) or Schedule F (Farm Income and Expenses).

If you receive a notice of audit where the IRS questions the same item(s) it questioned in a previous audit, call the agent and inform him or her that the IRS audited the same issue(s) in one of the two prior years with little or no change in tax. (And do note that the IRS has never bothered to define *little*. Changes of less than a few hundred dollars in tax, however, should meet this criteria.) The examining agent will ask you to furnish proof. Mail the examiner a copy of the IRS notice that your prior return was accepted without change, or mail the notice that adjusted your return.

If you can't document that the IRS is questioning items that it *already* questioned — with no change in tax — in one of the two preceding years, the lack of documentation doesn't mean that you can't get the current examination canceled. Just inform the examining agent by telephone about the prior year's tax examination. The agent will postpone the audit and request your tax account records from the two preceding years. If the transcript supports your contention, the IRS will cancel the audit.

Audit Preparation

Preparing for an audit is sort of like preparing for a test in school. The IRS informs you of which sections of your tax return the agency wants to examine. The first decision you face when you get an audit notice is whether to handle it yourself or turn to a tax advisor to represent you. Hiring representation costs money but saves you time, stress, and possibly money.

If you normally prepare your own return and are comfortable with your understanding of the areas being audited, represent yourself. If the IRS is merely asking you to substantiate deductions, you'll probably do all right on your own.

What constitutes substantiation may at times involve a somewhat complicated interpretation of the law and the accompanying regulations. If the amount of tax money in question is small in comparison to the fee you'd pay the tax advisor to represent you, self-representation is probably the answer. However, if you're likely to turn into a babbling, intimidated fool and are unsure how to present your situation, hire a tax advisor to represent you.

Even if you choose to represent yourself and find yourself over your head in an audit, you've got a back-up. Any time during the examination — when you feel a dizzy sensation — the Taxpayer Bill of Rights allows you to request that the audit be suspended until you have time to consult with either an enrolled agent, a certified public accountant, or an attorney. When you make this request, the IRS agent must stop asking further questions or making requests for documents until you are properly represented.

But if you do decide to handle the audit yourself, get your act together sooner rather than later. Don't wait until the night before to start gathering receipts and other documentation. You may discover, for example, that you can't find certain documents.

You need to document and be ready to speak with the auditor about the areas the audit notice said were being investigated. Organize the various documents and receipts into folders. You want to make it as easy as possible for the auditor to review your materials. *Don't* show up, dump shopping bags full of receipts and paperwork on the auditor's desk, and say, "Here it is — *you* figure it out."

Don't bring documentation for parts of your return that are not being audited, either. Besides creating more work for yourself, you're required to discuss only those areas mentioned in the audit letter.

Whatever you do, *don't ignore your audit request letter.* The IRS is the ultimate bill-collection agency. And if you end up owing more money (the unhappy result of most audits), the sooner you pay, the less interest and penalties you'll owe.

Who can represent you in an audit?

The IRS permits three types of individuals to represent taxpayers before the IRS: enrolled agents, certified public accountants, and attorneys. All three are bound by IRS rules of practice.

Enrolled agents become enrolled to practice before the IRS by passing a two-day written examination administered by the IRS in which their knowledge of the tax code is tested. Or they have had at least five years of experience as an IRS tax auditor. Attorneys and certified public accountants are the other two groups permitted to represent taxpayers before the IRS. Many states have continuing education requirements for CPAs and attorneys. The IRS requires that EAs also meet continuing education requirements.

Probably the best way to find a qualified tax professional is to ask a relative or friend for a recommendation of someone whose level of service and performance the relative or friend is more than satisfied with. For more information and background about these different tax practitioners and who may be best suited to help you in an audit, be sure to read Chapter 2.

Winning Your Audit

Two people with identical situations can walk into an audit and come out with very different results. The loser can end up owing much more in taxes and have the audit expanded to include other parts of the return. The winner can end up owing less tax money.

Here's how to be a winner:

Treat the auditor as a human being

Obvious advice, but often not practiced by taxpayers. You may be resentful or angry about being audited. You're a busy person with better things to do with what little free time you have, so you might be tempted to gnash your teeth and tell the auditor how unfair it is that an honest taxpayer like you had to spend scores of hours getting ready. You might feel like ranting and raving about how the government wastes too much of your tax money or that the party in power is out to get you.

Bite your tongue.

Believe it or not, most auditors are decent people just trying to do their job. They are well aware that taxpayers don't like seeing them. Don't suck up, either — just relax and be yourself. Behave as you would around a boss you like — with respect and congeniality.

Stick to the knitting

You're there to discuss *only* the sections of your tax return in question. The more you talk about other areas or things that you're doing, the more likely the auditor will probe into other items.

Don't argue when you disagree

State your case. If the auditor wants to disallow a deduction or otherwise increase the taxes you owe and you don't agree, state only once why you don't agree. If the auditor won't budge, don't get into a knock-down, drag-out confrontation. He or she may not want to lose face and is inclined to find additional tax money — that's the auditor's job. Remember that you can plead your case with several layers of people above your auditor. If that course fails and you still feel wronged, you can take your case to tax court.

Don't be intimidated

Just because IRS auditors have the authority of the government behind them, that doesn't make them right or all-knowing. The audit is only round one. If you disagree with the results, you have the right to appeal.

Appeal the results of an audit, if necessary

If you're dissatisfied with the results of an audit, see the section "Results of an audit notice" in Chapter 14 on how to make an appeal.

Go to Tax Court

If you receive a Statutory Notice of Deficiency, you have 90 days to appeal your case. If you don't appeal, the IRS can enforce collection on the 91st day. See the section "Statutory Notice of Deficiency" in Chapter 14.

The Statute of Limitations on Audits (or, How Long the IRS Can Keep You in Mind)

The IRS must make any assessment of tax, or of penalties and interest, within three years from the due date for filing a tax return. If the IRS grants you an extension of the filing deadline, the statute of limitations is extended to include the extension period. Where the due date falls on a legal holiday or a Saturday or Sunday, the due date is postponed to the next business day.

Here's how the statute of limitations works. The IRS must make an assessment regarding a 1994 tax return by April 17, 1998, three years from the April 17, 1995, due date. *After this date, the IRS can make no demand for additional tax.* If a return is filed after the due date, the three-year period starts on the date the return was filed. (Why April 17? In 1995, April 15 falls on a Saturday, so the due date is extended to Monday, April 17.) However, if you filed your return on or before April 15, 1995, the three-year statute of limitations expires on April 15, 1998, and *not* on April 17, 1998.

If more than 25 percent of the income required to be reported is omitted from a return, the statute of limitations extends to six years. No statute of limitations runs on a false or fraudulent return. Thus, where a false or fraudulent return (or no return at all) was filed, there is no time limit on when the government can assess additional tax.

Extending the statute of limitations

If the statute of limitations is about to expire and you haven't resolved your problems with the IRS, you will be asked to agree to extend the statute of limitations. If you don't agree, the IRS will immediately assess your tax based on the information it has. The only way to stop the IRS from forcing you to pay the tax is to file a petition with the tax court within a 90-day period. Although IRS Publication 1035 (*Extending the Assessment Period*) explains this process, our advice is to see a professional if you ever get into water *this* hot.

The statute of limitations on tax collection is...

Ten years — period. After that, the IRS can't collect a dime. The ten-year assessment period starts on the day the IRS receives your return. If the ten-year period is about to expire, the IRS usually attempts to extend the period by getting you to sign Form 900 (Tax Collection Waiver). More often than not, the IRS will threaten to seize everything under the sun that you own unless you agree to sign.

Your state tax return and the IRS

The IRS and 48 states have an agreement calling for the exchange of information on taxpayers. The only states that don't exchange information are Texas and Nevada, two states that don't have a personal income tax. Under these agreements, individual states and the IRS notify each other about taxpayers who failed to file returns and when either a state or the IRS has adjusted a taxpayer's taxable income.

The tax laws of most states provide that, if the IRS has adjusted your tax return, you must file an amended state income tax return with that state within 30 to 90 days of the IRS's adjustment. The amended state return must reflect the adjustments made by the IRS, and you must pay any additional tax plus interest. If an amended return isn't filed, your state's tax collector, upon receiving notice of the adjustments from the IRS, will send a demand for additional tax and interest, and possibly a penalty for not notifying the state within the required time frame.

Chapter 16

Fixing Boo-Boos the IRS Makes

· ·

In This Chapter

▶ Demystifying IRS mistakes

▶ Responding to notices

▶ Mastering the generic response form

▶ Dealing with a nonresponsive IRS

▶ Finding a lost refund

· ·

*G*et out your boxing gloves! Just kidding. It's best to leave your boxing gloves and attitude somewhere else — you definitely don't want to antagonize the IRS. When you're dealing with a bureaucracy and bureaucrats, you don't want them angry. Remember, they have the power to bring you to your knees. This is true whether you're dealing with an entry-level clerk, a phone assistant, or a manager.

You'll face many tax problems only once in your lifetime. That's a relief, we know. But it also means that you probably don't have a clue how to legally, swiftly, and inexpensively get Uncle Sam off your back. Stay tuned as we explain how to fix a variety of problems caused by the IRS — without breaking a sweat or an IRS employee's limbs!

Although reluctant to admit it, the IRS does make mistakes. In fairness to the IRS, collecting taxes from more than 100 million individuals and businesses under an extraordinarily complex tax system is, to say the least, difficult. The number of errors can appear to be limitless, but most errors occur for simple reasons.

Common IRS Flubs

We wish we could explain why the IRS can't get it right the first time. We can't.

But we can give you an idea of the number of mistakes made, the types of mistakes, and action you can take. We also can (and will!) offer tips to keep you away from the IRS paper trail.

The IRS processes just over a billion transactions a year. So, math wizards, what does an error rate of, say, one percent translate into? A hundred, you say. Wrong! Try adding six zeroes to that. Now, what do you have? 100 million errors, and way to go, that's right; take the rest of the day off.

That's a whole bunch of errors — the following is a long list of the types of flubs the IRS can make.

Misapplied payments

The IRS may not have posted tax payments to your tax account (under your Social Security number) that you made. Payments are sometimes posted to the wrong year or type of tax. Perhaps the IRS did not properly post overpayments from a preceding or subsequent year.

Misunderstood date

The IRS may claim that a taxpayer didn't file or pay tax on time. Computers at a service center may not acknowledge that the due date for filing or paying fell on a legal holiday or on a Saturday or Sunday and blame you for filing late, when in fact you filed on the first business day following a legal holiday or a Saturday or Sunday. Or perhaps you had a valid extension of time to file, but the IRS said you filed your tax return late.

Wrong Social Security/ID number

A data processing clerk may incorrectly input your Social Security number, or you may have been assigned two numbers. Because all data on a joint return are recorded under the Social Security number of the spouse whose name is listed *first*, any payments or credits that the other spouse made may not be posted under the first spouse's number. This situation frequently occurs where taxpayers file jointly for the first time or where a taxpayer files separately after having filed jointly in a prior year.

Wrong income

Income earned by another person may be inadvertently reported under your Social Security number. This often happens when you open a bank account for a child or another relative.

Exempt income

A payer may incorrectly classify income earned on your IRA, on a Keogh, on a pension account, or from municipal bond interest, and report it to the IRS as being taxable.

Income double-counted

Income earned from a trade, business, or profession may have been recorded as income from wages — or vice versa — and the IRS moved the income to the line or schedule on the taxpayer's return where it correctly belongs. That's okay, but sometimes the IRS does this *without* removing the income from the line or schedule where it was incorrectly entered!

Lost return

The IRS or the U.S. Postal Service may have lost your return and payment, leaving you in the unenviable position of having to prove the timely filing of the return. Hope you made a copy!

Partially corrected error

The service center may have corrected only one of the errors that was previously made. For example, an IRS error may be corrected, but the penalties and interest that were incorrectly charged were not removed.

Data processing error

A computer bug — or another unexplained phenomenon — may have caused a notice to be issued stating that a math error on your return was made where no error exists. Or someone may have failed to input all the data from the schedules attached to your return into the IRS computer.

Data processing errors are common with Form 2210 (Underpayment of Estimated Tax by Individuals and Fiduciaries), where a taxpayer claims an exemption from the penalty for underestimating the amount of his or her required estimated tax payments. This kind of error usually causes the IRS either to assess a penalty where it shouldn't have or to issue a refund for the underestimating penalty that the taxpayer has paid.

Incorrect 1099

The IRS may receive an incorrect Form 1099 from a bank or brokerage firm — either the amount of income reported on the form is wrong or the income isn't yours.

Fixing IRS Mistakes — Fight Fire with Fire

There is elegance in simplicity when corresponding with the IRS. Keep to the point. No letter should be longer than one page. A half page gets even quicker results. Remember, the tax examiner reviewing your inquiry could have little experience in the area you're writing about. Such people are, however, extremely conscientious in performing their duties. You stand a better chance of achieving the results you want by making their job as easy as possible. Don't succumb to the temptation to go into a narrative on how unfair our tax system is or how you are paying more than your fair share. Save that stuff for your representative in Congress.

What your letter should include

Your letter should contain the following items — and nothing more:

- ✔ vital facts: name, mailing address, Social Security number on the tax return, and the year of the disputed tax return
- ✔ document locator number (DLN), type of tax, and a copy of the notice you received
- ✔ what type of mistake the IRS made
- ✔ what action you want the IRS to take
- ✔ copies of the documents necessary to prove your case — canceled checks, corrected Form 1099s, mailing receipts — but *never* the originals

Address your letter to the Adjustments/Correspondence (A/C) Branch at the service center that issued the notice. You should note the type of request you are making at the extreme top of the letter — REQUEST TO ADJUST FORM [form number]. Use the bar-coded envelope that was sent with the notice to mail your letter.

Include a simple thank you and the telephone number where you can be reached if the tax examiner has any questions. Telephone contact between you and the tax examiner can take weeks off of the Adjustments/Correspondence process. See Figure 16-1 for an example of a generic Dear John, er, we mean Dear IRS, letter. This example addresses an adjustment to be made to form CP-2000.

Upon receipt of your letter, the A/C Branch will stop the computer from sending further notices until the matter is resolved. If your problem can't be resolved in seven days, you will be sent a letter indicating when it can. If you receive a second notice, don't be alarmed. This delay isn't unusual. The IRS doesn't move all that fast.

If 30 days go by and you haven't heard from the IRS or you receive a third notice, see the section "When the IRS Ignores You" later in this chapter.

Request to Adjust Form CP-2000

[your address]
[date]

Adjustments/Correspondence Branch
IRS Service Center Address
Re: [your name, Social Security number]
[tax year, DLN]

Dear IRS:

I have received your notice dated [date], in which you claim that I failed to report [$] of interest on my tax return.

Please be advised that your notice, a copy of which is enclosed, is incorrect. The interest that you claimed I earned was in fact earned on my daughter's bank account. Her Social Security number is [number], which should have been given to the bank — instead of mine — when the account was opened.

Please adjust your notice to reflect that no additional tax is due. Thank you for your prompt attention to this request. I can be reached at [phone number] should you require any additional information.

Very truly yours,
[your name]

Figure 16-1: Here's how to compose a Dear IRS letter that gets right to the point.

Simple Response to a Balance Due Notice

If you receive a balance due notice for a tax that has already been paid, simply mark the front of the notice: THIS BALANCE HAS BEEN PAID. SEE REVERSE SIDE OF NOTICE FOR PAYMENT INFORMATION. PLEASE REMOVE ALL PENALTIES AND INTEREST CHARGES THAT WERE ASSERTED.

Then fill in the payment information on the tear-away flap of the return envelope that the IRS supplies. The information that the IRS requires to properly credit your payment can be obtained from the back of your check. On the back of the check, you will notice the date, where it was endorsed, and the serial number stamped on it.

If any of this information isn't legible or you can't readily cull it from the back of the check, simply photocopy the check (front and back) and send the photocopy — along with the notice — in the envelope provided. Write across the notice: COPY OF CHECK ENCLOSED.

Generic Responses to Generic Notices

If you're like us, you probably dislike form letters with a passion. There are times, however, where you have no choice but to fight fire with fire. To simplify things, we have included an all-purpose generic response letter (see Figure 16-2).

You can use this letter simply by inserting any one of the following responses to frequent IRS errors. In order to keep it simple, we list the IRS error you want to address as the heading, and the response you can use right below it in quotes. We also include some explanatory text without quotes.

Misapplied payments

"Enclosed is a copy of my canceled check, front and back, showing that the tax was paid."

Figure 16-2:
You can get
down-and-
dirty with
the IRS folks
with this
battle-
proven
generic
letter. Just
insert the
correct
generic
paragraph
from the
appropriate
section
where
indicated.

Generic Response Letter

Request to adjust Form [number]

[date]

Adjustments/Correspondence Branch
Internal Revenue Service Center
[address]

Re: [your name, Social Security number]
Year, DLN, Form [number]

Dear IRS:

I am in receipt of your notice dated [date] (copy enclosed). Please be advised that your notice is incorrect.

[Insert generic paragraph(s) pertaining to one of the issues to be corrected.]

I would appreciate your adjusting the notice that you sent me now that you have the information contained in this letter that was previously unknown to you.

I would also appreciate your abating any penalties and interest that were incorrectly assessed.

May I thank you in advance for your prompt attention to this request. I can be reached at [number], should you have any questions.

Very truly yours,
[your name]

Enclosed: Notice [number]

Misunderstood due date

Here are several solutions to common problems with due dates.

Due date for filing or paying fell on Saturday, Sunday, or legal holiday

"Please be advised that your notice incorrectly penalizes me for filing/paying late. The due date for filing/paying fell on a [Saturday] and I made payment/filed on the next business day. Enclosed is a copy of my check dated [date], which is dated the date of the extended due date, as allowed by law. The serial number on the back of the check clearly indicates that the IRS negotiated my check on [date].

Please correct your records to reflect that my return/payment was timely and remove all penalties and interest that were charged."

If you don't have a mailing receipt and you know your return was mailed on time, you may have to request a copy of the envelope in which you mailed your return from the service center before requesting an adjustment. Your mailing envelope becomes a permanent part of your return.

Valid extension of time to file

"Your notice incorrectly assesses a penalty for late filing. Enclosed is a copy of an extension that granted an extension of time until [date] in which to file. I filed my return prior to the expiration of the extension on [date].

"Please correct your records by removing the penalties and interest that were incorrectly assessed."

Enclose a copy of any canceled check that might have accompanied the extension and make reference to the check in the letter.

Late filing

If you mailed your return on time with a balance due that you didn't pay — and the IRS sent a notice demanding the balance plus an erroneous late filing penalty — be prepared for lengthy correspondence with the IRS. If you don't have a postal mailing receipt, you will have to write to the service center and request a copy of the mailing envelope in which your tax return was mailed so that you can check the postmark.

"Your notice incorrectly assessed a late filing penalty in the amount of [amount]. Please be advised that my return was timely filed on [date].

"By checking the postmark on the envelope in which my return was mailed, you will see that I didn't file late and therefore no penalty should be asserted. I would appreciate your sending me a copy of my mailing envelope when responding to this inquiry."

If the IRS can't locate your envelope (which sometimes happens) or the envelope bears a crazy postmark date, you have a problem. If this is the only time you were ever notified that you filed your return late, you will have to request that the penalty be abated due to reasonable cause — and to your record of always filing on time. (For more on reasonable cause, see Chapter 17.)

Wrong income

"The income on which you claim I owe additional tax per your notice is not my income. The bank/broker/insurance company [or whatever] incorrectly reported the income that was earned on this account as belonging to me. This account, in fact, belongs to my [mother, for example], who reported it on her tax return for the year in question. Her Social Security number is [123-45-6789].

"Enclosed please find a copy of my [mother's] tax return and a statement from her stating that the balance in the account you question belongs to her. I have instructed the bank to correct its records. Please correct yours so that my tax account will show that no tax is owed your agency."

Exempt income

We are constantly amazed when we review returns that clients prepared themselves. One of the things that crops up all the time is how often they pay tax on income they don't have to. Here are two prominent examples and the appropriate response when the IRS tries to include these as taxable income.

Keogh — IRA

"The income on which you claim I owe additional tax is income earned from my [Keogh or IRA] account and is exempt from tax. Enclosed is a copy of my year-end statement of that account. Please notice that the number of this account is the same as the number that appears on your notice. Please correct your records so that my account will show that no additional tax is owed your agency."

Munibonds

"The income on which you claimed I owe additional tax is exempt municipal bond interest. Enclosed is a corrected statement from my broker/bank that clearly identifies that the amount of income reported on your notice, is tax exempt municipal bond interest. Please correct your records so that my tax account will show that no tax is owed your agency."

Income double-counted

"The interest income you claim I failed to report on my tax return for the year in question was, in fact, reported on Schedule C of my return (copy enclosed). By adjusting Schedule B (Interest and Dividend Income) of my tax return without adjusting my Schedule C, you require me to pay tax on the same item of income twice by double-counting it. Please correct your records so that my tax account reflects that no tax is owed your agency."

Lost return

This is a tough one. But one secret that the IRS hates to admit is that it frequently loses or misplaces tax returns. The IRS even has a form letter for when this happens. The letter requests that you send a duplicate. Unfortunately, when you do, you're likely to receive a follow-up notice saying that the IRS received the duplicate, but that it was filed late!

Refund return

"Enclosed is a copy of my return that your notice claimed was not filed. Please be advised that this return, which indicated a refund due, was filed on [date]."

If you have a postal mailing receipt, enclose a copy of it.

If your return was mailed by someone other than yourself, or if another person saw you mail your return, get a statement to that effect and enclose it.

Balance due return

"Enclosed is a copy of the return that your notice (copy enclosed) dated [date] claimed was not filed. Please be advised that my return was mailed on [date]. However, as of this date my check number dated [date] that accompanied my tax return hasn't been returned to me by my bank.

"I call your attention to the *ESTATE OF WOOD*, 92TC No.46 case in which the court held that a timely mailed return is presumed to have been received by the IRS.

"I would appreciate your correcting your records to reflect that this return was timely filed. If you would be kind enough to send me a bill for the balance I owe without reference to any penalties, I will remit full payment on receipt of your bill."

Enclose any proof of mailing that you have.

Lost check

"Please be advised that my check, number [number], dated [date], was attached to my return that I filed on [date]. Because my check still hasn't been returned by my bank I am placing a stop payment on it and have issued a new check for the same amount as the original check, which I have enclosed. Kindly abate the interest that you charged on your notice. It would be unfair to charge me interest because your agency can't locate my check."

Tax assessed after statute of limitations

By filing a Form 911 (Taxpayer Assistance Order), you put the IRS on notice that it could be liable for damages and costs up to $100,000 resulting from its reckless and intentional behavior in dunning you. TAOs are covered under the Taxpayer Bill of Rights. To cover all bases, write to the Adjustments/Correspondence Branch at the service center that issued the assessment.

"Please be advised that your assessment for additional tax, penalties, and interest was issued in violation of the statute of limitations. The time for making an additional assessment for the year in question expired on [date].

"Please remove this assessment from my tax account, along with any interest or penalties that were charged. The assessment you made is in direct violation of law. An assessment must be made within three years after the return is filed. This assessment doesn't comply with that requirement."

Partially corrected error

"Please make the following adjustment [insert] as requested in my original letter of [dated] (copy enclosed) that your current notice [date] failed to adjust."

At this point you may want to refer the matter to the Problems Resolution Office (PRO). (See "When the IRS Ignores You" later in this chapter.)

Erroneous refund

Remember what your mother told you about keeping money that doesn't belong to you? She was right, of course — maybe because she had to deal with the IRS. As a practical matter, if you want to save yourself a great deal of time corresponding with the IRS, deposit the check, but don't spend the money (sorry). You ultimately will receive a bill for it. You can also send it in, if you want to get rid of it.

You returned a refund check

"Enclosed is a refund check that was incorrectly issued to me."

Return the check to the service center where you filed your return, not to the Treasury Department office that issued the check. Send this letter by certified mail.

You didn't return a refund check sent to you by mistake

"Your notice demanding interest on a refund sent to me in error is assessed in violation of the law. I discovered the error only when I received your notice demanding repayment. I call your attention to the fact that IRC Section 6404(e)(2) states that no interest may be charged if a taxpayer who receives an erroneous refund of $50,000 or less repays it when the IRS demands payment. Enclosed please find my check in the amount of the tax that was incorrectly refunded. Please correct your notice by removing the interest that you shouldn't have charged me."

If this approach doesn't work, you should contact the PRO.

Data processing error

This problem is probably the most difficult to cope with.

"Your notice incorrectly states that [choose appropriate problem(s)]:

     (a) a mathematical error was made.

     (b) I used the wrong tax table in computing my tax.

     (c) I incorrectly claimed a credit.

"Please be advised that I *rechecked* my return and do not believe that any error was made. Enclosed is a copy of my return. Please review it and advise me exactly where you think an error was made.

"I thank you in advance for your prompt attention to this request."

Incorrect 1099

Use (a) or (b) where appropriate.

     (a) "Your notice incorrectly claims that I failed to report all the income I received from [name].

     (b) "Please be advised that the 1099 information that you received from [name] is incorrect.

" I enclose a copy of a corrected 1099 that [name] has issued to me.

"I would appreciate your adjusting my tax account to reflect the information contained in the corrected 1099. When this is done, you will readily see that no additional tax is due."

Wrong year

"The miscellaneous income your notice claims I failed to report for the year in question was not received until the following year and was reported on that year's return (copy enclosed). Additionally, I am enclosing a copy of my bank statement for the month in which this income was received. You will notice that this bank statement bears the following year's date."

Never received prior notices

"Your records don't have my correct address, which is probably why I never received your prior notices. Please send me copies of these notices so that I can determine whether the most current notice that I enclose is correct. If it is, I will pay the amount I owe upon receipt of the notices I request. If it is not correct, I will contact you. I thank you in advance for your prompt attention to this request."

To speed up this process, call the IRS at the number indicated on the notice and request copies of the prior notices. Also, send the IRS Form 8822 (Change of Address).

When the IRS Ignores You

At times, it seems that a black hole ravages every IRS service center, devouring loads of taxpayer correspondence. Naturally, the IRS won't respond right away in these cases. If this happens to you, the IRS has a special office that handles these problems — the good old Problem Resolution Office (PRO). That's a solid-sounding acronym, isn't it?

The Problem Resolution Office (PRO)

Since 1977, the Problem Resolution Office has been the complaint department of the IRS. There is a PRO in every one of the 61 IRS districts, as well as at the ten service centers. Their function is to resolve taxpayer problems that can't be resolved through normal channels.

The PRO is headed by the Office of the Taxpayer Ombudsman, which was established to provide taxpayers with an advocate within the IRS. *Ombudsman* is a fancy Swedish word that means, "Hey, we're on your side, bud — really!"

The PRO is independent from all other IRS offices, which enables a problem resolution officer to cut through red tape.

PRO officers don't interpret tax law, give tax advice, or provide assistance in preparing tax returns. But they do resolve procedural, refund, notice, billing, and other problems that couldn't be fixed after one or more attempts by a taxpayer. A PRO officer can abate penalties, trace missing tax payments, and credit them to a taxpayer's account. This officer can also approve replacement refund checks that were either lost or stolen, and he or she can release a lien.

PRO criteria for accepting a case

The PRO accepts cases for a variety of reasons. The following cases are certain to be considered:

- ✔ You call or write the IRS about a problem. After 30 days, you contact the IRS again, but the IRS still ignores you.

- ✔ You file your return expecting a nice refund, but after 60 days you're still waiting. You contact the IRS, but nothing happens.

- ✔ You receive a letter from the IRS promising to respond to your particular inquiry by a certain date, but the IRS forgets about you.

Established IRS procedures often fail to correct a problem — but don't count on the PRO to be overly charitable. However, if the PRO won't take your case, the PRO will refer it to another IRS office for resolution.

Contacting the Problem Resolution Office

Except in emergency cases, such as where a levy has been filed although the taxpayer owes the IRS no money, taxpayers should write to the PRO in the district your where they reside. Your letter should contain the following:

- ✔ a complete description of the problem

- ✔ copies of the fronts and backs of checks (if applicable)

- ✔ a signed copy of your tax return (if applicable)

- ✔ copies of all notices received from the IRS

- ✔ copies of previous letters written to the IRS regarding this problem

- ✔ the number of phone calls you made to the IRS, whom you spoke with, the dates, and what was discussed

- ✔ any other documents or information that might help the problem resolution officer in expediting the resolution of this problem

- ✔ a telephone number where you can be reached during the day

If the PRO takes your case

Problem resolution officers are committed to resolving your problem in seven working days. If they can't, you will be informed, usually by telephone, when you can expect the problem to be resolved. Most cases are closed in 30 days or less. If a problem resolution officer asks for certain information and it isn't sent, the case won't be held open indefinitely. After two weeks, it will be closed, in which case you will have to make a new PRO contact. A problem resolution officer closes a case by informing a taxpayer in writing what corrective action has been taken.

In an emergency situation, you should contact the PRO by phone. When you do call, an officer can immediately take a variety of actions. For example, the officer can issue a Taxpayer Assistance Order (TAO) — Form 911 — where a notice of levy has been incorrectly issued.

You Haven't Received Your Refund

If you don't receive your refund, you may be one of about 92,000 taxpayers whose refund checks are returned to the IRS by the U.S. Postal Service. According to the IRS, these checks are undeliverable because of incorrect addresses or because the taxpayer moved and failed to leave a forwarding address. So if you move, notify the IRS by filing Form 8822 (Change of Address). That way, you'll be sure to get your refund.

The actual figures on how many taxpayers never receive their refund checks are substantially higher when one takes into account the refund checks that are either lost or stolen. There are also a number of other reasons why a taxpayer may not have received a refund; for instance, it could have been used to offset another year's tax bill or to pay what you owed on a delinquent student loan.

How to locate your refund

Yes, there is a lost-and-found department. You can find out about the status of your refund by using the IRS automated Tele-Tax System. By dialing 1-800-829-4477 on a touch-tone phone, you are prompted through a series of computerized instructions.

Refund inquiries shouldn't be made until at least six weeks from the date the return was filed. It takes about that much time for the IRS to process a tax return and program the information into Tele-Tax. After the IRS inputs the information requested, you will be informed of the status of your refund.

If a mistake was made, the refund might have to be processed manually, which may take an additional four to six weeks. Whatever the reason for the delay, the Tele-Tax System usually explains it. Tele-Tax also informs you of the date your check was mailed or when it will be mailed.

If it has been more than ten days to two weeks since the date a refund check was scheduled to be mailed and you still haven't received it, the check was probably lost or stolen. If this is the situation, you can do one of three things:

- ✔ Fill out Form 3911 (Taxpayer Statement Regarding Refund) and send it to the service center where you filed. This is a one-page form that asks whether you ever received the check , or whether you received it and lost it. Allow four to six weeks for processing.

- ✔ Contact the Problems Resolution Office in your district. See "When the IRS Ignores You" earlier in this chapter for more information.

- ✔ Contact the IRS refund section at 1-800-829-1040 where you will have the opportunity to speak to an IRS employee instead of a machine.

Uncashed refund checks

You must cash a refund check within 12 months. If your refund check isn't cashed within the required 12-month period, it doesn't mean you're not entitled to your refund. You are. A new refund check will have to be issued and the uncashed one returned to the IRS. This procedure can be accomplished by filing Form 3911 (Taxpayer Statement Regarding Refund) with the service center where you filed your return. Check Box 16, cross out the wording next to the box, and in its place insert THE ENCLOSED REFUND CHECK CANNOT BE CASHED; 12 MONTHS HAVE EXPIRED SINCE IT WAS ISSUED. PLEASE ISSUE A REPLACEMENT CHECK.

You aren't entitled to additional interest on a replacement check because you failed to deposit or cash your refund.

Interest on refunds

If the IRS doesn't issue your refund within 45 days of filing your return, it must pay you interest. So if you file by April 15 and you don't receive your refund by May 31, interest is due.

Refunds and estimated tax payments

If you requested that your refund be applied to next year's tax, you can't change your mind and subsequently request a refund. You can get your overpayment back only by taking credit for it on next year's tax return. No interest is paid on an overpayment of tax credited to next year's tax.

Joint refunds

Where married couples have divorced or separated, or where there is a dispute as to how much of the refund each is entitled to, Revenue Ruling 80-7 provides a formula for determining each spouse's share of the refund. Again, this is one of those times when consulting a tax advisor is a must. If the parties can't decide how to divide the refund, either spouse may request that the IRS issue a separate refund check by filing Form 1040X (Amended U.S. Individual Income Tax Return) and making the computation required by Revenue Ruling 80-7. The IRS will accept a joint 1040X with only one signature from a divorced or separated taxpayer requesting a separate refund check.

Revenue Ruling 80-7 must be modified for taxpayers residing in community property states (California, Nevada, New Mexico, Arizona, Idaho, Washington, Louisiana, and Texas).

Joint estimated payments

Where joint estimated payments have been made, and a husband and wife file separate returns, the estimated payments may be divided in any manner the couple sees fit. However, if a couple can't agree on how these estimated payments are to be divided, the payments will be divided in accordance with Revenue Ruling 80-7.

Deceased taxpayer

If a refund is due a deceased taxpayer, Form 1310 (Statement of Person Claiming Refund Due a Deceased Taxpayer) must be attached to the return. If the form isn't attached, the IRS will send back the return along with Form 1310. The refund will be processed once the IRS receives Form 1310. This form need not be filed if a joint return is being filed by a surviving spouse.

Statute of limitations

To get a refund, you must file a return within three years of its due date, including extensions of time to file (or within two years from the date tax was paid, if later). After that time, you forfeit the refund. A return filed before the due date is considered to have been filed on the due date. For example, if the due date for filing a return is April 17, 1995, an amended return must be filed by April 17, 1998. After that date, no refund will be allowed.

If the April 17, 1995 filing date was extended to August 17, 1995, an amended return must be filed by August 17, 1998. Your acceptance of a refund doesn't bar a future claim for a refund if you subsequently discover that you made a mistake in computing the refund you were entitled to.

Erroneous refunds

If you receive an erroneous refund and don't repay it, the IRS cannot enforce collection by use of a lien or levy. Its only remedy is to sue you or to issue a deficiency notice.

Refund offset program

If the IRS intercepts a joint refund where only one spouse owes for support or a government debt, the IRS must notify the other spouse of the action the agency must take to get its share of the refund. The IRS can't keep the entire refund. The nonobligated spouse must file Form 8379 (Injured Spouse Claim and Allocation) to claim a share of the refund. Revenue Ruling 80-7, as previously discussed, explains how to divide the refund.

Just remember that to err is human, to forgive divine. And we never accused the IRS of not being human.

Reprinted with permission

Chapter 17

Fixing IRS Problems That Are (Generally) Your Fault

*W*e all make mistakes. To make them is human; to admit that they're our fault is untypically human. In most cases, the sooner you fix a problem, the happier and less poor you'll be. In some cases, you'll need to complete more paperwork; in others you'll have to speak with and cajole IRS employees. Regardless, here's our advice for how to do it now, do it right, and be done with it!

Amending a Return

Through the years, when taxpayers discovered that they failed to claim a deduction or credit in a prior year, they often asked whether they could claim the deduction in the current year. They couldn't and you can't, either.

If you discover that you forgot to claim a deduction and the statute of limitations hasn't expired, you have to file an amended return. Similarly, if you discover that a deduction was improperly claimed, you must file an amended return and pay any additional tax plus interest.

Not surprisingly, more amended returns are filed where the flow of funds is going in the taxpayers' direction than in the government's. Although this isn't a startling discovery, it has more to do with *letting sleeping dogs lie* than with people's honesty. It will take a sociologist to properly address this issue, and we're not quite qualified to pull it off.

If you forgot to claim a deduction in a prior year, you must file an amended return within three years from the date of filing your original return or within two years from the time the tax was paid, whichever is later. Form 1040X (Amended Individual Income Tax Return) is used to correct a prior year's tax return.

Suppose that you file your 1994 return on April 17, 1995. If you want to amend this return, you must do so by April 17, 1998. However, if you filed your return on or before April 15, 1995, the three-year statute of limitations expires on April 15, 1998, and *not* on April 17, 1998. If you had an extension of time to file until October 16, 1995 the three-year period starts to run from that date.

Filing an amended return doesn't affect the penalty for underestimating your tax. For example, suppose that you were assessed a $1,000 penalty for under-payment of your estimated tax. Your amended return is for half the tax on your original return. The $1,000 underestimating penalty can't be reduced. This is one mistake that can't be amended.

Amended returns are also useful in changing how you reported an item on your original return. You can change your mind in the following situations:

- ✔ You filed separately but now want to file jointly. It is important to note that you *cannot* do this in reverse — you can't switch back to filing separately if you originally filed jointly.

- ✔ You want to switch between five- and ten-year averaging on paying tax on a lump-sum retirement payment.

- ✔ You want to change from itemizing your deductions to claiming the standard deductions, or vice-versa.

- ✔ You want to revoke the election to exclude the first $125,000 of profit on the sale of your home. Revoking this election may make sense if you claimed the $125,000 exclusion when there was only a modest profit.

- ✔ You reported something incorrectly. This situation may occur if you claimed a deduction or an exemption of income that you weren't entitled to. An example could be where a noncustodial parent incorrectly claimed an exemption for a child or claimed head of household filing status.

Some decisions to treat an item in a certain manner are irrevocable, such as using the straight-line depreciation method and taking a net operating loss forward instead of backwards.

More expenses than income

An amended return is permitted if you incur a net operating loss (NOL). You have an NOL if you lost money (in a business or profession) that exceeds all your other income. You can carry back an NOL to offset your taxable income in the three previous years, and this action will entitle you to a refund. If the NOL is not used up by the last time you carry it back, it can be carried over for 15 years until it is.

Additionally, when filing your return for the NOL year, you can carry the NOL forward instead of having to amend your returns for the three preceding years. This choice may make sense when tax rates are rising. The reverse would be true if tax rates are declining.

You need Form 1045 (Application for Tentative Refund) to carry back an NOL. This form can be used only if it is filed within one year of the year you had the NOL. If it isn't, Form 1040X (Amended U.S Individual Income Tax Return) must be used.

The tax benefit rule

Usually, if you deduct an expense in one year and part or all of that expense is reimbursed in a subsequent year, you have to report the reimbursement as income. For example, suppose that you deducted $10,000 in medical expenses in 1994 and were reimbursed $3,000 by your insurance company in 1995. You have to report the $3,000 in 1995.

However, if the original deduction didn't result in a tax savings, you don't have to report the reimbursement. For example, you may receive a state tax refund for a year in which you claimed the standard deduction instead of itemizing your deductions — you don't have to report the refund.

When You Can't Pay Your Taxes

"If you can't pay," goes the old saw, "you can owe." That's certainly the way the Internal Revenue Service looks at things. Taxpayers currently owe the IRS almost $120 billion in back taxes, a number that increases at the rate of $15 billion a year.

If you are one of the millions of Americans who can't pay all they owe, you've got four options:

- ✔ You can pay it off in installments.
- ✔ You can put it off until you have more money.
- ✔ You can try to convince the IRS to take less than it wants.
- ✔ You can file for bankruptcy — in the absolute worst-case scenario.

Whatever you do, don't confuse filing and paying. More people get into hot water because they mistakenly believe that they should put off filing until they can pay. If you are one of the five to ten million nonfilers that the IRS is currently looking for, file your return as soon as possible — even if you can pay only part of what you owe. Owing the IRS money is expensive. Nine percent interest compounds daily on the balance you owe, in addition to a late-payment penalty of half a percentage point per month. This adds up to big bucks! Every month you're late in filing, you'll have to tack on an extra 5 percent penalty, up to a maximum of 25 percent.

At first, the IRS will come after you through the mail. If you owe money, either from the findings of an audit or because you simply couldn't pay it all on April 15 (or April 17 in 1995!), you'll get four notices from the IRS at four- to five-week intervals, the last one threatening in tone. If you didn't pay everything you owe on April 15, the last letter will arrive by certified mail around Labor Day.

Let's say you allow all four letters to go by without paying any money. Your account is now considered delinquent and forwarded to the IRS Automated Collection System (ACS), which means you will start getting telephone calls demanding payment — at home, at work, at your club, anywhere the IRS has a number for you. Although the IRS has been advertising itself as a friendlier place in recent public-service announcements, the agency is anything but congenial when demanding payment. If the ACS isn't successful in getting you to pay up, your account might be transferred to an IRS revenue officer, who will contact you in person.

In many cases, however, the agency already has what it refers to as *levy-source information.* Your file won't go to an agent. The IRS will place a levy on your assets or salary, or it may seize your property. Remember, if you file a return, the government knows where your income comes from and how much you make. Not only does the IRS know about your assets from your tax return, but it also has the right to get more information about you from credit and governmental agencies, such as the Department of Motor Vehicles, the Passport agency, and the U.S. Postal Service. It can make you pay in more ways than one.

Here's a tip to help you avoid that hassle: If there's any way you can get the money together, send a partial payment when filing your return, a partial payment with each of the first three notices, and the balance (including interest and penalties) with the fourth notice.

Installment agreements

In some cases, people need more time to pay off what they owe. If you need more time, you can make a request to pay in installments by attaching Form 9465 (Installment Agreement Request) either to your return or to any of the notices you receive and send it to the IRS Service Center where you file or the center that issued the notice. You can get Form 9465 by calling 800-829-3676. You also can request an installment agreement by telephoning the IRS Taxpayer Services office. This number is in the telephone directory. It's also printed on the notice you receive.

Unless you owe more than $10,000 or want more than 36 months to pay it off, you'll usually get your wish. A mailing will come from the IRS saying your request has been accepted and telling you where to send the money. You won't have to show a financial statement, but you will have to sign installment agreement Form 433-D. Nor will a federal tax lien be filed — that's no small matter because a tax lien can affect your credit rating for seven years, even if you pay off your tax liability in a shorter period of time.

Be careful not to fall behind in your payments, because you may have to apply for an installment plan all over again. If things are tight and you can't make a payment, contact the IRS. You stand a good chance of being able to skip a payment if you have a plausible reason. Although the IRS isn't all that charitable, it reserves its wrath for taxpayers who ignore the agency.

Installments get trickier if you owe more than $10,000 or want to stretch your payments over more than 36 months. Here, you're going to have to skip the Form 9465 and go straight to the IRS, either by mail or by phone. (A representative, such as an enrolled agent, a CPA, or an attorney, can make this request on your behalf.) You'll need to file a four-page financial statement listing your assets, liabilities, and monthly income and expenses. This is IRS Form 433-A (Collection Information Statement for Individuals).

After reviewing the form, the IRS will recommend one of the following courses of action, or a combination of them. The IRS may tell you to:

- make immediate payment by liquidating some of your assets.
- obtain a cash advance from a credit line.
- borrow against the equity in any assets you might have, such as your residence.
- make an installment agreement.

There is a fifth option: If there's just no way you're going to pay, the IRS will stop bothering you for the money. Yes, if you get the fifth option, the IRS will prepare Form 53 (Report of Taxes Currently Not Collectible) and you'll be off the hook for a while. But the IRS will contact you every nine to twelve months for a new financial statement, to see whether your financial condition has changed. Remember, the IRS has ten years to collect what you owe before the statute of limitations on collections expires.

Make an offer

What if you think there's no way you'll ever be able to pay it all off? The IRS, believe it or not, often takes partial payment. First you'll need to fill out Form 656 (Offer in Compromise). This is a one-page form that requires you to complete only three lines besides your name, address, and Social Security number. You merely state the amount you can pay in relation to your net worth and give the simple statement `I cannot pay these taxes` as the reason for making the offer. Then comes the hard part — you also have to supply a financial statement. And, unlike the application for an installment plan, this financial statement will be audited, not merely reviewed.

An Offer in Compromise is a matter of public record and, if accepted, may come with strings attached. You may have to agree that, for a period of years, perhaps as many as five, you will pay more than you offered should your financial condition improve. An aging Joe Louis had to accept such terms, in case he ever started earning millions again by going back into the boxing ring.

Who are candidates for offers in compromise? All types of taxpayers: senior citizens with few or no assets or in poor health, spendthrifts who earned large sums of money and squandered it, athletes and actors whose earning potential has diminished, casualties of the recession, and people whose relatives are reluctant to leave them money because of their tax problems.

Bankruptcy

If things are really dire, you may decide that declaring personal bankruptcy is the only way out. When you file a bankruptcy petition, it puts a legal stop to all IRS collection action, and the government can no longer garnish your salary or seize your property. Income taxes that are more than three years old are forgiven.

Even if your tax liability isn't completely wiped out in bankruptcy court, as often happens, the IRS probably won't have as much power over you anymore. For example, you don't have to get IRS approval on an installment plan. If the bankruptcy court allows your repayment plan, because the bankruptcy judge finds it fair and equitable, the IRS has to accept it.

However, remember that bankruptcy is a drastic step and shouldn't be undertaken unless you're guided by an attorney experienced in this area. It will damage your credit report, but with all the liens the IRS has filed, your credit is already damaged.

How to prevent all this?

The best defense is to make adequate provisions for paying your taxes in the first place. Routinely review your withholding allowances (Form W-4) to make sure that the proper amount of tax is being withheld from your salary. If you are self-employed or have income that isn't subject to withholding, you should be making quarterly estimated payments (Form 1040-ES). Look at it this way. On average, a third of what you earn isn't yours. You're only its temporary custodian until mid-April.

Abating a Penalty

Although the Internal Revenue Code contains about 150 penalties, some are more common than others. These common penalties include:

- ✔ accuracy errors (The IRS defines accuracy errors as either negligence or disregard of the rules.)
- ✔ failure to file
- ✔ failure to pay
- ✔ false Withholding Exemption Certificate (Form W-4)
- ✔ underestimating tax.

Many taxpayers who receive a penalty notice believe that a penalty wouldn't have been charged unless it was correct, and they simply pay it. After all, penalties are asserted on an official-looking document. Never think that any notice is correct. This is the primary requirement in making sure that you don't pay what you don't owe.

In 1992, the IRS assessed 34 million penalties for a total of $12 billion. Twelve million of these penalties totaling $3 billion were abated for reasonable cause. Penalties are never deductible. Because penalties are considered an addition to the tax you have to pay, interest is computed on the total amount due — tax plus penalties.

Reasonable cause — an important definition

With the exception of fraud penalties, just about every penalty can be abated for what is known as reasonable cause. The IRS defines reasonable cause as follows:

"If the taxpayer exercised ordinary business care and prudence and was nevertheless unable to file or pay within the prescribed time, then the delay is due to reasonable cause."

Estimated taxes

The penalty for underestimating your tax may be abated because of a casualty, disaster, or another unusual circumstance. It can also be abated by filing Form 2210 (Underpayment of Estimated Tax) if you meet one of the following conditions:

✔ You paid in 100 percent of last year's tax. However, if your last year's income exceeds $150,000, you must pay in 110 percent of last year's tax.

✔ You met the 90 percent tax payment requirement.

If you have income that isn't subject to withholding, the IRS doesn't want to wait until April 15 to be paid. The agency wants you to pay what you owe in quarterly estimates.

✔ You filed a return for the previous year that showed no tax liability.

✔ You retired at age 62 or later, or became disabled.

✔ If you operate a seasoned business or didn't earn your income evenly throughout the year, you may be able to reduce or eliminate the penalty by using the annualized income installment method. Not many taxpayers use it because of its complexity. But if you think it will save you money, IRS Publication 505 (Tax Witholding and Estimated Tax) explains how it works.

To get the penalty waived, attach an explanation to Form 2210 along with any documentation that will prove you shouldn't be charged a penalty.

Taxpayers can look to three sources — the Internal Revenue Manual, court cases, and IRS Rulings and Announcements — to determine if they meet the definition of reasonable cause.

Internal Revenue Manual (IRM)

This manual is the IRS bible. It contains the rules that IRS employees must follow in applying the law. According to the manual, the following situations constitute reasonable cause for abating a penalty:

✔ Your return was mailed on time, but was not received until after the filing date, regardless of whether or not the envelope bears sufficient postage.

✔ Your return was filed on time, but was received by the wrong IRS office.

✔ You relied upon erroneous information provided to you by an IRS officer or employee.

✔ Your return was filed late due to death or serious illness of the taxpayer, or to the death or illness of a family member.

- You were unavoidably away on the filing date.

- Your place of business, residence, or business records were destroyed due to fire or other casualty.

- You applied to the IRS district director for proper tax forms prior to the filing deadline — but these forms were not furnished in sufficient time.

- You presented proof of having visited the office of the IRS district director before the expiration date for filing returns in order to secure information on how to properly complete your return — but you were not able to meet with an IRS representative.

- You were unable, for reasons beyond your control, to obtain the records necessary to determine the amount of tax due or for reasons beyond your control you weren't able to pay. For example, you couldn't get your money out of a bankrupt S & L to pay your taxes, or your account was attached by lien or court order. Perhaps you earned money in a foreign country that you couldn't convert into dollars, or a person needed to cosign a check was ill or away.

- Your tax advisor incorrectly advised you that you didn't need to file a return, even though you provided him or her with all the necessary and relevant documents.

Your ignorance of the law may be considered as reasonable cause for a late-filed return if other factors, such as a situation where you are filing a return for the first time, support this contention. However, you must demonstrate having exercised ordinary care and prudence.

Court cases: defining reasonable cause

The following is a list of court precedents that can be handy to know when dealing with the IRS. Precedents are good things because they act like rules that the IRS will obey. You can use these arguments when appropriate. The IRS should listen. But be careful: when you start citing court cases, the eyes of IRS officials (or anyone else for that matter) may start to glaze over.

Ignorance

The taxpayer's limited education and business experience, together with her reliance on the advice of an attorney, caused her failure to file to be due to reasonable cause. _C.R. Dexter,_ 306 F.supp 415.

Litigation

The taxpayer's late filing was due to reasonable cause when litigation was necessary to determine the taxability of income received. _F.P. Walker_ (CA-9), 326 F. 2nd 261(nonacq).

Timely mailed and presumed received

Even though a taxpayer didn't have a certified or registered mailing receipt, the Tax Court held that the IRS is presumed to have received a timely mailed return when a postal official testified that she had accepted and postmarked the envelope prior to the due date of the return. The Court found it a mere coincidence that the taxpayer's state return hadn't been received by the state tax authority either, *Estate of Wood,* 92 TC 793. One could safely infer that the court would have been equally convinced if an employee or other individual had given the same testimony.

Return executed but misplaced

Where returns were signed and given to an employee whose duty was to mail the returns, who by error then placed them in a file together with copies of the returns of many other corporations, and on notice from the IRS a year later, the error was discovered and the returns filed, there was reasonable cause. *Bouvelt Realty,* 46 BTA 45.

Return misplaced by the IRS

The Commissioner failed to refute the taxpayer's evidence that the tax returns were timely filed, but misplaced by the IRS. *J.J. Carlin,* 43 TCM(CCH) 22.

Mailing of return on time

The Commissioner asserted that a return due on the 15th had not been received for filing until the 17th. The corporate officer who had mailed the return had died and because of the Commissioner's failure to produce the envelope in which the return was mailed, it was held that no penalty should attach. *Capento Securities Corp.,* 47 BTA 691 (Nonacq) Aff'd CA-1.

Honest belief

The taxpayer's honest but mistaken belief that an extension of time to file allowed him to delay the filing of his tax return until he had sufficient funds to pay his tax constituted reasonable cause for the late filing of his tax return. *M.S. Alba,* DC, East.Dist.MO.No.80-764.

A taxpayer who — while separated from her husband — attached her W-2 to a joint return that she gave back to her husband to file. The honest belief that the return was filed didn't constitute willful neglect. *E. Barker,* 22 TCM 634.

Illness

The taxpayer's illness and hospitalization constituted reasonable cause for failure to file a tax return. *C. Freeman,* 40 TCM 1219, Dec. 37,236(M).

Reliance on accountant

Where a corporate taxpayer selects a competent tax expert, supplies him with all necessary information, and requests him to prepare proper tax returns, we think the taxpayer has done all that ordinary business care and prudence can reasonably demand. *Haywood Lumber & Mining Co. v. Comm.*, (CA-2) 178 F.2nd 769.REV'D CA-2.

Excuses that won't fly

The dog-ate-my-homework excuse won't work. Nor will these three.

Delegation of authority

In a landmark case, the Supreme Court held that the reliance on an attorney as to the filing date of a return didn't constitute reasonable cause, *R.W Boyle, SCT. 105 S. Ct. 687.* A qualified tax advisor's incorrect advice as to whether a tax return should be filed constitutes reasonable cause, but his or her mistaken advice as to the correct date a return must be filed does not.

Disabled taxpayer

But subsequent to *Boyle v. U.S.,* a disabled taxpayer's reliance on an attorney to timely file a return was considered reasonable cause. *C. Brown v. U.S.,* 57 AFTR 2d (M.D. Tenn. 1985).

Incarceration

The Tax Court rejected a taxpayer's claim that incarceration constituted reasonable cause. *R. Llorente,* 74 TC 260.

IRS rulings and announcements

Taxpayers are amazed when they discover that most of the rules they must follow are created by the IRS — not the Congress. That's because most tax laws include the following language: "in accordance with rules and regulations to be promulgated by the Secretary of the Treasury." Therefore, we must pay special attention to the IRS rulings and announcements — there's a whole lot of promulgating going on.

Partnership returns—rev.proc.84-35

If the partnership is composed of ten or fewer partners and each of the partners reports his or her share of the partnership's income and deductions, the partnership won't be charged a penalty for not filing its return.

Erroneous advice given by IRS employees over the telephone

According to IRS Information Release IR-88-75, incorrect advice given over the telephone by an IRS employee may constitute reasonable cause. The only problem with this is how you prove that you called the IRS and received erroneous advice. The IRS will consider that a taxpayer received incorrect advice over the telephone if a taxpayer provides the following information:

- whether the taxpayer tried to find the answer to the question in IRS forms, instructions, or publications
- the questions asked and the specific facts given to the IRS employee
- the answer the taxpayer received
- the employee's name
- the date and time of the call

If you're reading this provision for the first time, it's probably too late. But please use it the next time you call the IRS for advice.

IRS criteria in determining reasonable cause

This IRS ruling spells out the criteria for reasonable cause. Here they are:

- Do the taxpayer's reasons address the penalty that was assessed?
- Does the length of time between the event that caused the late filing and the actual filing negate the fact that the taxpayer attempted to correct the situation in a timely fashion?
- Does the continued operation of a business after the event that caused the taxpayer's noncompliance negate the taxpayer's excuse?
- Should the event that caused the taxpayer's noncompliance or increased liability have been reasonably anticipated?
- Was the penalty the result of carelessness, or does the taxpayer appear to have made an honest mistake?
- Has the taxpayer provided sufficient detail (dates, relationships) to determine whether he or she exercised ordinary business care and prudence? Is a nonliable individual being blamed for the taxpayer's noncompliance? What is the nature of the relationship between the taxpayer and this individual? Is the individual an employee of the taxpayer or an independent third party, such as an accountant or a lawyer?
- Has the taxpayer documented all pertinent facts?
- Does the taxpayer have a history of being assessed the same penalty?
- Does the amount of the penalty justify closer scrutiny of the case?
- Could the taxpayer have requested an extension or filed an amended return?

Critical to getting the IRS to accept your reasons for late filing or paying is the time frame between the event that was clearly beyond your control and the date of your ultimate compliance with your obligation to file or pay. What the IRS considers to be an acceptable amount of time between these two events is based on the facts and circumstances in each case. Figure 17-1 shows a reasonable cause sample letter.

Penalty appeals

If the Adjustments/Correspondence Branch rejects your request to have a penalty abated, you may appeal. Every service center has a penalty appeals unit. The A/C Branch notice informing taxpayers that their request was rejected will also inform them of their appeal rights and how to exercise them. The rejection notice will simply use the IRS standard generic phrase: "Your explanation of why your return was filed late did not meet the criteria of reasonable cause."

Payment of the penalty is not a prerequisite to requesting an appeal. There is no official IRS form for requesting this type of appeal. Although some appeals within the IRS need not be in writing, this one must. Your original letter requesting an abatement can be used with one simple modification: your opening sentence should state that you are requesting an appeal from a tax examiner's determination (which you are enclosing) that you failed to establish reasonable cause.

You may want to include any additional reasons that constitute reasonable cause, or any documentary evidence, such as your passport showing that you were out of the country, medical records stating that you were ill, a statement from a third party who saw you mail the return on time, or a police or insurance report showing that the loss of your records was due to a theft or other casualty. These documents, if available, should have been sent with the original abatement request. Hold nothing back!

At times, for inexplicable reasons, tax examiners take the position that taxpayers should have quickly estimated their income and filed a return based on this estimate. In such instances, you should point out that the event that you considered reasonable cause prevented you from preparing an estimate.

It is IRS policy that no collection action will be taken while a penalty appeal is pending — unless the case has already been assigned to a collection officer who has determined that the appeal was requested solely to postpone or delay payment. If you are being bugged for the penalty, contact the appeals office in order to get the IRS Collection Division off your back. An appeals officer has authority to do this.

Be patient when requesting an abatement of a large penalty or when appealing a penalty abatement decision. The process is not speedy.

Sample Reasonable Cause Letter

Request to abate penalty
[your name and address]
[today's date]

Adjustments/Correspondence Branch
Internal Revenue Center
[address]

Re: [your name]
[Social Security number]
[tax year]

Dear IRS:

I am in receipt of your notice of [date] in which you asserted a late filing and payment penalty in the amount of [amount] plus interest on this amount of [interest].

Please be advised that my late filing and payment were due to reasonable cause and according to tax law should be abated.

On [date] I was ill with [illness]. I was hospitalized and didn't recover sufficiently until [date]. When I was well enough to assemble the data necessary to file a return and pay what was owed, I immediately did so. Enclosed is a letter from my physician confirming the nature of my illness and the length of my recovery, as well as the hospital bill.

Regulation 301.6651-1(c) provides that:

"If a taxpayer exercised ordinary business care and prudence and was nevertheless either unable to file the return or pay within the prescribed time, the delay is due to reasonable cause."

I thank you in advance for your prompt attention to this request. If you require further clarification of any point, I may be reached at [telephone number].

Very truly yours,
[your name]

Enclosed: Form 8488 (Penalty Notice)
           Letter from Physician & hospital

Figure 17-1:
Sample
reasonable
cause letter.

Abating Interest

Whereas the IRS has the power to abate a penalty for reasonable cause, it doesn't have — as a general rule — the authority to abate interest. But like every IRS rule, here are some limited exceptions when interest *can* be abated.

When interest is incorrectly charged

If interest was assessed after the expiration of the statute of limitations or was assessed illegally, then it's probably correct to assume that the underlying tax was also incorrectly assessed. If this is the case, then the interest, as well as the tax, can be abated.

Interest and tax that were incorrectly or illegally assessed may be abated in one of two ways. First, you can use Form 911 (Taxpayer Assistance Order). Or you can write to the Adjustments/Correspondence Branch at the service center (or district office) that issued the notice. Figure 17-2 shows a sample letter designed to abate interest with two possible reasons.

Erroneous refunds

The IRS is required to abate interest on a demand for repayment of a refund issued by error. In order for this rule to apply, the refund must be less than $50,000, and the taxpayer must be in no way responsible for causing the refund. On an erroneous refund, the IRS can charge interest only from the point in time when it demanded repayment and not for the period prior to the taxpayer being asked to repay it.

For example, suppose that you should have received a $100 refund, but instead, received a $1,000 refund. No interest may be charged on the $900 for the period of time you held the money. If interest is assessed on the $900, the filing of Form 843 (Claim for Refund and Request for Abatement) will get back the interest that you paid.

IRS delays

The Tax Reform Act of 1986 gives the IRS the authority to abate interest on any tax deficiency when an IRS official fails to perform a *ministerial act* and instead moves at a snail's pace in handling routine matters. The IRS has the right to abate interest, but it is not compelled to do so. Where the failure to perform a ministerial act has occurred, interest is required to be abated from the period of time when the IRS first contacted you, not from the due date of your tax return, which normally is the case.

Sample Letter

[date]

IRS Service Center
[address]

Re: [your name]
[Social Security number]
[tax year]

Dear IRS:

I respectfully request that you abate the tax assessment in the amount of [amount] that your agency made by error pursuant to the enclosed notice.

Reason (1) Section 6404(e) specifically allows for the abatement of tax that was assessed as the result of an IRS mathematical or clerical error.

Reason (2) Your assessment was made after the three-year statute of limitations had expired. Such assessments are prohibited by law.

I may re reached by telephone during the day at [telephone number] should you require any further information.

Very truly yours,
[your name]

Enclosed: Copy of Notice

Figure 17-2:
A sample
letter to
abate
interest.

Here's how the IRS decides whether it is moving slowly:

- ✔ You moved from one state to another. Your return was selected for audit. You request the audit to be transferred to your new location, and the transfer is approved. But the IRS delays in transferring your case. Interest can be abated.

- ✔ An audit reveals that additional tax is due. You and the IRS have agreed on the amount of additional tax due, but the IRS delays in sending you a bill. Interest can be abated.

✔ You deducted a loss from a tax shelter that is being audited. It takes a long time to complete the audit of the shelter. Interest can't be abated.

✔ The agent auditing your return is assigned to a training course, and, during the training course, no work is done nor is the audit reassigned to a different agent. Interest *can't* be abated. Sounds crazy, doesn't it?

Form 843 (Claim for Refund and Request for Abatement) is used to abate interest where the IRS has caused a delay. Check Box 4a (Interest Caused by IRS Errors and Delays). Getting interest abated on an IRS delay is a tough nut to crack.

When the IRS doesn't send a bill

When you sign off on the results of a tax examination or notice of proposed adjustments to your return, the IRS must send you a bill for payment within 30 days. If it doesn't, the agency can't charge interest until a bill is sent. Use Form 843 to abate any interest charges after the 30-day period.

Taxpayer Bill of Rights

This great republic was founded on the principle that taxation without representation is tyranny. But if you've ever had a run-in with the IRS, you know that taxation with representation isn't so hot either. To feed its insatiable appetite for spending, Congress has given the IRS almost unlimited authority to collect taxes — an authority that, sadly, can be abused in all sorts of horrible ways.

A few years ago, lawmakers decided to do something about the monster they created. Responding to a flurry of taxpayer horror stories, in 1988 Congress enacted the so-called Taxpayer Bill of Rights. The idea: to lay out in writing what the IRS can get away with when collecting your money, and what you can do to fight back.

Now, whenever you get a notice of any kind from the IRS, you'll get a four-page summary of the Taxpayer Bill, entitled "Your Rights as a Taxpayer." This remarkably readable document explains how to appeal an IRS decision, suggests where you can get "free information," and assures that you are entitled to "courtesy and consideration" from IRS employees. Reading it, you could almost get the impression that the IRS is a friendly place that only wants what's best for you. That assumption, of course, would be a terrible mistake.

It's not that the Taxpayer Bill of Rights is worthless. On the contrary, it contains two very significant points:

- At any time during an audit or interview, you may ask to speak with an enrolled agent, attorney, or CPA. The IRS must stop what it's doing and let you do so.

- The IRS may not take money or property from you on the same day that you comply with a summons. In other words, the IRS can't demand that you appear and then seize your car when you get to its office — something that used to happen a lot.

Despite those important rights, the Taxpayer Bill still leaves much to be desired — in too many cases it allows the IRS *itself* to interpret your rights. It's like having the same person as prosecutor, judge, and jury.

Part IV
Training for a Better Race Next Time

In this part...

Taxes are not a financial island unto themselves. Just about every major financial decision you make involves a tax angle and has tax consequences. With just a little bit of knowledge and advance planning, you can make your money work much harder for you. In fact, the worse you are at managing your finances, the more money you can put back into your hands if you learn how to make tax-wise financial decisions.

Chapter 18

Fitting Taxes into Your Financial Planning

In This Chapter

▶ Understanding the importance of the Big Picture

▶ Learning from mistakes

▶ Overcoming tax planning hurdles

▶ Spending less to reduce taxes

*T*axes build and fix the roads, allow local libraries to stay open over the summer months — and pay for the military's $600 toilet seats! These are some of the many benefits that we derive from our tax dollars.

But what do you really get out of taxes?

Most people get a headache — from filling out all those complicated forms — and feel terribly disorganized because they've got better things to do during the year than keep all those receipts and records they may need in April. And if that isn't enough, most of us get angry when we see how little money is left over *for us* after Uncle Sam takes his share.

Fitting Taxes into Your Financial Puzzle

You probably work hard for your money. Between actual hours in the office and commuting, you probably spend 50 hours per week on work stuff. That's about 2,500 hours per year. Think about that amount — 2,500 hours per year, *year after year after year*, spanning several decades.

That's a lot of time spent working to earn money.

Now, how much time do you spend planning how to make the most of this money? Yeah, we thought so — are you blushing?

Planning your finances involves much more than just managing and investing money — it includes making all the pieces of your financial life fit together. And, just like planning your vacation, it means developing a plan to make the best use of your limited time and dollars.

Taxes are a vital and large piece of your financial puzzle. Here are a few ways that taxes permeate sound financial decisions:

- ✔ **Spending.** The more you spend, the less you will be able to take advantage of the many tax benefits in our tax code — which require that you have money to invest in the first place. And because taxes are a hefty portion of your expenditures (probably one of your top items), a spending plan that overlooks tax reduction strategies is doomed to failure.

- ✔ **Retirement planning.** In no other aspect of your financial situation do taxes play a greater role than contributing to retirement accounts. You may not even know what you're missing out on, nor may you know that not taking advantage of these outstanding tax reduction opportunities could mean tens, perhaps even hundreds, of thousands, fewer dollars in your pocket come retirement.

- ✔ **Investing.** There are many tax angles that enable you to invest wisely. In addition to investing in stocks, bonds, and mutual funds, you may also invest in real estate and your own business. It's not enough to choose investments that generate favorable rates of return. What matters is not what you make but what you keep — after paying taxes and understanding and capitalizing on the many tax breaks available to investors.

- ✔ **Insuring.** Some of your insurance decisions (such as you learn in Chapter 24) also affect the taxes you'll pay. You'd think that after a lifetime of tax payments, your heirs would be left alone when you pass on to the greater beyond. Wishful thinking. Estate planning may enable you to pay less to the government.

As you see, taxes infiltrate all areas of financial planning. Often, people make important financial decisions without factoring in taxes as well as other important variables. Although you learn in the pages ahead that taxes are an important component to factor into your major financial decisions, taxes should not drive or dictate the decisions you make. Sometimes, in an obsession to minimize or avoid taxes, people make decisions that are counterproductive to achieving their personal and financial goals.

Taxing Mistakes

Ever since you were a wee little tot, you've been learning from your mistakes. For example, how many times did you try to pet that nasty pet parakeet! As you grew older, you not only learned from your mistakes, but you also learned by watching others screw up. We think that learning from others' mistakes is a much more pleasant way to learn. Therefore, we want you to meet a good friend of ours — Wally. You're going to learn a lot from him.

Wally the Tax Dunderhead

Over the years that we have worked as tax and financial practitioners, certain people stand out in our minds — some for good reasons and others for not-so-good reasons. Wally stands out because he made so many of the financial mistakes that can be made when factoring taxes into important financial decisions.

When he used to work full-time, Wally worked long hours. He held a senior-level management job with great benefits and enjoyed an annual income of about $100,000 per year. Work wasn't the only thing that Wally did to excess. Everything that Wally could focus on seemed to become a habit, including drinking, smoking, eating fast food, and constantly complaining about all the taxes he paid.

To be sure, Wally did pay a bunch in taxes — tens of thousands of dollars per year. He seemed to have at least one criticism for every dollar he paid in taxes:

- ✔ "Half my taxes go to pay for all these do-good social programs for immigrants. Most of them are here illegally and should be kicked out of my country."

- ✔ "The government should leave wage slaves like me alone and instead tax all these overpaid baseball players and movie stars who earn millions for doing little work."

- ✔ "I can't believe the bureaucrats who want to extend public transit farther into the suburbs. Why should I pay for something I won't use?" (It's worth noting that Wally also complained about the traffic jams on highways that ran through the area proposed for a new rapid-transit rail line!)

One of the other things that Wally did a lot of, besides getting cranky about taxes, was spending money. Despite his income, Wally hadn't started to save any money towards his retirement until he reached his 50s. He carried a wallet full of credit cards and enough credit card and other high-interest consumer debt — such as car loans — to choke his earnings.

Because he spent all his earnings and then some, he had no discretionary income to put into his employer's tax-deductible retirement savings plan. Besides missing out on great tax benefits, he also missed out on the generous matching funds his employer provided — his company matched *dollar for dollar* the first 5 percent of employee contributions. Thus, every year he didn't contribute to this terrific plan, Wally missed out on about $5,000 his employer was otherwise happy to give him.

Feeling that he wasn't ever going to be able to retire if he didn't start saving, Wally did start investing during the 1980s. He had been called at the office one day by a *"financial consultant"* who — almost paternalistically — seemed quite concerned that Wally wasn't planning for his future. So Wally bought the sales pitch about some limited partnerships; one partnership invested in biotechnology, another in real estate, and a third in oil and gas. The financial consultant also recommended some cash-value life insurance so that Wally could squirrel away more money for his old age (see Chapter 21).

Wally didn't understand any of these purchases — he went for them because he was relying on the consultant's professional judgment.

In the end, these decisions turned out to be terrible financial decisions for Wally. He didn't need life insurance because no one was dependent on his income. His limited partnership investments would turn out to be pretty much worthless. Even if these limited partnerships hadn't been such lousy investments, he could have had more tax-favored ways of saving and investing through his company's retirement account. The financial consultant — who sold investments, insurance, and other financial products on commission — had no incentive to recommend that Wally take advantage of his employee benefits.

For Wally's sake, we wish these mistakes were the extent of his financial and tax blunders, but they weren't. While on vacation at a ski resort, Wally went to a *free* seminar that discussed the tax benefits of owning real estate. He liked what he heard and was frustrated that he couldn't ever seem to come up with the necessary down payment needed to buy a home. In addition to the large amount of consumer debt he carried, Wally also rented a luxury condominium for $3,200 per month in an affluent community an hour from his office.

Wally ended up buying two time shares — generally bad-news real estate investments — from the *real estate consultant* who led the seminar. The time shares sounded like such an easy low-cost way for Wally to own some real estate. Wally has since learned that these are not good investments.

In addition to his investment blunders, with all the long hours that Wally put in at the office, he hardly had any time to understand his employee benefits package. This ignorance proved costly, because he wasn't able to take advantage of his health care spending account to pay, with pre-tax dollars, all the doctor's visits that he needed because he did not take care of his health.

Wally only took time to think about his taxes when he had to complete his annual tax return. This was a time of year when he was usually his grumpiest. Wally's taxes had grown more complex after he had set up an independent consulting business in order to earn more money. Because Wally worked so hard now juggling a job and a half, he often filed his tax return late and owed additional money in the form of late interest and penalties.

Because Wally didn't understand the tax implications of his various financial moves, the total additional taxes were extraordinary — easily in excess of $100,000 over the course of his working years. If you factor in the lost interest, dividends, and growth that Wally would have realized had he invested even somewhat wisely, his mistakes cost him in the neighborhood of half a million dollars ($500,000)!

If only Wally had planned better! If you read the remaining chapters in this part, you can avoid the tax and financial mistakes that Wally made.

P.S. It turned out that Wally hated paying his taxes so much that, when he got audited a couple of years ago, the IRS discovered that he hadn't been reporting all his consulting income. He had been cheating by underreporting his income in order to escape paying income taxes on his freelance income.

When Wally was last heard from, he was forced to retire at age 65, and he had just come home after a lengthy hospital stay with a poor prognosis. He had developed cancer — maybe because he abused his body for so long. He's been racking up tens of thousands of dollars in Medicare costs — a program that's funded through tax dollars. At least Wally is getting some of his tax dollars back now.

We feel sorry for Wally — we really do. We hope that you can learn from the financial, tax, and personal mistakes that he made.

Ten costly financial planning tax mistakes

Most tax-reducing strategies discussed in this book require that you plan ahead. Lack of foresight is one of the reasons why Wally the Tax Dunderhead paid so much in taxes.

Even if the tax system is hopelessly and unreasonably complicated, there's no reason why you can't learn from the mistakes of others to save yourself some money. With this goal in mind, we list here the most typical tax blunders people make when it comes to managing their finances.

Not saving and investing through retirement accounts

All the tax deductions and tax deferrals that come with accounts such as 401(k)s and IRAs were put in the tax code to encourage people to save for retirement. So why not take advantage of the benefits? You probably have your reasons or excuses — but most excuses for missing out on this strategy just don't make good financial sense. Most people underfund retirement accounts because they spend too much and because retirement seems so far away. See Chapter 19 to learn about retirement accounts.

Ignoring tax considerations when investing money

Suppose that you have some stock that you want to unload so you can buy a new car. You figure out which of your stocks is currently riding high — but also seems to have the poorest future prospects. You sell this stock at a significant capital gain, and you feel pretty good about your financial genius. But, come tax time, you may feel differently.

Don't forget to factor the taxes due from the sale of investments (except those in retirement accounts) into all your decisions about what you sell and when you sell it. Your tax situation should factor into *what* you invest in. If you're in a relatively high tax bracket, you probably don't want investments that pay much in taxable distributions, because such things only add to your tax burden (see Chapter 21 for more details).

Not buying a home

In the long run, owning should cost you less than renting. And because mortgage interest and property taxes are deductible, the government, in effect, subsidizes the cost of home ownership. Wow! So treat yourself to your own abode. Be sure not to let the lack of money for a down payment stand in your way — there are many ways to buy real estate with very little money up front. (See Chapter 22.)

Ignoring the financial aid tax system

The college financial aid system in this country assumes that the money you save outside of tax-sheltered retirement accounts is available to pay educational expenses. As a result, middle- and upper-income families qualify for far less financial aid than they otherwise would. So in addition to normal income taxes, an extra financial-aid tax is effectively being exacted. Be sure to read Chapter 23, which talks about the right and wrong ways to save and invest for educational costs.

Getting advice after a major decision

Too many people hire help *after* a disaster when we all know that it is generally wiser and less costly to seek preventive help. Don't use a tax preparer just to fill in the numbers on your return. During the year you may need assistance in making decisions *before* it's time to file the tax return — at which time it's probably too late to change many of the previous year's activities.

Get advice prior to making any major financial decisions. The wrong move when selling a piece of real estate or when taking a large sum from a retirement account can cost you thousands of dollars in taxes!

Not withholding the right amount of taxes

If you're self-employed or earn significant taxable income from investments outside of retirement accounts, you should be making quarterly tax payments. Likewise, if during the year you sell a major asset at a profit, you may need to make a quarterly tax payment.

Don't be a "should've" victim. People often don't discover that they "should've" paid more taxes during the year until after they complete their return in the spring — or get a penalty notice from the IRS and their state. Then they have to come up with a sizable sum all at once.

Some self-employed people dig themselves into a perpetual tax hole. They get behind during their first year of self-employment and are always playing catch-up.

Call the IRS at 800-TAX-FORM and ask for Form 1040-ES (Estimated Tax for Individuals). This form explains how to calculate quarterly tax payments and includes payment coupons and envelopes in which to send your checks. If you can't figure it out or if you just hate forms, call a tax preparer, without delay.

Then again, some people have too much tax withheld during the year, and this overpayment can go on year after year. Although it's nice to get a hefty refund check every spring, why should you loan money to the government interest-free? If you work for an employer, complete a new W-4 form (get it from your payroll department) to adjust your withholding.

If you know that you would otherwise spend the money, then this forced-savings strategy may have some value. But you can find other, better ways to make yourself save. You can set up all sorts of investments funded by automatic contributions from your paycheck (or from a bank or investment account). Of course, if you *prefer* to loan the IRS more money — interest-free — go right ahead.

Not taking legal deductions

In most cases, folks miss out on perfectly legal deductions because they just don't know about them. Ignorance is not bliss in this case . . . it's costly. If you're not going to take the time to learn about the tax system (you bought this book, so why not read it?), then spring for the cost of a competent tax advisor at least once. If you have a computer, try one of the user-friendly software packages we recommend in Chapter 2.

Fearing an audit, some taxpayers (and even some tax preparers) avoid taking deductions that they have every right to take. Unless you have something to hide, this oversight is expensive and silly. Remember that a certain number of returns are randomly audited every year, so even when you do nothing wrong or inappropriate, you may get audited anyway! And how bad is an audit, really? If you read Chapter 15, you can deal with your audit like a pro. An afternoon with the IRS is not as bad as you think, and it's probably worth the risk if you consider the amount you can possibly save by taking the legitimate deductions that you've been avoiding.

Ignoring the timing of events you can control

The amount of tax you pay on certain transactions can vary, depending on their timing. If you're nearing retirement, for example, you may soon be in a lower tax bracket. To the greatest extent possible, you should delay and avoid investment income until your overall income drops, and you should take as many deductions or losses as you can now while your income is still high. Here are two tax-reducing timing strategies you should be aware of, which you may someday be able to put to good use:

Income shifting

This tax-reduction technique is more esoteric and is available only to those who can control *when* they receive their income.

For example, suppose that your employer tells you in late December that you're eligible for a bonus. You are offered the option to receive your bonus in either December or January. Looking ahead, if you're pretty certain that you will be in a higher tax bracket next year, you should choose to receive your bonus in December.

Or suppose that you run your own business and operate on a cash accounting basis and think that you'll be in a lower tax bracket next year. Perhaps you plan to take time off to be with a newborn or take an extended trip. You can send out some invoices later in the year so that your customers won't pay you until January, which falls in the next tax year.

Shifting or bunching deductions

If, when you total up your itemized deductions on Schedule A (see Chapter 8), the total is lower than the standard deduction, then you should take the standard deduction. This total is worth checking each year, because you may have more deductions in some years than others, and you may occasionally be able to itemize.

Because you can control when you pay particular expenses that are eligible for itemizing, you can *shift* or *bunch* more of them into the select years when you have enough deductions to take advantage of itemizing. Suppose, for example, that you are using the standard deduction this year, because you don't have many itemized deductions. Late in the year, though, you become certain that you'll be itemizing next year because of large medical expenses that you'll pay for. It makes sense, then, to shift and collect as many deductible expenses as possible into next year. For example, if you're getting ready to donate old clothes and household goods to charity, wait until January.

If you're sure that you won't have enough deductions in the current year to itemize, try to shift as many expenses as you can into the next tax year.

Not using tax advisors effectively

If your financial situation is at all complicated, it's usually a mistake to go it alone and rely only on the IRS booklets to figure out your own taxes. The IRS instructions are certainly not going to highlight opportunities for tax reduction, and these instructions are often hopelessly complicated. Start by reading the relevant sections of *Taxes For Dummies*.

The danger of overemphasizing taxes

Perhaps you've heard the expression "Don't let the tail wag the dog." Sometimes, in an effort to avoid taxes today, people make financial decisions that are costly in the long term. Consider the case of Dave, a former IBM manager.

Dave was with IBM from the early days and retired in the mid-1980s. He had accumulated a great deal of IBM stock outside of tax-sheltered retirement accounts — stock that he was reluctant to sell because he would have to pay capital gains tax. So he held onto it. IBM was the Rock of Gibraltar and would keep on growing. Anyway, if IBM got into trouble, the whole country would be in the hopper, Dave thought.

Unfortunately for Dave, IBM's fortunes changed for the worse and its stock plummeted precipitously — more than 70 percent since Dave's retirement. Dave had a large chunk of his total assets — about half — tied up in IBM stock, so its plunge took Dave's dreams of a financially comfortable retirement with it.

Dave planned to sell his stock someday, so he was going to have to pay the tax eventually. While — generally speaking — it's better to postpone paying taxes, in Dave's case, it was a mistake to postpone selling the IBM stock, because he had half his money invested in it. It would have been prudent for him to sell off at least some of the stock so he could better diversify his portfolio.

It's important to note in Dave's case that we're not saying with the benefit of 20/20 hindsight that Dave should have dumped a stock that declined in value. The point is that he had such a large chunk of his money in one stock — and that's a risky proposition for a retiree.

If you're overwhelmed with the complexity of financial decisions, get advice from tax and financial advisors who are selling their time and nothing else. Protect yourself by checking references, clarifying the total expected fees up-front, and exactly what advice, analysis, and recommendations the advisor will provide for the fees charged.

And if you're not willing to make an effort to read this book, at least don't make the mistake of not hiring a competent tax advisor. You can figure out taxes for yourself, or you can pay someone to figure them out for you, but doing nothing is not a permissible option. Sorry!

If your tax situation is complicated, you'll probably more than recoup a preparer's fee. Remember that it's most beneficial to use a tax advisor when you're faced with new tax questions or problems. If your situation remains complicated, or if you know you would do a worse job on your own, by all means keep using a preparer. But don't pay a big fee year after year to a tax advisor who simply fills in the blanks. If your situation is unchanging or not that complicated, consider hiring and paying someone to figure out your taxes just the first time. But, after that, go ahead and try completing your own tax return. You probably can do it.

Challenges to Making Tax-Wise Decisions

When bad things happen, it's usually for a variety of reasons. And so it is with making financial blunders that cause you to pay more tax dollars. Here are the common culprits that may be keeping you from making tax-wise financial maneuvers:

Financial illiteracy

Lack of education is at the root of almost all financial blunders. You don't understand the tax system and how to manage your finances probably because you were never taught how to manage them in high school or college.

Financial illiteracy is a widespread problem — and not just among the poor and uneducated. Wally was well-educated on paper (and a high-income earner), but look at all the errors he made.

Most people don't plan ahead and educate themselves with financial goals in mind. People react — or worse — do nothing at all. We may dream, for example, about retiring and never having to work again. Or perhaps we hope that someday we can own a house or even a vacation home in the country.

You need to understand how to plan your finances in order to accomplish your financial goals. You also need to comprehend how the tax system works and how to navigate within it to work toward your objectives.

Beware financial planners' and brokers' advice

Wanting to hire a professional to help you make better financial decisions is a logical and sensible inclination if you are a time-squeezed, financially clueless person. But if you pick a poor planner or someone who isn't a financial planner, but a salesperson in disguise, watch out!

Unfortunately, more than 90 percent of the people who call themselves financial planners, financial consultants, or financial advisors work on commission, which creates enormous conflicts of interest for impartial financial planning.

Brokers and commission-based financial planners structure their advice around selling you investment and other financial products that provide them with a commission. As a result, they tend to take a narrow view of your finances and frequently ignore the tax and other consequences of financial moves.

The few planners who work on a fee basis primarily provide money management services and charge 1 to 2 percent per year of the money they manage. Fee-based planners who work on this basis have their own conflicts of interest as well, because, all things being equal, they want you to hire them to manage your money. Thus, they can't objectively help you decide if you should pay off your mortgage and other debts, invest in real estate or a small business, or invest more in your employer's retirement plan.

Be especially leery of planners, brokers, and the like who lobby you to sell investments that you've held for a while and that show a profit. If you sell these investments, you may have to pay a hefty tax burden. (See Chapter 21 for more insight on how to make these important investing decisions.)

Beware of advertising

Another reason we make financial missteps is advertising. Although many reputable firms with terrific products advertise, the firms that spend most heavily on advertising are those with mediocre or downright lousy offerings.

Bad financial moves result from responding to most ads, whether the product being pitched is good, bad, or so-so, because the company placing the ad typically is trying to motivate you to buy a specific product. The company doesn't care about your financial alternatives, whether its product fits with your tax situation, and so on. Many ads try to catch your attention with supposed tax savings that its product generates.

Beware of articles offering financial advice

You start reading an article that's recommending some mutual funds. Tired of not taking charge and making financial decisions, you get on the phone, call the appropriate 800 numbers, and — before you know it — you've invested. You feel a sense of relief and accomplishment. You've done something.

Come tax time, you get all these confusing statements detailing dividends and capital gains that you must report on your tax return. Now you can see that these mutual funds pay all sorts of taxable distributions that add to your tax burden but also require more forms to be completed on April 15. You wish you had known.

 Articles in magazines, newspapers, and newsletters can help you stay informed, but they also can cause you to make ill-advised financial moves that overlook tax consequences. Writers have limited space and often are not thinking of the big picture or how their advice could be misunderstood or misused.

Spending Less Slashes Your Taxes

Too many tax guides go on and on and on (like the Energizer bunny), talking about this tax break and that tax break. The problem is that, in order to take advantage of many of the best tax breaks, you need to have some money to invest. If you spend all that you earn, as most Americans do, you may miss out on many terrific tax benefits that we tell you about in this book. And the more you spend, the more taxes you pay, both on your income and on the purchases (sales taxes) you make.

Spending less *sounds* good, but most people have a hard time living within their financial means. Living within your means requires more than spending less than you earn. Living within your means requires that you *spend, save,* and *invest* your money so that you can accomplish your financial goals. At a *minimum,* this implies that you must save some money — that is, spend less than you earn.

Perhaps you already know where the fat is in your spending. If you don't, it's a real eye-opener to figure where all your monthly income is going. It takes a little bit of detective work — looking throught your credit card statement and your checkbook register to track your cash purchases and categorize your spending.

 Because this is a tax-focused book, if you need more help with these issues, we can recommend a useful resource, *Personal Finance For Dummies.* We're not biased in the least (okay, maybe a little, but, hey, the publisher made us say it).

Chapter 19

Retirement (Tax-Reduction) Accounts

Saving and investing through retirement accounts is one of the simplest and best ways to reduce your tax burden. You learn a lot about such strategies in this chapter. Unfortunately, most people can't take full advantage of these plans because they spend everything they make. So not only do they have less savings, they also pay higher income taxes — a double whammy. And don't forget, the more you spend, the more sales tax you pay on purchases.

In order to take advantage of the tax savings that come with saving through retirement savings plans, you must first spend less than you earn. Only then can you afford to contribute to these plans.

Retirement Account Benefits

For some baby boomers and generation Xers, age 65 may seem like the distant future. For many people, it's not until middle age that some warning bells start to stimulate thoughts about what money there will be to live on in the golden years.

The single biggest mistake we see people at all income levels make with retirement accounts is not taking advantage of them — thereby delaying the age at which they start to sock money away. The sooner you start to save, the less painful it is each year, because your contributions have more years to compound. Each decade you delay approximately doubles the percentage of your earnings you should save to meet your goals. For example, if saving five percent per year in your early 20s would get you to your retirement goal, waiting until your 30s may mean socking away ten percent; waiting until your 40s, 20 percent ... it gets ugly beyond that.

So the longer you wait, the more you have to save and the less you'll have to spend. As a result, it could mean that your golden years may be more unpleasant and restrictive than you expected.

We use this economics lesson to emphasize the importance of considering *now* the benefits you achieve by saving and investing in some types of retirement accounts.

Contributions are (generally) tax-deductible

Retirement accounts are misnamed. For most people, particularly those in their 20s, 30s, and even 40s, saving for retirement is like eating a dozen plain rice cakes for dinner. It might be healthier and help you to live longer, but you want to *live* life.

Retirement accounts should really be called tax-reduction accounts. If they were, people might be more excited about contributing to them. For many people, avoiding higher taxes is the motivating force that opens the account and starts the contributions.

Suppose that you are paying about 35 percent between federal and state income taxes on your last dollars of income (see Chapter 1 to identify your tax bracket). For most of the retirement accounts described in this chapter, for every $1,000 you contribute into them, you'll save yourself about $350 in taxes in the year that you make the contribution. Contribute five times as much, or $5,000, and whack $1,750 off your tax bill!

Tax-deferred compounding of investment earnings

Once money is in a retirement account, any interest, dividends, and appreciation add to the amount of your account without being taxed. Of course, there's no such thing as a free lunch — these accounts don't allow for permanent avoidance of taxes. Yet you can get a really great lunch at a discount — you get to defer taxes on all the accumulating gains and profits until you withdraw the money down the road. Thus, more money is working for you over a longer period of time.

You can save less money and spend more

That's right! Because of all the terrific tax benefits you get by saving and investing in retirement accounts, you end up with more money now than if you had saved the money elsewhere.

You incur penalties for early withdrawal

WARNING!

If you withdraw funds from retirement accounts before age 59^1/$_2$, you not only have to pay income taxes on the withdrawals, but you also may pay early withdrawal penalties — 10 percent in federal and varied state charges.

Huh? Doesn't sound like an advantage, you say. Yes, this is an advantage! The system is built to save you from your bad habits.

Retirement accounts are there for just that reason — saving toward retirement. If you could easily raid them without penalties, the money wouldn't be there when you really need it. But if you have an emergency, catastrophic medical expenses, or a disability, you may be able early withdrawals from retirement accounts for these reasons.

TIP

For all you worriers about your retirement tax rates

You may get an added bonus from deferring taxes on your retirement account assets if you are in a lower tax bracket when you withdraw the money. You may very well be in a lower tax bracket in retirement because most people have less income when they're not working.

Some people fret that their taxes will increase when they retire. Although it could happen, the following simple example shows you why your time is better spent worrying about more important issues—like whether there will be a World Series next year.

Take the case of a woman earning $35,000 per year who pays 35 percent in federal and state taxes on her last dollars of income. She contributes 10 percent, or $3,500, per year into a retirement savings plan, thereby decreasing her current year's taxes by $1,225. Assume that the money she contributes grows at the rate of 8 percent per year until she withdraws the money at age 65. After paying taxes at the same rate on her with-

drawal at age 65 as she pays today, she'll have about $15,580 left. If she hadn't saved this money through a retirement plan, she would have had only $8,080 at age 65.

Now, suppose that her career takes off and she earns more money (and pays more taxes) as she gets closer to retirement. How high would her retirement tax rate have to be before she should regret having saved in the retirement account? Answer: She would have to pay about 67 percent in taxes on the retirement account withdrawals to be worse off — a very unlikely occurrence.

Note: If you are near retirement and already have money in a tax-sheltered type of retirement account (for example, at your employer), by all means continue to keep it in a tax-sheltered account if you leave. You can accomplish this goal, for example, by rolling the money over into an IRA account. Never pass up an opportunity to continue the tax-deferred compounding of your money.

What if you just run out of money because you lose your job? Although you can't bypass the penalties, if you're earning so little income that you need to raid your retirement account, you'll surely be in a low tax bracket. So even though you pay some penalties to withdraw retirement account money, the lower income taxes you pay as compared to the taxes you would have incurred when you earned the money originally should make up for most or all of the penalty.

If you get in a financial pinch while you're still employed, some company retirement plans allow you to borrow against your cash balance (it's like loaning money to yourself). Another strategy to meet a short-term financial emergency is to withdraw money from your IRA and return it within 60 days to avoid paying penalties. We don't generally recommend this maneuver because of the penalties invoked if you don't make the 60-day deadline.

If your borrowing option right now is a high-interest credit card, you should save three to six months' worth of living expenses in an accessible account before funding a retirement account.

Get started, now!

Despite all these great tax benefits of saving in retirement accounts, many people aren't taking advantage of them. Unless you're accumulating an emergency reserve, saving for a home purchase, paying off high-interest consumer debt such as on credit cards, or planning to work for the rest of your life, get started contributing now!

Types of Retirement Accounts

If you earn employment income (or receive alimony), you have the option to put money away in a retirement-type account that compounds without taxation until you withdraw the money. And in most cases, your contributions are tax-deductible. The following list includes the major types of accounts and explains how to determine whether you are eligible for them.

Employer-sponsored plans

You should be thankful that your employer values your future enough to offer such benefits. Also be grateful that your employer has gone to the trouble of doing all the legwork setting the plan up, including , in most cases, selecting investment options, which you'd have to hassle with if you were self-employed and setting up your own plan. All you have to do with an employer plan is learn how it works and save enough to invest. Is that cool or what?

401(k) plans

For-profit companies offer 401(k) plans. The silly name comes from the section of the tax code that establishes and regulates these plans. The 401(k) generally allows you to save up to $9,240 per year (for 1994). Your contributions to a 401(k) are excluded from your reported income and thus are free from federal and state income taxes but not FICA taxes. Your employer's plan may have lower limits, though, because not enough employees save enough.

Some employers don't allow you to start contributing to a 401(k) plan until you've worked for them for a full year. Others allow you to start contributing right away. Some employers also match a portion of your contributions. They may, for example, match half of your first 6 percent of contributions (so in addition to saving a lot of taxes, you get a bonus from the company). Check with your company's benefits department for your plan's details.

Thanks to technological innovations and the growth of the mutual fund industry, smaller companies (those with fewer than 100 employees) can consider offering 401(k) plans, too. In the past, it was prohibitively expensive for smaller companies to administer 401(k)s. If your company is interested in this option, contact a mutual fund organization, such as T. Rowe Price, Vanguard, or Fidelity, or a discount brokerage house, such as Charles Schwab or Jack White.

403(b) plans

Many nonprofit organizations offer 403(b) plans to their employees. As with a 401(k), your contributions to these plans are federal and state tax-deductible. The 403(b) plans often are referred to as tax-sheltered annuities, the name for insurance-company investments that satisfy the requirements for 403(b) plans. For the benefit of 403(b) retirement-plan participants, no-load (commission-free) mutual funds can now be used in 403(b) plans.

Nonprofit employees are allowed to contribute up to 20 percent or $9,500 of their salaries, whichever is less. Employees who have 15 or more years of service may be allowed to contribute a few thousand dollars beyond the $9,500 limit. Ask your employee benefits department or the investment provider for the 403(b) plan (or your tax advisor) about eligibility requirements and details about your personal contribution limit.

If you work for a nonprofit or public-sector organization that doesn't offer this benefit, make a fuss and insist on it. Nonprofit organizations have no excuse not to offer a 403(b) plan to their employees. This type of plan includes virtually no out-of-pocket set-up expenses or ongoing accounting fees like a 401(k). The only requirement is that the organization must deduct the appropriate contribution from employees' paychecks and send the money to the investment company handling the 403(b) plan.

Self-employment plans

If you work for yourself, you obviously don't have an employer to do the legwork to set up a retirement plan. You need to take the initiative. Although there's more work for you, you get to select and design a plan that meets your needs. And your trouble will be rewarded — self-employment retirement plans allow you to put more money away on a tax-deductible basis than most employers' plans do.

If you have employees, you are required to provide coverage for them under these plans with contributions comparable to the company owners' (as a percentage of salary). Some part-time (fewer than 1,000 hours per year) and newer employees (less than a few years of service) may be excluded. Not all small-business owners know about this requirement — or they choose to ignore it, and they set up plans for themselves but fail to cover their employees. The danger is that the IRS and state tax authorities may discover if you neglect to make contributions for eligible employees, sock you with big penalties, and disqualify your prior contributions. Because self-employed people and small businesses get their taxes audited at a relatively high rate, it's dangerous to mess up in this area. In fact, the IRS has set up a program to audit small pension plans in the past few years.

Don't avoid setting up a retirement savings plan for your business just because you have employees and you don't want to make contributions on their behalf. In the long run, you build the contributions you make for your employees into their total compensation package — which includes salary and other benefits like health insurance. Making retirement contributions need not increase your personnel costs.

To get the most from contributions as an employer, consider the following:

- Educate your employees about the value of retirement savings plans. You want them to understand, but more importantly, you want them to appreciate your investment.

- Select a Keogh plan that requires employees to stay a certain number of years to vest in their contributions and allows for "Social Security integration" (see discussion in Keogh section).

- Consider offering a 401(k) plan if you have more than 20 employees.

SEP-IRAs

Simplified employee pension individual retirement account (SEP-IRA) plans require little paperwork to set up. They allow you to sock away from about 13 percent (13.04 percent, to be exact) of your self-employment income (business revenue minus expenses) up to a maximum of $22,500 (1994) per year. Each year, you decide the amount you want to contribute — there are no minimums. Your contributions to a SEP-IRA are deducted from your taxable income, saving you big-time on federal and state taxes. As with other retirement plans, your money compounds without taxation until withdrawal.

Keoghs

Keogh plans require a bit more paperwork to set up and administer than SEP-IRAs. The appeal of certain types of Keoghs is that they allow you to put away a greater percentage (20 percent) of your self-employment income (revenue less your expenses), up to a maximum of $30,000 per year.

Another appeal of Keogh plans is that they allow business owners to maximize their contributions relative to employees in two ways that they can't with SEP-IRAs. First, all types of Keogh plans allow vesting schedules, which require employees to remain with the company a number of years before they earn the right to their retirement account balances. If an employee leaves prior to being fully vested, their unvested balance reverts to the remaining plan participants.

Second, Keogh plans allow for Social Security integration. Integration effectively allows those in the company who are high-income earners (usually the owners) to receive larger percentage contributions for their accounts than the less highly-compensated employees. The logic behind this idea is that Social Security taxes top out once you earn more than $60,600 (for 1994). Social Security integration allows you to make up for this ceiling.

Just to make life complicated, Keoghs come in four main flavors:

- ✔ **Profit-sharing plans.** These plans have the same contribution limits as SEP-IRAs. So why would you want the headaches of a more complicated plan when you can't contribute more to it? These plans appeal to owners of small companies who want to use of vesting schedules and Social Security integration. This cannot be done with SEP-IRA plans.

- ✔ **Money-purchase pension plans.** You can contribute more to these plans than you can to a profit-sharing plan or SEP-IRA. The maximum tax-deductible contribution here is the lesser of 20 percent of your self-employment income or $30,000 per year. While allowing for a larger contribution, there is no flexibility allowed on the percentage contribution you make each year — it's fixed. Thus these plans make the most sense for high-income earners who are comfortable enough financially to know that they can continue making large contributions.

  If the simplicity of the money-purchase pension plan appeals to you, don't be overly concerned about the consequences of some unforeseen circumstance that might make you unable to make the required contribution. You can amend your plan and change the contribution percentage starting the next year.

As long as you have a reason, the IRS generally allows you to discontinue the plan altogether. Prior contributions can remain in the Keogh account — you can even transfer them to other investment companies if you like. Discontinuing the plan simply means that you won't be making further contributions. You don't lose the money.

Usually, the reason people reduce contributions is that their business income drops off. The silver lining to your shrinking income is that Keogh plan contributions are set as a percentage of your earnings. So less income means proportionately smaller contributions.

✔ **Paired plans.** These plans combine the preceding profit-sharing and money-purchase plans. Although it requires a little more paperwork to set up and administer, a paired plan takes the best of both individual plans.

You can attain the maximum contribution possible (20 percent) that you get with the money-purchase pension plan but have some of the flexibility that comes with a profit-sharing plan. You can fix your money-purchase pension plan contribution at 8 percent and contribute anywhere from 0 to 12 percent of your net income to your profit-sharing plan.

✔ **Defined-benefit plans.** These plans are for people who are able and willing to put away more than $30,000 per year. As you can imagine, only a very small percentage of people can afford them. Consistently high-income earners older than age 45 to 50 who want to save more than $30,000 per year in a retirement account should consider these plans. If you are interested in defined-benefit plans, hire an actuary to crunch the numbers to calculate how much you can contribute to such a plan.

Individual Retirement Accounts (IRAs)

Anyone with employment (or alimony) income can contribute to IRA accounts. You may contribute up to $2,000 each year. If you don't earn $2,000 a year, you can contribute as much as you'd like (and can afford) up to the amount of your employment or alimony income. If you are a nonworking spouse, you're eligible to put $250 per year into a so-called spousal IRA.

Your contributions to an IRA may or may not be tax deductible. If you're single and your adjusted gross income is $25,000 or less for the year, you can deduct your IRA contribution. If you're married and file your taxes jointly, you're entitled to a full IRA deduction if your AGI (adjusted gross income) is $40,000 per year or less.

If you make more than these amounts, you can take a full IRA deduction if and only if you (or your spouse) are not an active participant in any retirement plan. The only way to know for certain whether you're an active participant is to look at your W-2 Form: that smallish (4 by 8$\frac{1}{2}$-inch) document your employer sends you early in the year to file with your tax returns. Little boxes in Box number 15 on that form indicate whether or not you are an active participant in a pension or deferred-compensation plan. If either of these boxes is checked, you're an active participant.

If you are a single income earner with an adjusted gross income above $25,000 but below $35,000, or part of a couple with an AGI above $40,000 but below $50,000, you're eligible for a partial IRA deduction, even if you're an active participant. The size of the IRA deduction that you may claim depends on where you fall in the income range. For example, a single income earner at $30,000 is entitled to half ($1,000) of the full IRA deduction because his or her income falls halfway between $25,000 and $35,000.

A couple earning $42,500 loses just a quarter of the full IRA amount because their incomes are a quarter of the way from $40,000 to $50,000. Thus, the couple can take a $1,500 IRA deduction. (See Chapter 7 for how to calcuate your exact deductible IRA contribution.)

Even if you can't deduct a portion or all of a $2,000 IRA contribution, you can still contribute the full $2,000 to an IRA as long as you had that much employment income during the year. This misunderstanding is common among people who used to contribute to IRAs before tax laws changed in 1986. (Before, anyone could deduct his or her IRA contributions, but lots of restrictions on deductions were added in 1986.)

An IRA contribution that is not tax deductible is called, not surprisingly, a *nondeductible* IRA contribution. The benefit of this type of contribution is that the money can still compound and grow without taxation. For a person who plans to leave contributions in the IRA for a long time (a decade or more), this tax-deferred compounding makes even nondeductible contributions worthwhile. However, you should consider such an IRA only *after* you have exhausted the possibilities of contributing to retirement accounts that do provide an immediate tax deduction (for example, 401(k)s, SEPs, Keoghs, and so on).

Because you've already paid income tax on the nondeductible contribution, how will the IRS know not to tax you again on those portions of IRA withdrawals in retirement? You guessed it, there's another form to fill out, Form 8606 that you file each year with your tax return to track these nondeductible contributions.

Retirement account inequities

If you don't have access to a retirement plan through your place of employment, you can try lobbying your employer to set one up — or you could look elsewhere for a job that offers this valuable benefit. Failing these options, you've got a right to be angry about the inequities in terms of access to tax-deductible retirement accounts.

To put everyone on more equal footing, we believe those who work for employers without retirement savings plans should be allowed to contribute more to their IRAs. It's not fair that people who work for companies that have no retirement savings plans can deduct only $2,000 per year from their taxable income for an IRA. In some cases, they may not be able to deduct anything!

Take an example of two households that each have annual employment income of $50,000. One household has access to a 401(k) plan, while the other household has no access to retirement plans other than an IRA. The house-hold with the 401(k) can put away and deduct from its taxable income thousands of dollars more per year than the household with just the IRA.

The inequity can be even larger with higher-income earners. A self-employed person, for example, making $100,000 per year can sock away a tax-deductible $20,000 per year. $150,000+ per year earners may be able to do $30,000, perhaps even more, if they establish defined-benefit plans and other types of plans.

These inequities have persisted because of the federal government's budget deficit. Allowing more people to make larger tax-deductible contributions to retirement accounts would reduce government revenue in the short term.

Tax deductions for retirement savings are included in the tax system to encourage people to provide for their own retirement. It's hypocritical for the government and our tax laws to tell people the importance of saving for retirement and not give them equal access to do so. Okay, we'll get off our soapbox.

Annuities

Annuities, like IRAs, allow your capital to grow and compound without taxation. You defer taxes until withdrawal. Annuities carry the same penalties for withdrawal prior to age 59$\frac{1}{2}$ as do IRAs. But, unlike an IRA that has a $2,000 annual contribution limit, you can deposit as much as you want in any year into an annuity — even a million dollars if you've got it! As with a so-called nondeductible IRA, you get no up-front tax deduction for your contributions.

Annuities are peculiar investment products. They are contracts that are backed by an insurance company. If you, the annuity holder (investor), die during the so-called accumulation phase (that is, prior to receiving payments from the annuity), your designated beneficiary is guaranteed to receive the amount of your original investment.

I need how much for retirement?

On average, most people need about 70 to 80 percent of their preretirement income throughout retirement to maintain their standard of living.

For example, if your household earns $40,000 per year before retirement, you're likely to need $28,000–$32,000 (70 to 80 percent of $40,000) per year during retirement to live the way that you're accustomed to living. The 70 to 80 percent is an average. Some people may need more money simply because they have more time on their hands to spend their money. Others adjust their standard of living and need less.

Remember that 70 to 80 percent is just an average. You need more or less. If you currently save little or none of your annual income and expect to have a large mortgage payment or growing rent to pay in retirement (and anticipate wanting to travel and do other expensive things in retirement) you may need 90 percent, perhaps even 100 percent of your current income to maintain your retirement standard of living.

On the other hand, if you now save a high percentage of your earnings, are a high-income earner, expect to own your home free of debt by retirement, and anticipate leading a modest lifestyle in retirement, you may be able to make do with 60 percent of your current income.

If you've never thought about what your retirement goals are, looked into what you can expect from Social Security (stop laughing), or calculated how much you should be saving for retirement, now's the time to do it. *Personal Finance For Dummies* goes through all the necessary details and even tells you how to come up with more to invest and how to do it wisely.

Because the initial contribution to an annuity is not tax deductible, it makes sense to contribute to an annuity only after you have exhausted contributing to employer-sponsored and self-employed plans. And because annuities carry higher fees (which reduce your investment returns) due to the insurance that comes with them, you should first make the maximum contribution that you can to an IRA, even if it's not tax-deductible.

Taxing Issues about Retirement Accounts

In addition to knowing about the different types of retirement accounts available and the importance of using them, we know you're going to have other problems and questions. It's not that we're so darn smart, but our clients have trained us! Here are the sticky issues you may be struggling with, along with our recommendations.

Prioritizing retirement contributions

If you have access to more than one type of retirement account, prioritize which accounts to use by what they give you in return. Your first contributions should be to employer-based plans that match your contributions. After that, contribute to any other employer or self-employed plans that allow tax-deductible contributions. If you've contributed the maximum possible to tax-deductible plans or do not have access to such plans, contribute to an IRA. If you've maxed out on contributions to an IRA or don't have this choice because you lack employment income, consider an annuity or tax-friendly investments (see Chapter 21).

We hate to bring it up, but some spouses worry too much about retirement contributions going into the other spouse's account. You may be concerned about this situation because of the realities of divorce. Or perhaps you're sure that your spouse doesn't read books like this one and may make big investing mistakes. You can handle this second worry by educating yourselves and by making decisions together where your retirement money is concerned.

You should also know that in a divorce, money in retirement accounts (regardless how much is in which person's name) can be divided up like the other assets. But rather than worrying about the possibility of divorce, how about investing in the effort to make your relationship stronger in order to avoid this problem?

Transferring existing retirement accounts

With plans maintained by your employer, such as 401(k)s, you usually have limited investment options. Unless you are the employer or can convince the employer to change, you're stuck with what is offered. If your employer offers four mutual funds from say the Lotsa Fees and Lousy Performance Fund Company, you can't transfer this money to another investment company.

Once you leave your employer, however, you generally have the option of leaving your money in the plan or transferring it to an IRA at an investment company of your choosing. (See Chapter 21 for some recommendations of good investment firms). The process of moving this money from an employer plan to investments of your choosing is called a *rollover*. And you thought you weren't going to be learning anything fun today!

When you roll money over from an employer-based retirement plan, never take personal possession of the money. If your employer gives the money to you, the employer must withhold 20 percent of it for taxes. This situation creates a tax nightmare for you because you must then jump through more hoops when you file your return. You should also know that you need to come up with the extra 20 percent when you do the rollover because you won't get the 20 percent that your employer withheld in taxes until you file your tax return. If you can't come up with the 20 percent, you have to pay taxes on this money as a distribution.

You can move your money held in SEP-IRAs, Keoghs, IRAs, and many 403(b) plans (also known as *tax-sheltered annuities*) to most any major investment firm you please. Moving the money is pretty simple. If you can dial an 800 number, fill out a couple of short forms, and send them back in a postage-paid envelope, you can transfer an account. The investment firm to which you are transferring your account does the rest.

Taking money out of retirement accounts

Someday, hopefully not until you retire, you'll need or want to start withdrawing and enjoying all the money that you socked away in your retirement accounts. Some people, particularly those who are thrifty and good at saving money (a.k.a. cheapskates and tightwads) have a hard time doing this.

You saved and invested money in your retirement accounts to use at a future date. Perhaps you're in a pinch for cash and the retirement account looks as tempting as a catered buffet meal after a day of fasting. Whatever the reason, here's what you need to know about taking the money out of your retirement accounts.

Penalty-free distributions

Despite the innumerable types of retirement accounts and special rules each one has, the IRS did do one thing to make understanding these things just a bit less complicated. All retirement accounts allow you to begin withdrawing money, without penalty, after age $59^{1}/_{2}$. (They couldn't pick a round number now could they?!) You will, of course, pay current income taxes, both federal and state, when you withdraw the money.

If you withdraw money from your retirement accounts prior to age $59^{1}/_{2}$, in addition to paying current income tax on the distribution, you must also pay penalties — 10 percent at the federal level and whatever penalties your state charges.

What if you have an emergency or unexpected expense prior to age $59^{1}/_{2}$? As detailed earlier in this chapter, there are a variety of circumstances under which you can access your money without penalty. Some employers also allow borrowing from their plans, which may help in a pinch.

When should you start withdrawing from retirement accounts?

Most people start withdrawing *when* they retire. This may or may not be the best financial decision for you. Generally speaking, you're better off postponing drawing on retirement accounts until you need the money. But don't wait if it means that you must scrimp and cut corners — especially if you have the money to use and enjoy. On the other hand, the longer the money resides inside of the retirement account, the longer it can compound and grow tax-deferred.

Suppose that you retire at age 60 and, in addition to money inside your retirement accounts, you have a bunch available outside as well. If you can, you're better off living off the money outside of retirement accounts *before* you commence tapping the retirement account money.

If you're not wealthy, odds are you'll need and want to start drawing on your retirement account soon after you retire. By all means, do it. But have you figured out how long your nest egg will last and how much you can afford to withdraw? Most folks haven't. It's worth taking the time to figure how much of your money you can afford to draw on per year even if you think you have enough. Many good savers have a hard time spending and enjoying their money in retirement. If you knew how much you could safely use, it may get you to loosen up the purse strings.

Don't forget these elections

By April 1 on the year following the year you turn 70½ you've got to make some important decisions about how the money will come out of your IRA. The first choice: whether you receive yearly distributions based on your life expectancy or based on the joint life expectancies of you and your beneficiary. If your aim is to take out as little as possible, you'll want to use a joint life expectancy. That will stretch out the distributions over a longer period.

Next you've got to decide how you want your life expectancy to be calculated. With the method know as *term-certain,* you pick the current IRS estimate of your life expectancy, then reduce it by one year every year. So if the IRS figures you'll live 23.1 years this year, next year you'd divide the balance of the account by 22.1, and so on. See IRS Publication 590 on how to calculate your life expectancy.

Under the second method, you go back to the IRS tables and look up your new life expectancy each year. Over time, this method has you taking out a little less money per year than with the term-certain approach. (According to the IRS tables, your life expectancy doesn't decrease by a full year every 12 months.) But there are some serious drawbacks to using this method, which is known as recalculation. Namely, if one spouse dies, only the survivor's life expectancy is used. When you both die, the entire balance must be paid out within a year to whoever is next in line for the money. That could mean a big tax bill for whoever is getting the balance of your account — presumably an heir. If you use the term-certain approach, the heir gets to keep taking money out in dribs and drabs, just as you have been doing. To us, the term-certain method is the clear winner.

One danger of leaving your money to compound inside of your retirement accounts for a long time — once you are retired — is that the IRS will eventually require you to start making withdrawals by April 1st of the year *following* the year you reach age 70¹/₂. It's possible that because of your delay in taking the money out at a later age — and the fact that it will have more time to compound and grow — you may need to withdraw a hefty chunk per year. This procedure could push you into higher tax brackets in those years that you are forced to make larger withdrawals.

For high rollers, be aware that your delay in withdrawing retirement account money may cause you to pay an excess distribution penalty of 15 percent tax to the IRS on top of the regular income tax you owe *if* you are forced to withdraw more than $150,000 in a year from all your retirement accounts. There are also some penalties if you take a hefty lump-sum distribution (in the neighborhood of half to three-quarters of a million dollars) if you perform a tax reducing technique called *forward averaging*. Forward averaging is just a fancy way of saying that — although you take money out in a lump — the IRS allows you (under certain circumstances) to treat the payment as if it were received out over five to ten years, although the tax is paid out in the year of distribution.

If you want to plan how you withdraw money from your retirement accounts in order to meet your needs and minimize your taxes, hire a tax advisor to help. This process is definitely worthwhile if you are considering a large lump sum withdrawal and want to explore issues such as forward averaging. If you have a lot of money in retirement accounts and have the luxury of not needing the money until you're well into retirement, tax planning will likely be worth your time and money as well.

Naming beneficiaries

With any type of retirement account, you're supposed to name beneficiaries who will receive the assets in the account when you die. You usually name primary beneficiaries (your first choices for receiving the money) and secondary beneficiaries — who receive the money in the event the primary beneficiaries are also deceased when you pass away. The designations are not cast in stone; you can change them whenever and as often as your little heart desires by sending written notice to the investment company or employer holding your retirement account.

Do the best that you can in naming beneficiaries and be thankful that you're not having to designate someone to raise your children in your absence. You should also know that you can designate charities as beneficiaries. If you want to reduce the amount of money you are required to distribute from your retirement accounts annually, name beneficiaries who are all at least ten years younger than yourself. The IRS allows you to calculate the required minimum distribution based on the joint life expectancy of you and your oldest named beneficiary. However, you can't use a difference of greater than ten years for a non-spouse. If your spouse is named as the beneficiary and is more than ten years younger than you that's fine — so Hugh Hefner is in luck (maybe that's why he likes marrying much younger women)!

The dreaded pension decision

As discussed earlier in the chapter, if you've worked for a larger company for a number of years, you may have earned yourself what is known as a *pension benefit*. This term simply means that upon attaining a particular age, usually 55 to 65, you can start to receive a monthly check from the employer(s) you worked for. With pension plans today, you earn ("vest") a benefit once you have completed five years of full-time work.

Make sure that you keep track of the employer(s) where you have earned pension benefits as you move to new jobs and around the country. Mail address changes to your previous employer's benefits department. If they lose track of you and you forget you've earned a benefit, you could actually lose a lot of money.

What age to start?

You may be able to start drawing your pension as early as 50 years of age — so long as you have worked enough years somewhere. The majority of plans, however, won't give you payments until age 55 or 60. Some plans even make you wait until age 65.

If you don't have a choice as to what age you want to start drawing benefits, that situation surely simplifies things for you. Before you get perplexed and overwhelmed if you do have options, remember one simple thing: There are smart actuaries who have created the choices you have. Actuaries are the kinds of people that score 800s (perfect scores) on their math SATs. These folks work, eat, breath, and sleep numbers.

The choices you confront will show you that the younger you elect to start drawing benefits, the less you will be paid. Conversely, the longer you can wait to access your pension, the more you should receive per month.

Some pensions stop offering higher benefits once you reach a certain age — make sure you don't delay starting your benefits after you've reached this plateau. Otherwise, make your decision as to what age to start drawing benefits based on when you need them and/or can afford to retire. Run the numbers or hire a financial advisor.

If you're still working and earning a healthy income, think twice before starting pension benefits — these pension benefits are likely to be taxed at a much higher rate. You're probably going to be in a lower income tax bracket after you cease working.

If you know that you're in poor health and will not live long, you better start drawing your pension as soon as possible. Otherwise, it's not worth your time to try to calculate which age option will lead to your getting more money. So many assumptions, such as the rate of inflation and how long you'll live, are beyond your abilities to accurately predict. The actuaries have done their homework on these issues and that's why the numbers vary the way they do.

Which payment option for you married folks?

Besides deciding at what age you will elect to start receiving benefits, if you're married you may have other options as to how much money you'll receive now versus how much your spouse will receive if you pass away. Remember, actuaries are smart — don't make your selection based upon age differences between you and your spouse.

For example, if you were Hugh Hefner and married to someone young enough to be your daughter, you may be tempted to choose the pension option that maximizes how much your wife receives upon your death because you're likely to pre-decease her. Each person's pension options already reflect the age differences between spouses, so don't waste your time with this line of thinking. Remember those smart actuaries.

The following are some of the typical options, which are ranked in order of providing the most to the fewest dollars at the beginning of retirement. The first choices are the riskiest, and the last ones are the least risky — but therefore less financially rewarding in the beginning:

- ✔ Single Life Option — pays benefits only as long as the pensioner is alive. Survivor receives nothing. Offers the highest monthly benefits but is also the riskiest option. For example, pensioner receives $1,500 per month for as long as he or she is alive. Spouse receives nothing after pensioner's death.

- ✔ Ten Years' Certain Option — pays benefits for at least ten years, even if pensioner passes away within first ten years of drawing pension. Pensioner continues to receive benefits for as long as he or she lives even if greater than ten years. For example, pensioner receives $1,400 per month for at least ten years until his or her death. Spouse then receives nothing.

- ✔ 50 Percent Joint and Survivor Option — Survivor receives 50 percent of pensioner's benefit after his or her death. For example, pensioner receives $1,350 per month. Upon pensioner's death, spouse receives reduced benefit of $675 per month.

- ✔ ²/₃ Joint and Survivor Option — Survivor receives 66 percent of pensioner's benefit after his or her death. For example, pensioner receives $1,310 per month. Upon pensioner's death, spouse receives reduced benefit of $865 per month.

- 75 Percent Joint Survivor Option — Survivor receives 75 percent of pensioner's benefit after his or her death. For example, pensioner receives $1,275 per month. Upon pensioner's death, spouse receives reduced benefit of $955 per month.

- 100 Percent Joint and Survivor Option — Survivor receives 100 percent of pensioner's benefit after his or her death. For example, pensioner receives $1,200 per month. Upon pensioner's death, spouse also receives $1,200 per month.

Choosing the best pension option for you is not unlike selecting investments. What's best for you depends upon your overall financial circumstances and desire, comfort, and ability to accept risk. The Single Life Option is the riskiest and should be used only by couples who don't really need the pension — it's frosting on the financial cake and they're willing to gamble in order to maximize benefits today. If the surviving spouse is very much dependent on the pension, select one of the survivor options that leaves a high amount.

Beware of insurance salespeople and financial planners who also sell life insurance advocating that you purchase life insurance and take the Single Life Option. They argue that this option allows you to maximize your pension income and protect the surviving spouse with a life insurance death benefit if the pensioner dies. Sounds good, but the life insurance expense will outweigh the potential benefits. Choose one of the survivor pension options that gives you life insurance protection. This method is a far more cost effective way to buy *life* insurance.

Chapter 20

Your Small Business and Taxes

*W*hether you are your entire company or you have many employees for whom you are responsible, running a business can be one of the most frustrating, exhilarating, rewarding — and financially punishing — endeavors of your adult life.

Many Americans fantasize about being their own boss. Tales of entrepreneurs becoming multimillionaires focus our attention on the financial rewards without teaching us about the business and personal costs associated with being in charge.

Business owners know the good and the bad. Consider all the activities that your company has to do well in order to survive and succeed in the rough-and-tumble business world. You have to develop products and services that the marketplace will purchase. And you have to price your wares properly and promote them. What good is a better mousetrap if you're the only one who knows about it? After you've been successful in developing offerings that meet a need, new worries begin: competitors. Your success will likely spur imitators.

Even though you never desired a career in real estate, you may find yourself poring over lease contracts and evaluating office space. Perhaps you must struggle with the decision of whether to continue operating out of that spare bedroom or pony up for some office space. If that worry isn't enough, you need to read trade and professional journals to keep current with changes in your field. Although you never desired to be a human resource manager, you need to know about the right ways to hire, train, and retain good employees. You soon become an expert on insurance and other employee benefits.

With all that money flowing into your coffers, you need to keep appropriate records documenting your income and expenses. Unlike working for a corporation, owning a small business makes you responsible for ensuring that the right amount of taxes is withheld and paid on both the state and federal level.

The biggest challenges business owners face are the personal and emotional ones. It's sad to say, but these challenges rarely get discussed among all the glory tales of rags-to-riches. Major health problems, divorces, the loss of friends, and even suicides have been attributed to the passions of business owners consumed with winning or overwhelmed by their failures. Although careers and business success are important, if you really think about it, at best these things should be no higher than fourth on your overall priority list. Your health, family, and friends can't be replaced — but a job or business can.

Real versus Bogus Businesses

This chapter is about how small business owners can make tax-wise decisions in running their businesses. It is *not* about how to start up a sideline business for the primary purpose of generating tax deductions.

Unfortunately, some self-anointed financial gurus claim that you can slash or even completely eliminate your tax bill by setting up a sideline business. They say that you can sell your services while doing something you enjoy (something legal, of course!). The problem, they argue, is that — as a regular wage earner who receives a paycheck from an employer — you can't write off many of your other (that is, personal) expenses. These hucksters usually promise to show you the secrets of tax reduction if you shell out a few bucks for their audio tapes and notebooks of inside information. "Start a small business for fun, profit, and huge tax deductions" one financial book trumpets, adding that "the tax benefits alone are worth starting a small business." Gee, sounds good. Where do we sign up?

Suppose that you are interested in photography. You can take pictures on your next vacation and then sell the pictures. Some experts claim this activity allows you to deduct many expenses (including airfare for travel) that you previously couldn't deduct.

According to the same so-called experts, you can write off part of your utility bills and rent for your home office. Then you can turn your restaurant meals with potential clients (that is, your friends) into tax deductions. Entertain your clients at your health club and deduct those dues, too! Before you know it, you have wiped out most of your taxes. You're entitled to these deductions (according to our experts) because lots of big corporations and wealthy people also pay next to nothing in taxes.

The pitch is enticing, but the reality is something quite different. First off, don't forget that you have to *spend* money to get tax deductions. Second, the spending needs to be *legitimate* for purposes of generating an income. Sideline or hobby businesses are audited at a very high rate by the IRS, so you're more than likely to get caught deducting personal expenses if you try anything funny. Furthermore, as discussed later in the chapter, the IRS has significantly tightened the rules for writing off meals, entertainment, and so on.

The bottom line is that you need to operate a legitimate business for the purpose of generating income and profits — not tax deductions. For example, your sideline business (in most cases) must realize a profit three out of the last five years of operation for you to take deductions. Even if your sideline business meets this requirement, as well as other IRS requirements, it's *illegal* to deduct any expenses not directly applicable to your business.

Here's another detail to consider. After a full week of work do you really want to be keeping records and accounting for expenditures on something you do just a few hours per week?

Hobby loss rules

If you're considering deducting expenses for activities that are really more of a hobby for you than a genuine business, you should also be aware of the hobby loss rules. Suppose that you enjoy collecting baseball cards or writing poetry — or maybe you do both! After going to one of the seminars that advocate setting up a sideline business to slash your taxes, you decide to enlist the IRS in your hobby.

Year after year, your "business" shows a loss because it creates no (or little) income and lots of expenses. The IRS will likely disallow your claiming of the losses. Losses from hobbies are not deductible — of course, if you make a profit, you must pay tax.

An activity is considered a hobby if it shows a loss for three or more of the past five tax years. (Horse racing, breeding, and so on is considered a hobby

if it shows a loss for five or more of the past seven tax years.) Certainly, some businesses lose money. But a real business can't afford to do so year after year and remain in business. Who likes losing money unless the losses are really just a front for a hobby?

If these hobby loss rules indicate that you're engaging in a hobby and you still want to claim your losses, you must convince the IRS that you are seriously trying to make a profit and run a legitimate business. The IRS will want to see that you are actively marketing your services, building your skills, and accounting for income and expenses. The IRS also wants to see that you're not having too much fun! If you're deriving too much pleasure from an activity, in the eyes of the IRS, the activity must not be a real business!

Getting and Staying Organized

If you're thinking of starting a business or are already in the thick of one, you need to keep a proper accounting of your income and expenses. If you don't, when it comes time to file the necessary tax forms for your business, you won't be able to complete them accurately.

Besides helping you over the annual tax-filing hurdle, you want accurate records so that you can track the health and performance of your business during the year. How are your profits running? Are they going up, sideways, or down? Should you and can you afford to hire new employees? Can you afford the ones you've got? Analyzing your monthly or quarterly business financial statements can help you to answer these questions.

Here's a final reason to keep good records. The IRS may audit you and ask you that dreaded question: "Can you prove it?" Small business owners who file Schedule C (Profit or Loss From Business) with their tax return are audited at a much higher rate than other taxpayers. Although that dubious honor may seem like an unfair burden to business owners, the IRS targets small businesses because more than a few small business owners bend the tax rules — and there are so many areas where small business owners can mess up.

Here are the key tax things business owners should do.

Keep records

When it comes time to file your annual return, you want to be able to find the documentation that allows you to figure your business income and expenses. At a minimum, set up some file folders into which you can collect information and receipts — perhaps one for tabulating your income and another for compiling your expenses. Computer software may help you with this chore as well, but you must still go through the hassle of entering the data (see Chapter 3).

Leave a spending trail

Odds are very good that you'll lose some of those little pieces of paper needed to document your expenses. One big advantage of charging expenses on a credit card or of writing a check is that these transactions leave a paper trail. This trail makes it easier to total up your expenses come tax time — and not miss expenses.

Be careful when using a credit card, because you may buy more things than you can really afford. Then you're stuck with a lot of debt to pay off. On the other hand (as many a small business owners know), it's difficult to find lenders when you need money. Using the credit on a low-interest rate credit card can be an easy way for you to borrow money without shamelessly begging from a banker.

Separate business from personal accounts

One of the IRS' biggest concerns is that — as a small business owner — you'll try to minimize your business profits (and therefore taxes) by hiding business income and inflating your business expenses. Uncle Sam thus looks suspiciously at business owners who use personal-checking and credit-card accounts for business transactions. You may be tempted to use your personal account this way (because it's a hassle to open separate accounts — not because you're dishonest). Take the time to open separate accounts. It not only makes the feds happy, but it also makes your accounting easier.

Keep current on income and payroll taxes

When you're self-employed, you're responsible for the accurate and timely filing of all taxes owed on your income. Without an employer and a payroll department to handle on a regular schedule the paperwork for withholding taxes, you need to make estimated tax payments on a quarterly basis.

If you have employees, you also need to withhold taxes on their income from each paycheck they receive. And you then must make timely payments to the IRS and to the appropriate state authorities. In addition to federal and state income tax, you also need to withhold and send in Social Security and any other state or locally mandated payroll taxes.

For paying taxes on your own self-employment income, you can obtain Form 1040ES (Estimated Tax for Individuals) with instructions from the IRS (call 800-TAX-FORM). This form comes complete with an estimated tax worksheet and the four payment coupons to send in with your quarterly tax payments. It's amazing how user-friendly government people can be when they want our money.

To learn about all the amazing rules and regulations of withholding and submitting taxes from employees' paychecks, ask the IRS for Form 941. Once a year, you also need to complete Form 940 for unemployment insurance payments to the feds.

Unless you're lucky enough to live in a state with no income taxes, don't forget to call for your state's estimated income tax package. Check your local telephone directory for the number of your state tax authorities or the instruction booklet that you used to prepare last year's state income taxes.

If you aren't going to keep current on taxes for yourself and your employees, hire a tax advisor who will force you to jump through the necessary tax hoops. (See "Hired Help" in Chapter 2 for advice on selecting a tax advisor.) Many small businesses have been ruined by falling behind in taxes. When you hire employees, for example, you are particularly vulnerable to multiple tax land mines. Payroll companies and tax advisors are there for a reason, so use them selectively.

To Incorporate or Not to Incorporate

Starting a business is hard enough between mustering up the courage and swinging it financially. Many business owners meet their match deciding what should be a reasonably straightforward issue: whether to incorporate. Just about every book that addresses the subject (or just about every lawyer or accountant who advises business owners) steers clear of giving definitive answers.

In some instances the incorporation decision is complicated, but in most cases it need not be a difficult choice. Taxes may be important to the decision but are not the only consideration. The following section is an overview of the critical issues to consider.

Liability protection

If you're one of the millions of small-business owners in America, the chief reason to consider incorporation is for purposes of liability protection. Attorneys speak of the protection of the *corporate veil*. Don't confuse this veil with insurance — you don't get any insurance when you incorporate. You may need or want to buy insurance instead of (or in addition to) incorporating. Liability protection doesn't insulate your company from being sued, either.

When you incorporate, what you do get is the separation or division of your *business* assets and liabilities from your *personal* finances. Why would you want to do that? Suppose that your business is doing well and you take out a bank loan in order to expand. The next year, however, the government enacts a regulatory change that makes your services or product obsolete. Before you know it, your business is losing money and you're forced to close up shop. But if you can't repay the bank loan because of your business failure, the bank shouldn't be able to go after your personal assets if you're incorporated.

Unfortunately, many small-business owners who need money find that bankers ask for a *personal guarantee*, which negates part of the liability protection that comes with incorporation. Also, if you play games with your company (such as shifting money out of the company in preparation for defaulting on a loan), a bank may legally be able to go after your personal assets. You must adhere to a whole host of ground rules and protocols to prove to the IRS that you are a bona fide company. For example, you need to keep corporate records and hold an annual meeting — even if it's just with yourself!

A business can also be sued if it mistreats an employee or if its product or service causes harm to a customer. But the owner's personal assets should be protected if the business is incorporated.

Liability insurance — a better alternative if you can get it

Before you incorporate, ask yourself (and perhaps others in your line of business or advisors who work with businesses like yours) what could cause you to be sued. Then see if you can purchase insurance to protect against these potential liabilities. Insurance is superior to incorporation because it pays claims.

Suppose that you perform professional services but make a major mistake that costs someone a lot of money — or worse. You can still be sued even if you're incorporated. If you're incorporated and someone successfully sues you, your company has to cough up the money. This situation not only costs a lot of money, but can also sink your business. Only insurance can cover such destructive claims.

You can also be sued if someone slips and breaks a bone or two. To cover these types of claims, you can purchase a property or premises liability policy from an insurer.

Accountants, doctors, and a number of other professionals can buy liability insurance. A good place to start searching for liability insurance is through the associations that exist for your profession. Even if you're not a current member, check out the associations anyway — you may be able to access the insurance without membership, or you can join the association long enough to get signed up.

Before you call your neighborhood lawyer or your state offices to figure out how to incorporate, you should know that incorporating takes time and costs money. So if incorporating doesn't offer some small benefits to outweigh the hassles and costs, you shouldn't do it. Likewise, if the only benefits of incorporating could be better accomplished through some other means (such as purchasing insurance), save your money and time and don't incorporate.

Taxes

Corporations are taxed as entities separate from their individual owners. This situation can be both good and bad. Suppose that your business is doing really well and making lots of money. If your business is not incorporated, all the profits from your business are taxed on your personal tax return in the year that those profits are earned.

On the other hand, if you intend to use these profits to reinvest in your business and expand, incorporating can potentially save you some tax dollars. If your business is incorporated (as a regular or so-called C Corporation), the first $75,000 of profits in the business should be taxed at a lower rate in the corporation than on your personal tax return (see Table 20-1). One exception to this rule is personal service corporations, such as accounting, legal, and medical firms (which actually pay a higher rate up to $335,000 in profits).

A possible tax advantage of a corporation is that corporations can pay — on a tax-deductible basis — for employee benefits such as health insurance, disability, and up to $50,000 of term life insurance. (See "Insurance" later in this chapter for more details.) Sole proprietorships and other unincorporated businesses can only take tax deductions for these benefit expenses for employees. Benefit expenses for owners who work in the business are not deductible.

Resist the temptation to incorporate just so that you can have money left in the corporation taxed at a lower rate. Don't be motivated by this seeming short-term gain. If you want to pay yourself the profits in the future, you could end up paying *more* taxes. Why? Because you end up paying double taxes. First you pay taxes at the corporate tax rate in the year your company earns the money. Then you pay taxes again on these profits — this time on your personal income tax return — when you pay yourself from the corporate till in the form of a dividend.

Another reason not to incorporate (especially in the early days of a business) is that you can't immediately claim the losses for an incorporated business on your personal tax return. Because most businesses produce little revenue in their early years and have all sorts of start-up expenditures, losses are common.

Table 20-1 Corporate Tax Rates for Regular (C Corporations) — 1994	
Income	*Tax Rate*
$0 – $50,000	15%
$50,001 – $75,000	25%
$75,001 – $100,000	34%
$100,001 – $335,000	39%
$335,001 – $10,000,000	34%

Personal service corporations, such as accounting, legal, and medical firms, pay a flat 35 percent on all income.

S Corporations

Subchapter S Corporations, so named for that part of the tax code, can offer some business owners the best of both worlds. You get the liability protection that comes with being incorporated, and the business profit or loss passes through to the owner's personal tax returns. So if the business shows a loss in some years, the owner may claim those losses in the current year of the loss on the tax returns. If you plan to take all the profits out of the company, an S Corporation may make sense for you.

The IRS allows most small businesses to be S Corporations, but not all. In order to be an S Corporation by the almighty IRS, a company must

- ✔ be a U.S. company.
- ✔ have just one class of stock.
- ✔ have no more than 35 shareholders (who are all U.S. residents or citizens and are not partnerships, corporations or, with certain exceptions, trusts).

Limited liability companies (LLCs)

Limited liability companies (LLCs) offer business owners benefits similar to those of S Corporations but are even better in some cases. Like an S Corporation, an LLC offers liability protection for the owners. LLCs also pass the business' profits through to the owner's personal income tax returns.

Limited liability companies have fewer restrictions regarding shareholders. For example, LLCs have no limits on the number of shareholders. The shareholders in an LLC can be foreigners. Corporations and partnerships can also be shareholders.

Compared with S Corporations, the only additional restriction LLCs carry is that sole proprietors and professionals cannot always form an LLC (although Texas allows this). Most state laws require you to have at least two partners and not be a professional firm. LLCs are not available in all states.

Other incorporation issues

Because corporations are legal entities distinct from their owners, they offer other features and benefits that a proprietorship or partnership doesn't. For example, corporations can have shareholders who own a piece or percentage of the company. These shares can be sold or transferred to other owners, subject to any restrictions in the shareholders' agreement.

Corporations also offer *continuity of life,* which simply means that they can continue to exist despite the death of an owner — or the owner's transfer of his or her share (stock) in the company.

Don't incorporate for ego purposes. If you want to incorporate in order to impress friends, family, or business contacts, few people will be impressed or ever know. If you operate as a sole proprietor, you can choose to operate under a different business name ("doing business as" or d.b.a.) without the cost — or the headache — of incorporating.

If you're in doubt ...

If you've weighed the factors and there are offsetting pros and cons, our advice is to keep it simple. Don't incorporate. Remember that once you incorporate, it takes time and money to *un*-incorporate. Start off as a sole-proprietorship and then take it from there.

Where to get advice

If you're totally confused about whether to incorporate because your business is undergoing major financial changes, it's worth getting competent professional help. The hard part is knowing where to turn, because it's a challenge to find one advisor who can put all the pieces of the puzzle together. And be aware that you may get wrong or biased advice.

Attorneys who specialize in advising small businesses can help explain the legal issues. Tax advisors who do a lot of work with business owners can help explain the tax considerations. If you find you need two or more advisors to help make the decision, it may help to get them together in one room with yourself for a meeting — which saves you time and money.

Spending to Minimize Taxes

Every small business has to spend money to make money. Most businesses need phone service, paper, a computer and printer, software, a bottle of extra-strength aspirin, and a whole bunch of other things you probably never thought you'd be purchasing.

But don't spend money on business stuff just for the sake of generating tax deductions. In some cases, business owners we know buy all sorts of new equipment and other gadgets at year's end for their business so that they can pay less taxes. While we endorse reinvesting in your business and making things more efficient, the more you spend the less you earn — and it's the same with your personal finances. There's nothing wrong with paying taxes. In fact, it's a sign of the success of your business!

What follows is a brief overview of what to do and what not to do in order to spend for your business in a tax-wise way.

Depreciation versus deduction

As a small business owner, you can take up to a $17,500 deduction for purchases of equipment for use in your business. When you buy things such as computers, office furniture, bookshelves, and so on, each of these items is supposed to be *depreciated* over a number of years. Depreciation simply means that each year, you get to claim, as a tax deduction, a portion of the original cost of purchasing an item, until you depreciate it all.

For example, suppose that you spend $3,000 on computer equipment. According to the IRS, computer equipment is to be depreciated over five years. Thus, each year you can take a $600 deduction for depreciation of this computer if you elect straight-line depreciation (defined in Chapter 10). By expensing or deducting (through what's called a section 179 deduction) rather than depreciating, you can take the entire cost of $3,000 immediately (unless it contributes to your business showing a loss or a larger loss).

It's tempting to want to expense the full amount immediately, but that action isn't always the best thing to do. In the early years of your business, for example, your profits may be low. Therefore, because you won't be in a high tax bracket, the value of your deductions is limited. Looking ahead — if you have reason to be optimistic about your future profits — you may actually save tax dollars by choosing to depreciate your purchases. Why? By delaying some of your tax write-offs until future years (when you expect to be in a higher tax bracket because of greater profits), you save more in taxes.

Cars

If you use your car for business, you can claim a deduction (see "Line 10: Car and truck expenses" in Chapter 10 for details). The mistake that some business owners (and many other people) make is to buy an expensive car. Such a purchase causes two problems. First, the car may be a waste of money that could be better spent elsewhere in the business. Second, the IRS limits how large an annual auto expense you can claim for depreciation.

The IRS gives you a choice in how to account for business automobile expenses. You can either expense a mileage charge (29 cents per mile for 1994) *or* keep track of the actual operation expenses (such as gas, insurance, repairs, and so on) plus take depreciation costs.

For cars that were *placed in service* (bought or began to be used in the business) after 1986, depreciation is done over five years. If you bought a car in 1994, for example, the maximum amount of depreciation that you can take is $2,960 in the first year, $4,700 in the second year, $2,850 in the third year, and $1,675 in the fourth and following years until the car is depreciated down to nothing. The way the math works out, you are effectively limited by these caps if you spent more than about $14,800 on a car in 1994.

With expensive cars, the mileage expense method will probably shortchange your deduction amounts for auto usage. If you buy a reasonably priced car, you won't need to go through the headache of tracking your actual auto expenses (in addition to not wasting money). It's so much easier just to track mileage and use the mileage expense method.

Auto dealers increasingly push leasing. For the auto dealers and salespeople in the showrooms, leases have the marketing appeal of monthly payments (like auto loans) for buyers — but without the perceived noose of a large loan around the neck. Don't be fooled. If you do your homework and hunt for a good deal on a car, buying with cash is the best way to go. Borrowing with an auto loan and leasing are much more expensive (leasing generally being the highest cost) and encourage car buyers to spend more than they can afford.

Travel, meal, and entertainment expenses

The IRS has clamped down on writing off expenses in these areas because there has been so much abuse by business owners and employees writing off non-business expenses. Some books, seminars, and unscrupulous tax preparers have effectively encouraged such abuse.

Be honest — not only because it's the right thing to do but also because the IRS looks long and hard at expenses claimed in these areas. Travel must be for a legitimate business purpose. If you take a week off to go to San Francisco, spend one day at a business convention, and then spend the rest of the time sightseeing, you may have a great time — but only a portion of your trip expenses may be deductible.

There is one exception: if you extend a business trip to stay over on a Saturday in order to qualify for a lower airfare — and you save money in total travel costs by extending your stay — you can claim the extra costs incurred to stay over through Sunday. If your spouse or friend tag along, their costs are most definitely not deductible.

With meal and entertainment expenses, only 50 percent of your business expenses are now deductible. In addition, the IRS no longer allows any deduction for club dues such as health, business, airport, social clubs, or entertainment facilities like executive boxes at sports stadiums, apartments, and so on. (See Chapter 10 for more details.)

Home alone, or outside office space?

If you have a truly small business, you may have a choice between having an office in your home or getting outside office space. There are many financial and non-financial considerations. At home, are you going to have the discipline to get to work, or will you be tempted to sleep until 10 a.m., watch soap operas, and play solitaire on your computer? Will you argue with your spouse — who expects you to pick up the dry cleaning and go grocery shopping because you're *at home*?

And then there's the issue of being home alone, where the social highlights of the day may be greeting the postal carrier and having lunch with your cat or dog. (Although, compared to lunch with some of the bosses you've had, lunch with a pet may be welcome relief!)

The financial and tax sides of this issue are actually not important — certainly not nearly as important as many business owners make them out to be. Why? First off, the cost of office space you rent or purchase outside your home is an expense that can be deducted on your business tax return. In a home-based office, if you own your home, you already get to claim the mortgage interest and property taxes as tax deductions on your personal tax return. So don't set up a home office thinking you'll be getting all sorts of extra tax breaks. (You will qualify for some minor ones such as deductions for utilities, repairs, and insurance for the portion of a home devoted to business. See Chapter 10.)

The one extra home-based office expense that you can take if you are a homeowner is depreciation. Be warned, however, that when you sell your home in the future, the IRS won't allow you to rollover a capital gain on the portion of your home that was depreciated for your business. Currently, a way exists around this problem — simply use the home office space for some additional personal purpose during the year that you sell your home. Then you can roll over the entire gain (see Chapter 22).

If you don't need to move into a larger apartment or home to accommodate your business, then you may feel that your home provides "free" office space. This situation may be true. However, if your home is larger than you need, you *could* move to a smaller, less expensive home!

Try as best you can to make your decision about your office space based on your business and customer needs, along with your personal preferences. If you're a writer and don't need fancy office space to meet with anyone (or to impress anyone), working at home may be just fine. On the other hand, one writer we know rents space because, at home, he has munchkins running around who can't understand why daddy has to work. If you operate a retail or service business that requires your customers to come to you, getting outside office space is probably the best choice for all involved — and the best legal way to go as well. Check with the governing authorities of your town, city, and county to learn what regulations exist for home-based businesses.

Independent contractors versus employees

If you really want to give yourself a headache, read the tax laws applying to the classification of people that a business hires as either employees or independent contractors. If a business hires an employee, the business is required to withhold federal and state taxes and then send the taxes to the appropriate tax authorities. The government likes this arrangement because independent contractors (as a group) pay less taxes by underreporting their income. Contractors are also entitled to take more business deductions than employees.

If a business hires independent contractors to perform work, the contractors are responsible for paying all their taxes. However, business owners are now required to file with the IRS and some states Form 1099, which reports the amount of money paid to contractors who receive $600 or more from the business. This form allows the IRS to keep better tabs on contractors who may not be reporting all their income.

Unless a company offers an employee benefits (insurance, retirement savings plans, and so on), a hired hand should prefer to be an independent contractor. Contractors have more leeway to deduct business expenses, including the deduction for a home office. Contractors can also tax-shelter a healthy percentage in a retirement savings plan (see Chapter 19). But one additional expense for contractors is their obligation to pay the full share of Social Security taxes (although they can then deduct half as a tax deduction). An employer would pay half the Social Security taxes.

So how does the business owner decide if someone is a contractor or an employee? Some cases are hard to determine, but the IRS has a 20-point set of guidelines to make most cases pretty clear cut.

The classic case of independent contractor status is most professional service providers such as legal, tax, and financial advisors. These people are considered contractors because they generally train themselves and — when hired — figure out how they can accomplish the job without much direction or instruction from the employer. Contractors usually perform work for a number of other companies and people, and they hire others to work with them.

On the other hand, employees usually work for one employer and have set hours of work. For example, a full-time secretary hired by a business would be considered an employee because he or she takes instructions from the employer regarding when, where, and how to do the desired work — and the secretary is an integral part at the work site in completing the work.

What do you do if your situation falls in between these two types and you're perplexed about whether the person you're hiring is a contractor or employee? Ask a tax advisor or contact the IRS for their handy-dandy Form SS-8 (Determination of Employee Work Status). Complete the form, mail it in, and let the IRS make the call for you. That way the IRS can't blame you!

All in the family

If you hire family members to perform real work for fair wages, you may be able to reduce your tax bill. If your children under the age of 18 are paid for work performed, they are probably in a much lower tax bracket than you are. And they need not pay any Social Security like you do.

Get your kids started on investing by having them contribute some of their earnings to an IRA account.

Likewise, if you pay your spouse (who has no other income) at least $2,000 to do some work, your spouse becomes eligible to contribute to an IRA. (See Chapter 19 for more information on IRAs.)

But if you earn more than the $61,600 cap (in 1995) for full Social Security taxes, this strategy may lead to more Social Security taxes being paid by your family. Run the numbers or talk to a tax advisor.

Insurance and other benefits

A variety of insurance and related benefits are tax deductible to corporations for all employees. These benefits include the following:

- health insurance
- disability insurance
- term life insurance (up to $50,000 in benefits per employee)
- dependent care plans (up to $5000 per employee may be put away on a tax-deductible basis for child care and/or care for elderly parents)
- cafeteria or flexible spending plans (which allow employees to pick and choose which benefits to spend their benefit dollars on)

If your business is not incorporated, the business owner(s) can't deduct the cost of the preceding insurance plans for themselves — but they can deduct these costs for employees.

In 1993, self-employed people could deduct 25 percent of their health insurance costs for themselves and covered family members. This provision of the tax code expired at the end of 1993. However, a number of proposals before Congress could revive some version of this tax benefit if passed.

Retirement plans

Retirement plans are a terrific way for business owners and their employees to tax-shelter a healthy portion of their earnings. (These plans are discussed in detail in Chapter 19.)

Investing in a Business

Putting money into your own business (or someone else's) can be a high-risk but potentially high-return investment. The best options are those you understand well. If you hear about a great business idea or company from someone you know and trust, do your research and make your best judgment. It may well be a terrific investment. But keep in mind that people are always willing to take more risk with other people's money than with their own — and that many well-intentioned people fail at their businesses.

A new provision in the tax law allows investors to exclude half their capital gains (profits) from small business investments held for five or more years in small businesses (small being defined as businesses with gross assets at less than $50 million). With the maximum federal capital gains rate at 28 percent, this new provision lowers the capital gains tax to 14 percent. So if you have a knack for identifying up-and-coming entrepreneurs, you may be able to make rewarding investments that aren't too taxing.

Before investing in a project, ask to see a copy of the business plan. Talk to others (who aren't involved with the investment!) about the idea and learn from their comments and concerns. But don't forget that many a wise person has rained on the parade of what turned out to be a terrific business idea.

Avoid limited partnerships and other small-company investments pitched by brokers, financial planners, and the like. They want you to buy limited partnerships because they earn a hefty commission from them. If you want a convenient way to invest in a businesses and earn tax breaks, buy some stock mutual funds inside a retirement account.

Buying and Selling a Business

If you are buying or selling an existing business, get the help and advice of competent tax and legal advisors. These financial transactions are important in your overall personal finances.

If you are a buyer, good advisors can help you inspect what you're buying and look for red flags in the company's financial statements. Advisors can also help to structure the purchase to protect what you're buying — and to gain maximum tax benefits.

If you are a seller, your advisors can help you prepare your business for maximum sale value and minimize taxes from the sales price.

If your business is worth a lot, make sure to read the chapter on estate planning, because hefty taxes may be owed upon your death if you don't structure things properly. Your heirs may be forced to sell your business to pay estate taxes! (See Chapter 24 for more information.)

Chapter 21

Investments and Taxes

· ·

In This Chapter

▶ Making tax-friendly investments

▶ Deciding what to sell and how to sell it

▶ Reinvesting and dollar cost averaging

▶ Tax-favored "investments" to avoid

· ·

*N*ote: This chapter focuses on tax issues relating to investments in mutual funds, stocks, bonds, and other securities. Other chapters cover tax matters for investing in real estate, in small businesses, in your children's names, and in your estate.

If you have money to invest, or if you're considering selling current investments that you hold, taxes should be an important factor in your decision. But tax considerations alone should not dictate how and where you invest your money. You should also weigh investment options such as your desire (and the necessity) to take risk, personal likes and dislikes, and the number of years you plan to hold the investment.

Tax-Friendly Investments

Lots of folks invest their money in ways that increase their tax burdens. In many cases, they (and sometimes their advisors) don't consider the tax impact of their investment strategies.

For investments that you hold in *tax-sheltered* retirement accounts such as IRAs and 401(k) plans (discussed in detail in Chapter 19), you don't need to worry about taxes. This money is not taxed until you actually withdraw funds from the retirement accounts. Thus, you should never invest money that is inside retirement accounts in tax-favored investments such as tax-free money market funds and bonds (discussed later in this chapter).

You are far more likely to make tax mistakes investing assets held outside retirement accounts. Distributions, such as interest, dividends, and *capital gains* (profits from the sale of an investment at higher than purchase price) produced by nonretirement account investments, are all exposed to taxation.

Another mistake many people make is investing in securities that produce tax-free income even though these people are not in a high enough tax bracket to benefit. But how high is high enough?

- ✔ **31 percent or higher federal tax bracket.** If you're in this bracket, you should definitely avoid investments that produce taxable income. For tax year 1994, the 31 percent federal bracket started at $55,100 for singles and $91,850 for married couples filing jointly.

- ✔ **28 percent federal tax bracket.** In most cases, you should be as well or better off in investments that do not produce taxable income when investing outside retirement accounts. This may not be the case, however, if you're in tax-free money market and bond funds whose yields are depressed due to high operating expenses.

- ✔ **15 percent federal bracket.** Investments that produce taxable income are just fine for you. You will likely end up with *less* if you purchase investments that produce tax-free income.

In this section are some of the best methods to reduce the taxes on investments exposed to taxation.

Your capital gains (may be) taxed at a different rate

Just to make matters even more complicated, the IRS doesn't tax all distributions equally. A long-term capital gain, which is the profit (sales price minus purchase price) on a security that you own more than one year, is taxed on a different tax-rate schedule. However, if your taxable income places you in the federal 28 percent or lower tax brackets, your capital gains tax rate is identical to your ordinary income tax rate. Short-term capital gains (securities held less than one year) are taxed at your ordinary income tax rate.

If you fall in the 31 percent or higher federal tax bracket, the good news is that your long-term capital gains tax rate is capped at 28 percent.

That's why higher-income earners should avoid non-retirement account investments that produce taxable income — these people pay a high income tax rate on such investments. They should seek out investments that produce tax-free income or capital gains — although they may not want capital gains because such money is still taxable.

Besides the possibility that the IRS wants to make our tax lives more difficult, there is some logic behind the capital gains tax limit. Some argue that this limit encourages investment for long-term growth. On the other hand, some complain that it's a tax break for the affluent.

Fund your retirement accounts

Make sure that you take advantage of opportunities to direct your employment earnings into retirement accounts. If you work for a company that offers a retirement savings plan such as a 401(k), try to fund it at the highest level you can manage. If you earn self-employment income, look into SEP-IRAs and Keoghs. (All retirement plan options are discussed in Chapter 19.)

You get two possible tax bonuses by investing more of your money in retirement accounts. First, your contributions to the retirement accounts may be immediately tax deductible. Second, the distributions and growth of the investments in the retirement accounts aren't taxed until withdrawal.

Funding retirement accounts makes particular sense if you're currently in a high tax bracket and can allow the money to compound over many years (at least 10 years, preferably 15 to 20 years or more).

If you need to save money outside retirement accounts for other short-term purposes (for example, for buying a car or a home), keep doing what you're doing. But if you continue to accumulate money outside retirement accounts with no particular purpose in mind (other than that you like seeing the balances with all those nice, fat numbers), why not get some tax breaks *too* by contributing and investing through retirement accounts?

Investing money outside retirement accounts requires greater thought and consideration because your investments can produce taxable distributions. This is another reason to shelter more of your money in retirement accounts.

Pay off high-interest debt

Many folks have credit card or other consumer debt, such as auto loans, that costs more than 10 percent per year in interest. Paying off this debt with savings is like putting your money in an investment with a guaranteed tax-free return equal to the rate you pay on the debt.

For example, if you have credit-card debt outstanding at 15 percent interest, paying off that loan is the same as putting your money to work in an investment with a certain 15 percent annual return. Remember that the interest on consumer debt is *not* tax deductible, so you would actually need to earn *more* than 15 percent investing your money elsewhere in order to net 15 percent after paying taxes.

Banks and other lenders charge higher rates of interest for consumer debt than for debt for investments (such as real estate and business). Debt for investments is generally available at a lower rate of interest, and it's tax deductible. Consumer debt is not only hazardous to your long-term financial health (because it encourages you to borrow against your future earnings) but is also more expensive.

Paying off your mortgage quicker may make sense, too. This financial move isn't as clear because the interest rate is lower than that on consumer debt and is usually tax deductible (for more details on this decision, see Chapter 22).

Use tax-free money market and bond funds

If you're in a high enough tax bracket (federal 28 percent to 31 percent, or higher), you may find that you come out ahead with tax-free investments. Tax-free investments yield less than comparable investments that produce taxable earnings. But because of the difference in taxes, the earnings from tax-free investments *can* end up being greater than what you're left with from taxable investments.

What's a mutual fund?

Mutual funds are one of the best, if not the best, investment vehicles ever created. Why? Because mutual funds take most of the hassle and cost out of figuring out which securities (stocks, bonds, and so on) to invest in. Mutual funds allow you to diversify your investments — that is, to invest in many different industries and companies instead of just one or two. Mutual funds allow you to give your money to the best money managers in the country — some of the same folks who manage money for the already rich and famous.

Mutual funds, which you can purchase from the comfort of your own home, can pay you over the long haul a better rate of return than a dreary and boring bank or insurance company account. No-load (no commission) funds can be bought directly from the mutual fund company with no broker (and therefore no sales commission) involved.

Mutual funds, like all investments, carry their own unique risks that you'll need to be aware of before you leave the seemingly safe havens of banks and insurers. Funds that invest in stocks and bonds, for example, fluctuate in value with overall changes in the stock and bond markets.

What's really cool about mutual funds is that once you understand them, you soon realize that they can help you meet a bunch of different financial goals. Maybe you have an emergency savings stash of three to six months' living expenses (a prudent idea, by the way). Perhaps you're starting to think about saving for a home purchase or for your retirement. You may know what you need the money for, but you may not know how to protect the money you have and make it grow. To learn more, check out *Mutual Funds For Dummies.*

Tax-free money market funds, offered by mutual fund companies, can be a better alternative to bank savings accounts that pay interest subject to taxation. The best money market funds pay higher yields and give you check-writing privileges. And if you're in a high tax bracket, you can select a *tax-free* money market fund, which pays interest that is free from federal and/or state tax. You can't get this feature with a bank savings account.

Companies offering competitive yields on tax-free money market funds and bonds are Vanguard (800-662-7447) and Fidelity (800-544-8888). Fidelity's Spartan series of funds require much higher minimums to open ($20,000+ versus Vanguard's $3,000). These firms also offer terrific tax-free bond mutual funds that pay tax-free income. Bond funds are intended as longer-term investments (they offer daily liquidity but fluctuate in value).

Invest in tax-friendly stock mutual funds

Too often, when selecting investments, people mistakenly focus on past rates of return. We all know that the past is no guarantee for the future. But an even worse mistake is choosing an investment with a reportedly high rate of return without considering tax consequences.

Determining whether tax-free funds pay more

If you're in the federal 31 percent tax bracket (which starts at $55,100 of taxable income for singles and $91,850 for married couples filing jointly for tax year 1994), you will *usually* come out ahead in tax-free investments. If you're in the federal 28 percent tax bracket, you may or may not earn more in tax-free investments.

In order to do the comparison properly, factor in federal as well as state taxes. Suppose, for example, that you call Vanguard, which tells you that their Prime Portfolio money market fund currently yields 4.5 percent. The yield or dividend on this fund is fully taxable.

Suppose further that you are a resident of the great state of California — home to beautiful beaches and rumbling earthquakes — and that Vanguard's CA money market fund currently yields 3.0 percent. The California tax-free money market fund pays dividends that are free from federal *and* California state tax. Thus, you get to keep all 3.0 percent that you earn. The income you earn on the Prime Portfolio, on the other hand, is taxed. So here's how you compare the two:

yield on tax-free fund ÷ yield on taxable fund

.03 (3 percent) ÷ .045 (4.5 percent) = 0.67

In other words, the tax-free fund pays a yield of 67 percent of that on the taxable fund. Thus, if you must pay more than 33 percent (1 minus 0.67) in federal and California state tax, you net more in the tax-free fund (see Chapter 1 for details on how to determine your federal and state tax rate).

If you do this analysis comparing some funds today, be aware that yields bounce around. The difference in yields between tax-free and taxable funds widens and narrows a bit over time.

Investors often make this mistake when investing in stock mutual funds. Historically, however, many mutual fund investors and publications have not focused on the tax-friendliness of some mutual funds versus others. Just as you should avoid investing in funds with high sales commissions, high annual operating expenses, and poor relative performance, you should also avoid tax-unfriendly funds.

When comparing two similar funds, most people prefer a fund that averages returns equaling 14 percent per year to a fund earning 12 percent. But what if the 14-percent-per-year fund causes you to pay a lot more in taxes? What if, after factoring in taxes, the 14-percent-per-year fund nets just 9 percent, while the 12-percent-per-year fund nets an effective 10 percent return? In such a case, you'd be unwise to choose a fund solely on the basis of the higher reported rate of return.

Numerous mutual funds effectively reduce their shareholders' returns because of their tendency to produce more taxable distributions (capital gains and dividends, which were discussed earlier). Many mutual fund investors are affected by taxable distributions, because more than half the money in mutual funds resides outside tax-sheltered retirement accounts.

All mutual fund managers buy and sell stocks during the course of a year. Whenever a mutual fund manager sells securities, any gain or loss from those securities must be distributed to fund shareholders. Securities sold at a loss can offset those liquidated at a profit. If a fund manager has a tendency to cash in more winners than losers, significant capital gains distributions can result.

Choosing mutual funds that minimize capital gains distributions helps investors defer taxes on their profits. By allowing their capital to continue compounding as it would in an IRA or other retirement account, fund shareholders receive a higher total return. Long-term investors benefit most from choosing mutual funds that minimize capital gains distributions. The more years that appreciation can compound without being taxed, the greater the value to the fund investor.

In addition to capital gains distributions, mutual funds produce dividends that may be subject to higher income tax rates for some investors due to the 1993 tax law changes (both for high-income earners and Social Security recipients).

Investors who purchase mutual funds outside tax-sheltered retirement accounts should also consider the time of year they purchase shares in funds. December is the most common month in which mutual funds make capital gains distributions. When making purchases late in the year, investors may want to find out whether and when the fund may make a significant capital gains distribution. The December payout generally happens when a fund has had a good performance year.

Index mutual funds are tax-friendlier

Some funds have a greater tendency to produce capital gains distributions. Mutual fund mangers of actively managed portfolios, in their attempts to increase their shareholders' returns, buy and sell individual securities more frequently. This process increases the chances of a fund needing to make significant capital gains distributions.

Index funds are mutual funds that invest in a relatively fixed portfolio of securities. They don't attempt to beat the market. Rather, they invest in the securities to mirror or match the performance of an underlying index.

Although index funds cannot beat the market, they have several advantages over actively managed funds. First, because indexed funds trade much less than actively managed funds, index fund investors benefit from lower brokerage commissions. Second, because significant ongoing research need not be conducted to identify companies to invest in, index funds can be run with far lower operating expenses. All things being equal, lower brokerage and operating costs translate into higher shareholder returns. Finally, because index funds trade less, they tend to produce lower capital gains distributions. For mutual funds held outside tax-sheltered retirement accounts, this reduced trading effectively increases an investor's total rate of return.

The Vanguard Group (800-662-7447), headquartered in Valley Forge, Pennsylvania, is the largest mutual fund provider of index funds with about $20 billion in index funds. Vanguard also recently introduced a series of "Tax-Managed" mutual funds, which are index funds that seek to maintain low capital gains distributions.

San Francisco-based Charles Schwab & Co. (800-526-8600) also offers tax-friendly stock index funds. What makes the Schwab Index funds tax-friendly is that whenever its fund managers need to sell securities because of changes in the index or shareholder redemptions, they make sure to offset capital gains with losses. The fund can achieve this result by having the flexibility to temporarily deviate from index weightings by small amounts.

Selling Decisions

Once you've owned a stock, bond, or mutual fund for a while, you may kick around the idea of selling some or all of it. Taxes should factor into the decision when you consider selling investments that you hold outside tax-sheltered retirement accounts. If the investments are inside retirement accounts, taxes aren't an issue because the accounts are sheltered from taxation (unless you're withdrawing funds from the accounts — see Chapter 19).

In most cases, you need not waste your money or precious free time consulting a tax advisor. In the sections that follow, we outline the concepts that you should apply to your situation.

Accounting headaches — selling selected shares

Before we get into specific types of investment decisions you're likely to confront, we must deal with a rather unpleasant but important issue: inventory accounting methods. Although this stuff gets a little complicated, with minimal advance planning, you'll learn sound ways to reduce your tax burden.

If you sell all your shares of a security that you own, you can ignore this issue. Only when you sell a portion of the shares of a security should you consider *specifying* which shares you are selling. Suppose that you own 200 shares of stock in Intergalactic Computer Software and you plan to sell 100 shares. You bought 100 of these shares ten years ago at $50 per share, and then another 100 shares two years ago for $100 per share. Today, the stock is at $150 per share. What a savvy investor you are!

Which 100 shares should you sell? The IRS gives you a choice from a tax and accounting standpoint. You can identify the *specific* shares that you sell. With your Intergalactic shares, you may opt to sell the last or most recent 100 shares you bought in order to minimize your tax bill — because these shares were purchased at a higher price. If you do it this way, identify the shares you want the broker to sell by original date of purchase and/or cost when you sell the shares through your brokerage account. The broker should include this information on the confirmation slip you receive for the sale.

The other method of accounting for which shares are sold is the method the IRS forces you to use if you don't specify before the sale which shares are to be sold — the *first-in-first-out* (FIFO) method. FIFO means that the first shares you sell are simply the first shares that you bought. Not surprisingly, because most stocks appreciate over time, the FIFO method leads to paying more tax sooner. In the case of Intergalactic, FIFO considers that the 100 shares sold are the 100 that you bought ten years ago at the bargain basement price of $50 per share.

Although you will save taxes today if you specify selling the shares that you bought first, don't forget (and the IRS won't let you) that when you finally sell the other shares, you'll then owe taxes on the larger profit. The longer you expect to hold these other shares, the greater the likely value that you'll derive from postponing realizing the larger gain and paying more in taxes. Of course, the risk always exists that the IRS will raise tax rates in the future or that your particular tax rate will rise.

Mutual funds and the average cost method

In America, you never have a shortage of choices — so why not with accounting methods, too? When you sell shares in a mutual fund (this information doesn't apply to money market funds, which don't fluctuate in value), the IRS allows you an additional method — the _average cost method_ — for determining your profit or loss for tax purposes.

If you bought shares in chunks over time and/or reinvested the fund distributions (such as from dividends) into more shares of the fund, tracking and figuring what shares you're selling could be a real headache. So the IRS allows you to take an average cost for all the shares you bought over time.

Be aware that once you elect the average cost method, you can't change to another method for the remaining shares. If you plan on selling only some of your fund shares and it would be advantageous for you to specify that you're selling the newer shares first, choose that method.

In order to choose or _specify_ which shares you are selling, you must select them before you sell. If you don't, the IRS says you must use the FIFO method. You may wonder how the IRS knows whether you specified which shares before you sold them. The IRS doesn't know. But if you are audited, the IRS will ask for proof.

Selling securities with (large) capital gains

Of course, no one likes to pay taxes. But if an investment you own has appreciated in value, someday you will have to pay tax when you sell (unless you plan on passing the investment onto your heirs upon your death — see Chapter 24).

Capital gains tax applies when you sell a security at a higher price than you paid for it. As explained earlier, the capital gains tax rate is different than the tax rate you pay on ordinary income (such as from employment earnings, or interest on bank savings accounts).

Odds are, the longer you've held securities such as stocks, the greater the capital gain you'll have, because stocks tend to appreciate over time. Suppose that your parents bought you 1,000 shares of XYZ company stock ten years ago when it was selling for $10 a share (your folks probably didn't, but let's pretend!). Today it's selling for $20 per share, but you also vaguely recall that the stock split two-for-one a few years ago so now you own 2,000 shares. Thus, if you sell XYZ stock for $40,000 today, you'd have a gain of $30,000 to pay taxes on. So why would anyone want to sell?

The answer depends on your situation. If, for example, you need the money for some other purpose — buying a home, taking a year-long trip around the world — and the stock is your only source of funds, go for it. If you can't do what you want to do without selling, don't let the taxes stand in the way. (We aren't endorsing frivolous spending, but far be it for us to tell you how to live your life). Even if you have to pay state as well as federal taxes totaling some 35 percent of the profit, there will be lots left over. Before you sell, however, do some rough figuring to make sure that you'll have enough to accomplish what you want.

What if you hold a number of stocks? In order to diversify and meet your other financial goals, all you have to do is prioritize. Give preference to selling your largest holdings (total market value) with the smallest capital gains. If you have some securities that have profits and some with losses, you can sell some of each in order to offset the profits with the losses. (Gains and losses for securities held less than one year are taxed at your ordinary income tax rates — see Chapter 11 for more details).

Don't expect to obtain objective, disinterested tax-wise advice regarding what to do with your current investments from a stock broker or from most financial planners. If they earn commissions from the products they sell, their bias will be to tell you to sell. Ditto for financial planners who earn fees from managing money. Even though some financial planners don't get commissions, they can't charge fees on what they aren't managing. If you need help here, turn to a tax or financial advisor who works on an hourly basis.

Selling securities with losses

Perhaps you own some turkeys in your portfolio. If you need to raise cash for some particular reason, you may consider selling some securities at a loss. Losses can be used to offset gains — as long as both offsetting securities were held for more than one year ("long-term") or both held for less than one year ("short-term"). The IRS makes this delineation since long-term gains and losses are taxed on a different rate schedule than short-term gains and losses (see Chapter 11).

If you are in a high federal tax bracket (31 percent and higher), both short-term and long-term losses can be deducted against ordinary income, subject to limitations.

If you need to sell securities at a loss to raise money for some other purpose, be advised that you cannot claim more than $3,000 in short-term or long-term losses in any one year. If you sell securities with losses totaling more than $3,000 in a year, the losses must be carried over to future tax years. This situation not only creates more tax paperwork, it also delays realizing the value of deducting a tax loss. So try not to have *net losses* (losses + gains) that exceed $3,000 in a year.

Some tax advisors advocate doing *year-end tax-loss selling*. The logic goes that if you hold a security at a loss, you should sell it, take the tax write-off, and then buy it (or something similar) back.

When selling for tax loss purposes, be careful of the so-called *wash sale* rules. The IRS will not allow deduction of a loss for a security sale if you buy that same security back within 30 days. As long as you wait 31 or more days, no problem. If you're selling a mutual fund, you can easily sidestep this rule simply by purchasing a fund similar to the one you're selling.

If you own a security that has ceased trading and appears worthless (or have made a loan that hasn't been repaid — even if to a friend), you can probably deduct this loss. (See Chapter 11 for more information on what situations are deductible and how to claim these losses on your annual tax return.)

Selling securities whose costs are unknown

When you sell a security or a mutual fund that you've owned for a long time (or that your parents gave you), you may not have any idea what it originally cost (also known as its *cost basis*). If you could only find the original account statement that shows the original purchase price and amount...

If you can't find that original statement, start by calling the firm where the investment was bought. Whether it's a brokerage firm or mutual fund company, it should be able to send you copies of old account statements. You may have to pay a small fee for this service. Also, increasing numbers of investment firms (particularly mutual fund companies) will automatically calculate and report cost basis information on investments you sell. The cost basis they generally calculate is the average cost for the shares that you purchased. See Chapter 3 for more ideas of what to do when original records aren't available.

Reinvesting and Dollar Cost Averaging

You may be asking yourself if you should make small purchases in a particular investment over time — simply because such an action increases the accounting complexity and tax-filing headaches (this situation applies only to non-retirement accounts). For example, when you buy shares in a mutual fund, you'll be asked if you want the dividends and capital gains paid out to you as cash or reinvested into buying more shares in the fund. (Increasing numbers of individual companies allow you to reinvest dividends on individual stock holdings. These plans are known as *dividend reinvestment plans* or DRIPs. Discount broker Charles Schwab also offers this service for free for individual stocks.)

If you are retired or if you otherwise need to live off your investment income, receiving cash payments probably works best. If you don't need the money, reinvesting allows your money to continue compounding and growing in the investment. While reinvesting complicates your tax situation because you're buying shares at different times at different prices, this reinvestment benefit should outweigh the hassles. (But please take note: You still must pay current taxes on reinvested distributions in nonretirement accounts.)

Another investing approach is *dollar-cost averaging,* which can also cause headaches with your taxes when it comes time to sell investments held outside retirement accounts. Dollar cost averaging simply means that you're investing your money in equal chunks on a regular basis, such as once a month. For example, if you have $60,000 to invest, you can invest $2,000 per month until it's all invested, which takes a few years. The money that awaits future investment isn't lying fallow. You keep it in a money-market-type account, where it earns a bit of interest while it waits its turn.

The attraction of dollar cost averaging is that it allows you to ease into riskier investments instead of jumping in all at once. The benefit may be that if the price of the investment drops after some of your initial purchases, you can buy more later at a lower price. If you had dumped all your money at once into an investment and then it dropped like a stone, you'd kick yourself for not waiting.

The flip side of dollar-cost averaging is that if your investment of choice appreciates in value, you may wish that you had invested your money faster. Another possible drawback of dollar-cost averaging is that you may get cold feet as you continue to invest money in an investment that's dropping in value. Many people who are attracted to dollar-cost averaging out of fear of buying before a price drop are scared to continue boarding a sinking ship.

Dollar-cost averaging has its advantages, but it also has its drawbacks. It's most valuable when the money you want to invest represents a large portion of your total assets and you can stick to a schedule. It's best to make it automatic so that you're less likely to chicken out. Most investment firms recommended in the next few chapters can provide automatic exchange services.

If you buy an investment via dollar-cost averaging or dividend reinvestment at many different times and prices, accounting is muddied as you sell blocks of the investment. Which shares are you selling?

For recordkeeping purposes, save your statements detailing all the purchases in your accounts. Most mutual fund companies, for example, provide year-end summary statements that show all transactions throughout the year. For purchases made now and in the future, fund companies should also be able to tell you what your average cost was per share when you need to sell your shares.

Tax-Favored "Investments" to Avoid

Investment and insurance brokers and financial planners who sell products and work on commission — and therefore who are also salespeople — love to pitch investment products that will supposedly save you on your taxes. In all cases, you have better options available. Most of the time, the salesperson won't examine your entire financial situation. Therefore the salesperson may sell you an inappropriate or lousy investment that pays (the salesperson!) hefty commissions. Here are the main investments these commission-driven folks try to sell you — along with the reasons why you shouldn't buy them.

Limited partnerships

Limited partnerships (LPs) sold through brokers and financial planners should be avoided at all costs. They are inferior investment vehicles. That's not to say that no one has ever made money on one, but they are burdened with high sales commissions and ongoing management fees that deplete your investment. You can do better elsewhere.

Limited partnerships invest in real estate and a variety of businesses, such as cable television, cellular phone companies, and research and development. They pitch that you can get in on the ground floor of a new investment opportunity and make big money. They also usually tell you that while your investment is growing at 20 percent or more per year, you get handsome dividends of 8 percent or so each year. Sound too good to be true? It is.

Many of the yields on LPs have turned out to be bogus. In some cases, partnerships propped up their yields by paying back investors' principal (without clearly telling them, of course). The other hook with LPs is tax benefits. What few loopholes did exist in the tax code for LPs have largely been closed. (Amazingly, some investment salespeople hoodwink investors to put their retirement account money — which is already tax-sheltered — into LPs!) The other problems with LPs overwhelm any small tax advantage, anyway.

The investment salesperson who sells you such an investment stands to earn a commission of up to 10 percent or more — so only 90 cents, or less, per dollar of yours gets invested. Each year, LPs typically siphon off another several percentage points for management and other expenses. Most partnerships have little or no incentive to control costs. In fact, there is pressure to charge more to enrich the managing partners. Efficient, no-load mutual funds, in contrast, put 100 percent of your capital to work and charge 1 percent per year or less in management fees.

Unlike a mutual fund, you can't vote with your dollars. If the partnership is poorly run and expensive, you're stuck. LPs are *illiquid.* You can't get your money that is left until the partnership is liquidated, typically seven to ten years after you buy in.

The only thing limited about a limited partnership is its ability to make you money. If you want to buy investments that earn profits and have growth potential, stick with stocks (preferably using mutual funds), bonds, real estate, or your own business.

Life insurance with a cash value

Life insurance should *not* be used as an investment, especially if you haven't exhausted contributing money to retirement accounts. Agents love to sell cash value life insurance for the high commissions. Life insurance that combines life insurance protection with an account that has a cash value is usually known as *universal, whole,* or *variable life.*

It's true that the cash value portion of your policy grows without taxation until you withdraw it. But if you want tax-deferred retirement savings, you should *first* take advantage of such retirement savings plans as 401(k)s, 403(b)s, SEP-IRAs, and Keoghs that give you an immediate tax deduction for your current contributions in addition to growth without taxation until withdrawal.

Money paid into a cash value life policy gives no up-front tax breaks to you. If you've exhausted the tax-deductible plans, variable annuities and/or a nondeductible individual retirement account (IRA) can provide tax-deferred compounding of your investment dollars (see Chapter 19).

The only real advantage cash value life insurance offers is that the proceeds paid to your beneficiaries can be free of estate taxes. You need to have a fairly substantial estate at your death to benefit from this feature. (See Chapter 24 for more estate planning strategies.)

Loaded mutual funds and the like

Loaded mutual funds aren't those that send firearms with their marketing materials. "Load" simply means sales commission — and that means anywhere from 4 percent to 8.5 percent of your investment dollars are siphoned off to pay a broker.

While mutual funds are good investment vehicles, there is no need to pay a sales commission or load. Loads are additional and unnecessary costs that are deducted from your investment money. Load funds don't perform any better than no-load (commission-free) funds. Why should they? Commissions are paid to the salesperson, not to the fund manager.

Another problem with buying load funds is that you miss out on the opportunity to assess objectively whether you should buy a mutual fund at all. Maybe, for example, you should pay off debt or invest somewhere else. But salespeople almost never advise you to pay off your credit cards or mortgage or invest through your company's retirement plan instead of buying an investment through the salespeople.

Salespeople who sell mutual funds usually push other stuff as well. Limited partnerships, life insurance, annuities, futures, and options hold the allure of big commissions. Salespeople tend to exaggerate the potential benefits and obscure the risks and drawbacks of what they sell — they don't seem to take the time to educate investors.

In addition to load mutual funds, you may be pitched to buy a *unit investment trust* or *closed-end fund.* These funds are basically similar to other mutual funds, and they also pay brokers a commission. Also beware of the increasing numbers of brokers and financial planners selling bogus no-loads — which are actually funds that just hide the sales commission.

You may be told something along the line that — as long as you stay in a fund for five to seven years — you needn't pay the back-end sales charge that would apply upon sale of the investment. This claim may be true, but it's also true that these funds pay investment salespeople a hefty commission. The salespeople are able to receive this commission because the fund company charges you very high ongoing operating expenses (usually 1 percent more per year than the best funds). So one way or another, these salespeople get their pounds of flesh (that is, commissions) from your investment dollars.

Invest in no-loads and avoid load funds and investment salespeople. The only way to be sure that a fund is truly no-load is to look at the prospectus for the fund. Only there, in black and white and without marketing hype, must the truth be told about sales charges and other fund fees. Never buy an investment without looking at a prospectus.

Annuities

Annuities are a peculiar type of insurance and investment product. They are a sort of savings-type account with slightly higher yields that are backed by insurance companies.

Insurance agents and financial planners working on commission happily sell annuities to anyone with money to invest. The problem is, annuities are suitable for a relatively small portion of people with money to invest. If annuities make sense for you, you can buy no-load (commission-free) annuities by bypassing salespeople and dealing directly with mutual fund companies.

The major selling hook of annuities is supposed tax savings. "Why pay taxes each year on your investment earnings?" the agent or financial planner will say. As in other types of retirement accounts, money that is placed in an annuity compounds without taxation until withdrawal. However, unlike most other types of retirement accounts — 401(k)s, SEP-IRAs, and Keoghs — your contributions into an annuity give no up-front tax deductions. The only tax benefit is that the earnings on the investment compound without tax until withdrawal. Thus it makes sense to consider contributing to an annuity only after you fully fund tax-deductible retirement accounts.

Because annuities carry higher annual expenses due to the insurance that comes with them, they only make sense if you have 15 or more years to go until you need the money. So annuities are *not* appropriate if you are already in retirement or near retirement. (Read Chapter 19 to learn more about retirement account options and annuities.)

Chapter 22

Real Estate Decisions and Taxes

- -

- -

*T*ax benefits are a significant reason why many people engage in plug-fests for property ownership — especially people in the real estate business, such as real estate agents and bankers, loan brokers, and others in the mortgage business.

Buying a home or investing in real estate *can* provide many financial and psychological rewards. And taxes help reduce the cost of owning real estate. On the other hand, purchasing and maintaining property can also be extremely time-consuming, emotionally draining, and financially painful.

Don't make the mistake of looking at someone's property that's worth $200,000 today (bought 20 years ago for $40,000) and assume that real estate investment is the inside track to wealth creation. Consider all the expenditures the owner likely made over the years, such as fixing plumbing and electrical problems, updating appliances, replacing the roof, and repainting. And then there are the annual carrying costs — the interest alone over the life of the loan can total more than the original purchase price of the property! Of course, when you buy and sell real estate, you should add all those transaction costs, such as real estate broker's commissions, loan fees, title insurance, and so on. Also, don't forget that $40,000 sounds cheap, but two decades ago when the cost-of-living was much lower, 40 grand actually bought a lot.

Real Estate Tax Breaks

Just as contributing money to retirement accounts (See "Retirement Account Benefits" in Chapter 19) yields tax breaks, so does buying a home and investing in other real estate. Our tax system favors property ownership, because it is widely believed that owners take better care of their property when they have a financial stake in its future value. It's hard to argue with this logic, if you visit most government-subsidized tenements.

All the powerful real estate lobbies also contribute to the addition and retention of real estate tax benefits in our tax code. Builders, contractors, real estate agents, the banking industry, and many other real estate sectors have an enormous financial stake in the American hunger to own and improve properties.

You should understand the tax aspects of home ownership and other real estate investing so that you can make the most of these tax-reduction opportunities and make informed real estate decisions. Making wise real estate moves requires that you also know how to fit real estate decisions into your overall financial picture. After all, you have limited income and other options on which to spend your money. But don't make the mistake of depending on those involved in your typical real estate deal to help you see the bigger picture — they make their livings off your decision to buy, and the more you spend, the more they make.

We know that you can't wait to uncover the real estate tax breaks for the taking. But before we get to them, we kindly ask that you never forget two important caveats to gaining these property tax advantages:

> ✔ You have to *spend* money on real estate — acquiring property, paying the mortgage and property taxes over the years, improving the property while you own it — to even be eligible for the tax breaks. As you'll learn in this chapter, if you earn enough income or make the wrong financial moves, you may not be able to claim some of the tax benefits available.

> ✔ Always remember that you're not the only one who knows that the U.S. tax code offers these real estate tax breaks. What difference does that make? The price of real estate in America reflects the fact that buyers and sellers know about the tax deductions, and this is a major reason why so many people are willing to pay sums with many zeroes for a piece of the American Dream. Other countries that don't offer tax breaks for home ownership, such as Canada, have comparably lower prices, because buyers can't afford to pay higher prices when they can't bank on a tax deduction to help subsidize the cost.

> In fact, if the folks in Washington who make and forever change our tax laws yanked away the current tax goodies for real estate, it would have a depressing effect on U.S. property values. It's unlikely that politicians would take away these benefits, because property owners, who make up the majority of voters, would likely bounce the offenders out of office.

The following sections offer an overview of the tax goodies available to homeowners. The benefits are similar to, but different from, the tax benefits for rental or income property owners, which are discussed later in this chapter.

Keep track of your tax bracket

When you first go to purchase a home, it may pay to plan ahead and push as many so-called itemizeable deductions as you can into the tax year in which you expect to buy your home.

Suppose, for example, that this year you are using the standard deduction because you don't have many itemized deductions. You decide late in the year that you'll probably buy a home in the coming year. Because you'll have mortgage interest and property taxes to write off, you'll be able to itemize next year. It makes sense, then, to collect as many deductible expenses as possible and shift them into next year. For example, if the solicitations surrounding the December holidays prompt you to contribute to many charities, you can wait until January to donate. Take a look at the deductible items on Schedule A (discussed in Chapter 8) to determine what else you may want to postpone paying.

Also, be aware that your income tax bracket may change from year to year. Thus, where possible, you can choose to pay more or less of some itemizeable expenses in one year versus another. Suppose that you receive your annual property tax bill in the fall of the year, and it's payable in two installments. You must pay one installment before the end of the year, whereas you have until the next spring to pay the other installment. If for some reason you expect to be in a lower tax bracket next year — perhaps you're going to take a sabbatical and will earn less income — you may choose to pay the entire property tax bill before this year ends.

Be sure to read the section in Chapter 1 about figuring your current and future expected tax bracket for planning purposes to minimize your taxes.

Mortgage interest and property tax write-offs

When you buy a home, you can claim two big ongoing expenses of home ownership on Schedule A of IRS Form 1040. These expenses consist of the interest on your mortgage and your property taxes.

You are allowed to claim mortgage-interest deductions on a primary residence (where you actually live) and on a second home for mortgage debt totaling $1,000,000. You are also allowed to deduct the interest on a home-equity loan of up to $100,000 (See Chapter 8).

Property taxes are also fully deductible on Schedule A whether you purchase a $15,000 one-room shack in an unpopulated rural area without electricity or a multimillion-dollar mansion on several acres overlooking the ocean.

Home office deductions

When you run your business out of your home, you may be able to take additional tax deductions beyond the mortgage interest and property taxes you already get to claim as a homeowner. See "Home alone, or outside office space?" in Chapter 20 for a discussion of this issue.

Capital gains rollover

Normally, when you make an investment in a stock or business, for example, and you later sell it for a profit (also known as a *capital gain*), you owe tax on the profit. Some real estate, however, receives special treatment in this regard. If you buy a home in which you plan to live (your so-called primary residence), the IRS allows you to roll over (defer) paying tax on your profit when you sell as long as you meet certain criteria.

Suppose that on December 1, 1995, you sell your home at a profit — for more than you paid originally. You sell the home for $250,000 and after paying real estate commissions and other costs of sale, you realize $225,000. (Ignore the size of the mortgage you must pay off, because this, as well as the down payment you make on your next home purchase, does not affect the rollover rule.)

The capital gains rollover rule for your residence says that you then have 24 months, until December 1, 1997, to purchase and move into another home that costs at least as much — that is, $225,000. The IRS is strict and inflexible on this rule, so don't push your luck. Two years, they feel, is more than ample time to buy again. If it takes you 24 months and two days to buy and move into another home, you're stuck with paying the tax. (Some members of the armed forces and those affected by disaster losses, such as Hurricane Andrew in Florida, get more time — see Chapter 11 for more details.) You should also know that you can use this rollover provision only once every two years unless your employer transfers you to another location or you must relocate because you take a new job.

If you move from your home, rent it out for a period of time, and then sell it, you may lose the privilege of rolling over the profit on the sale as your primary residence. The IRS may consider that you have converted your home from a primary residence to a rental property. The only exception: you actively tried to sell the home after you moved and only rented it temporarily to help defray the costs of keeping it until you sold it.

All is not lost if you want to purchase a less expensive home when you sell your current one. If you're over 55, you can take advantage of another real estate tax break, discussed in the next section. You should know as well that the 24-month window of time that you have to buy a more expensive home also allows you to include the improvements you make to your new home. So in the example earlier in the section where you realized $225,000 from your home sale, if you buy a replacement home for $200,000, you can spend $25,000 improving the replacement home to meet the roll over requirement. This additional $25,000 must be spent within the two-year period of selling your old home. (See "Tracking what you spend on your home," later in this chapter regarding what constitutes improvements.)

(An eighth of) a million-dollar tax-free gain!

You know the expression "Once in a lifetime..." The IRS grants you a real estate capital gains tax break that you can use once, and only once, in your lifetime. And no, you can't change your name to take advantage of it twice, because to the IRS you're just a number — your Social Security number won't change, even if you legally change your name.

When you reach the magic age of 55, the IRS allows you, when you sell your primary residence, to buy a home that costs as much as $125,000 less and not pay any capital gains tax. Such a deal! As discussed in the preceding section, you can normally avoid paying capital gains tax only when you buy a new home that is more expensive than the one you sold.

If you are a single homeowner over the age of 55 and you're considering selling your home and taking advantage of this one-time tax break, do it *before* you get married (if marriage is in your plans). The IRS allows only one person in a married couple to take this tax break. So you and your spouse-to-be can each take the $125,000 capital gains exclusion.

Buying Your Own Abode

It really doesn't matter why you're thinking of buying a home. This type of decision is seldom motivated by just financial considerations. Whether your five-story walkup has lost its bohemian appeal or you can't get the crayon stains off the kitchen floor, in our book that's a good enough reason to buy a home.

Financially speaking, you really shouldn't buy your own place unless you anticipate being there for at least three years, and preferably five years or more. Many expenses are included in buying and selling a property, such as the cost of getting a mortgage (points, application and credit report fees, and appraisal fees), inspection expenses, moving costs, real estate agents' commissions, and title insurance. And remember — most of these expenses are *not* tax-deductible. To cover these transaction costs plus the additional costs of ownership, a property needs to appreciate a fair amount before you can be as well off financially as if you had continued renting. A property needs to appreciate about 15 percent just to offset these expenses, even factoring in the tax benefits homeowners enjoy.

If you need or want to move in a couple of years, it's risky to count on that kind of appreciation. If you're lucky (that is, if you happen to buy before a sharp upturn in housing prices), you may get it. If you're not, you will probably lose money on the deal.

Some people are willing to buy a home even when they don't expect to live in it for long and would consider turning it into a rental. Doing so can work well financially in the long haul, but don't underestimate the responsibilities that come with rental property. (Rent the movie *Pacific Heights* and talk to friends and colleagues who have been landlords.)

Renting's OK; you're OK if you rent

Don't feel that you're not a success if you're not a homeowner. And as we discussed earlier in this chapter, don't feel pressured to buy a home because of the tax breaks. The value of those tax breaks is reflected in the higher home prices we pay versus the home prices in other countries where real estate owners don't get tax deductions.

Some financially successful long-term renters we've seen include people who pay low rent — either because they've made sacrifices to live in a smaller rental, for example, or live in a rent-controlled building. One advantage of low rental costs is that you may be able to save more money. If you can consistently save ten percent or more of your earnings, you will probably meet your future financial goals.

As a long-term renter, you won't have a lot of money tied up in your home. Many homeowners enter their retirement years with a substantial portion of their wealth in their homes. As a renter, you have all your money in financial assets that you can probably tap into more easily.

Some renters are tempted to invest in a property elsewhere and rent it to others or use it when they want. Make sure you read the sections later in this chapter that discuss investment property and second homes. Such a decision is neither straightforward nor simple.

Tax savings in home ownership

To quickly determine your tax savings in home ownership, try this simple shortcut: Multiply your marginal federal tax rate (discussed in Chapter 1) by the total amount of your property taxes and mortgage. Technically, not all your mortgage payment is tax deductible; only the portion of the mortgage payment that goes to interest is tax-deductible. In the early years of your mortgage, the portion that goes toward interest is nearly all of the payment. On the other hand, your property taxes will probably rise over time and you can also earn state tax benefits from your deductible mortgage interest and property taxes.

To figure out more precisely how home ownership may affect your tax situation, try plugging some reasonable numbers into your tax return to *guesstimate* how your taxes will change. You can also speak with a tax advisor.

When you buy a home, make sure that you refigure how much you need to pay in income tax, because your mortgage interest and property tax deductions should help lower your tax bill. If you work for an employer, ask your payroll/benefits department for Form W-4. If you're self-employed, you can complete a worksheet that comes with Form 1040-ES. (Call 800-TAX-FORM for a copy.) Many homebuyers skip this step, and they end up getting a big tax refund in the next year. Although getting money back from the IRS may feel good, it means that at a minimum, you made an interest-free loan to the IRS. In the worst case, the reduced cash flow during the year may cause you to accumulate debt or miss out on contributing to tax-deductible retirement accounts.

How much should you spend on a home?

Real estate agents and mortgage lenders will be more than happy to tell you the maximum that you are qualified to borrow. They want your business, and the more money you spend, the more they make. But that doesn't mean that you should borrow the maximum.

If you fall in love with a home and buy it without looking at your monthly expenditures and long-term goals, you may end up with a home that dictates much of your future spending. For example, how much should you save monthly to reach your retirement goals? Suppose two different home buyers with identical incomes consider buying the same home. Kathy is 30 years old and has already put away $40,000 in her retirement accounts. James, on the other hand, is 10 years older (he's 40) yet has no money stashed in retirement accounts.

Because she has a head start, Kathy is in a much better position overall to afford the home purchase because she doesn't need to save as much toward retirement as James to reach the same retirement goal. But real estate agents and mortgage lenders would tell them that they can borrow the same amount because they have identical incomes.

In addition to analyzing your retirement planning, other questions you should ask yourself before you buy may include whether you spend (and want to continue spending) on fun stuff like travel and entertainment. If you want to continue your current lifestyle (and the expenditures inherent in it), be honest with yourself about how much you can really afford to spend as a homeowner.

Often, first-time homebuyers are apt to run into financial trouble because they don't know their spending needs and priorities and don't know how to budget for them. Buying a home can be a wise decision, but it can also be a huge burden. Some people don't decrease their spending, as they should due to the large amount of debt they just incurred; in fact, they often spend even more on all sorts of gadgets and furnishings for their homes. Many people prop up their spending habits with credit. For this reason, a surprisingly large percentage — some studies say about half — who borrow additional money against their home equity use the funds to pay other debts.

Don't let your home control your financial future. Take stock of your overall financial health — especially where you stand in terms of retirement planning if you hope to retire by your mid-60s — *before* you buy property or agree to a particular mortgage.

Tracking what you spend on your home

Although it may be a bit of a hassle, it's in your best interest to document and track when you spend money improving your property. You can add the cost of these improvements to your original purchase price for the home. So, when you someday sell the property, you get to reduce your profit, for tax purposes, accordingly. In fact, when you sell your home, you'll need to report to the IRS what you sold the home for and how much you spent improving it.

Set up a simple file folder into which you deposit receipts for your expenditures. The challenging part for most people is simply keeping the receipts separate. Another challenge is to correctly distinguish between spending on *improvements,* which the IRS allows you to add to your cost of the home, and spending for *maintenance and repairs,* which you can't add to the original purchase price of the home.

Improvements include expenses such as installing an alarm system, adding or remodeling a room, planting new trees and shrubs in your yard, and purchasing new appliances. These improvements increase the value of your home and lengthen its life.

Maintenance and repairs include expenses such as the cost of hiring a plumber to fix a leaky pipe, repainting, repairing a door so that it closes better, and recaulking around your bathtub to prevent leaks.

It's interesting to note that if you hire a contractor to do the home improvements, the IRS allows you to effectively add the cost of the contractor's time (the labor charges) into the overall improvements that reduce your home's profit for tax purposes. On the other hand, if you elect to do the work yourself, you gain no tax benefit for your sweat. You cannot add in a cost for the value of your time — the IRS says that you work for free. Now you may have another reason to hire someone to do the work for you.

One home is usually the best number

Part of the allure of a second home is the supposed tax benefits. Even when you qualify for some or all of them, tax benefits only partially reduce the cost of owning a property. We've seen more than a few cases in which the second home is such a cash drain that it prevents its owners from contributing to and taking advantage of tax-deductible retirement savings plans.

If you can realistically afford the additional costs of a second, or vacation home, we're not going to tell you how to spend your extra cash. But please don't make the all-too-common mistake of viewing a second home as an investment. The way most people use them, they're not.

Investment real estate is property that you rent out. Most second-home owners rent their property out very little — ten percent or less of the time. As a result, second homes are usually money drains.

If you don't rent out a second home property most of the time, ask yourself whether you can afford such a luxury. Can you accomplish your other financial goals — saving for retirement, paying for your primary residence, and so on — with this added expense? Keeping a second home is more of a consumption than an investment decision if you don't rent it out.

Also, be aware that if your vacation home appreciates in value, the IRS does not allow the rollover without taxation on your capital gains, as they do on primary residences (discussed in the section, "Capital gains rollover," earlier in this chapter).

In the blizzard of paperwork that you sign and receive when you buy your home, you should find a *settlement statement*. Don't lose this! These valuable pieces of paper itemize many of the expenses associated with the purchase of your home. You can add many of these expenses to the original cost of the home and reduce your taxable profit when it comes time to sell. Also, don't forget to toss into your receipt folder proof of other expenditures that the settlement statement may not document, such as inspection fees that you paid for when buying your home.

Declare income if you rent a room

The IRS allows you to rent your home or a room in your home for up to 14 days each year without having to declare the rental income and pay income taxes on it. Rental of your home or a portion thereof for more than 14 days requires that you report the income when you file your annual tax return. You can declare rental income simply by filing Schedule E (See Chapter 12 for more information.)

Selling Your Home

As discussed in the section "Capital gains rollover" earlier in this chapter, home-owners can roll over the profit (capital gain) when they sell their home so long as they buy another home that costs as much or more within two years. When-ever you sell a home, even if you are going to rollover a gain, you must file Form 2119 (Sale of Your Home) with Form 1040 from the same tax year. Both the IRS and you receive Form 1099-S from the firm that handles the sales transaction of your home.

If you've made a profit and don't plan on rolling over your gain, you must pay capital gains tax. If you plan on rolling over the gain but haven't done so yet, you can indicate on Form 2119 that you plan to do so.

If the two-year period elapses after you sell your home at a profit and you don't buy a replacement home, you owe not only capital gains tax but also the IRS interest from date of sale. So file an amended return as soon as you know you won't be buying another home. If you do buy a replacement home, make sure that you complete another Form 2119 to inform the IRS that you have satisfied the rollover requirements and to document the purchase price of the new property. Forgetting to file this form a second time triggers many an audit.

"I don't want to sell at a loss"

Many homeowners are tempted to hold on to their properties when they need to move if the property is worth less than when they bought it or if the real estate market is soft. We recommend not doing this. It's probably not worth the hassle of renting out your property or the financial gamble to hold on to the property.

You may reason that in a few years, the real estate storm clouds will clear and you can sell your property at a much higher price. Here are three risks associ-ated with this way of thinking:

- ✔ First, you can't know what's going to happen to property prices in the next few years. They may rebound, but they can stay the same or drop even further. A property generally needs to appreciate at least a few percentage points each year just to make up for all the costs of holding and maintaining it.

- ✔ If you haven't been a landlord, don't underestimate the hassle and head-aches associated with the job.

- ✔ After you convert your home into a rental property, you need to pay capital gains tax on your profit when you sell (the only exception being if you tem-porarily rent your home while you're still actively trying to sell it — see "Capital gains rollover" earlier in this chapter). This tax wipes out much of the advantage of having held onto the property until prices recovered. (If you want to be a long-term rental property owner, you can, under current tax laws, do a *tax-free exchange* into another rental property after you sell.)

You would think that, because the IRS makes you pay capital gains if you sell your home at a profit, they would allow you to deduct a loss when you sell your home for less than you paid. After all, you can do this with other investments such as stocks and mutual funds. Well, you can't claim a capital loss if you lose money on your home.

"Does it make sense to keep my home as investment property when I move?"

One advantage to keeping your current home as an investment property after you move is that you already own it. Locating and buying a property takes time and money. Also you know what you have with your current home. If you go out and purchase a property to rent, you're starting from scratch.

On the other hand, don't consider converting your home into a rental when you move unless it really is a long-term proposition. As discussed in the preceding section, selling rental property has tax consequences.

Also, be aware that you may not be able to deduct as much for depreciation expenses when you convert your home to rental property as you could on a rental bought separately. If your home has appreciated since you bought it, the IRS forces you to use your original (lower) purchase price for purposes of calculating depreciation. To make matters worse, if your home has declined in value since you originally purchased it, you must use this lower value, at the time you convert the property, for purposes of depreciation.

If the idea of keeping the home you move from as a long-term investment appeals to you, take stock of your overall financial situation *before* you make the final call. Can you afford to purchase your next home given the money that's still tied up in the home you're considering keeping as a rental? Can you afford to contribute to tax-deductible retirement plans, or will the burden of carrying two properties tie up too much of your cash flow? Will your overall investments be well diversified or will you have too much of your money tied up in real estate (perhaps in one area of the country)?

What happens in the event of divorce?

A divorce complicates many financial issues. Real estate is no different. It used to be that if ownership of a home that has appreciated in value were transferred between spouses because of a divorce, capital gains tax was owed. Fortunately, this is no longer one of the additional costs of divorce. Transfers of property between spouses are not taxed if the transfers are made within one year of divorce (and both spouses are U.S. residents or citizens).

If you are selling your home because of a divorce, when you sell the home and what each spouse does in terms of replacement properties can have large tax ramifications. If you agree to sell the home in the divorce settlement, you can each choose whether to roll over your share of the capital gains into another home. If you split the home 50/50 and the home sells for $300,000, you would each need to spend at least $150,000 on your repacement homes to avoid capital gains tax.

If both you and your spouse are over the age of 55, and you plan on selling the home at a large profit, it may be to your advantage to get divorced first and then sell the home so that you can take the $125,000 capital gains exclusion. If you sell the home while still married; the IRS allows only one exclusion of $125,000.

Be careful if you sell your home before divorcing. If one of you *does* purchase a replacement home and rolls over the capital gain and the other person doesn't, it's possible the spouse who *did* repurchase may be saddled with the capital gains tax for the one who didn't. There are real life cases where this has happened.

Competent divorce attorneys and tax advisors can help you work out an equitable financial and tax settlement.

Real Estate as an Investment

For most people, the only real estate they own or consider owning are the homes in which they live. If that's all you desire, we're not going to push you into the business of investing in and managing rental property. It's a lot of work and there certainly are other investments, such as mutual funds that own stocks, that are far more convenient and as financially rewarding.

But some people just have that itch to own something tangible. Real estate is, well, *real,* after all. You can fix it up, take pictures of it, and drive your friends by it!

Is real estate investing for you?

Whether you should invest in real estate versus other investments, such as stocks, bonds, or mutual funds, depends on many factors. The first and most important question to ask yourself is whether you're cut out to handle the responsibilities that come with being a landlord. Real estate is a time-intensive investment — it's not for couch potatoes. Investing in stocks can be time-intensive as well, but it doesn't have to be if you use professionally managed mutual funds. Conversely, you can hire a property manager with real estate experience to reduce your workload.

An often-overlooked drawback to investing in real estate is that you earn no tax benefits while you're accumulating your down payment. Rental property usually is a cash drain as well in the first few years of ownership. Retirement accounts, on the other hand, such as 401(k)s, SEP-IRAs, Keoghs, and so on (discussed in Chapter 19) give you immediate tax deductions as you contribute money to them. Although real estate offers many tax deductions, as we discussed earlier in the chapter, the cost of real estate reflects the expected tax breaks. So don't invest in real estate because of the tax deductions. Exhaust contributing to retirement accounts before considering property as an investment.

A final consideration with regard to whether real estate investing is for you — if you think that you have an above-average understanding of real estate and how to improve its value, you have reason enough to invest in it.

Rental property tax breaks

When you purchase property and rent it out, you're essentially running a business. You take in revenue — namely rent from your tenants — and incur expenses from the property. You hope that, over time, your revenue exceeds your expenses so that your real estate investment produces a profit (cash flow, in real estate lingo) for all the money and time you've sunk into it. You also hope that the market value of your investment property appreciates over time. The IRS helps you make a buck through a number of tax benefits. Here are the major ones:

Operating expense write-offs

In addition to the deductions allowed for mortgage interest and property taxes, just as on a home in which you live, you can deduct on your tax return a whole variety of other expenses for rental property. Almost all these deductions come from money that you spend on the property, such as money for insurance, maintenance and repairs, and food for the Doberman you keep around to intimidate those tenants whose rent checks always seem to be in the mail.

But one expense — depreciation — doesn't involve your spending money. Depreciation is an accounting deduction that the IRS allows you to take for the overall wear and tear on your building. The idea behind this deduction is that, over time, your building deteriorates and needs upgrading, rebuilding, and so on. The IRS tables now say that for residential property, you can depreciate over $27^1/_2$ years; for nonresidential property, 39 years. Only the portion of a property's value that is attributable to the building(s) — and not the land — can be depreciated.

If your rental property shows a loss for the year (when you figure your property's income and expenses), you may be able to deduct this loss on your tax return. If your *adjusted gross income* (as defined in Chapter 12) is less than $100,000 and you actively participate in managing the property, you are allowed to deduct your losses on operating rental real estate — up to $25,000 per year. Limited partnerships and properties in which you own less than ten percent are excluded. (See Chapter 12 for more details.)

Good versus bad real estate investments

You can invest in real estate in a number of ways. The traditional and best method is to purchase property in an area that you've researched and are familiar with. Single-family homes and multi-unit buildings generally work best for most investors. Make sure that you do your due diligence; have the property professionally inspected and secure adequate insurance coverage.

If you want a stake in real estate but don't want the responsibilities and hassles that come with being a landlord, consider *real estate investment trusts (REITs).* REITs offer the benefits of property ownership without the headaches of being a landlord. REITs are a collection of real estate properties, such as shopping centers, apartments, and other rental buildings. REITs trade as securities on the major stock exchanges and can also be bought through mutual funds such as Fidelity and Cohen & Steers.

Some real estate investments rarely make sense because they're near-certain money losers. Many investors get sucked into these lousy investments because of the supposed high expected returns and tax breaks. Limited partnerships, for example, that are sold through stock brokers and financial planners who work on commission are burdened by high sales commissions and ongoing management fees as well as illiquidity (see Chapter 21).

Time shares are another nearly certain money loser. With a time share, you buy a week or two of ownership, or usage, of a particular unit, usually a condominium in a resort location. If you pay $8,000 for a week (in addition to ongoing maintenance fees), you're paying the equivalent of $400,000 for the whole unit year-round, but a comparable unit may sell for only $150,000. All the extra mark-up pays the salespeople's commissions, administrative expenses, and profits for the time-share development company.

In order to deduct a loss on your tax return, you must *actively participate* in the management of the property. This rule doesn't necessarily mean that you have to perform the day-to-day management of the property. In fact, you can hire a property manager and still *actively participate* by doing such simple things as approving the terms of the lease contracts, tenants, and expenditures for maintenance and improvements on the building.

If you make more than $100,000 per year, you start to lose these write-offs. At an income of $150,000 or more, you cannot deduct rental real estate losses from your other income. People in the real estate business (for example, agents and developers) who work more than 750 hours per year in the industry may not be subject to these rules. (See Chapter 12 for more information.)

You start to lose the deductibility of rental property losses above the $100,000 limit whether you are single or married filing jointly. It's a bit unfair to couples because it's easier for them to break $100,000 with two incomes than for a single person with one income. Sorry!

Tax credits for low-income housing and old buildings

If you invest in low-income housing or particularly old commercial buildings, the IRS grants you special tax credits. The credits represent a direct reduction in your tax bill because you're spending to rehabilitate and improve such properties. The IRS wants to encourage investors to consider investing in and fixing up old or run-down buildings that likely would continue to deteriorate otherwise.

The amounts of the credits range from as little as 10 percent of the expenditures to as much as 90 percent, depending on the property type. The IRS has strict rules governing what types of properties qualify.

Rollover of capital gains

Suppose that you purchase a rental property and nurture it over the years. You find good tenants and keep the building repaired and looking nice. You may just find that all that work wasn't for naught. The property may be worth much more than you originally paid for it.

However, if you simply sell the property, you owe taxes on your gain or profit. Even worse is how the government defines your gain. If you bought the property for $100,000 and sell it for $150,000, you not only owe tax on that difference, but you also owe tax on an additional amount, depending on the property's depreciation. The amount of depreciation that you deducted on your tax returns reduces the original $100,000 purchase price, making the taxable difference that much larger. For example, if you deducted $25,000 for depreciation over the years that you owned the property, you owe tax on the difference between the sale price of $150,000 and $75,000 (= $100,000 purchase price minus $25,000 depreciation).

All this tax may just motivate you to either hold on to your property or roll over your gain into another property. You *can* avoid paying tax on your profit when you sell a rental property by rolling over your gain into another property, similar to deferring tax from the sale of your residence at a profit. (You may not receive the proceeds — they must go into an escrow account.) The rules, however, are different for rolling over profits (called *1031 exchanges,* for the section of the tax code that allows them) from the sale of rental property.

Under current tax laws, the IRS continues to take a broad definition of what *like kind* property is. They'll allow you, for example, to exchange from undeveloped land into a multi-unit rental building.

Should you form a real estate corporation?

When you invest in and manage real estate with at least one other partner, you can set up a company through which you own the property.

The main reason you may want to consider this action is liability protection. A corporation can reduce the chances of lenders or tenants suing you.

See the discussion in Chapter 20 about incorporating, the different entities under which you may do business, and the pros and cons of each.

The rules for properly doing one of these exchanges are complex. Third parties are usually involved. Make sure that you find an attorney and/or tax advisor who is expert at these transactions to ensure that you do it right.

Tax-Wise Mortgage Decisions

The largest expense of property ownership is almost always the monthly mortgage payment. In the earlier years of a mortgage, the bulk of the mortgage payment covers interest that is generally tax deductible. In this section, we'll discuss some important mortgage decisions and how to factor taxes, and your financial circumstances, into making intelligent decisions.

What type mortgage?

There are, unfortunately, thousands of mortgage options. Fixed-rate and variable-rate mortgages come with all sorts of different bells and whistles. The number of permutations is mind-numbing.

The good news from a tax angle is that the major and most complicated decisions, namely whether to choose a fixed-rate or an adjustable-rate mortgage and then how to get the best deal on the mortgage you've chosen, have little to do with tax issues. This decision is covered thoroughly in *Personal Finance For Dummies*.

From a tax perspective, one of the most important mortgage selection issues is whether to take a 15-year or 30-year mortgage. To afford the monthly payments, most homebuyers need to spread the loan payments over a longer period of time, and a 30-year mortgage is the only option. A 15-year mortgage has higher monthly payments because you pay it off more quickly.

If you can afford these higher payments, it's not necessarily better to take the 15-year option. The money for making extra payments doesn't come out of thin air. You may have better use for your excess funds. What you're really asking is whether you should pay off your mortgage slowly or quickly. And the answer isn't as simple as you think.

First, think about *alternative uses* for the extra money you're throwing into the mortgage payments. What's best for you depends on your overall financial situation and what else you can do with the money. If you would blow the extra money on a new car, for example, you're better off paying down the mortgage.

Suppose that you take the extra $100 or $200 per month that you were planning to add to your mortgage payment and contribute it to a retirement account instead. That step may make financial sense. Why? Because additions to 401(k)s, SEP-IRAs, Keoghs, and other types of retirement accounts are tax deductible (see Chapter 19).

When you dump that $200 into a retirement account, you get to subtract that $200 from the income on which you pay taxes. If you're paying 35 percent in federal and state income taxes, you shave $70 (that's $200 multiplied by 35 percent) off your tax bill. (You're going to pay taxes when you withdraw the money from the retirement account someday. In the meantime, the money that would have gone to taxes is growing on your behalf.) When you add $200 to your mortgage payment to pay off your mortgage faster, you get *no* tax benefits.

With kids, you have an even greater reason to fund your retirement accounts before you consider paying down your mortgage quickly. Under current rules for determining financial aid for college expenses, money in your retirement accounts is not counted as an asset (see Chapter 23, "Taxes and Educational Expenses").

If you're uncomfortable investing and would otherwise leave the extra money sitting in a money market fund or savings account, or worse, if you would spend it, you're better off paying down the mortgage. If the investments in your retirement account plummet in value, the impact of the tax-deferred compounding of your capital may be negated. Paying down the mortgage, on the other hand, is just like investing your money in a sure thing — but with a modest rate of return.

In most cases, you get to deduct your mortgage interest on your tax return. So if you're paying 8.5 percent interest, it really may cost you only around 6 percent after you factor in the tax benefits. If you think you can do better by investing elsewhere, go for it. Investments such as stocks and real estate have generated better returns over the long haul. These investments carry risks, though, and are not guaranteed to produce any return.

If you *don't* have a burning investment option, it's usually wise to pay down your mortgage as your cash flow allows. If you have extra cash and have contributed the maximum allowed for retirement accounts, you may want to invest in real estate or perhaps a business. You have to decide whether it is worth the extra risk to make that particular investment instead of paying less interest on your mortgage.

How large a down payment?

What if you're in the enviable and fortunate position of having so much money that you can afford to put down more than a 20 percent down payment? Perhaps you're one of those wise people who don't want to get stretched too thin financially and you're buying less house than you can afford. How much should you put down?

Some people, particularly those in the real estate business (and even some tax and financial advisors), say that you should take as large a mortgage as you can for the tax deductions — that is, don't make a larger down payment than you have to. This is silly reasoning. Remember, you have to pay out all this money in interest charges to get the tax deductions.

Again, what makes sense for you depends on your alternative uses for the money. If you're considering other investment opportunities, determine whether you can expect to earn a higher rate of return than the interest rate you'll pay on the mortgage.

During this century, stock market and real estate investors have enjoyed average annual returns of around 10 percent per year (just remember the past doesn't guarantee the future). So if you borrow mortgage money at around 8 percent today, you may come out ahead by investing in these areas. Besides possibly generating a higher rate of return, other real estate and stock investing can help you diversify your investments, which is always a good thing. (Don't forget that although your mortgage interest is generally tax deductible, you have to pay income tax on your investment earnings.)

There is, of course, no guarantee that you can earn 10 percent each year. And don't forget that all investments come with risk. The advantage of putting more money down for a home and borrowing less is that a home is essentially a risk-free investment.

If you prefer to put down just 20 percent and invest more elsewhere, that's fine. Just don't keep the extra money (beyond an emergency reserve) under the mattress, in a savings account, or in bonds that pay less interest than the mortgage costs you in interest.

Should I refinance?

When you refinance a mortgage, you have to spend money and time to save money. So you need to crunch a few numbers, and factor taxes in, to determine whether refinancing makes sense for you.

If your loan has a higher rate of interest than loans currently available, you may save money by refinancing. Because refinancing almost always costs money, it's a bit of a gamble whether you can save enough to justify the cost. Ask your mortgage lender or broker how many months it will take you to recoup the costs of refinancing, such as appraisal expenses, loan fees and points, title insurance, and so on.

For example, if the refinance costs you $2,000 to complete and reduces your monthly payment by $100, the lender or broker typically says that it will take 20 months for you to save back the refinance costs. This isn't accurate, however, because you lose some tax write-offs if your mortgage interest rate and payments are reduced. You can't simply look at the reduced amount of your monthly payment (mortgage lenders like to look at it, however, because it makes refinancing more attractive).

If you want a better estimate but don't want to spend hours crunching numbers, take your tax rate as specified in Chapter 1 (for example, 28 percent) and reduce your monthly payment savings on the refinance by this amount. That means, continuing with the example in the preceding paragraph, if your monthly payment drops by $100, you *really* save only around $72 a month after factoring in the lost tax benefits. So it will take 28 months ($2,000 divided by $72) — not 20 months — to recoup the refinance costs.

If you can recover the costs of the refinance within a few years or less, go for it. If it takes longer, it may still make sense if you anticipate keeping the property and mortgage that long. If you estimate it will take more than five to seven years to break even, it is probably too risky to justify the refinance costs and hassles.

When you refinance, don't forget to change the amount of tax you are paying during the year. See the section "Tax savings in home ownership" in this chapter for more information on how to change your tax withholding.

Another reason people refinance is to pull out cash from the house for some other purpose. This strategy can make good financial sense, because under most circumstances, mortgage interest is tax deductible. If you're starting a business or buying other real estate, consider borrowing against your home. You can usually borrow against your home at a lower cost than on a business or rental property loan. (If you are a high-income earner, you may be losing some of the tax deductibility of your home mortgage interest deductions — see Chapter 8.)

If you've run up high-interest consumer debt, you may be able to refinance your mortgage and pull out extra cash to pay off your credit cards, auto loans, or other costly credit lines, thus saving yourself money. You can usually borrow at a lower interest rate for a mortgage and get a tax deduction as a bonus, which lowers the effective borrowing cost further. Consumer debt, such as auto loans and credit cards, is not tax deductible.

Borrowing against the equity in your home can be addictive. An appreciating home creates the illusion that excess spending isn't really costing you. But debt is debt, and you have to repay all borrowed money. In the long run, you wind up with greater mortgage debt, and paying it off takes a bigger bite out of your monthly income. Refinancing and establishing home-equity lines also cost you more in terms of loan application fees and other charges (points, appraisals, credit reports, and so on).

Should I take out a home-equity loan?

This special type of mortgage loan allows you to borrow against your home in addition to the mortgage you already have (a first mortgage). The allure of home equity loans today is simple. Borrowing against real estate is relatively low-cost and (usually) tax deductible to boot. Generally, the interest on a home-equity loan of up to $100,000 is tax-deductible (see Chapter 8).

The problem, however, with home-equity loans is that they allow, and even encourage, people to overspend. It's no wonder that many people have them (and, in some cases, for frivolous reasons), because they can be as easy to use as credit cards — you can access some home equity loans simply by writing a check.

Borrowing more against your home makes financial sense in some cases: for example, when you decide to build an addition to your home instead of selling the home to buy a larger one. But taking out a second mortgage is usually an inferior option. Second mortgages or home equity loans have higher interest rates than comparable first mortgages. They are also riskier from a lender's perspective, because the primary mortgage lender gets first dibs if you file bankruptcy or the property ends up in foreclosure.

A home-equity loan may be beneficial if you need more money for just a few years or if your first mortgage is at such a low interest rate that refinancing to get more cash would be as costly — otherwise, avoid home-equity loans. If you've racked up high-interest credit card or other consumer debt, refinancing your mortgage to pay it off can be a good financial move. Mortgage interest rates are lower and tax deductible.

Chapter 23

Kids and Taxes

. . . .

In This Chapter

▶ Judging the costs and benefits of a second income

▶ Getting a Social Security number and other child tax goodies

▶ Taxes, financial aid, and educational expenses

▶ The kiddie tax system

. . . .

Cloth diapers or disposables? Which is better for your baby's behind? Are you adding to landfills by using disposables? But what about all those harsh chemicals used to clean the cloth diapers? When should you send your youngster to preschool? And which school? Should you move to live in a better school district? And can you afford to move, or will it cause you to work so many hours that you'll never get to see your child? If you stay put, your child may end up in the junior high where last year a kid brought a gun to school and shot another student. And what about toys? You want your baby to be stimulated and have fun, but the toys need to be at least somewhat educational. And then you have to worry about the safety issue. Is your baby going to get hurt when some part comes loose?

Ahhhhhhhhhhhhhhhhhhhhhhhhhhhhhhhhhhhhhhhhhhhhhhhhhhhhhhhhhhhhhhhhhhhhhhhhhhhhhhhhh!

If you're raising children in the world today, you deserve an A+ for effort.

Bringing Up Baby

Deciding whether or not to have children and if so, how many, is probably one of life's more complex decisions. Money is certainly a factor in the kid equation. Although kids can cost a lot of money, the expenses, or thousands of diaper changes during the infant years, rarely deter people from wanting a family. And for good reason — kids are wonderful, at least most of the time.

Raising a family can be the financial equivalent of doing a triathalon and can stretch and break the budgets of even those who consider themselves financially well off and on top of things. Taxes are an important factor in quite a number of kid-related issues. Here's our take on some important tax issues that you might confront before conception and in the early years of bringing up baby.

Costs and benefits of the second income

In addition to less sleep at night and frequent diaper changing, children mean increased spending. At a minimum, expenditures for food and clothing will increase. Although you may have less time to shop for yourself, causing your personal spending to decrease, you're likely to spend more on housing, insurance, day care, and education. And don't forget the host of not-so-incidental incidentals. Toys, art classes, sports, field trips, and the like can rack up big bills, especially if you don't control them.

One of the most challenging decisions that new parents face is whether to work full time, part time, or not at all. We mean work at a paying job, that is — parenting is the lowest paid but potentially most rewarding job there is. The need or desire to work full time is obvious — doing so brings more money home. You may feel that working full time prohibits you from playing an active role in raising your children, so as you consider the additional expenses of raising children, you may also need to factor in a decrease in income.

Financially speaking, taxes can have a big impact on the value or benefit of working full time, especially for two-income couples. Remember that the tax brackets are set up so that the last dollars of earnings are taxed at a higher rate (see Chapter 1). So if you simply look at the salary that your employer quotes you as the value of that second income (for example, $30,000), you're making a potentially big financial mistake.

Take the case of Ron and Mary, a nice couple who struggled with how to handle their work schedules after the birth of their first child. They both worked full time. Mary, a marketing manager, earned $55,000 per year, and Ron, a school teacher, made $32,000 per year. Ron was considering working part time or not at all so that he could be at home with their daughter. Because of Ron and Mary's prior financial commitments, such as their home, they felt that they couldn't afford for Ron to work less than full time.

Ron and Mary took a closer look at their finances and taxes and started to see things a little differently. Taxes took a whopping 40 percent of Ron's income, so his take-home pay was just $19,200 per year, or $1,600 per month. Then they added up all the additional costs of both working full-time: day care, a second car, more meals eaten out, and so on. When they totaled up all these extra costs, which could be eliminated if Ron didn't work at all or worked on a greatly reduced basis, they figured that Ron was effectively contributing about $300 per month from his full-time job — or about $1.80 per hour!

Ultimately, because of his low after-tax effective hourly income, Ron decided to quit his job and work part time at home. This gave the family the best of both worlds — a more involved dad and husband and some income that didn't include the extra costs that come with a second job. And because he was able to work part time, Ron and his wife were able to earn some tax credits (discussed later in this chapter) for the part-time day care their daughter needed.

Of course, people enjoy other benefits of working besides income. But you should examine taxes and other expenses on that second income to ensure that you're making your financial decision to work based on complete and accurate information.

Rites of tax passage — getting Junior a Social Security number

When a child is born, he or she may be a bundle of joy to you, but to the federal government and the IRS, Junior is just a number — more specifically, a Social Security number. The IRS allows you to claim your children as dependents on your tax return. For tax year 1994, each child was "worth" a $2,450 deduction as your dependent. So if you're in the 28 percent federal tax bracket, each child saves you about $686 in federal taxes.

In order to claim your child as a dependent on your tax return, he or she must have a Social Security number (unless the child is not yet one year old by the end of the tax year in which you're claiming the tyke as a dependent). The IRS requires a Social Security number because people were inventing children — you know, telling the IRS they'd just had twins when the closest they actually came to becoming parents was babysitting their best friend's kid one evening! You also need a Social Security number for your child if you want to establish investment accounts in your child's name (although you might not want to after you understand the drawbacks to doing so, which are discussed later in this chapter).

Using the copious amount of free time you'll have during your child's first year to obtain a Social Security number, contact the Social Security Administration (800-772-1213) and ask for Form SS-5 (Application for a Social Security Card).

Child care tax goodies

In addition to the extra personal deduction that you can take with each new child and the tax savings that come with that deduction, you should also be aware of the tax perks for child care and related expenditures that may save you thousands of dollars.

Dependent care tax credit

If you need to hire child care assistance for your youngster(s), you may be able to claim a tax credit on your annual return (Form 2441). In order to be eligible for this credit, you (and your spouse, if you're married) must work at least part-time, unless you're a full-time student or you're disabled. Your kid(s) must be under the age of 13 or physically or mentally disabled.

This credit is better than a tax deduction, because a credit is a dollar-for-dollar reduction in your taxes owed — it may save you hundreds of tax dollars each year. And you not only count child care expenses toward calculation of the tax credit, but you also may be able to count the cost of a housekeeper or even a cook if the expense benefits your kids.

As discused in the last section, tax and other considerations will influence your desire as a parent to work. Working at least part time makes you eligible for this tax credit. If you elect to be a full-time mom or dad, you're not eligible for the dependent care tax credit.

If your employer offers a dependent care assistance plan (discussed in the next section), you may be able to reduce your taxes by taking advantage of that benefit rather than this tax credit. Your tax credit will be reduced or eliminated if you use your employer's dependent care plan spending account. To learn more about how to claim this credit on your annual tax return, see Chapter 13.

Dependent care spending accounts

Increasing numbers of employers offer flexible benefit or spending plans. These plans allow you to choose among a number of different benefits, such as health, life, and disability insurance; vacation days; and dependent care expenses.

These plans allow you to put away money from your paycheck on a pre-tax basis, which you can then use to pay for child care expenses. Doing so saves you federal, state, and even Social Security taxes. Plans allow you to put away up to $5,000 per year ($2,500 for those of you who are married filing separately). The exact amount that you can put away depends on the specifics of your employer's plan.

Dependent care spending accounts are a "use it or lose it" benefit. If you aren't able to spend the money for child care expenses in the current tax year, at the end of the year the IRS forces you to forfeit all the money not used. So be careful not to go overboard and contribute more than you are certain to use.

As mentioned in the preceding section, your participation in your employer's dependent care assistance plan reduces your tax credit. You can't do both. If you're in the federal 28 percent tax and higher, you should be able to save more in taxes by using your employer's plan rather than by taking the credit on your tax return. The only way to know for sure is to run the numbers.

The nanny tax

Someday you may want to run for or be nominated for an important public office. If you hire a nanny to take care of your child, you're best off to legally withhold and file the taxes necessary for employing help. Zoë Baird, President Clinton's nominee for Attorney General, and Michael Huffington, failed Senate candidate in California, didn't withhold and file these taxes, and the press found out. Baird was nixed and Huffington's blunder helped sink his political ship.

Even if you're not planning on running for political office someday, you need to know that you are legally required to withhold Social Security and other taxes if you have household employees who are U.S. citizens earning $1,000 or more in a tax year. You can now do this through the filing of your annual tax return.

In addition to complying with the law on employee withholdings, you also benefit because you may be allowed to take advantage of the tax breaks discussed in this section when the employee helps with child care. The employee benefits, of course, by building up Social Security credits — and these credits qualify an employee for monthly retirement income payments.

In addition to paying the taxes for household help on your annual tax return, you also need to pay unemployment tax for any household employee to whom you paid $1,000 or more per calendar quarter. Request Form 940 (*Employer's Annual Federal Unemployment Tax Return*) from the IRS to do so. Some states have similar requirements, so contact your state's employment tax office for information. Beginning in 1995, this tax can be paid on Form 1040.

The dependent care tax credit and spending accounts that are discussed in this section can also be used to pay for the costs of taking care of other dependents, such as an ill or elderly parent. See Chapter 13 and your employer's employee benefits manual for more information.

Teaching kids about taxes and money

Show your kids your paystub! Although you probably haven't shown what you earn to your parents, best friends, and perhaps even your spouse, sharing with your children what you earn and what you pay in taxes can be highly educational. It gets kids thinking about the realities of living within an income.

Your paystub helps kids see not only what you earn each month, but also how much goes out for things like taxes. You can then have discussions about the costs of rent and mortgages, utilities, food, and everything else. Your children may better understand your financial constraints, and they'll be on the road to financial literacy, prepared for the day when they'll be responsible for earning money and paying taxes and monthly bills themselves. You're not doing them (or yourself) any favors by keeping them in the dark.

In the absence of information, children have no conception of what their parents earn. Some have outrageously inflated ideas of how much their parents make — this is often true for children whose parents eagerly fulfill their requests for purchases.

Taxes and Educational Expenses

What do taxes have to do with educational expenses? A surprising amount. As you'll soon learn, how you invest money that will pay for educational expenses can have an enormous impact on your family's taxes, ability to qualify for financial aid, and overall financial well-being.

The (hidden) financial aid tax system

The financial aid system (which parents apply through so that their children are eligible for scholarships, grants, and loans) treats assets differently when held outside of rather than inside of retirement accounts. Under the current financial aid system, the value of your retirement plans is *not* considered an asset. Thus, the more money you stash in retirement accounts, the greater your chances of qualifying for financial aid and the more money you'll qualify for.

Most new parents do not place their savings into retirement accounts. Many nonwealthy parents make the mistake of saving and investing money in a separate account for their child (perhaps even in the child's name) or through some other financial product, such as a life insurance policy. Why is this a mistake? Because you'll end up being taxed at a much higher level than if you had employed other savings strategies.

Most important, you should be saving and investing through retirement accounts that give you significant tax benefits. Your initial contributions to a 401(k), SEP-IRA, Keogh, or other retirement accounts (described in Chapter 19) are usually tax-deductible. An additional and substantial benefit is that once your money is placed in these accounts, it grows and compounds without taxation until you withdraw it.

As a parent you incur an additional "tax" when you save money *outside* of retirement accounts. Money that you save *outside* of retirement accounts, including money in the child's name, is counted as an asset and reduces your eligibility for financial aid.

Therefore, it does not make sense to forgo contributions to your retirement savings plans in order to save money in a taxable account for Junior's college fund. When you do, you pay higher taxes both on your current income and on the interest and growth of this money. In addition to paying higher taxes, you are expected to contribute more to your child's educational expenses; therefore, you'll qualify for less financial aid.

Even worse is if you save money in your child's name. If you plan to apply for financial aid, it's a good idea to save money in your name rather than in your child's name (in a *custodial account*). Colleges expect a much greater percentage of money in your child's name (35 percent) to be used for college costs than money in your name (6 percent). This is the hidden financial aid tax. (Don't assume you can't qualify for aid — a fair amount of it, both loans and grants, is available without regard to financial need).

Note: As we discuss later in the chapter, if you're affluent enough that you expect to pay for your kid's entire educational costs, investing through custodial accounts can save on taxes. Prior to your child reaching age 14, the first $1,200 of interest and dividend income is taxed at your child's income tax rate rather than yours. After age 14, *all* income generated by investments in your child's name is taxed at your child's rate.

When a millionaire's kid gets more financial aid than a middle-class family's

What's truly amazing and sad about the way the current financial aid system works is that some affluent people who don't really need aid can get more than those who are not nearly as well off financially. Here's a real case that, although somewhat extreme, is not that unusual, and it highlights the shortcomings of the current procedures used to determine financial need.

Kent, a doctor who earned $200,000 per year, and his wife Marion, a housewife, had a son who applied for and received financial aid. By the time that Kent and Marion's son was ready to apply to college, Kent had quit working as a physician and was earning little money while doing some part-time teaching. However, he had more than $1,200,000 in his retirement savings plan, which he had accumulated over his years of work. Being savvy financial managers, Kent and Marion had little money invested and available outside of tax-sheltered retirement accounts. Because the financial aid system ignores retirement accounts in their analysis and because Kent's income was modest at the time their son applied for aid, the family got significant aid.

On the other hand, Rick and Liz, full-time employees with a combined income of $50,000, and their daughter received no financial aid. Why? Because Rick and Liz had been saving money in their daughter's name. By the time she was ready to apply for college, she had about $25,000 saved. Rick and Liz had also accumulated some other modest investments outside of retirement accounts but only had about $30,000 put away in retirement accounts. Because of the assets available outside of retirement accounts and their current income, they were deemed not needy enough for aid.

Minimizing your taxes and paying for college

Socking money away into your tax-sheltered retirement accounts helps you reduce your tax burden and may help your children to qualify for more financial aid. However, accessing retirement accounts before age $59\frac{1}{2}$ incurs tax penalties.

So how do you pay for your children's educational costs? There isn't one correct answer, because it depends on your overall financial situation. Here are some ideas to consider that will help meet expected educational expenses as well as minimize your taxes.

- *Don't try to do it all yourself.* Unless you're affluent, don't even try to pay for the full cost of a college education for your children. You can't afford it. You and your child will, in all likelihood, have to borrow some money.

- *Apply for aid, regardless of your financial circumstances.* A number of loan programs, such as Unsubsidized Stafford Loans and Parent Loans for Undergraduate Students (PLUS), are available even when your family is not deemed financially needy. Only Subsidized Stafford Loans, on which the federal government pays the interest that accumulates while the student is still in school, are limited to those students deemed financially needy.

  In addition to loans, a number of grant programs are available through schools and the government, as well as through independent sources. Specific colleges and other private organizations (including employers, banks, credit unions, and community groups) also offer grants and scholarships. Some of these have nothing to do with financial need.

- *Save in your name.* If you've exhausted your retirement account contributions, it's fine to save money that you're earmarking to pay for college. Just do it in your name.

- *Get your kids to work.* Your child can work and save money to pay for college costs during junior high, high school, and college. In fact, if your child qualifies for financial aid, he or she is expected to contribute a certain amount to education costs from employment held during the school year or summer breaks and from savings. Besides giving Junior a stake in his or her own future, this training encourages sound personal financial management down the road.

- *Borrow against your home equity.* If you're a homeowner, you can borrow against the equity (market value less the outstanding mortgage loan) in your property. Doing so is usually best because you can borrow against your home at a relatively low interest rate, and the interest is tax-deductible.

- *Borrow against your company retirement plans.* Many larger firms' retirement savings plans, such as 401(k)s, allow borrowing. Just make sure that you are able to pay the money back. Otherwise, you'll owe big taxes for a premature distribution.

If your parents want to gift money to your children for college expenses, it's generally better if the money is kept in your name, or have the grandparents keep the money until the kids are ready to enter college and are in need of the money.

Don't let them scare you into paying more taxes

More than a few investment firms and financial planners argue that in the long run, it's far cheaper for you to save for your children's college expenses rather than borrow for them. This claim is not true. If you are able to save in retirement accounts and you can find other ways to pay for college costs (such as those discussed in the preceding section), you can come out far ahead, thanks to the tax benefits that retirement accounts provide and the increased financial aid that your children may receive by not accumulating so much outside retirement accounts.

The conflict of interest of these organizations and planners is that they can't sell you investments if you channel your savings into your employer's retirement plan. They have every reason to scare you into their hands and into paying more taxes.

Taxes on Your Kiddies' Investments

As mentioned earlier, parents of all different financial means must be aware of the financial aid implications of putting money into a child's name. If you haven't read the section "Taxes and Educational Expenses" earlier in this chapter, please read it before you jump into investing money in your children's names.

Parents used to have a significant tax incentive to transfer money into their children's names, because the earnings on those investments would be taxed at the child's tax rate. In 1986, the tax rules changed, however, and this benefit was greatly reduced. Also as a result of these tax law changes, increasing numbers of children need to file tax returns. (Actually, parents normally do the filing.)

Kiddie taxes for children under age 14

Prior to reaching the magical age of 14, kids have a special tax system that applies to them. Specifically, the first $600 of *unearned income* (income from interest and dividends on investments) that a child earns is not taxed at all.

It's tax-free! In contrast, *earned income* is considered income earned from work. For example, the money that Macaulay Culkin of *Home Alone* fame gets from his movies is earned income. (See Chapter 13 to learn about when you need to file a tax return for your child.)

The next $600 of unearned income for this age set is taxed at the federal level at 15 percent. Everything over $1200 is taxed at the parent's income tax rate. The system is set up in this fashion to discourage parents from transferring a lot of assets into their children's names, hoping to pay lower taxes.

Because the first $1200 of unearned income for the child is taxed at such a low rate, many parents are tempted to transfer some money into the child's name to save some income taxes. Quite a number of financial books and advisors recommend this strategy. Consider this passage referring to transferring money to your children, from a tax book written by a large accounting firm, "Take advantage of these rules. It still makes sense to shift some income-producing assets to younger children."

Wrong! As discussed in "The hidden financial aid tax system," earlier in this chapter, your short-sighted desire to save a little in taxes today can lead to your losing out on some financial aid. And what about your limited discretionary income? You don't want to put money in your child's name if it means you're not fully taking advantage of your retirement accounts.

The only parents who should seriously consider putting money into their children's names are parents who meet both of the following criteria:

✔ You expect to pay for the full cost of a college education yourselves and not apply for or use any financial aid, including loans that are not based on financial need.

✔ You are comfortable with the notion that your children will have legal access to the money at age 18 or 21 if the money is in a custodial account in the child's name. At that age, the money is legally theirs and they can blow it on something other than a college education.

If after all the caveats and warnings, you're still thinking about putting money into an account bearing your child's name, consider buying tax-friendly investments that will not generate many taxes, if any, until after the child turns 14. (See Chapter 21 for tax-friendly investment ideas.) As you learn in the next section, after your kids turn 14, all income they earn is taxed at their rate, not yours. You can also buy investments in your name and then transfer them to your child's name once Junior turns 14. (Each parent is limited to gifting $10,000 to each child per year.) That way, if the investment declines in value, you can take the tax loss; if it has turned a profit, you should save on your taxes by transferring the investment to your child and having them pay tax on it after turning 14. This won't work if your child is like Macaulay Culkin and in a higher tax bracket than you are!

Children 14 and older: adults to the IRS

Although your gangly teenager may still be wearing braces, using Clearasil, and spending two hours a day on the phone, to the IRS he or she is a warm-blooded, tax-paying adult, just like you, as soon as he or she turns age 14. Because most 14-year-olds don't earn a lot of income, taxes on their investments don't need to be a concern. However, the same negative financial aid considerations discussed earlier apply to money held in their name versus yours.

Tax-wise investments for educational funds

Mutual funds, which offer investors of all financial means instant diversification and low-cost access to the nation's best money managers, are an ideal investment when saving money for educational expenses. See Chapter 21 for a discussion of the tax-wise ways to invest in funds.

Treasury bonds issued by the federal government are often recommended by many tax and financial books as a college investment. We're not enthusiastic about some of these (see the following sidebar). Zero-coupon treasuries are a particular tax headache. Zero-coupon treasuries are sold at a discount to their value at maturity instead of paying you interest each year. Guess what? You still have to report the effective interest you're earning each year on your tax return. And just to give you a headache or pad your tax preparer's bill, this implicit interest needs to be calculated. Yuck!

Life insurance policies that have cash values are some of the most oversold investments to fund college costs. The usual pitch is this: Because you need life insurance to protect your family, why not buy a policy that you can borrow against to pay for college? Makes sense, doesn't it? Insurance agents will also emphasize that the cash value in the policy is growing without taxation over time. Although this part of their sales pitch is true, you have better alternatives.

The reason you shouldn't buy a cash value life insurance policy is that, as discussed earlier in this chapter, you're better off contributing to retirement accounts. These investments give you an immediate tax deduction that you don't receive when saving through life insurance. Because life insurance that comes with a cash value is more expensive, parents are more likely to make a second mistake — not buying enough coverage. If you need and want life insurance, you're better off buying lower-cost term life insurance.

An investment that fails to keep you ahead of inflation, such as savings or money market accounts, is another poor investment for college expenses. You need your money to grow to afford educational costs down the road. The interest on these accounts is also taxable, which doesn't make sense for many working parents.

Double-what bonds?

Among the many forms of bonds (debt) that our fine government issues are *EE* (double "E") bonds. These are one of the many classes of Treasury bonds issued by that national organization with a penchant for borrowing money. You may hear about these as a suggested investment for children's college expenses.

EE bonds purchased after 1989 have a unique tax twist if you use the proceeds when liquidated to pay for educational tuition and fees. (Room and board and other education-related costs are not covered.) The interest earned on the bonds is exempted from federal taxation (interest on all Treasury bonds is already state tax-free) as long as two other requirements are met: the purchaser of the bond must be at least 24 years of age; at the time the bonds are sold to pay for educational tuition and fees, the holder of the bond may not have adjusted gross income in excess of $41,200 if single or $61,850 if married and filing a joint return.

Just to make matters more complicated, if you are somehow able to know years in advance what your income will be when your toddler has grown into a college-bound 18-year-old, you gotta file yet another tax form, Form 8815, to claim the exclusion of the interest on EEs from federal taxation. And don't forget that not a year goes by without Congress messing with the Federal tax laws. So the income requirements for the tax exemption can be changed.

You should also know that EE bonds generally pay a lower rate of interest than other, simpler Treasury bonds. The yield or interest rate on EE bonds is also a chore to understand. You must hold these bonds for at least five years in order to receive a return of 85 percent of the average yield payable on five-year Treasury notes during the period held, or 4 percent, whichever is higher.

Regardless of how the EE bond proceeds are used, taxation of the interest on them is deferred until cashed. Although in most cases this is beneficial, don't forget that children under age 14 can earn $600 of interest tax-free every year. So if you buy the bond and register it in your child's name, he or she may end up actually paying more in taxes when the bonds are cashed in, because all the interest income will be recognized at once. Buying the bond in your child's name, however, may hurt his or her chances of obtaining financial aid.

Our advice: don't waste your time on these needlessly complicated bonds. They are testimony to the absurdly complicated tax code and government rules. You're better off investing in mutual funds that offer some growth potential. But if we haven't dissuaded you, make sure that you buy these bonds from the Federal Reserve in your area and hold them in an account with the Federal Reserve so that you'll always get a statement on your account and won't lose track of them when you're no longer being paid interest!

Chapter 24

Estate Planning

● ●

In This Chapter

▶ Paying taxes on your death — should you care or worry?

▶ Reducing expected estate taxes

▶ Trusts, wills, and more trusts

▶ Finding help if you need it

● ●

*A*mong the dreariest and least interesting financial topics is the issue of what happens to your money when you die. Depending on how you have your finances structured, you (actually, your estate) may get stuck paying *estate taxes* when you die. Unfortunately, the time when the grim reaper pays a visit cannot be predicted. This scenario doesn't mean that we all need to participate in complicated estate planning. To the contrary — if your assets are not substantial, a few simple moves may be all you need to get your affairs in order.

Estate planning takes time and money, which are precious commodities for most of us. Whether it's worthwhile to spend your time and money on estate planning depends on your personal and financial circumstances, both now and in the near future.

When planning for the time they kick the bucket, people can make more than a few errors. Some errors can be easily avoided and are not too costly. Others can cost you and your family a small fortune. Ironically, some of these mistakes result from your best intentions when you consult with "experts" who render inappropriate or self-serving advice.

We know that your days are just packed with excitement, and you bound out of bed most mornings, racing off to a job that you love. Who can blame you for not wanting to plan for the day when you won't see the sun rise? Unlike filing your tax return annually, arranging your financial affairs for your death is easy to put off. You're not breaking any laws if you don't arrange your financial affairs, as you are when you fail to file your tax return and pay your taxes.

Unless you're leaving a lot of money behind when you die, planning your estate won't save your heirs much in the way of money. In some cases, your good intentions to prepare documents and trusts now can actually be a waste of your money.

For most people who don't plan on leaving a fortune to their heirs, the major benefit to arranging things now is that it helps ensure that the heirs are not left with an administrative mess or difficult decisions you should have made. So even if you're not a Rockefeller or Getty, estate planning simplifies things for your survivors and shows that you took the time to arrange everything because you care about them.

Will I Owe Estate Taxes?

One may think that, with all the attorneys, estate planning specialists, and insurance agents warning us about the enormous estate taxes that will be owed upon our deaths, owing estate taxes is a common problem. It's not. But insurance agents, attorneys, and some investment firms use this scare tactic to attract prospective clients, often by luring them to free estate planning seminars.

Under current tax laws, an individual can pass $600,000 and a couple, *if* they have their assets properly structured (as discussed later in this chapter), can pass $1,200,000 to beneficiaries without federal estate taxes. Because most people are still trying to accumulate enough money so that they can someday retire or take a trip around the world, it's hardly a normal problem for folks to have this much when they die.

Whether your assets will face estate taxes depends on the amount of your assets that you use up during your retirement, unless you already possess great wealth. How much of your assets are used up depends on how your assets grow over time, as well as how rapidly you spend money.

Reprinted with permission

To calculate the value of your estate upon your death, the IRS totals up your assets and subtracts your liabilities. Assets include your personal property, home and other real estate, savings and investments (such as bank accounts, stocks, bonds, and mutual funds held both inside as well as outside of retirement accounts), and life insurance death benefits (unless properly placed in a trust as described later in this chapter). Your liabilities include any outstanding loans (such as a real estate mortgage), bills owed at the time of your death, legal and other expenses to handle your estate, and funeral expenses.

If you are married at the time of your death, all assets that you leave to your spouse are excluded from estate taxes, thanks to the *unlimited marital deduction* (discussed later in this chapter). Also, any charitable contributions or bequests made via your will are deducted from your assets before calculating your *taxable estate*.

How much are estate taxes?

Thanks to inflation, more people in the years ahead will be affected by the $600,000 threshold limits. At your death, if your estate totals more than $600,000, you will owe federal estate taxes. The tax rates are fairly hefty (see Table 24-1).

Table 24-1	Federal Estate Taxes
Value of Estate	**Tax Rate**
$ 600,000 to $ 750,000	37%
$ 750,001 to $ 1,000,000	39%
$ 1,000,001 to $ 1,250,000	41%
$ 1,250,001 to $ 1,500,000	43%
$ 1,500,001 to $ 2,000,000	45%
$ 2,000,001 to $ 2,500,000	49%
$ 2,500,001 to $ 3,000,000	53%
$ 3,000,001 to $10,000,000	55%
$10,000,001 to $21,040,000	60%
Over $21,040,000	55%

States can also levy additional estate and inheritance taxes. Most states don't — they simply share in the federal taxes that the IRS collects from each estate. So if your residence at the time of your death is any of the following states, you only need concern yourself with federal estate taxes: Alabama, Alaska, Arizona, Arkansas, California, Colorado, Florida, Georgia, Hawaii, Idaho, Illinois, Maine,

Minnesota, Nevada, New Mexico, North Dakota, Oregon, Rhode Island, South Carolina, Texas, Utah, Vermont, Virginia, Washington, West Virginia, Wisconsin, and Wyoming — along with the District of Columbia.

Some states have elected to assess their own estate taxes and, therefore, do not share in the federal estate taxes collected. These states include Massachusetts, Mississippi, New York, Ohio, and Oklahoma. Rhode Island and South Carolina do both. Not surprisingly, these states opt out of the federal tax sharing so that they can assess and collect an even higher rate of estate tax than they would receive from the federal government. Thus, if you live in one of these states, your estate taxes will be higher due to the additional state levy.

The following states also impose an inheritance tax: Connecticut, Delaware, Indiana, Iowa, Kansas, Kentucky, Louisiana, Maryland, Michigan, Montana, Nebraska, New Hampshire, New Jersey, North Carolina, Pennsylvania, South Dakota, and Tennessee

Reducing Expected Estate Taxes if You're Rich

You've got your work cut out for you as you search around and try to educate yourself about estate planning. You'll find many attorneys and nonattorneys selling estate planning services, and you'll encounter lots of insurance agents hawking life insurance. All will be more than happy to sell you their services and products. Most people don't need to do fancy-schmancy estate planning with high-cost attorneys. We'll give you the straight scoop on what, if anything, you should be concerned with now and at other junctures in your life, and we'll tell you the conflicts of interest that these "experts" have in rendering advice.

Thanks to all the changes in the tax laws and the thousands of attorneys and tax advisors working to find new ways around paying estate taxes, a dizzying array of strategies exist to reduce estate taxes (including taking up residence in a foreign country!) We start with the simpler stuff and work toward the more complex.

Gifting

There's nothing wrong with making, saving, and investing money. But someday, you have to honestly look at yourself in the mirror and ask, "For what purpose?" It's easy to rationalize hoarding money — you never know how long you'll live or what medical expenses you may have. Besides, your kids are still paying off their VISA cards and don't seem to know a mutual fund from an emergency fund.

Current tax law allows you to gift up to $10,000 each year to as many people and organizations — such as your children, grandchildren, best friends, or favorite charities — as you desire (no tax forms required!). If you're married, your spouse can do the same. The benefit of gifting is that it removes the money from your estate and therefore reduces your estate taxes. Even better is the fact that all future appreciation and income on the gifted money also is removed from your estate, because the money belongs to your gift recipient.

Upon your death, your money has to go somewhere. By directing some of your money to people and organizations now, you'll be able to pass on far more later, because you'll be saving anywhere from 37 to 60 percent in estate taxes. Plus, while you're still alive, you'll experience psychological and emotional satisfaction seeing the good that your money can do.

Gifting can be used to remove a substantial portion of your assets from your estate over time. Suppose you have three children. You and your spouse could both give each of your children $10,000 per year for a total gift of $60,000 per year. If your kids are married, you could make an additional $10,000 gift to their spouses for another $60,000 per year. You can also gift an unlimited amount to pay for current educational tuition costs and medical expenses. Just be sure to make the payment directly to the organization charging the fees.

If you're thinking of gifting, learn enough *now* to make up your mind and then do it. Some in Congress view this as a loophole in the estate tax laws that should be closed in order to increase tax revenue.

As you gift money, most people have options in terms of what money or assets ar gifted. Start with cash or assets that haven't appreciated since you purchased them. If you want to transfer an asset that has lost value, consider selling it — claim the tax loss and transfer cash.

Be careful to avoid gifting assets that have appreciated greatly in value. Why? Because if you hold appreciated assets until your death, your heirs will receive what is called a *stepped-up basis*. The IRS assumes that the price that your heirs paid for an asset is the value on your date of death — this wipes out the capital gains tax that would otherwise be owed when selling an asset that has appreciated in value.

A more complicated way to gift money to your heirs and still retain some control over the money is to set up a *Crummey Trust*. Although the beneficiary has a short window of time (a month or two) to withdraw money that's contributed to the trust, you can make it clear verbally to the beneficiary that future gifts are dependent on their leaving the money in the trust. You can also specify, in the trust document itself, that the trust money be used for particular purposes, such as tuition. Some of the other trusts discussed later in this chapter may meet your needs if you want to have more control over the money you intend to pass to your heirs.

A trick to pay some gift taxes now to avoid estate taxes later

You can gift $10,000 tax-free per year to as many people or organizations as you like. However, you can gift more than $10,000 in a year to your heirs if you like.

If you have substantial assets now (several million dollars, for example), and you're worried that your advancing age may prohibit you from moving the money out of your estate quickly enough to get down to the $600,000 limit, you may be able to pass on more money to your heirs by transferring a larger lump of money now. This strategy is particularly useful if you wish to focus your gifting to one or two people.

Suppose you want to gift $500,000 to your son (why can't you be *our* parents?) and you do it this year. You'll owe $155,800 to the IRS in gift tax. So

you write the IRS a check for $155,800. By doing this, you've accomplished two positives for maximizing how much you pass to your son and other heirs. First, you've transferred $500,000 to your son and eliminated accumulating more growth on that money in your estate. Secondly, because you've paid the gift tax out of your estate, you've reduced your taxable estate by that amount. This maneuver saves your estate the tax on the $155,800.

Note: You could opt instead to not pay gift tax and now and take the $500,000 gift against your $600,000 limit. You may pass the estate tax free to your heirs. But, if you expect to pass more than $600,000 at your death to your heirs, paying the gift tax now may help.

Leave it all to your spouse

Tax laws wouldn't be tax laws without exceptions and loopholes. If you are married at the time of your death, any and all assets that you leave to your spouse are exempt from estate taxes normally due upon your death. In fact, you may leave an unlimited amount of money — millions and millions of dollars if you've got it — to your spouse. Hence the name *unlimited marital deduction.* Assets that count are those willed to your spouse or for which he or she is named as the beneficiary (such as on retirement accounts).

Although this is a tempting estate planning strategy for married couples, it can backfire. First, the surviving spouse may end with an estate tax problem upon his or her death because he or she will have all the couples' assets. (See the next section for a way around this issue.) Two other less likely but potential problems: You and your spouse could die simultaneously. And this exemption is not allowed if your spouse is not a U.S. citizen. You should also be aware that some states don't allow unlimited marital deduction, so be sure to find out about your state.

Establish a bypass trust

As we discussed in the last section, a potential estate tax problem is created upon the death of the first spouse if all his or her assets pass to the surviving spouse. When the second spouse passes away, just $600,000 can be passed on free of federal estate taxes.

If you have substantial assets, you and your spouse can each take advantage of the $600,000 estate tax-free rule and pass to your heirs $1,200,000 estate tax-free. By shielding an additional $600,000 from estate taxes, you save a whopping $235,000 in estate taxes, so your heirs receive $235,000 more. How? Each of you can arrange through your will a *bypass* (also known as *credit shelter* or *exemption equivalent*) trust.

Upon the death of the first spouse, assets held in that spouse's name go into a trust. The income from those assets and even some of the principal can still be used by the surviving spouse and/or other heirs. They can receive 5 percent of the value of the trust or $5,000, whichever is greater, each year. They can also draw additional principal if it's needed for educational, health, or living expenses. Ultimately, the assets in the bypass trust pass to the designated beneficiaries (usually, but not limited to, children).

In order for a bypass trust to work, you will likely need to rework how you hold ownership to your assets (for example, jointly or individually). You may need to individually title your assets so that each spouse has $600,000 in assets in order to take full advantage of the $600,000 estate tax-free limit. See "Where to get advice and help" later in this chapter for more information.

Cash value life insurance

Two major types of life insurance exist. Most people who need life insurance — and who have someone dependent on their income — should buy *term* life insurance, which is pure life insurance: You pay an annual premium for which you receive a predetermined amount of life insurance protection. If the insured person passes away, the beneficiaries collect; otherwise, the premium is gone. In this way, term life insurance is similar to auto or homeowner's insurance.

The other kind of life insurance, called *cash value* life insurance, is probably one of the most oversold financial products in the history of Western civilization. Cash value policies (whole, universal, variable, and so on) combine life insurance with a supposed savings feature. Your premiums not only pay for life insurance, but some of your dollars are also credited to an account that grows in value over time, assuming that you keep paying your premiums. On the surface, this sounds potentially attractive.

It's true that life insurance, when bought and placed in an irrevocable life insurance trust (discussed later in this chapter), receives special treatment with regards to estate taxes. Specifically, the death benefit or proceeds paid on the policy upon your death can pass to your designated heirs free of estate taxes. (Some states don't allow this).

People who sell cash value insurance — that is, insurance salespeople and others masquerading as "estate planning specialists" and "financial planners" — too often advocate life insurance as the best, and only way to reduce estate taxes. But the other methods discussed in this chapter are superior in most cases because they don't require spending money on life insurance.

Insurance companies aren't stupid. In fact, they're quite smart. If you purchase a cash value life insurance policy that will provide a death benefit of $1,000,000, for example, you have to pay substantial insurance premiums, although far less than $1,000,000. Isn't that a good deal for you? No, because the insurance company invests your premium dollars and earns a return just as you would have, had you not bought the life insurance and invested the money instead.

Using this estate planning strategy is beneficial when your estate has assets that you don't want to be subjected to a forced sale to pay estate taxes after you die. For example, small-business owners whose businesses are worth $1 million or more may want to consider cash value life insurance under specialized circumstances. If your estate will lack the other necessary assets to pay expected estate taxes and you don't want your beneficiaries to be forced to sell the business, you can buy cash value life insurance to pay expected estate taxes.

If you want to get advice on whether cash value life insurance is appropriate for you, don't expect to get objective information from anyone who sells cash value life insurance.

Among the best places to shop for cash value life insurance policies are the following:

- ✔ **USAA** (800-531-8000)
- ✔ **Ameritas** (800-552-3553)
- ✔ **Wholesale Insurance Network** (800-808-5810)

Trusts, trusts, and more trusts

If estate planning hasn't already given you a headache, understanding the different types of trusts will. A *trust* is a legal device used to pass to someone else management responsibility and, ultimately, ownership of some of your assets. We've already discussed some trusts in this chapter, such as bypass, Crummey, and life insurance trusts.

Here are some other trusts you may hear about when doing estate planning.

Living trusts

Because of our quirky legal system, even if you have a will, some or all of your assets must go through a court process known as *probate*. Probate is the legal process for administering and implementing the directions in a will. Living trusts keep your assets out of probate but do nothing to help you deal with estate taxes.

BEWARE

Don't get seduced into buying cash value life insurance for the wrong reasons

Cash value policies are aggressively pushed by insurance salespeople because of the high commissions (50 to 100 percent of the first year's premium paid by you) that insurance companies pay the agents.

These policies are expensive ways to purchase life insurance. Because of the high cost of these policies (about eight times the cost of the same amount of term life insurance), you are more likely to buy less life insurance coverage than you need — that's the sad result of the insurance industry pushing this stuff. The vast majority of life insurance buyers need more protection than they can afford to buy with cash value coverage.

Agents know which buttons to push to get you interested in buying the wrong kind of life insurance. Agents will show you all sorts of projections that imply that after the first 10 or 20 years of paying your premiums, you'll have such a large cash value in your policy that you won't need to pay more premiums to keep the life insurance in force. The only reason that you may be able to stop paying premiums is that you've poured too much extra money into the policy in the early years of payment. Remember that cash value life insurance costs eight times as much as term.

Agents will also argue that your cash value grows tax-deferred. But if you want tax-deferred retirement savings, you should first take advantage of such retirement savings plans as 401(k)s, 403(b)s, SEP-IRAs, and Keoghs, which give you an immediate tax deduction for your current contributions in addition to growth without taxation until withdrawal. Money paid into a cash value life policy gives no up-front tax breaks to you. If you've exhausted the tax-deductible plans, then variable annuities or a nondeductible individual retirement account (IRA) can provide tax-deferred compounding of your investment dollars (see Chapter 19).

Life insurance tends to be a mediocre investment anyway. The insurance company quotes you an interest rate for the first year only. After that, it's up to the company's discretion for what it pays you. If you don't like the future interest rates, you can be penalized for quitting the policy. Would you ever invest your money in a bank account that quoted an interest rate for the first year only and then penalized you for moving your money in the next seven to ten years?

Property and assets that are owned in joint tenancy or inside retirement accounts (such as IRAs or 401(k)s) and have designated beneficiaries generally pass to heirs without going through probate. (Many states also allow a special type of revocable trust for bank accounts called a *Totten* trust, which insulates the bank accounts from probate, as well.)

A *living trust* effectively transfers assets into a trust. If you use a *revocable living trust*, you control those assets and can revoke the trust whenever you desire. The advantage of a living trust is that upon your death, assets can pass directly to your beneficiaries without going through probate. Probate is a lengthy, expensive hassle for your heirs. Attorney probate fees run around 5 to 7 percent of the value of the estate. In addition, your assets become a matter of public record as a result of probate. Living trusts are also useful in naming someone to administer your affairs in the event that you become incapacitated.

Wills

Wills — legal documents that detail your instructions for what you want done with your personal property and assets upon your death — won't save you on taxes or on probate. They are, however, an estate planning basic that most people should have but don't. Most of the world doesn't bother with wills, because laws and customs divvy up a person's estate among the spouse and children or other close relatives.

The main benefit of a will is that it ensures that your wishes for the distribution of your assets are fulfilled. If you die without a will (known in legalese as *intestate*), your state decides how to distribute your money and other property, according to state law. Therefore, your friends, more-distant relatives, and favorite charities will probably receive nothing. For a fee, the state will appoint an administrator to supervise the distribution of your assets.

If you have little in the way of personal assets and don't really care who gets your possessions and other assets, (state law usually speci-

fies closest blood relatives), you can forget about creating a will. You'll save yourself the time and depression that inevitably accompanies this gloomy exercise.

If you have minor (dependent) children, a will is necessary to name a guardian for them. In the event that you and your spouse should both die without a will, the state (courts and social service agencies) decides who will raise your children. Therefore, even if you cannot decide at this time who would raise your children, you should *at least* appoint a trusted guardian who could decide for you.

Living wills and medical power of attorney are useful additions to a standard will. A living will tells your doctor what, if any, life-support measures you would accept. A medical power of attorney grants authority to someone you trust to make decisions with a physician regarding your medical care options. These additional documents are usually prepared when a will is drawn up.

Living trusts are likely to be of greatest value to people who are age 60 and older, single, and own assets worth more than $100,000 that must pass through probate (including real estate, non-retirement accounts, and business). Small estates may actually be less expensive to probate in some states than the cost and hassle of setting up a living trust.

Charitable trusts

If you're feeling philanthropic, charitable trusts may be for you. With a *charitable remainder trust*, you or your designated beneficiary receives income from assets you donate to a charity. On your death or after a certain number of years, the principal is donated to the charity and is thus removed from your taxable estate.

In a *charitable lead trust,* the roles of the charity and beneficiaries are reversed. The charity receives the income from the assets for a set number of years or until you pass away, at which point the assets pass to your beneficiary. You get a current income tax deduction for the value of the expected payments to the charity.

Where to get advice and help

The number of people who will happily charge you a fee or sell you some legal device or insurance far exceeds the number actually qualified to render objective estate planning advice. Attorneys, accountants, financial planners, estate planning specialists, investment companies, insurance agents, and even some nonprofits stand ready to help you figure out how to dispense your wealth.

Most of these people and organizations have conflicts of interest and lack the knowledge necessary to properly do sound estate planning for you. Attorneys are biased towards drafting legal documents and devices that are more complicated than you may need. Insurance agents and financial planners who work on commission try to sell you cash value life insurance. Investment firms and banks want you to establish a trust account that requires that in the future the assets be managed through them.

Although the cost of *free* estate planning seminars is tempting, you get what you pay for — or worse.

Start the process of planning your estate by looking at the big picture first. Talk to your family members about your financial situation. Many people never take this basic but critical step. Your heirs likely have no idea what you're considering or what you're worried about. Conversely, how can you develop a solid action plan without understanding your heirs' needs and concerns? Be careful not to use money to control or manipulate other family members.

For professional advice, you need someone who can objectively look at the big picture. Attorneys and tax advisors who specialize in estate planning are a good starting point. Ask the persons you're thinking of hiring if they sell life insurance or manage money. If they do, they can't possibly be objective and likely aren't sufficiently educated about estate planning, given their focus.

For preparation of wills and living trusts, check out the high-quality software programs on the market. Legal software may save you from the often difficult task of finding a competent and affordable attorney. Preparing documents with software can also save you money.

Using legal software is generally preferable to using fill-in-the-blank documents. Software has the built-in virtues of directing and limiting your choices and keeping you from making common mistakes. Quality software also incorporates the knowledge and insights of the legal eagles who developed the software.

If your situation isn't unusual, legal software may work well for you. As to the legality of documents that you create with software, remember that a will, for example, is made legal and valid by your witnesses; the fact that an attorney prepares the document is *not* what makes it legal. Here are two good software packages worth considering:

- ✓ For will preparation, check out WillMaker (available in Windows, DOS, and Macintosh versions) by Nolo Press. In addition to allowing you to prepare wills (in every state except Louisiana), WillMaker can help you prepare a *living will* and *medical power of attorney* (as discussed earlier in the chapter).

- ✓ Nolo's Living Trust software (available in Windows and Macintosh versions) allows you to create a living trust that serves to keep property out of probate in the event of your death (remember that it does *not* address the issue of estate taxes). Like wills, living trusts are fairly standard legal documents that you can properly create with the guidance of a top-notch software package. The Living Trust package also advises you to seek professional guidance for your situation, if necessary.

If you want to do still more reading on estate planning, pick up a copy of *Plan Your Estate* by attorney Denis Clifford (Nolo Press). If you have a large estate that may be subject to estate taxes, it's probably worth your time and money to consult an attorney or tax advisor who specializes in estate planning.

Part V
The Part of Tens

Reprinted with permission

In this part...

Okay, so we're not as funny as David Letterman. But how much money has he saved you on your taxes? And does he care as much as we do about your financial health? These short chapters, which can be read just about anytime you may have a few spare minutes, are packed with other tax-saving and planning ideas. Maybe you have your own idea for a list of Ten Tax somethings. Send us the idea for a list, and if we incorporate it into our next edition of *Taxes For Dummies*, we'll send you next year's edition for free.

Chapter 25

Ten Frequently Asked Tax Questions

O ver the years, we've had a great number of people ask us all sorts of tax questions. We've also noted the conspicuous absence of some questions that people should be asking — sometimes you don't know what to ask because you don't know what you don't know. We also realize that there are some questions that more of you would really like to ask but don't feel comfortable asking. We answer these questions for you right now in the privacy of your own home.

Why do I pay so much in taxes?

We actually pay less in taxes than people in most developed countries. It's easy to overlook all the stuff our tax dollars pay for, such as national defense, roads, bridges, schools, libraries, police departments, Social Security income, and health care benefits — and $600 toilet seats!

The best and legal way to reduce your taxes is to master the strategies that we discuss in this book, some of which can be applied when preparing your annual return (Part II) and others that involve advance planning (Part IV). Some taxes, such as sales taxes, can be reduced by simply spending less money. Besides, you're probably not saving enough anyway. Now you have another reason to cut your spending. A double bonus!

It's tempting to want to blame the government for high taxes. You're not going to get it to change. But if you can change your financial behaviors, that's where you can save big tax dollars.

Haven't they closed all the tax loopholes?

Yes, it's true that many of the financial schemes concocted to reduce taxes have been eliminated by changes in the tax laws over the past decade. This elimination of many loopholes has put a number of investment salespeople and *creative* financial planners out of business — which has reduced the likelihood of you being hoodwinked into buying bad investments. Fortunately, with fewer loopholes, we have a more level playing field. Just about all the tax-reduction strategies discussed in this book are open to people of any economic means.

Why do the wealthy and corporations pay so little in taxes?

This myth is perpetuated by those rare but highly publicized cases where — because of large write-offs — affluent people and mighty corporations appear to slide by without paying their fair share of taxes. Yet, the truth is that the highest-income earners typically pay more in taxes than most of us earn in a year! That's why so many of these folks moan and complain about how much they pay in taxes. (The polite ones complain to their tax and financial advisors lest others think they are ungrateful for their high wages!.)

The only way a person or company with a big income can end up paying less taxes is if a great deal of money is spent on tax-deductible stuff like mortgage interest, property taxes, and reinvesting in business. These perfectly legal write-offs are available to anyone, regardless of income. In fact, low-income earners have tax deductions, such as the earned income tax credit that others can't take. A wealthy person cannot deduct the mortgage interest on anything larger than a million dollar first mortgage.

Shouldn't I buy real estate to reduce my taxes?

You can write off mortgage interest and property taxes on most pieces of real estate (for more details, see Chapter 22). Such a write-off can help, but you shouldn't buy real estate *because* of these tax breaks. You should own a home because you need a place to live long term. Besides, owning should cost you less than paying an ever-escalating rent over the years.

Real estate property sellers aren't stupid. The tax benefits available on homes are factored into the current selling prices. This is one of the reasons why real estate is so expensive.

How can I avoid scrambling for documents at the last minute when it comes time to file my annual tax return?

One of the easiest tax headaches to avoid is the search for tax forms at midnight on a rainy Sunday night. Make sure to pick up the forms the next time you are at the local Post Office or call 800-829-3676. Another easy way to avoid the midnight search is to use some of the tax preparation software we recommend in Chapter 2. It is also your responsibility to take care of your personal forms, like your W-2s.

Setting up a filing system can be a big time saver for the missing-form phenomenon. If you have limited patience for setting up neat file folders and you lead an uncomplicated financial life (that is, you haven't saved the receipts that you need for tax purposes throughout the year), you can confine your filing to January and February. During those months, you find in the mailbox your tax booklets from the IRS and your state tax authority, along with tax summary forms on wages paid by your employer (W-2), investment income (1099), and home mortgage interest (1098). Find a file folder or big envelope and label it something easy to remember — "1994 Taxes" is a brilliant choice — and then dump all these forms in as they arrive. When you're ready to crunch numbers, just open the file or envelope and away you go. See Chapter 3 for more organizing tips.

How can I know that I'm not overlooking deductions?

Educate yourself. You don't know what you're missing until you know the goodies available. This book, particularly Part II and Part IV, can help you see the light. If you're currently working with a tax preparer and aren't confident of his or her capabilities, consider getting a second opinion by taking your tax returns to another preparer and seeing whether other tax-reduction opportunities can be uncovered.

Why should I work so hard if I have to pay all these taxes?

Here's a question more of you should be asking, especially two-income families. Although we don't want to get into trouble by suggesting that someone may not be spending enough time at home with the kids, couples pay a very high effective rate of tax on the second income. That second-income earner may be making only the minimum wage when you factor in all the commuting costs, lunches out, work clothing expenses, child care expenses, and so on. Of course, there are other benefits to working besides money. But you have to ask yourself whether those commuting traffic jams and office politics are really worth the minimum wage!

Most people don't make the most of their money. We work hard at earning money but not at educating ourselves about how to make it stretch further. That's why you owe it to yourself to read this book, especially Part IV.

Why does my brother-in-law get a larger tax refund than me?

Because you aren't your brother-in-law. Seriously, though, a large refund is not a sign of victory over the IRS. In fact, it's more likely a sign of failure. Large refunds result from having paid the IRS too much in taxes *during* the year. You essentially give the federal government an interest-free loan when you overpay your taxes during the year and wait until the next spring to get the money returned.

If your brother-in-law pays little in the way of taxes relative to his income, he probably takes advantage of all the tax breaks we've told you about in this book. Good thing you got the book!

How long do I have to keep my tax forms?

Easy one. The quick answer is three years from your official filing date (usually April 15). But check out Chapter 3 for a few exceptions to this rule — remember the IRS loves exceptions to the rules.

I can't make (or already missed) the deadline for filing my return and paying what I owe. What do I do?

Don't panic but get on the stick. And unless you lost your records in a fire or some other catastrophe (your dog eating them doesn't count), you'll owe interest and penalties if you miss the April 15 filing deadline and owe taxes. Every day you delay coming clean, the more it's going to cost you as the interest and penalties mount.

If it's before midnight on April 15, you're in luck. You can get yourself an additional four months to procrastinate by filing Form 4868. (You can find it in our Appendix — you'd think the IRS would put this form in their booklet since this is a form many people realize they need at the last minute. But the IRS doesn't) You need not have a good excuse for the extension — you get it even if you were too busy having fun.

If you file an extension, you are still obligated to pay the tax that you owe. Because you haven't completed your tax return (that's why you need the extension, right), you won't know how much you owe. You're going to have to estimate. Better to overestimate and send them a bit more than you think you need to.

If you don't have the money to pay your taxes, it's far better to contact the IRS and tell them your situation. The IRS is actually understanding and will work out a payment plan (with interest, of course). See Chapter 17 for tips on what to do if you can't pay. If you don't have the necessary records to prepare your return, see Chapter 3.

I learned that I forgot to deduct something last year. May I go back and fix my mistake now?

It depends on what you forgot and how long ago you filed your return. Unfortunately, one of the best deductions available, for retirement accounts, cannot be claimed on an amended return (unless the money was legally contributed by the time you filed your return). Other oversights you made in reporting your income and deductions and expenses can generally be handled on Form 1040X (Amended U.S. Individual Income Tax Return).

You must file your amendments within three years from April 15 of the year you filed the original return. (If you filed after April 15 because you got an extension, count the three years from the date you actually filed your completed return.) See Chapter 17 to see how to amend your return.

Chapter 26

Ten Best Ways to Avoid an Audit

*I*f you've never been audited, you probably fall into one of these categories: you're not old enough yet, you haven't made gobs of money, or you're just plain lucky. The fact is that many taxpayers do get audited during their adult lives.

Even well-meaning and humble authors of well-meaning and humble tax-advice books are not exempt. One of us, Eric, has stared down an audit and says that the audit wasn't too bad — sort of like preparing for an exam . . . in a course you're not taking for credit.

There are some common-sense steps (honesty being the star of the show) you can take to reduce your chances of winning this most unwelcome lottery. After all, instead of wasting your day in some IRS office, you want to make sure that you have sufficient time for jury duty and to run down to the Department of Motor Vehicles to renew your driver's license.

Dot your i's and cross your t's

Audit your own return first *before* you send it in. If the IRS finds mistakes through its increasingly sophisticated computer-checking equipment, you're more likely to get audited. So your undotted i's and uncrossed t's are probably more likely than ever to make some computer beep at IRS Central (beeps are bad).

Have you included all your income? And think about the different accounts you had during the tax year. Do you have interest and dividend statements for your accounts? Finding these statements is easier if you've been keeping your financial records in one place. Check your W-2s and 1099s against your tax form to make sure you wrote the numbers down correctly.

Don't forget to check your math. Have you added, subtracted, multiplied, and divided correctly? Are your Social Security number and your address correct on the return? (Just use that handy-dandy, pre-printed label the IRS gives you with your federal return — as long as *it* is accurate.) Did you sign and date your return?

These infractions will not, on their own, trigger an audit. In some cases the IRS simply writes you a letter asking for your signature or the additional tax you owe (if the math mistake is not too fishy or too big). In some rare instances, they'll even send you a refund if the mistake they uncover was in your favor (really!). Regardless of how they handle the mistake, it can be a headache to clear up and, more importantly, it can cost you extra money.

Declare all your income

When you prepare your return, you may be tempted to shave off a little of that consulting income you received in the form of a check. Who will miss it, right? The IRS will, that's who.

Thanks largely to computer cross-checking, the IRS has many ways to find unreported income. Be particularly careful if you're self-employed: anyone who pays you more than $600 in a year is required to file a Form 1099, which basically tells the IRS how much you got.

Don't itemize

People who itemize their deductions on Schedule A are far more likely to get audited because they have more opportunity and temptation to cheat. By all means, if you can legally claim more total deductions on the Schedule A than you can with the standard deduction (this deduction stuff is all spelled out in Chapter 8), we say "itemize, itemize, itemize." If it's basically a toss up between Schedule A and your standard deduction, it's safer to take the standard deduction, which the IRS can't challenge.

Earn less money

At first glance this may seem like an odd statement, but there really are costs of affluence. One of the costs of a high income — besides higher taxes — is a dramatic increase in the probability of getting audited. If your income is more than $100,000, you have about a 1 in 20 chance of being audited. But you have less than a 1 in 100 chance if your income is under $50,000. You see, there *are* advantages to earning less!

Tax protesters take note

Why should you take note? Because the IRS may be. The IRS may flag returns that are accompanied by protest notes. Threats are bad, too — even if it's meant in fun (humor is not rife at the IRS, we suspect). The commandment is: Thou shalt not draw attention to thyself.

The protest issue is interesting. There are congressional hearings where tax protesters will stand up and tell members of the Congress that the income tax is unconstitutional. They say they have proof. If we can get our hands on the proof, we'll include it in the next edition.

Don't cheat

It may have taken the IRS a while to wisen up, but now the government is methodically figuring out the different ways that people cheat. The next step for the IRS — after they figure out how people cheat — is to come up with ways to catch them. And with the enormous size of the federal deficit, the pressure on the IRS to produce more revenue is huge. Cheaters beware! Also, the IRS offers rewards for informants. If you are brazen enought to cheat and the IRS doesn't catch you, you may not be home free yet. Someone else may turn you in. Besides, you'll sleep better at night knowing that you're not breaking the law.

Stay away from back-street refund mills

This advice does not apply to the majority of tax preparation firms, but unfortunately there are some firms out there that fabricate deductions. Be careful, and refer to Chapter 2 for ways to determine the quality of a tax preparer.

Be careful with hobby losses

Some people who have full-time jobs also have side businesses or hobbies with which they try to make a few bucks. But be careful if you report the side business as showing a loss year after year on your tax forms.

Here's an extreme example: You like to paint surreal pictures and you even sold one in 1991 for $150. But since then you haven't sold any paintings (the surreal market has bottomed out). Nevertheless, you continue to write off your cost for canvas and paint in the following years. The IRS will take a close look at that record, and you may be a candidate for an audit.

Don't be a nonfiler

The IRS has a special project in order to go after the estimated five to ten million nonfilers. Lest you think the IRS does things in small ways, the IRS has assigned 2,000 agents to this project.

Work for an employer

People who are self-employed have more opportunities to make mistakes on their taxes — or to creatively add deductions — than company-payroll wage earners. As a business owner, you're responsible for reporting not only your income but also your expenses. You have to be even more honest when it comes to dealing with the tax authorities because the likelihood of getting audited is higher than average.

There's nothing wrong with being self-employed. But resist the temptation to cheat because you are far more likely to be scruntinized.

Don't disguise employees as independent contractors

This maneuver is covered by another IRS project. You remember the old barb: You can't put a sign around a cow that says "This is a horse." You don't have a horse — you have a cow with a sign around its neck. Okay, we're reaching a bit … but the point is this: Just because you call someone an independent contractor doesn't mean that this person is not your employee. If you aren't sure about the relationship. See Chapter 20.

Carry a rabbit's foot

Try as you may to be an obedient taxpayer, you can get audited simply because of bad luck. Every so often, the IRS audits thousands of people at random. Although such an undertaking may seem like a colossal waste of time to a tax neophyte like yourself, this effort provides the IRS with valuable information on the areas of tax returns where people make the most (or least) mistakes — and on the areas where people like to cheat!

(Did you notice how many items we put in this part of ten? Okay, it's eleven, but we didn't know if you thought the last one was particularly helpful; if you did find it helpful, call it a bonus tip.)

Chapter 27

Ten Commonly Overlooked Deductions

● ●

*D*eductions are just what they sound like: You subtract them from your income before you calculate the tax you owe. So the more deductions you take, the smaller your income — and the smaller your tax bill. Nothing could be easier, right? But you don't want to be like all those other people who miss out on perfectly legal deductions simply because they don't know what they can and what they can't deduct. Here's ten that we don't want you to overlook.

Check if you can itemize

The IRS gives you two methods to determine your total deductions. You get to pick the method that leads to the largest total deductions — and thus, lower tax bill. But sometimes the choice is not so clear, so be prepared to do some figuring.

Taking the standard deduction usually makes sense if you have a pretty simple financial life — a regular paycheck, a rented apartment, and no large expenses such as medical bills, moving expenses, or loss due to theft or catastrophe. Single folks qualify for a $3,800 standard deduction, and married couples filing jointly get a $6,350 standard deduction for 1994.

The standard deduction gets adjusted each year for inflation, so it always grows. And with fewer and fewer allowable deductions, many taxpayers who once itemized have realized that taking the standard deduction is in their best interest.

The other method to determine your allowable deductions is to itemize them on your tax return. This painstaking procedure is definitely more of a hassle, but if you can tally up more than the standard deduction amounts, itemizing saves you money. Schedule A of your 1040 is the page for summing up your itemized deductions, but you won't know whether you have enough itemized deductions unless you give this schedule a good examination (see Chapter 8) or talk to a tax advisor.

Shift and bunch (your deductions, that is)

If you total up your itemized deductions on Schedule A and the total is less than the standard deduction, take the standard deduction without fail. The total for your itemized deductions is worth checking each year, however, because you may have more deductions in some years than others, and you may occasionally be able to itemize.

Because you can control when you pay particular expenses that are eligible for itemizing, you can *shift* or *bunch* more of them into the select years when you have enough deductions to take full advantage of itemizing. Suppose, for example, that you are using the standard deduction this year because you just don't have many itemized deductions. Late in the tax year, though, you become certain that you'll buy a home sometime during the next year. Thanks to the potential write-off of mortgage interest and property taxes, you also know that you'll be able to itemize. It makes sense, then, to shift as many deductible expenses as possible into the next year.

Trade consumer debt for mortgage debt

Suppose that you own real estate and haven't borrowed as much money as the bank will allow. And also suppose that you've run up high-interest consumer debt. Well, you just may be able to trade one debt for another. You probably can refinance your mortgage and pull out extra cash to pay off your credit card, auto loan, or other expensive credit lines. You can usually borrow at a lower interest rate for a mortgage, thus lowering your monthly interest bill. Plus, you get a tax-deduction bonus because consumer debt — auto loans, credit cards, credit lines — is not tax deductible, but mortgage debt is. Therefore, the effective borrowing rate on a mortgage is even lower than the quoted rate suggests.

Don't forget that refinancing your mortgage and establishing home equity lines involve application fees and other charges (points, appraisals, credit reports, and so on). These fees have to be included in the equation to see whether it makes sense to exchange consumer debt for more mortgage debt.

This strategy involves one big danger. Borrowing against the equity in your home can be an addictive habit. We've seen cases in which people run up significant consumer debt during three or four distinct times and then refinance their home the same number of times over the years in order to bail themselves out.

At a minimum, continued expansion of your mortgage debt handicaps your ability to work toward other financial goals. In the worst case, easy access to borrowing encourages bad spending habits that can lead to bankruptcy or foreclosure against your debt-ridden home.

Charitable contributions and expenses

If you itemize, you can deduct contributions made to charities. For example, most people already know that when they write a check for $50 to their favorite church or college, they can deduct it. (**Note:** Make sure to get a receipt because a canceled check is no longer sufficient documentation for the IRS.)

Yet many taxpayers overlook the fact that they can also deduct expenses on work done for charitable organizations. For example, when you go to a soup kitchen to help prepare and serve meals, you can deduct your transportation costs to get there. You just need to keep track of your bus fares or driving mileage. The IRS currently allows a deduction of 12 cents per mile.

You also can deduct the fair market value of donations of clothing, household appliances, furniture, and other goods to charities — many of which will even drive to your home to pick up the stuff. Just make sure to keep some documentation: Write up a detailed list and get it signed by the charity. Consider taking pictures of more valuable donations (see Chapter 8).

Personal property and state taxes

If you don't currently itemize, you may be surprised to learn that your state income taxes are itemizable. If you must pay a fee to the state to register and license your car, you can itemize the expenditure as a deduction (line 7 on Schedule A, "Other Taxes"). The IRS allows you to deduct only the part of the fee that relates to the value of your car, however. The state organization that collects the fee should be able to tell you what portion of the fee is deductible. If it's a user-friendly organization, it even shows this figure for a fee on your invoice. What service!

Self-employment expenses

If you are self-employed, you already deduct a variety of expenses from your income before calculating the tax that you owe. If you buy a computer or office furniture, you can deduct those expenses (sometimes they need to be gradually deducted or *depreciated* over time). Salaries for your employees, office supplies, rent or mortgage interest for your office space, and phone expenses are also generally deductible.

Although more than a few business owners cheat on their taxes, some self-employed folks don't take all the deductions they should. In some cases, people simply aren't aware of the wonderful world of deductions. For others, large deductions raise the risk of audit. Taking advantage of your eligible deductions makes sense and saves you money.

If you're self-employed, you already know that you have a lot of responsibilities. Don't try to be an island unto yourself. It's usually a mistake to go it alone around tax time. Many issues can trip up even the sharpest solo shop. It's worth the money to hire tax help — either by paying a tax professional or by using a self-help book like the one you're reading.

Miscellaneous expenses

A number of so-called *miscellaneous expenses* are deductible on Schedule A. Most of these relate to your job or career; and managing your finances are deductible to the extent that they exceed 2 percent of your adjusted gross income (see Chapter 8).

Educational expenses

You may be able to deduct your tuition, books, and travel costs to and from classes if your education is related to your career. Specifically, you can deduct these expenses if your course work improves your work skills. Continuing education classes for professionals may be deductible. If the law or your employer requires you to take courses to maintain your position, these courses are also deductible. But note that educational expenses allowing you to change or to move into a new field or career are not deductible.

Job search and career counseling

After you obtain your first job, you may deduct legitimate costs relating to finding another job within your field. For example, suppose that you're a chef in a steak house in Chicago and you decide you want to do stir-fry in Los Angeles. You take a crash course in vegetarian cooking and then fly to L.A. a couple of times for interviews.

You can deduct the cost of the course and your trips — *even if you don't ultimately change jobs.* If you hire a career counselor to help you figure everything out, you can deduct that cost, too. On the other hand, if you're burned out on cooking and decide that you want to become a professional volleyball player in L.A., that's a new career. You might get a better tan, but you won't generate deductions from changing jobs.

Unreimbursed expenses related to your job

If you pay for your own subscriptions to trade journals to keep up to date in your field, or if you buy a new desk and chair to ease back pain, you can deduct these costs. If your job requires you to wear special clothes or a uniform, you can write off the cost of purchasing and cleaning them, as long as the clothes aren't suitable for wearing outside of work.

If you buy a computer for use outside the office at your own expense, you may be able to deduct the cost of the computer if it's for the convenience of your employer, or if it's a condition of your employment (and is used more than half the time for business). Union dues and membership fees for professional organizations are also deductible.

Investment and tax-related expenses

Investment and tax-advisor fees are deductible, as are subscription costs for investment-related publications. Accounting fees for preparing your tax return or conducting tax planning during the year are deductible, as are legal fees related to your taxes. If you purchase a home computer to track your investments or prepare your taxes, you can deduct that expense, too.

Appendix

Reaching Out to the IRS (Oh, Yuck!)

• •

*E*instein was fond of saying that the most complicated thing he ever encountered was the income tax. Evidently, he considered the Theory of Relativity to be simple mathematics in comparison. So if you go through a bottle of aspirin when filling out your forms, you're in good company. **Medical Disclaimer:** If you are filling out your tax forms in one day, don't finish the bottle!

This Appendix is our attempt to give you as much detailed information as we can so you don't have to run all over to get the information you need. To that end, we've got phone numbers; we've got addresses; we got tips; and we've got warnings. Enjoy!

Where to File

First things first. The address where you send your completed form is listed in Table A-1.

Table A-1	Where the Check (and Forms) Go
If an addressed envelope came with your return, please use it. If you do not have one, or if you moved during the year, mail your return to the **Internal Revenue Service Center** for the place where you live. No street address is needed.	
If you live in:	*Use this address:*
Florida, Georgia, South Carolina	Atlanta, GA 39901
New Jersey, New York (New York City and counties of Nassau, Rockland, Suffolk, and Westchester)	Holtsville, NY 00501
New York (all other counties), Connecticut, Maine, Massachusetts, New Hampshire, Rhode Island, Vermont	Andover, MA 05501
Illinois, Iowa, Minnesota, Missouri, Wisconsin	Kansas City, MO 64999

(continued)

Table A-1 *(continued)*

If you live in:	Use this address:
Delaware, District of Columbia, Maryland, Pennsylvania, Virginia	Philadelphia, PA 19255
Indiana, Kentucky, Michigan, Ohio, West Virginia	Cincinnati, OH 45999
Kansas, New Mexico, Oklahoma, Texas	Austin, TX 73301
Alaska, Arizona, California (counties of Alpine, Amador, Butte, Calaveras, Colusa, Contra Costa, Del Norte, El Dorado, Glenn, Humboldt, Lake, Lassen, Marin, Mendocino, Modoc, Napa, Nebraska, Nevada, Placer, Plumas, Sacramento, San Joaquin, Shasta, Sierra, Siskiyou, Solano, Sonoma, Sutter, Tehama, Trinity, Yolo, and Yuba), Colorado, Idaho, Montana, Nevada, North Dakota, Oregon, South Dakota, Utah, Washington, Wyoming	Ogden, UT 84201
California (all other counties), Hawaii	Fresno, CA 93888
Alabama, Arkansas, Louisiana, Mississippi, North Carolina, Tennessee	Memphis, TN 37501
American Samoa	Philadelphia, PA 19255
Guam: Permanent residents	Department of Revenue and Taxation, Government of Guam, 378 Chalan San Antonio, Tamuning, GU 96911
Guam: Nonpermanent residents, Puerto Rico (or if excluding income under section 933), Virgin Islands: Nonpermanent residents	Philadelphia, PA 19255
Virgin Islands: Permanent residents	V.I. Bureau of Internal Revenue, Lockhart Gardens No. 1A, Charlotte Amalie, St. Thomas, VI 00802
Foreign country (or if dual-status alien): U.S. citizens and those filing Form 2555, Form 2555-EZ, or Form 4563	Philadelphia, PA 19255
All A.P.O. and F.P.O. addresses	Philadelphia, PA 19255

Recorded Tax Information

Just like the Yellow Pages, quick answers to many of your tax questions are only a phone call away. It's called Tele-Tax and — drum roll, please — it's free!

Although the thought of calling the IRS creates visions of hours listening to subliminal elevator music spreading the message "Taxes are good, taxes are fun," you really can get answers quickly through this system. Admittedly, a question like "I am a U.S. citizen and have my primary residence in Lizard Lick, North Carolina; I own a business in Brazil; I bought a coffee farm there in 1994; I patented a new coffee bean and made gads of money off it; how much money can I deduct on my taxes?" will be difficult to answer through Tele-Tax. However, a question like "I am a U.S. citizen and have my primary residence in Lizard Lick, North Carolina; I own a business in Brazil; I bought a coffee farm there in 1994; I patented a new coffee bean and made gads of money off it; I filled out my tax forms; where do I send them?" can be answered quickly.

Tele-Tax

1-800-829-4477

This IRS system known as Tele-Tax provides recorded tax information on the most frequently asked tax questions. There are nearly 150 topics. You can listen to up to three topics on each call you make. Tele-Tax is available 24 hours a day, 7 days a week, 365 days a year. Isn't it great to know the IRS never closes! Call them at midnight on New Year's Eve to test it.

When you call, you're asked if you want to listen to a Tele-Tax topic or if you're inquiring about a refund. You have to use a touch-tone phone after the main recording gives the basic instructions. Tele-Tax also explains the neat function of the(R)EPEAT and (C)ANCEL buttons on the touch-tone phone. The R button (#7) repeats your message as many times as you want — maybe until you understand! If you only have a rotary phone, you are out of luck.

Your Form 1040 booklet has a complete listing of topics, or you can access the directory over the phone when you call into Tele-Tax.

Automated refund information

1-800-829-4477 (same number as Tele-Tax)

Want to find out where your refund check is? Wait! Before you pick up the phone, make sure you have a copy of your tax return ready: you will need to know the first Social Security number shown on your return, your filing status, and the exact whole-dollar amount of your refund. Then place your call and follow the cheerful recorded instructions.

Here's an important point: The IRS updates refund information every seven days. If you call to find out about the status of your refund and do not receive a refund mailing date, wait a few days before calling back. Also, it's important to note that touch-tone service is available Monday through Friday from 7:00 a.m. to 11:30 p.m.

Toll-free tax help

1-800-829-1040

The IRS prefers that you contact a local IRS office to rap about your tax questions. But there is also a toll-free 800 number that you can call. Remember to have all the information ready to get to the root of your question or problem with the IRS rep.

If the IRS provides an incorrect answer to your question, you are still responsible for the payment of the correct tax. But if this situation occurs, you will not be charged any penalty. (Gee, thanks IRS!)

It is therefore critical that you obtain the name of the person you spoke to and record the date (as well as the time of the call) in order to have abated for reasonable cause any penalty that may be imposed (see Chapter 17 for the low-down on abating stuff). It will save you lots of grief with the IRS. For example, when calling, you should always have in front of you your tax form, schedule, or notice to which your question relates. Don't be embarrassed if you don't understand the answer. If you don't, just say so, and ask the IRS representative to explain it again or to refer you to an IRS representative who is more familiar with your problem.

IRS Tax Forms and Publications

Call **1-800-TAX-FORM** to get more forms and publications than you ever wanted in your life. Let's start with the list of the most popular IRS forms.

Remember, you can obtain forms by visiting a local IRS office, many libraries, other government offices, and some banks.

Individual tax forms

1040
U.S. Individual Income Tax Return

1040A
U.S. Individual Income Tax Return

1040ES
Estimated Tax for Individuals

1040ES(NR)
U.S. Estimated Tax for Nonresident Alien Individuals

1040EZ
Income Tax Return for Single and Joint Filers With No Dependents

1040NR
U.S. Nonresident Alien Income Tax Return

1040X
Amended U. S. Individual Income Tax Return

Form 1040 schedules

A
Itemized Deductions

B
Interest and Dividend Income

C
Profit or Loss From Business

C-EZ
Net Profit From Business

D
Capital Gains and Losses

E
Supplemental Income and Loss

EIC
Earned Income Credit

F
Profit or Loss From Farming

R
Credit for the Elderly or the Disabled

SE
Self-Employment Tax

Form 1040A schedules

1
Interest and Dividend Income

2
Child and Dependent Care Expenses

3
Credit for the Elderly or the Disabled

EIC
Earned Income Credit

Other forms

TD F 90-22.1
Report of Foreign Bank and Financial Accounts

W-4
Employee's Withholding Allowance Certificate

W-4P
Withholding Certificate for Pension or Annuity Payments

W-5
Earned Income Credit Advance Payment Certificate

W-10
Dependent Care Provider's Identification and Certification

843
Claim for Refund and Request for Abatement

940
Employer's Annual Federal Unemployment (FUTA) Tax Return

940EZ
Employer's Annual Federal Unemployment (FUTA) Tax Return

942
Employer's Quarterly Tax Return for Household Employees

1045
Application for Tentative Refund

1116
Foreign Tax Credit

1127
Application for Extension of Time for Payment of Tax

1310
Statement of Person Claiming Refund Due a Deceased Taxpayer

2106
Employee Business Expenses

2106—EZ
Unreimbursed Employee Business Expenses

2119
Sale of Your Home

2120
Multiple Support Declaration

2210
Underpayment of Estimated Tax by Individuals and Fiduciaries

2210F
Underpayment of Estimated Tax by Farmers and Fishermen

2441
Child and Dependent Care Expenses

2555
Foreign Earned Income

2555-EZ
Foreign Earned Income Exclusion

2688
Application for Additional Extension of Time to File U.S. Individual Income Tax Return

3903
Moving Expenses

3903F
Foreign Moving
Expenses

4070
Employee's Report of
Tips to Employer

4070-A
Employee's Daily
Record of Tips

4136
Credit for Federal Tax
Paid on Fuels

4137
Social Security and
Medicare Tax on
Unreported Tip Income

4255
Recapture of Invest-
ment Credit

4506
Request for Copy of Tax
Form

4562
Depreciation and
Amortization

4684
Casualties and Thefts

4797
Sales of Business
Property

4835
Farm Rental Income and
Expenses

4868
Application for
Automatic Extension of
Time to File U.S.
Individual Income Tax
Return

4952
Investment Interest
Expense Deduction

4970
Tax on Accumulation
Distribution of Trusts

4972
Tax on Lump-Sum
Distributions

5329
Return for Additional
Taxes Attributable to
Qualified Retirement
Plans (Including IRAs),
Annuities, and Modified
Endowment Contracts

5884
Jobs Credit

6198
At-Risk Limitations

6251
Alternative Minimum
Tax — Individuals

6252
Installment Sale Income

6781
Gains and Losses from
Section 1256 Contracts
and Straddles

8271
Investor Reporting of
Tax Shelter Registration
Number

8275
Disclosure Statement

8275-R
Regulation Disclosure
Statement

8283
Noncash Charitable
Contributions

8300
Report of Cash
Payments Over $10,000
Received in a Trade or
Business

8332
Release of Claim to
Exemption for Child of
Divorced or Separated
Parents

8379
Injured Spouse Claim
and Allocation

8396
Mortgage Interest
Credit

8453
U.S. Individual Income
Tax Declaration for
Electronic Filing

8582
Passive Activity Loss
Limitations

8582CR
Passive Activity Credit
Limitations

8606
Nondeductible IRAs
(Contributions,
Distributions, and Basis)

8611
Recapture of Low-
Income Housing Credit

8615
Tax for Children under
Age 14 Who Have
Investment Income of
More Than $1,200

8801
Credit for Prior Year
Minimum Tax —
Individuals and
Fiduciaries

8814
Parents' Election to
Report Child's Interest
and Dividends

8815
Exclusion of Interest
from Series EE U.S.
Savings Bonds, Issued
After 1989

8818
Optional Form to
Record Redemption of
Series EE U.S. Savings
Bonds Issued after 1989

8822
Change of Address

8824
Like-Kind Exchanges

8826
Disabled Access Credit

8828
Recapture of Federal
Mortgage Subsidy

8829
Expenses for Business
Use of Your Home

8834
Qualified Electric
Vehicle Credit

9465
Installment Agreement
Request

IRS Tax Information Publications

If you want a more detailed explanation of the tax law (you glutton), go for the gusto and grab a good IRS publication that suits your tastes or needs. Again **1-800-TAX-FORM** is the magic (phone) number. IRS Publication 910 provides a complete list of its free publications by topic. Here's a shorter list that includes the most frequently used publications. Remember, this is not beach reading! It's more like detention-hall reading.

General guidelines

1
Your Rights as a Taxpayer

17
Your Federal Income Tax

225
Farmer's Tax Guide

334
Tax Guide for Small Business

509
Tax Calendars for 1995

553
Highlights of 1994 Tax Changes

595
Tax Guide for Commercial Fisherman

910
Guide to Free Tax Services

Specialized publications

3
Tax Information for Military Personnel (Including Reservists Called to Active Duty)

4
Student's Guide to Federal Income Tax

15
Circular E, Employer's Tax Guide

54
Tax Guide for U.S. Citizens and Resident Aliens Abroad

378
Fuel Tax Credits and Refunds

448
Federal Estate and Gift Taxes

463
Travel, Entertainment, and Gift Expenses

501
Exemption, Standard Deduction, and Filing Information

502
Medical and Dental Expenses

503
Child and Dependent Care Expenses

504
Divorced or Separated Individuals

505
Tax Withholding and Estimated Tax

508
Educational Expenses

513
Tax Information for Visitors to the United States

514
Foreign Tax Credit for Individuals

516
Tax Information for U.S. Government Civilian Employees Stationed Abroad

517
Social Security and Other Information for Members of the Clergy and Religious Workers

519
U.S. Tax Guide for Aliens

520
Scholarships and Fellowships

521
Moving Expenses

523
Selling Your Home

524
Credit for the Elderly or the Disabled

525
Taxable and Nontaxable Income

526
Charitable Contributions

527
Residential Rental Property

529
Miscellaneous Deductions

530
Tax Information for First-Time Homeowners

531
Reporting Tip Income Tax

533
Self-Employment Tax

534
Depreciation

535
Business Expenses

536
Net Operating Losses

537
Installment Sales

IRS Problem Resolution Program

Any problems you have that cannot be resolved through normal channels, as discussed in Chapter 16, may qualify for the IRS Problem Resolution Program (Don't worry this has nothing to do with the Witness Relocation Program!).

Just call **1-800-829-1040** for one-stop service. Explain your problem to a specially-trained operator who will try to fix it while you're on the line, if possible. If not, he or she will evaluate your case to see if it meets the necessary criteria for the program. The operator will then assign you to a caseworker at your local district service center.

This may take some time on the phone but don't worry about it — it's a taxpayer service. And although you may not enjoy the IRS muzak, it's better than corresponding by mail. It could take months if you send your letter to the wrong address (or sometimes even if you send it to the correct address). Use the IRS one-stop number as a starting point.

Form **4868**

Department of the Treasury
Internal Revenue Service

**Application for Automatic Extension of Time
To File U.S. Individual Income Tax Return**

OMB No. 1545-0188

1994

	Your first name and initial	Last name	Your social security number
Please Type or Print	If a joint return, spouse's first name and initial	Last name	Spouse's social security number
	Home address (number, street, and apt. no. or rural route). If you have a P.O. box, see the instructions.		
	City, town or post office, state, and ZIP code		

I request an automatic 4-month extension of time to August 15, 1995, to file Form 1040EZ, Form 1040A, or Form 1040 for the calendar year 1994 or to _____ , 19____ , for the fiscal tax year ending _____ , 19____ .

Part I   Individual Income Tax—You must complete this part.

1. **Total tax liability for 1994.** This is the amount you expect to enter on Form 1040EZ, line 9; Form 1040A, line 27; or Form 1040, line 53. If you expect this amount to be zero, enter -0-. . . . | **1** |

   Caution: You **MUST** enter an amount on line 1 or your extension will be denied. You can estimate this amount, but be as exact as you can with the information you have. If we later find that your estimate was not reasonable, the extension will be null and void.

2. **Total payments for 1994.** This is the amount you expect to enter on Form 1040EZ, line 8; Form 1040A, line 28d; or Form 1040, line 60 (excluding line 57) . . . . | **2** |

3. **BALANCE DUE.** Subtract line 2 from line 1. If line 2 is more than line 1, enter -0-. If you are making a payment, you must use the Form 4868-V at the bottom of page 3. For details on how to pay, including what to write on your payment, see the instructions . . . . ▶ | **3** |

Part II   Gift or Generation-Skipping Transfer (GST) Tax—Complete this part if you expect to owe either tax.

Caution: Do not include income tax on lines 5a and 5b. See the instructions.

4. If you or your spouse plan to file a gift tax return (Form 709 or 709-A) for 1994, generally due by April 17, 1995, see the instructions and check here . . . } Yourself ▶ ☐ Spouse ▶ ☐

5a. Enter the amount of gift or GST tax **you** are paying with this form. Also, you must use the Form 4868-V at the bottom of page 3 . . . . | **5a** |

   b. Enter the amount of gift or GST tax **your spouse** is paying with this form. Also, you must use the Form 4868-V at the bottom of page 3 . . . . | **5b** |

Signature and Verification

Under penalties of perjury, I declare that I have examined this form, including accompanying schedules and statements, and to the best of my knowledge and belief, it is true, correct, and complete; and, if prepared by someone other than the taxpayer, that I am authorized to prepare this form.

▶ _____   _____   ▶ _____   _____
Your signature   Date   Spouse's signature, if filing jointly   Date

_____   _____
Preparer's signature (other than taxpayer)   Date

If you want correspondence regarding this extension to be sent to you at an address other than that shown above or to an agent acting for you, please enter the name of the agent and/or the address where it should be sent.

Please Type or Print	Name
	Number and street (include suite, room, or apt. no.) or P.O. box number if mail is not delivered to street address
	City, town or post office, state, and ZIP code

For Paperwork Reduction Act Notice, see page 3.   Cat. No. 13141W   Form **4868** (1994)

4868-1

Figure A-1:
We know that none of you would need to refer to this type of form. But perhaps you have a good friend (wink!) that may need to seek an extension. Pass it on!

Index

The fun & easy way to learn about computers and more!

Title	Author	ISBN	Price
INTERNET / COMMUNICATIONS / NETWORKING			11/11/94
CompuServe For Dummies™	by Wallace Wang	1-56884-181-7	$19.95 USA/$26.95 Canada
Modems For Dummies™, 2nd Edition	by Tina Rathbone	1-56884-223-6	$19.99 USA/$26.99 Canada
Modems For Dummies™	by Tina Rathbone	1-56884-001-2	$19.95 USA/$26.95 Canada
MORE Internet For Dummies™	by John R. Levine & Margaret Levine Young	1-56884-164-7	$19.95 USA/$26.95 Canada
NetWare For Dummies™	by Ed Tittel & Deni Connor	1-56884-003-9	$19.95 USA/$26.95 Canada
Networking For Dummies™	by Doug Lowe	1-56884-079-9	$19.95 USA/$26.95 Canada
ProComm Plus 2 For Windows For Dummies™	by Wallace Wang	1-56884-219-8	$19.99 2 $26.99 Canada
The Internet For Dummies™, 2nd Edition	by John R. Levine & Carol Baroudi	1-56884-222-8	$19.99 USA/$26.99 Canada
The Internet For Macs For Dummies™	by Charles Seiter	1-56884-184-1	$19.95 USA/$26.95 Canada
MACINTOSH			
Macs For Dummies®	by David Pogue	1-56884-173-6	$19.95 USA/$26.95 Canada
Macintosh System 7.5 For Dummies™	by Bob LeVitus	1-56884-197-3	$19.95 USA/$26.95 Canada
MORE Macs For Dummies™	by David Pogue	1-56884-087-X	$19.95 USA/$26.95 Canada
PageMaker 5 For Macs For Dummies™	by Galen Gruman	1-56884-178-7	$19.95 USA/$26.95 Canada
QuarkXPress 3.3 For Dummies™	by Galen Gruman & Barbara Assadi	1-56884-217-1	$19.99 USA/$26.99 Canada
Upgrading and Fixing Macs For Dummies™	by Kearney Rietmann & Frank Higgins	1-56884-189-2	$19.95 USA/$26.95 Canada
MULTIMEDIA			
Multimedia & CD-ROMs For Dummies™, Interactive Multimedia Value Pack	by Andy Rathbone	1-56884-225-2	$29.95 USA/$39.95 Canada
Multimedia & CD-ROMs For Dummies™	by Andy Rathbone	1-56884-089-6	$19.95 USA/$26.95 Canada
OPERATING SYSTEMS / DOS			
MORE DOS For Dummies™	by Dan Gookin	1-56884-046-2	$19.95 USA/$26.95 Canada
S.O.S. For DOS™	by Katherine Murray	1-56884-043-8	$12.95 USA/$16.95 Canada
OS/2 For Dummies™	by Andy Rathbone	1-878058-76-2	$19.95 USA/$26.95 Canada
UNIX			
UNIX For Dummies™	by John R. Levine & Margaret Levine Young	1-878058-58-4	$19.95 USA/$26.95 Canada
WINDOWS			
S.O.S. For Windows™	by Katherine Murray	1-56884-045-4	$12.95 USA/$16.95 Canada
MORE Windows 3.1 For Dummies™, 3rd Edition	by Andy Rathbone	1-56884-240-6	$19.99 USA/$26.99 Canada
PCs / HARDWARE			
Illustrated Computer Dictionary For Dummies™	by Dan Gookin, Wally Wang, & Chris Van Buren	1-56884-004-7	$12.95 USA/$16.95 Canada
Upgrading and Fixing PCs For Dummies™	by Andy Rathbone	1-56884-002-0	$19.95 USA/$26.95 Canada
PRESENTATION / AUTOCAD			
AutoCAD For Dummies™	by Bud Smith	1-56884-191-4	$19.95 USA/$26.95 Canada
PowerPoint 4 For Windows For Dummies™	by Doug Lowe	1-56884-161-2	$16.95 USA/$22.95 Canada
PROGRAMMING			
Borland C++ For Dummies™	by Michael Hyman	1-56884-162-0	$19.95 USA/$26.95 Canada
"Borland's New Language Product" For Dummies™	by Neil Rubenking	1-56884-200-7	$19.95 USA/$26.95 Canada
C For Dummies™	by Dan Gookin	1-878058-78-9	$19.95 USA/$26.95 Canada
C++ For Dummies™	by Stephen R. Davis	1-56884-163-9	$19.95 USA/$26.95 Canada
Mac Programming For Dummies™	by Dan Parks Sydow	1-56884-173-6	$19.95 USA/$26.95 Canada
QBasic Programming For Dummies™	by Douglas Hergert	1-56884-093-4	$19.95 USA/$26.95 Canada
Visual Basic "X" For Dummies™, 2nd Edition	by Wallace Wang	1-56884-230-9	$19.99 USA/$26.99 Canada
Visual Basic 3 For Dummies™	by Wallace Wang	1-56884-076-4	$19.95 USA/$26.95 Canada
SPREADSHEET			
1-2-3 For Dummies™	by Greg Harvey	1-878058-60-6	$16.95 USA/$21.95 Canada
1-2-3 For Windows 5 For Dummies™, 2nd Edition	by John Walkenbach	1-56884-216-3	$16.95 USA/$21.95 Canada
1-2-3 For Windows For Dummies™	by John Walkenbach	1-56884-052-7	$16.95 USA/$21.95 Canada
Excel 5 For Macs For Dummies™	by Greg Harvey	1-56884-186-8	$19.95 USA/$26.95 Canada
Excel For Dummies™, 2nd Edition	by Greg Harvey	1-56884-050-0	$16.95 USA/$21.95 Canada
MORE Excel 5 For Windows For Dummies™	by Greg Harvey	1-56884-207-4	$19.95 USA/$26.95 Canada
Quattro Pro 6 For Windows For Dummies™	by John Walkenbach	1-56884-174-4	$19.95 USA/$26.95 Canada
Quattro Pro For DOS For Dummies™	by John Walkenbach	1-56884-023-3	$16.95 USA/$21.95 Canada
UTILITIES / VCRs & CAMCORDERS			
Norton Utilities 8 For Dummies™	by Beth Slick	1-56884-166-3	$19.95 USA/$26.95 Canada
VCRs & Camcorders For Dummies™	by Andy Rathbone & Gordon McComb	1-56884-229-5	$14.99 USA/$20.99 Canada
WORD PROCESSING			
Ami Pro For Dummies™	by Jim Meade	1-56884-049-7	$19.95 USA/$26.95 Canada
MORE Word For Windows 6 For Dummies™	by Doug Lowe	1-56884-165-5	$19.95 USA/$26.95 Canada
MORE WordPerfect 6 For Windows For Dummies™	by Margaret Levine Young & David C. Kay	1-56884-206-6	$19.95 USA/$26.95 Canada
MORE WordPerfect 6 For DOS For Dummies™	by Wallace Wang, edited by Dan Gookin	1-56884-047-0	$19.95 USA/$26.95 Canada
S.O.S. For WordPerfect™	by Katherine Murray	1-56884-053-5	$12.95 USA/$16.95 Canada
Word 6 For Macs For Dummies™	by Dan Gookin	1-56884-190-6	$19.95 USA/$26.95 Canada
Word For Windows 6 For Dummies™	by Dan Gookin	1-56884-075-6	$16.95 USA/$21.95 Canada
Word For Windows For Dummies™	by Dan Gookin	1-878058-86-X	$16.95 USA/$21.95 Canada
WordPerfect 6 For Dummies™	by Dan Gookin	1-878058-77-0	$16.95 USA/$21.95 Canada
WordPerfect For Dummies™	by Dan Gookin	1-878058-52-5	$16.95 USA/$21.95 Canada
WordPerfect For Windows For Dummies™	by Margaret Levine Young & David C. Kay	1-56884-032-2	$16.95 USA/$21.95 Canada

Fun, Fast, & Cheap!

CorelDRAW! 5 For Dummies™ Quick Reference
by Raymond E. Werner

ISBN: 1-56884-952-4
$9.99 USA/$12.99 Canada

Windows "X" For Dummies™ Quick Reference, 3rd Edition
by Greg Harvey

ISBN: 1-56884-964-8
$9.99 USA/$12.99 Canada

Word For Windows 6 For Dummies™ Quick Reference
by George Lynch

ISBN: 1-56884-095-0
$8.95 USA/$12.95 Canada

WordPerfect For DOS For Dummies™ Quick Reference
by Greg Harvey

ISBN: 1-56884-009-8
$8.95 USA/$11.95 Canada

Title	Author	ISBN	Price
DATABASE			
Access 2 For Dummies™ Quick Reference	by Stuart A. Stuple	1-56884-167-1	$8.95 USA/$11.95 Canada
dBASE 5 For DOS For Dummies™ Quick Reference	by Barry Sosinsky	1-56884-954-0	$9.99 USA/$12.99 Canada
dBASE 5 For Windows For Dummies™ Quick Reference	by Stuart J. Stuple	1-56884-953-2	$9.99 USA/$12.99 Canada
Paradox 5 For Windows For Dummies™ Quick Reference	by Scott Palmer	1-56884-960-5	$9.99 USA/$12.99 Canada
DESKTOP PUBLISHING / ILLUSTRATION/GRAPHICS			
Harvard Graphics 3 For Windows For Dummies™ Quick Reference	by Raymond E. Werner	1-56884-962-1	$9.99 USA/$12.99 Canada
FINANCE / PERSONAL FINANCE			
Quicken 4 For Windows For Dummies™ Quick Reference	by Stephen L. Nelson	1-56884-950-8	$9.95 USA/$12.95 Canada
GROUPWARE / INTEGRATED			
Microsoft Office 4 For Windows For Dummies™ Quick Reference	by Doug Lowe	1-56884-958-3	$9.99 USA/$12.99 Canada
Microsoft Works For Windows 3 For Dummies™ Quick Reference	by Michael Partington	1-56884-959-1	$9.99 USA/$12.99 Canada
INTERNET / COMMUNICATIONS / NETWORKING			
The Internet For Dummies™ Quick Reference	by John R. Levine	1-56884-168-X	$8.95 USA/$11.95 Canada
MACINTOSH			
Macintosh System 7.5 For Dummies™ Quick Reference	by Stuart J. Stuple	1-56884-956-7	$9.99 USA/$12.99 Canada
OPERATING SYSTEMS / DOS			
DOS For Dummies® Quick Reference	by Greg Harvey	1-56884-007-1	$8.95 USA/$11.95 Canada
UNIX			
UNIX For Dummies™ Quick Reference	by Margaret Levine Young & John R. Levine	1-56884-094-2	$8.95 USA/$11.95 Canada
WINDOWS			
Windows 3.1 For Dummies™ Quick Reference, 2nd Edition	by Greg Harvey	1-56884-951-6	$8.95 USA/$11.95 Canada
PRESENTATION / AUTOCAD			
AutoCAD For Dummies™ Quick Reference	by Bud Smith	1-56884-198-1	$9.95 USA/$12.95 Canada
SPREADSHEET			
1-2-3 For Dummies™ Quick Reference	by John Walkenbach	1-56884-027-6	$8.95 USA/$11.95 Canada
1-2-3 For Windows 5 For Dummies™ Quick Reference	by John Walkenbach	1-56884-957-5	$9.95 USA/$12.95 Canada
Excel For Windows For Dummies™ Quick Reference, 2nd Edition	by John Walkenbach	1-56884-096-9	$8.95 USA/$11.95 Canada
Quattro Pro 6 For Windows For Dummies™ Quick Reference	by Stuart A. Stuple	1-56884-172-8	$9.95 USA/$12.95 Canada
WORD PROCESSING			
Word For Windows 6 For Dummies™ Quick Reference	by George Lynch	1-56884-095-0	$8.95 USA/$11.95 Canada
WordPerfect For Windows For Dummies™ Quick Reference	by Greg Harvey	1-56884-039-X	$8.95 USA/$11.95 Canada

FOR MORE INFORMATION OR TO ORDER, PLEASE CALL ▶ 800. 762. 2974

For volume discounts & special orders please call
Tony Real, Special Sales, at 415. 312. 0650

11/11/94

Windows 3.1 SECRETS™
by Brian Livingston

ISBN: 1-878058-43-6
$39.95 USA/$52.95 Canada

Includes Software.

MORE Windows 3.1 SECRETS™
by Brian Livingston

ISBN: 1-56884-019-5
$39.95 USA/$52.95 Canada

Includes Software.

Windows GIZMOS™
by Brian Livingston & Margie Livingston

ISBN: 1-878058-66-5
$39.95 USA/$52.95 Canada

Includes Software.

Windows 3.1 Connectivity SECRETS™
by Runnoe Connally, David Rorabaugh, & Sheldon Hall

ISBN: 1-56884-030-6
$49.95 USA/$64.95 Canada

Includes Software.

Windows 3.1 Configuration SECRETS™
by Valda Hilley & James Blakely

ISBN: 1-56884-026-8
$49.95 USA/$64.95 Canada

Includes Software.

Internet SECRETS™
by John R. Levine & Carol Baroudi

ISBN: 1-56884-452-2
$39.99 USA/$54.99 Canada

Includes Software.
Available: January 1995

Internet GIZMOS™ For Windows
by Joel Diamond, Howard Sobel, & Valda Hilley

ISBN: 1-56884-451-4
$39.99 USA/$54.99 Canada

Includes Software.
Available: December 1994

Network Security SECRETS™
by David Stang & Sylvia Moon

ISBN: 1-56884-021-7
Int'l. ISBN: 1-56884-151-5
$49.95 USA/$64.95 Canada

Includes Software.

PC SECRETS™
by Caroline M. Halliday

ISBN: 1-878058-49-5
$39.95 USA/$52.95 Canada

Includes Software.

WordPerfect 6 SECRETS™
by Roger C. Parker & David A. Holzgang

ISBN: 1-56884-040-3
$39.95 USA/$52.95 Canada

Includes Software.

DOS 6 SECRETS™
by Robert D. Ainsbury

ISBN: 1-878058-70-3
$39.95 USA/$52.95 Canada

Includes Software.

Paradox 4 Power Programming SECRETS,™ 2nd Edition
by Gregory B. Salcedo & Martin W. Rudy

ISBN: 1-878058-54-1
$44.95 USA/$59.95 Canada

Includes Software.

Paradox For Windows "X" Power Programming SECRETS™
by Gregory B. Salcedo & Martin W. Rudy

ISBN: 1-56884-085-3
$44.95 USA/$59.95 Canada

Includes Software.

Hard Disk SECRETS™
by John M. Goodman, Ph.D.

ISBN: 1-878058-64-9
$39.95 USA/$52.95 Canada

Includes Software.

WordPerfect 6 For Windows Tips & Techniques Revealed
by David A. Holzgang & Roger C. Parker

ISBN: 1-56884-202-3
$39.95 USA/$52.95 Canada

Includes Software.

Excel 5 For Windows Power Programming Techniques
by John Walkenbach

ISBN: 1-56884-303-8
$39.95 USA/$52.95 Canada

Includes Software.
Available: November 1994

INFO WORLD

...SECRETS™

®

IDG BOOKS

Order Center: **(800) 762-2974** *(8 a.m.–6 p.m., CST, weekdays)*

11/11/94

Quantity	ISBN	Title	Price	Total

Shipping & Handling Charges

	Description	First book	Each additional book	Total
Domestic	Normal	$4.50	$1.50	$
	Two Day Air	$8.50	$2.50	$
	Overnight	$18.00	$3.00	$
International	Surface	$8.00	$8.00	$
	Airmail	$16.00	$16.00	$
	DHL Air	$17.00	$17.00	$

*For large quantities call for shipping & handling charges.
**Prices are subject to change without notice.

Ship to:

Name _____

Company _____

Address _____

City/State/Zip _____

Daytime Phone _____

Payment: ☐ Check to IDG Books (US Funds Only)

☐ Visa ☐ Mastercard ☐ American Express

Card # _____ Expires _____

Signature _____

Subtotal _____

CA residents add applicable sales tax _____

IN, MA and MD residents add 5% sales tax _____

IL residents add 6.25% sales tax _____

RI residents add 7% sales tax _____

TX residents add 8.25% sales tax _____

Shipping _____

Total _____

Please send this order form to:

IDG Books Worldwide
7260 Shadeland Station, Suite 100
Indianapolis, IN 46256

Allow up to 3 weeks for delivery.
Thank you!

IDG BOOKS WORLDWIDE REGISTRATION CARD

RETURN THIS REGISTRATION CARD FOR FREE CATALOG

Title of this book: Taxe$ For Dummie$, 1995 Edition

My overall rating of this book: ❑ Very good [1] ❑ Good [2] ❑ Satisfactory [3] ❑ Fair [4] ❑ Poor [5]

How I first heard about this book:

❑ Found in bookstore; name: [6]

❑ Advertisement: [8]

❑ Word of mouth; heard about book from friend, co-worker, etc.: [10]

❑ Book review: [7]

❑ Catalog: [9]

❑ Other: [11]

What I liked most about this book:

What I would change, add, delete, etc., in future editions of this book:

Other comments:

Number of computer books I purchase in a year: ❑ 1 [12] ❑ 2-5 [13] ❑ 6-10 [14] ❑ More than 10 [15]

I would characterize my computer skills as: ❑ Beginner [16] ❑ Intermediate [17] ❑ Advanced [18] ❑ Professional [19]

I use ❑ DOS [20] ❑ Windows [21] ❑ OS/2 [22] ❑ Unix [23] ❑ Macintosh [24] ❑ Other: [25]_____
(please specify)

I would be interested in new books on the following subjects:
(please check all that apply, and use the spaces provided to identify specific software)

❑ Word processing: [26]

❑ Data bases: [28]

❑ File Utilities: [30]

❑ Networking: [32]

❑ Other: [34]

❑ Spreadsheets: [27]

❑ Desktop publishing: [29]

❑ Money management: [31]

❑ Programming languages: [33]

I use a PC at (please check all that apply): ❑ home [35] ❑ work [36] ❑ school [37] ❑ other: [38] _____

The disks I prefer to use are ❑ 5.25 [39] ❑ 3.5 [40] ❑ other: [41]_____

I have a CD ROM: ❑ yes [42] ❑ no [43]

I plan to buy or upgrade computer hardware this year: ❑ yes [44] ❑ no [45]

I plan to buy or upgrade computer software this year: ❑ yes [46] ❑ no [47]

Name: _____ Business title: [48] _____ Type of Business: [49] _____

Address (❑ home [50] ❑ work [51]/Company name: _____)

Street/Suite# _____

City [52]/State [53]/Zipcode [54]: _____ Country [55] _____

❑ **I liked this book!** You may quote me by name in future IDG Books Worldwide promotional materials.

My daytime phone number is _____

IDG BOOKS

THE WORLD OF COMPUTER KNOWLEDGE

❑ YES!

Please keep me informed about IDG's World of Computer Knowledge.
Send me the latest IDG Books catalog.